❖| COMPANY C |❖

⁂| COMPANY C |⁂

An American's Life as a Citizen-Soldier in Israel

Haim Watzman

FARRAR, STRAUS AND GIROUX
NEW YORK

Farrar, Straus and Giroux
19 Union Square West, New York 10003

Distributed in Canada by Douglas & McIntyre Ltd.
Printed in the United States of America
First edition, 2005

Grateful acknowledgment is made to the following for permission to reprint previously
published material:
"What to Do When Surrounded," copyright © 2003 by David Wagoner. Used by permission
of the author.
"Odysseus's Secret," from *Different Hours* by Stephen Dunn. Copyright © 2000 by
Stephen Dunn. Used by permission from W. W. Norton and Company, Inc.

Some names have been changed.

Library of Congress Cataloging-in-Publication Data
Watzman, Haim.
    Company C : an American's life as a citizen-soldier in Israel / Haim Watzman.— 1st ed.
    p. cm.
    ISBN-13: 978-0-374-22633-6
    ISBN-10: 0-374-22633-4 (hardcover : alk. paper)
    1. Watzman, Haim. 2. Americans—Israel—Biography. 3. Israel—Armed Forces—
Reserves—Biography. 4. Arab–Israeli conflict—Anecdotes. 5. Arab–Israeli conflict—
Moral and ethical aspects—Israel. I. Title.

    DS113.8.A4W37 2005
    956.9405'092—dc22

                                                                    2004006578

Designed by Lisa Stokes

www.fsgbooks.com

10 9 8 7 6 5 4 3 2 1

For Ilana, with all my love

A man finds his shipwrecks,
tells himself the necessary stories.

—STEPHEN DUNN, "ODYSSEUS'S SECRET"

CONTENTS

·

❧| COMPANY C |❧

PROLOGUE
· *Actions* ·

A KHAKI-COLORED CANVAS BAG SLUMPS BEHIND THE FILING CABI-
net in the tiny basement storeroom that doubles as my study. It
bears faded Hebrew lettering—my name and serial number—and inside
is a pair of black army boots, a set of work fatigues, and a hat. There's
a battered pocket-sized prayer book, a pen and notepad, and sand from
the Negev desert, from Hebron and Jenin in the West Bank, from Mt.
Hermon, and from Lebanon.

In army slang it's called a *chimidan*, a word that, like so many others in the peculiar argot of this most Israeli of institutions, comes from
another language—in this case, the authorities say, from Tatar, by way
of Russian. After twenty years of intensive use, my chimidan is still
strong. The canvas handles have withstood the weight of thick novels
and extra ammunition, and the heavy-duty zipper has survived the
strain of chronic overstuffing. It could be used for camping trips or family vacations, since I no longer need it for the army. But I haven't had
the heart to unpack it. Too much history, too many memories, too much
of my biography is in there. It just won't do for anything else.

"Owl-necked looking back / to where you might have been / or what you could have done / . . . you can't believe this skintight *is* your skin," says Sharon Dolin, in a poem called "Regret" that I have pasted on my door. Memories are tricky; they don't really tell us what was, but rather what was through the scrim of what happened after. But I'm pretty sure that no one who knew me in high school would have predicted that in middle age I'd be sitting down to write about my military career. Not that bookish kid, so physically inept that any team forced to take him in gym class got two extra players as compensation. I am the antithesis of a warrior. I can't throw a grenade far enough to keep myself alive. I never use bad language, and I daydream under pressure. Yet for twenty years of my life I was a soldier. I was a soldier as I adjusted to a new country, as I sought and found love, as I raised my children, as I pursued my career. At times I patrolled and defended my country's borders; at other times I served beyond them, or in that gray area, the occupied territories, the West Bank and Gaza Strip. I served in uniform in conflicts that I demonstrated against in civilian clothes.

I never planned to or particularly wanted to join an army. No romantic images of heroic fighters were instilled in me when I was young. There was no family military tradition to speak of. My paternal grandfather, apparently the first Watzman in untold generations to bear arms, was drafted into the czar's army in 1914 and deserted at the first opportunity. My father served honorably as a rifleman in the U.S. army at the tail end of World War II, but he did not speak of this much when I was a boy and certainly never expressed any hope that I would follow in his footsteps.

In the 1960s, the years of my childhood, middle-class Jewish boys were not inculcated with a sense of military duty. The army was just not something we did. As the Vietnam War escalated, military service became first something one avoided, and then, as political opposition to the war burgeoned, something one criticized, even despised. This was certainly not World War II, when my father eagerly awaited his eighteenth birthday so he could join the fight against Hitler. Hitler had been a clear and immediate threat both to the Jewish people and to the United States. The Viet Cong were not, as far as my friends and I could make out.

Israel's wars—specifically the Six-Day War of 1967, which broke out when I was at the end of sixth grade, and the Yom Kippur War of 1973, which erupted at the beginning of my senior year in high school— seemed different. I wasn't one of those guys with romantic ideas about heroic Israeli citizen-soldiers battling evil Arabs, though some of my friends were, and aspired to go to Israel to become such men. But even without the romance, service in the Israeli army looked different. Israeli soldiers were defending their homes and families, not serving as pawns in a geopolitical game. And their cause, protecting the Jewish state from enemies who sought to destroy it, seemed just beyond dispute. Yet I felt no particular obligation to enlist in that cause. My family and friends were in America, and I had no thought of living elsewhere.

Unlike many of my Jewish friends at my high school in suburban Washington, I did not join one of the several Zionist youth movements that had active local chapters. Perhaps I would have, had someone invited me. But, at least in early adolescence, when those cliques formed, I didn't fit in well. Anyway, Zionism didn't fire me up the way it did others. Of course I was a Zionist—weren't all the Jews I knew? It went without saying that I supported the state of Israel. In my family, however, Zionism was but one of many aspects of our Jewish identity. Unlike the parents of one high school friend, my own parents had never tried to settle in Israel. Unlike some other classmates, I had no relatives there. Most of my friends went on summer trips to Israel with their youth groups. I did not.

Given my personality, it's not surprising that the part of Judaism that caught my attention was not Israel but books. At a communitywide after-school program for Jewish teens, I became aware of a vast corpus of Jewish texts—the Bible, commentaries, Talmud, Midrash—with which the Jews I knew seemed to have little acquaintance. Most of the teachers in this program were Orthodox, and I was surprised and intrigued to discover that the stereotype I had of religious Jews—dogmatic, rigid, afraid of new ideas—did not fit them. True, they were strictly observant—much more strictly than I could ever imagine myself being. But they liked nothing more than a lively argument. They seemed willing to entertain, dissect, analyze, and dispute any notion or idea my classmates and I could throw at them, no matter how heretical—even if, at the end of the discussion, they stuck to their Orthodox guns. I soon came to realize that this love of a good argument, and the keen talent for turning every proposition over every which way—stripping it of cant and emotion, and measuring its strengths and weaknesses—was rooted in the rabbinical texts that we studied. There was a lot more intellectual energy in Maimonides and the Talmud than in the bland American synagogue Judaism with which I'd grown up.

The *way* the rabbis argued was also intriguing and quite different from anything I had encountered in my secular reading. At first sight, the Talmud and other rabbinical works were legal arguments over fine points of observance. You are supposed to make a blessing when you eat bread, but what does eating bread mean? How much bread qualifies—a crumb, a bite, a slice, a loaf? You're supposed to light Hanukkah candles outside so that they can be seen by passersby, but what if you live somewhere where no one would see them? When Jewish men recite their morning prayers, they are obligated to wear tefillin—black boxes, containing passages from the Torah, strapped to their arms and foreheads. Why aren't women so obligated? What if a woman wants to put on tefillin when she prays? Is she allowed to, even if it's not required? And if she does, can she say the associated blessing, which contains a declaration that the person reciting it is fulfilling an obligation? Debates like these were based on the desire, and need, to act—on the obligation to do the right thing in the right way. Ideological and philosophical issues of import were at stake here, but they were framed in disputations over the detailed fulfillment of God's precepts.

My teachers' openness notwithstanding, I realized that to be a full participant in this discourse you had to observe the commandments. Otherwise the decisions resulting from the discussions didn't impinge on you; you didn't have to live with the concrete outcome of the argument. That one should live the practical consequences of one's thoughts seemed correct to me, but I was not one of those adolescents who jumped headfirst into an enthusiasm. Also, a lot of orthodoxy's elements ran against the grain of the late 1960s and early 1970s liberalism I'd absorbed. There was too much deference to authority, whether of ancient texts or living rabbis. Different roles were mandated for men and women, and the women got the worst of it. Beneath the rigorous rationalism that I found so stimulating was a mystical, messianic undercurrent that disturbed me. And beyond that, I was a child of the West, brought up to be a skeptic. The Talmud and Midrash fascinated me, and for a couple of hours a week I got to sample them, unlike the great majority of nonobservant American Jewish kids. But it was only a couple of hours a week, and that couldn't compare to my non-Jewish reading. I read Tolkien's mythology, and Plato, and Shakespeare and Shaw and Nabokov and Joyce. Judaism had to compete for space in my mind.

As for Israel, it remained for me an abstract concept rather than a real question that had to be acted on. That changed during my sophomore year in college. On November 10, 1975, the United Nations General Assembly passed a resolution declaring that "Zionism is a form of racism and racial discrimination." To me this was obviously absurd. I knew very well that the Jewish people were the victims, not the perpetrators, of racial discrimination. My parents, liberal Democrats to the core, had been active supporters of the civil rights movement and had brought me up to view securing rights for blacks and other minorities as a Jewish mission. Just as we had suffered discrimination and enslavement in our past, so we had the responsibility to speak up for those who suffered discrimination and enslavement in our own day. The defining holiday in our house was Passover, with this very message at the center of our observance.

At Duke University, I was one of only a handful of Jewish students who were active in the campus's Hillel club, the Jewish students' association. (Duke had many Jews, but they were for the most part assimilated, so we'd see them only at High Holiday services, if then.) After the UN vote, Rabbi Bob Siegel, the woefully underpaid but enthusiastic Hillel director, announced that we must take action. President Gerald Ford was due to take a swing through North Carolina; we'd present him with a petition, signed by hundreds if not thousands of Duke students, commending him for the U.S. condemnation of the Zionism-is-racism resolution and at the same time urging him to strengthen America's support for Israel. We drafted a text and drew up a duty roster.

My turn manning the petition table on the West Campus quad came the next afternoon. The girl I was relieving told me not to bother soliciting signatures from non-Jews—they weren't interested, and some were hostile. Just go for our own, she advised.

So as students passed by on the way from their dorms or the dining hall to classes, I'd call out to those I knew, or to those who looked Jewish, and it was going pretty well until I pulled over a guy I knew vaguely from my Conflict Resolution course in the Political Science Department. I explained the petition and asked him to sign.

He refused.

"Why?" I asked in astonishment.

"Because Zionism *is* racist," he said.

"How can you say that?" I exclaimed.

"Well, it's only for Jews, isn't it? Israel's a Jewish state, right? So where does that leave the Arabs who live there?" he said, and walked off.

I headed back to my dorm room in a daze.

How could the simplistic, snide comment of a misinformed acquaintance unbalance me so? I would prove him wrong. After all, everyone knew that Israel's Arab citizens had full and equal rights. It was common knowledge that Israel had occupied the West Bank and Gaza Strip only in response to Arab aggression, and that it would gladly return those territories to Arab sovereignty in exchange for peace. So I had always been told. But more than that, such a policy seemed the only one consistent with Judaism as I knew it.

Along with a good friend who'd had a similar experience, I started, for the first time in my life, to read books about Israel. I signed up for a course on the Middle East conflict. I pored over histories, political analyses, foreign policy papers. I began paying attention to articles about Israel in the newspapers. I made contact with Palestinian students at Duke and had long conversations with them.

Israel, I discovered, wasn't living up to my standards. It wasn't pursuing peace with sufficient energy, it wasn't all that eager to give up the territories, and it was beginning to set up civilian settlements in them, even in the midst of areas heavily populated by Palestinians. A messianic, chauvinistic nationalism seemed to be gaining sway among the Israeli populace. And the country's Arab citizens weren't getting a fair deal. If this was Zionism, I decided, it wasn't for me.

While I suffered from a twenty-year-old's tendency to see the world in black and white, I was luckily not afflicted with that age's other common malady, the assumption that having learned a little, I knew everything. My reading proved to me how vast the subject was and how risky it was to rely on what others told me. I needed to see for myself. So my friend and I signed up for a 1976–77 winter-vacation tour of Israel. Rabbi Bob, sensing our crisis, drafted an itinerary focusing specifically on the Palestinian question. In the end, not enough students registered and the trip was canceled. But my friend and I had already gotten the money together and were fired up, so we attached ourselves to a college tour from another region.

For two weeks we saw the usual sights, along with two dozen students from junior colleges in Long Island and a tour guide provided by the Jewish Agency, the body that oversees Israel's relations with the Jewish diaspora. We were hosted by Israeli families and heard from them the sentiments that would topple Israel's Labor party in the 1977 elections and, for the first time, put the right-wing, hard-line Likud party in power. The third week we were free to explore on our own, and my friend and I devoted a part of it to talking to Arabs in Jerusalem's Old City and in Nazareth, where three Palestinian brothers at Duke had relatives.

By the end of those three weeks I realized I'd made a mistake. The Jewish people had to have a country of their own. They needed a country as a refuge from those who sought to destroy them. But even more so, I came to realize, only in a state of their own could the Jews meet the challenge of God's commandment that they create a just society. Only in a polity in which they were a solid majority could they delve into and develop the rich cultural and religious heritage they received from previous generations and put that heritage to the test of real life.

The fact that the Jewish state wasn't perfect—didn't even come close—was no reason to reject it. That error, I'd later discover, is peculiar to left-wing Jewish intellectuals, whether Israeli, American, or European. They expect Israel to meet a higher standard of moral behavior than any other country, and when it fails the test, they conclude that the Jewish state ought not exist at all. My trip cured me of that fallacy. I realized that the issues that concerned me were more complex than I'd imagined. So I revised my postcollege plans. Instead of enlisting in the Peace Corps, I opted to spend a year as a volunteer in Israel—not at a kibbutz, as so many friends had done, but in a program that would place me in a small Israeli town inhabited by the economically disadvantaged "other Israel": families who had come from the Islamic world and who now constituted the bulk of the country's underclass.

When I finished that year of volunteer work in the fall of 1979, I was more aware than ever of how Israel fell short of being an ideal state based on Jewish and democratic values as I knew them. I also understood, as I had not before, that Israel was under constant attack. For the first three months I'd attended an intensive Hebrew course in Kiryat Shmonah, a town at the northern end of Israel's northern panhandle, a piece of the Galilee sticking up into Lebanon. The Palestinian guerrillas who'd ensconced themselves in southern Lebanon periodically fired rockets on Kiryat Shmonah and sent terrorists over the border to kill Israeli civilians. After the Hebrew course I moved half an hour's drive south, to a town at the base of the panhandle, Hatzor Hagelilit. Hatzor, like Kiryat Shmonah, was populated largely by Oriental Jews (commonly, if not quite accurately, called "Sephardim") who had come to Israel from the Muslim world, mostly from North Africa. The town, like others of its kind, had been jerry-built by the Israeli government in the 1950s to house the massive wave of immigrants who flowed into the state soon after its founding. Hatzor had no resources, indeed no economic rationale at all. Most everyone who was motivated and educated fled it at the first opportunity, leaving behind a town with rampant unemployment, delinquency, and poverty. Down the road was Tuba, a village of no longer nomadic Bedouin Arabs where some families were still living in corrugated aluminum shacks. The Israeli government establishment, made up mostly of Ashkenazi Jews—Jews whose roots lay in Europe—wasn't doing much to help. The new Likud government, led by Prime Minister Menachem Begin, had come to power largely because of its promises to assist and empower the Sephardim, but it seemed mostly to foster hypernationalism rather than offer solutions to the severe social problems places like Hatzor suffered. Begin offered the Israeli Arabs like those in Tuba nothing at all. The young people in both towns—the Sephardi kids in Hatzor and the Arab kids in Tuba—were growing up with a justified sense that they were second-class citizens.

Of course, so long as Israel had not made peace with its neighbors, such social and economic problems took second place to defense. Yet

Begin's government, like the Labor governments that preceded it, didn't seem to be doing enough to bring peace. True, Begin had begun a process of accommodation with Egypt, but he adamantly refused to deal with the core of Israel's conflict with the Arabs—the Palestinians. Begin viewed the West Bank and Gaza Strip, the Palestinian areas that Israel had occupied in the Six-Day War, as rightfully and historically Israel's. He encouraged Jewish settlement in the territories and seemed to think that the Palestinian Arabs who lived there (who were not Israeli citizens, as the Arabs of Tuba were) would accept a future as hewers of wood and bearers of water for the Jews of Israel. It was clear to me that Israel could never live in peace until it recognized that the Palestinians had a right to their own country.

Having met Israel's problems face to face, how could I simply walk away? If I were to return to the United States to live, I would, as a Jew, have to defend Israel in discussions with other Americans. Yet there was so much about the country that I opposed and felt needed to be reformed. The thought of leaving my family and friends in the United States was wrenching, nearly unbearable. But I knew I'd be ashamed of myself if I went back to the life of an American Jew, shaking my head sadly at the Jewish state from afar. The only responsible thing I could do, it seemed to me, was stay and try, in my own small way, to work for change. I didn't think I was capable of moving mountains, but I could do my bit of shoveling. I spent another year in Jerusalem to prove to myself that I could eke out a living as a freelance journalist and, that done, I took out Israeli citizenship. By law, that meant I'd be drafted within six months.

Had I been a few years older, or married, or if I had the right kind of back or knee pain, I would have gotten off with a couple months' service in an undemanding unit. But I didn't fit into any of those categories. Under the regulations in force at that time, the one consideration I got that an Israeli kid out of high school didn't was that my term of service would be only eighteen months, half the usual time.

Army service was not something I looked forward to but a duty that had to be done. As I expected, I passed my army physical with a perfect score (there being no test for klutziness) and was therefore in line for combat service. Perhaps if I'd cried and made a fuss about being alone in the country I could have landed a desk job, but I didn't try.

So my choices were limited to field units. Artillery was too loud; the paratroops were out because it was my considered opinion that no rational man jumps out of an airplane. To be in tanks you had to know how to operate a screwdriver. By default, I chose the infantry. If I had any physical ability at all, it was stamina. I'd begun running for exercise in college, though I couldn't say I enjoyed it. In the infantry you walk and run a lot, so maybe it was the place for me. And I had some American-born friends who had already done their service in the infantry. If they could do it, so could I, I supposed.

At their advice I volunteered for Nachal. This infantry brigade differed from the others in that its soldiers combined combat service with work on a kibbutz. My service would be too brief to fit in a kibbutz stint, but Nachal had more experience than other units in absorbing older, foreign-born soldiers like me.

As part of its assistance, Nachal arranged for kibbutzim to adopt soldiers who had immigrated without families. In exchange for a few months of work prior to enlistment, the kibbutz provided room and board for the duration of the soldier's service. While the kibbutzim hoped that these immigrants would join the commune after being discharged, both the kibbutzim and the soldiers knew this seldom happened, so the adoption was largely an altruistic, patriotic act. I gladly agreed—the thought of having to return to an empty apartment in Jerusalem on weekends off to do my own laundry and cook my own meals was depressing.

However, choosing which kibbutz's adoption offer to accept required me to make a long-delayed decision about where I was religiously. Within the American Jewish community is a broad spectrum of religious observance and the differences along it are institutionalized. In addition to Orthodox communities, there are Conservative, Reform, Reconstructionist, and independent communities, each with a different take on how and what to observe. Israeli society is more polarized between those who are observant in the Orthodox sense and those who are not observant at all. Even those who call themselves "traditional," meaning that they are partially observant, generally attend Orthodox synagogues.

The kibbutzim are even more polarized. Most of them are overwhelmingly secular—that is, not only are their members not religious, they are ideologically antireligious. Then there are a small number of kibbutzim that maintain an Orthodox lifestyle, though they tend to be more liberal than Orthodox communities in Israeli cities. Given the choice between no religion and Orthodox religion, I chose the latter without much hesitation.

I went to live at Tirat Zvi on the Jordan River, about a half hour's drive south of the Sea of Galilee. Established in 1937 as a lonely outpost in a wild and dangerous border region, Tirat Zvi was the oldest member of the small Religious Kibbutz Movement. Its founders had arrived from Germany and Poland as part of what they called a "holy rebellion"— against both the passivity of the European Orthodox Jewish world they had grown up in and the radically secular socialism of the majority of the Zionist pioneers in Palestine. The kibbutz's members had believed that settling and guarding the Jewish state's underpopulated regions was both a religious and a patriotic obligation. For them, helping an immigrant serving in the army was an extension of that mission. I easily adjusted to Tirat Zvi's religious norms, since I had been headed in that direction for some time. The most salient outward consequence was that I began wearing a *kipah*, the knitted cap that is the badge of an Orthodox male.

I'd hoped that my year and a half of mandatory service would coincide with a relatively quiet period in my country's history, but the Begin government had other plans. On June 6, 1982, two and a half months before my enlistment date, Israel embarked on a massive invasion of Lebanon. At first, like most Israelis, I supported what I thought would be a brief incursion aimed at destroying the Palestinian terrorist bases from which missiles were being launched against Kiryat Shmonah and other northern towns and villages. As the army pushed north through Lebanon, however, eventually invading the country's capital, Beirut, I began to have serious misgivings.

On August 16, 1982, a month after my twenty-sixth birthday, I reported to the draft office in Tiberias, a city on the Sea of Galilee. From Tiberias, the army bused me to its huge central induction base outside Tel Aviv, dressed me in a uniform and dog tags, and sent me off to basic infantry training with a bunch of eighteen-year-olds.

In mid-September, a month after I began basic training, Israeli soldiers stood by as Lebanese Christian militiamen slaughtered Palestinian civilians, including women and children, in two refugee camps in Beirut. One Saturday night in October, when I was on leave, I went to Tel Aviv to attend a mass demonstration demanding that a commission be established to investigate the massacre. The next morning I reported back to my unit.

Being an enlisted man was not particularly pleasant. My initial impression had been correct—I turned out to be not very good at nearly everything an infantryman is supposed to do. In basic, which lasted six months, most of the guys I served with were immature, even crude, and I felt like an outsider. Then I went straight into noncommissioned officers (NCO) course. This certainly wasn't because I'd excelled in boot camp. But a certain percentage of the privates at the end of basic had to go to the course and, again at the advice of more experienced friends, I volunteered. After completing the course with low marks in every category but personal responsibility and camaraderie—in which I excelled—I served with the Nachal Brigade in Lebanon until my discharge in February 1984.

On the long-awaited day, I took a bus back to the induction base outside Tel Aviv to turn in my gear. The army didn't take it all back, however. It left me with a pair of black combat boots. I'd need them because, although I was now a civilian, I remained an infantryman. I'd continue to serve in a reserve unit until I was forty-five. This, I knew, was no weekend camp assignment. In the Israeli army, the reserves are the bulk of the fighting force. When the country is attacked, the enlisted men only take the first blow and hold the line until the reserves can be mobilized. It's the reserves that then do the real fighting.

The boots weren't the only thing the army left me with. "I'm not the man who was, I'm the one who came after," wrote Chaim Guri, a poet who fought in the War of Independence, "an approximate extension of the same face." The transformation back into a civilian, which I'd so anticipated, was not instantaneous. In fact, I quickly realized that I'd never again be a civilian in the same sense I had been before enlisting. Army habits were too ingrained in me. My right hand kept feeling for the rifle that no longer hung at my waist. I briefly considered purchasing a pistol just so I'd have the familiar feel of a weapon at hand. I felt like a foreigner among my American-born friends, few of whom had done military service of the same rigor and difficulty that I had. I was both proud at having gotten through it and bewildered by how an entire part of my life now stood outside the awareness of most of the people I'd known before.

The army itself made sure that I didn't forget that, in the years to come, I'd be simultaneously civilian and soldier. Three months after my discharge I was summoned back to the army for a day to receive my reserve assignment. I was attached to Company C of a battalion in what had until a few years before been called the Jerusalem Brigade, a fabled infantry unit that had fought in the battle for Israel's capital in the Six-Day War and in the Sinai Peninsula in the Yom Kippur War. Three months after that, having resumed my career as a journalist and having met the woman I would marry, I packed my chimidan, donned my uniform, and became a soldier again.

Enlisted men are adolescents. Reservists are adults. It makes a big difference. The core group that crystallized during my first few years in Company C was made up of mature, thoughtful men who managed the trick of combining an easygoing ambience with determination and professionalism. Almost immediately, I felt a bond with them that made the unit a focal point in my life for the next eighteen years. The bond was so strong that it proved very difficult to release when age and disability dictated that I leave.

The stories that follow occurred during those years, through winter and summer maneuvers, through stints facing the Syrians on Mount Hermon and the Palestinian uprising in the West Bank. One of the many things I learned during those years is that reserve duty in Israel is not, in fact, mandatory. True, the law requires all able-bodied men to serve as reservists, but in practice those who don't want to serve can find their way out of the system without too much exertion. For all intents and purposes, I was a volunteer, and a rather determined one. When my company was called up, I reported for duty and missed only a small number of days over nearly two decades—even though I often had good reasons for staying home.

So the events here did not have to happen to me. I could have avoided them and remained free of the moral ambiguities of military service. In writing about myself as a soldier, I am attempting to understand why these are necessary stories.

Chapter One

· LANDINGS ·

MOUNT HERMON, AUGUST–SEPTEMBER 1984

ELDAD EVOKED MIRI AS I WAVED A WASP OFF MY NOSE. WE'D BEEN on this hilltop for an hour and a half already. There were more than six hours to go, though only two and a half until Brenner and Sharvit came in the jeep to bring us lunch.

We were on the peak of a spur jutting out from the lift station at the bottom of the ski slope on Mount Hermon, Israel's highest mountain. It had been captured from Syria in the Six-Day War, seventeen years and a couple of months ago. Our position gave us a commanding view of the Sion Gorge, which plunged westward down to the town of Kiryat Shmonah and the fields of the Hula Valley. On the far side, above the gorge, was Har Dov, or Bear Mountain, the summit's northwestern shoulder, along which snaked the perimeter road and border fence that another company in our battalion patrolled day and night. It was late August, so the bear's haunches were the drab brown of parched shrubs and desiccated spring flower stems. Through a lingering morning haze we could now make out Astra, the outpost above and beyond the perimeter road where the bulk of Company C was stationed.

Eldad and I, being new, had been shunted off doubly. First, we were separated from our platoon, One, and attached to Platoon Three, stationed at the small base next to the lift station. Second, being both newcomers to the company and outsiders to Platoon Three, we'd been given the most annoying assignment on the Lower Ski Lift base's duty roster—sitting on this wasp-infested high point to guard the approaches to the base where many of the more senior reservists who had shafted us now slept.

I half-listened—indulgently, for the moment—to yet another recounting of how Eldad met Miri. At a party? On a bus? The story didn't quite register. It had happened, in Eldad's hometown of Lod, just three days before our month of reserve duty began—that is, just a week and a few days before we ascended this hill. In the week intervening, he and I had become inseparable. We guarded together, patrolled together, sat next to each other at meals. While others called us Sarfati and Watzman, we called each other by our first names (the mysterious general rule in the Israel Defense Forces being that while soldiers are usually called by their surnames, officers nearly always go by their first names). It occurred to me as I listened to him that he and I had spent more time together, in closer quarters, and in more intensive activity, than he and Miri had. I didn't realize that this friendship, based on our common status as Platoon One's novices, would fade the next year, when we became veterans in Company C. For the moment, he was my anchor in this new milieu, the other guy who didn't yet understand the tacit rules, the pecking order, the cause-and-effect processes at work. A reserve unit, we'd realized soon after arriving, works differently from a unit of enlisted men, but we hadn't yet entirely fathomed what the difference was.

Eldad was no poet, but his boyish enthusiasm and his absolute confidence in the permanence of the love that he and Miri (by his report) shared imbued his story with the vastness of an epic romance. His longish face and light brown eyes gave him a dreamy look. Uncombed hair, growing longer and mussier after three years of close cropping, made him look like a minstrel in olive green fatigues. He and Miri would marry, he asserted, and buy an apartment, and have a given number of children. Specific plans were to be made as soon as our stint of reserve duty was over.

I leaned back on a boulder and thought that Eldad would probably not marry Miri. True, at twenty-two, six months past his three years of mandatory army service, he was at that stage in life when many Israeli men establish their families. But his romance sounded to me more like a high school crush. And frankly, the question of whether Eldad would marry Miri was much less interesting to me than the question of whether I would marry Ilana.

I took a swing at three circling wasps and rummaged through my chimidan, fumbling for the spiral notebook I used for letter writing. Told we would be out here for eight hours straight, I'd decided to bring the chimidan and everything in it. There was the small (spare socks and extra shoelaces) and the warm (sweatshirt, army-issue stocking cap, and the gloves I'd worn until the morning chill passed). There were things that army experience taught me always to have at hand, like a box cutter and a roll of toilet paper. There were cookies and Cokes, and a coffee kit (camp stove, long-handled pot, sugar, glasses, and Turkish coffee)—mandatory for any lengthy assignment. My recently used prayer gear was lodged in a blue velvet bag. It included my prayer book (the complete, though still compact green plastic–bound version, as opposed to the small one with only the brief afternoon and evening services and the grace after meals, which I kept permanently in my shirt pocket). Also my tallit, the large, fringed, rectangular piece of cloth draped over the shoulders and back during prayers, and my tefillin. By delaying my morning prayers until we were on-site, I'd gained another twenty minutes of sleep that morning. The chimidan also contained a radio, a backgammon set, and four books, one of them the hefty first volume of Henry Kissinger's memoirs. These items were stowed in thematic groups in plastic bags that rustled as I searched them, harmonizing with the buzz of the wasps.

I pulled out the notebook and located a pen, but wasps kept landing on my hand. They didn't sting as long as I didn't move, but this kept me from writing much of a letter. Eldad suggested various strategies. We poured a quantity of sugar on a rock some meters distant, hoping that, as social insects, the wasps would organize a party where food was plentiful and cheap. But they seemed to prefer whatever was coming out of our sweat pores. Eldad said that the best way to confuse and frustrate wasps was to hang a plastic bag full of water from a tree. I recalled, but did not quote to Eldad, an adage from a Tom Stoppard play: "There is no problem that can't be solved if one has a large enough plastic bag." Not true. We had a plastic bag, and a jerrycan full of water, but no tree.

"Did you ever shoot anyone?" Eldad asked, gazing down into the gorge. He slipped the magazine from his M-16 rifle, examined it absentmindedly, and clicked it back in. "In Lebanon?"

"No," I said. I was thrown off balance by the question. "I mean, we returned fire a few times when we were attacked. But I never saw who we were firing at." I paused for a short battle between my sense of humor and my pride. Self-deprecation won. "Anyway, I'm sure that if I'd aimed at anyone in particular I would have missed."

Eldad was still looking at the vegetation below us. His usually cheerful face seemed to have gone dark. I sensed that he was waiting for me to ask him the same question, so I did.

"We were at a roadblock in Beirut," he said. "And this car drove up, and three guys got out with rifles and began spraying us. We opened fire, and within a few seconds we'd finished them all off."

There was tension in his voice. And fervor. The adrenaline of that moment, the joy of finding himself alive just seconds after dozens of bullets flew by him, had returned.

"One of them wasn't dead," he continued. "He was lying by the car on his back. I went up to him and raised my rifle and switched it to automatic. He put up his hands as if to fend me off, or maybe beg for mercy. But I just pulled the trigger and filled his body up with bullets."

"If he was already wounded, why did you kill him?" I asked. "That's against orders."

"He could still use his hands. And he might have had a grenade," Eldad said testily. "He was going to die anyway. And he deserved it."

He looked at me angrily. Was I accusing him of a crime?

"You would've done the same thing."

Would I have? I thought I wouldn't. Also I thought: in not doing so, I might have been wrong.

"If I had," I half joked, "I would have missed."

The radio crackled. "Alterman to Uri Alef."

Eldad picked up the handset. "Root," he said, which is how you say "roger" in Hebrew radio talk.

"Situation report, avor"—avor meaning "over"—replied a voice that we couldn't identify. We still didn't know the other guys well enough.

"Okay. Nothing to report, avor."

"Root. Hang in there." The radio went silent.

"Have you told Miri that story?" I asked.

Eldad's bushy eyebrows descended. This was what had troubled him before. "No." He paused. "Do you talk to Ilana about the army?"

"Not a whole lot," I said, "but still more than she cares for."

"If you thought the Lebanon war was wrong, why were you there?" Eldad put the question directly. He must have guessed that I asked myself the same question, over and over, and that I didn't have a clear answer.

I was Company C's only American. Along with two Russians whom I barely knew, I differed from the rest of the men in that I made my decision to live in Israel—and, by corollary, to serve in its army—as an adult. I could have decided otherwise. I need not have served in the war in Lebanon. And I could have been elsewhere this summer morning.

The rest of the men grew up expecting, and largely wanting, to be soldiers. They knew that at age eighteen they would begin three years of mandatory service, and continue, through their twenties, thirties, and forties, to be soldiers for a couple months each year, more in case of emergency. The greater part of them were veterans of the Yom Kippur War, when the reserves had been on active duty for months on end.

"When was your first time in Lebanon?" Eldad needled me.

"At the beginning of NCO course," I replied. "The very first week."

"Hell week?"

"Hell week."

When I volunteered to go straight from basic to NCO course, I had to choose between two opposite views current among my fellow foot soldiers. One was that anyone would be crazy to go to the course voluntarily: "Three more months of basic training? Forget it." The second was that it was wise to make a move up the command ladder as soon as possible, so as to enjoy the perks, such as having inferiors to scream at.

All agreed, however, that the first week of NCO course was one of the great horrors known to man. You got dumped out in the middle of nowhere to do exercises and maneuvers and forced marches day and night, with insufficient quantities of canned rations and no showers and barely any sleep. Since it was the beginning of February in a particularly cold and wet winter, when we did sleep, it would be in our damp uniforms and muddy boots, which we wouldn't be able to change or clean until hell week was over.

The horror stories were true. No sooner had we arrived at the NCO school base and been given our gear than we were hastily preparing our weapons and packs—elephant packs, they were called—as our corporals and sergeants barked orders. We shouted advice to one another about things worth taking and things worth leaving behind to minimize the elephant's weight. We packed and polished and tied for an entire afternoon and night, covering everything we could with plastic sheeting and putting anything loose into plastic bags. We slept two hours, only to be jarred awake at 3:30 a.m. We threw chimidans, duffel bags, anti-tank missiles, mortars, stretchers, submachine guns, jerrycans, and boxes of rations onto trucks, climbed on ourselves, and were driven over unpaved roads through a freezing drizzle as we dozed for a few more minutes. We woke with a start when the trucks stopped in a clearing surrounded by tiny, exhausted oak trees that seemed themselves to have buckled under excess weight and lack of sleep. At this point, a thunderstorm broke out so violently that even our commanders were not willing to get out of the trucks and we sat inside for two hours. When the barrage died down to a drizzle, we threw our gear onto the freshly churned mire below us, jumped down, and began to set up camp. There was no conversation, only muttered curses as the rain penetrated gloves, coats, and uniforms, and as the chill that would be our companion for the entire week worked itself into our skin. Then we began running uphill and downhill, shooting at targets—over and over until another night in which we barely slept melded into another morning, which dragged on into a dismal afternoon. Suddenly, without explanation, exercises ceased and we were told to ready our equipment and stand for inspection.

Suddenly, we heard beating propellers, then more shouts and orders as three helicopters descended onto the flat hill above us. We looked up, puzzled, and the commanders shouted at us to pack up everything and lug it all up the hill. Emergency orders from Central Command. We're going to Lebanon. Never were soldiers so happy to get sent to a war zone.

The helicopters took us to Tyre, the southern Lebanese port, where we were installed in a warm, dry warehouse as another thunderstorm raged outside. We had nothing to do for the entire day but sleep and do guard duty, an hour each. Then we piled onto buses and rushed north to southern Beirut, where we were installed in the concrete shell of a large, unfinished, and more than half-destroyed house. There we began patrolling the neighborhood. A couple of days later my platoon was dispatched to an improvised outpost not far to the southeast, on the slope of Mount Lebanon.

It was now Sunday, and I was on guard duty. That we might have the most commanding view of the territory around us, the guard position was the commander's seat of one of our armored personnel carriers, or APCs. A chill sea wind scoured my face, the only exposed part of my body. A *hermonit*, the padded coverall that is every soldier's most precious piece of gear in the winter, kept my body warm, but my fingers were icy and my immobile feet almost dead with cold. I was angry.

The Lebanese capital was spread like a map below me. I could identify the airport, the presidential palace, and the business district, and was able to trace clearly the line along which Israeli and Syrian troops faced each other. I could also see Sabra and Shatila, the two refugee camps where Lebanese Christian militias had massacred Palestinians.

I was reading a newspaper—from the previous Tuesday, the latest we had. This was against the rules, so I kept the pages on my lap, out of sight under the rim of the commander's hatch. We weren't allowed to read, listen to the radio, or talk to any other soldier except on operational business, so that we'd devote our full attention to guard duty. Now a veteran of more than half a year in the army, I'd come to realize that trying to focus exclusively on guard duty during a four- to six-hour stint was the best way to get bored and doze off. A measured bit of reading, music, or conversation always helped keep you alert.

Also keeping me alert was the fact that I was scared stiff. My platoon's mission on this hill was one with which the Israel Defense Forces found itself preoccupied during its lengthy occupation of southern Lebanon: keeping Lebanese of different confessional communities from murdering one another.

The hill on which we had stationed ourselves stood above a neighborhood at the edge of Beirut, really a village that was in the process of being engulfed by the expanding city. Its homes, belonging to Christians and Druze, lay below us along a green wadi whose seasonal creek now flowed down its center toward the sea. The houses were expansively spaced, generous structures, two or three stories tall. Each had two, three, even four automobiles parked on the muddy roads that wound up and down and across the valley. Most of the homes had chicken runs and sheep pens in the yards. On the flat roof of the house directly north of me, a family was taking breakfast. Through my binoculars I could see a mother in a navy blue skirt and frilled white blouse, a father in a brown jacket and tie, small boys in vests and trousers—dressed, perhaps, for church. The father was speaking with an older woman, maybe his mother or mother-in-law, and two young men—the father's brothers?—were leaning over the roof's railing, talking to someone below. Not far from where the mother sat, an RPG antitank rocket launcher was mounted, aimed at the house across the way.

I was angry because I'd been had. I was reading a special newspaper supplement, a report on how the Israeli government, *my* government, had decided to embark on this war that had already claimed the lives of more than two hundred soldiers.

According to the newspaper, the minister of defense, Ariel Sharon, and the army's chief of staff, Rafael (Raful) Eitan, had deliberately misled Prime Minister Menachem Begin and his cabinet as to the aims and extent of the military operation. Sharon and Eitan wanted to reach Beirut and install the leader of the Phalangist Christian militias as president of Lebanon. He would head a pro-Israeli regime that would prevent Palestinian guerrillas from attacking northern Israel. Sharon and Eitan were aware, though, that the government would not likely approve a grandiose plan to remake the Middle East. So, the newspaper report claimed, the pair asked the cabinet to approve a limited incursion aimed at flushing the PLO out of southern Lebanon. All the while, they intended to send the army on to Beirut. According to the paper, the cabinet—Prime Minister Begin included—were not informed that the army had leapfrogged over the forty-kilometer limit that the cabinet had authorized, not until the Israeli forces were well on their way north to Beirut and the Beka'a Valley. In other words, the country's army had trumped its civilian government in a manner that a democracy must not tolerate.

"Pepper?" I looked down from my perch and saw Shmuel, a freck-led, short, but sturdily built guy, holding out a handful of bright red fruit glistening with morning dew. We had no oranges, apples, toma-toes, or cucumbers, just boxes of canned rations and ten crates of red peppers.

"Have you seen this?" I stage-whispered, holding up the newspaper supplement, then quickly concealing it again under the hatch.

Shmuel gazed at the village below us. "Do you think we could send a detachment down to that store to buy some coffee?" he wondered, half serious.

"We've been duped," I hissed. "We shouldn't be here." And in a few sentences I explained to Shmuel the gist of the report.

Shmuel was exasperated. He tore open a pepper with his bare hands and demanded, "Why are you always talking about politics? Is that something American?"

"Doesn't it bother you that you're here risking your life for Sharon and Raful in a war that your elected government didn't approve?"

He shrugged. "I don't want to be here. But here we are. I'm not risk-ing my life for Sharon and Raful. I'm risking my life to defend you and you're risking your life to defend me." He turned his attention to the roof-mounted RPG. "They just need to rotate that twenty degrees and raise the supports and it'll be aimed at us." He tossed me a red pepper and headed back to his tent.

I fell silent. Sometime during this story I'd gotten up and begun to pace. I looked down into the valley and up at the slope beyond. All was still. Eldad was lying on his side, his head on his arm.

"You could have picked up and gone, like Eli Geva," Eldad said, referring to a senior officer who had resigned his commission during the invasion of Beirut.

"Oh, right," I snapped. "Just packed up my stuff and walked home."

"You could have pretended to be sick. You could have said your grandmother died."

I kicked at a rock and missed.

"And left the guys to get shot at instead of me?" I asked, looking at Eldad out of the corner of my eye.

"Right. So you stayed."

"We weren't there for that much longer. They sent us back to the course, and I finished it."

"And then?"

"Most of the nine months I had left were also in Lebanon. Then I was discharged."

"And when did you meet Ilana?"

"Oh, I was out of the army by then," I said.

I told him how mutual friends had introduced us, and how I'd nearly insulted her irremediably by not asking for her phone number at that first encounter. Also, how I'd made my first visit to her apartment in Holon, where she lived with her mother, on the same May morning that I went to the infantry base where I'd been assigned to Company C.

There was a cloud of dust down by the Lower Ski Lift base, and a rumble as the cloud rolled toward us. Inside it were Brenner and Sharvit on a jeep. Lunchtime already. They greeted us, told us what was up back at the base, and presented us with a pair of orange plastic plates covered with orange plastic bowls. The plates were heaped with lukewarm chicken, rice, cabbage salad, and eggplant mush. After chatting a few moments, they wheeled the jeep around and headed back. Eldad and I sat down to eat.

"Actually," I said, "this is more like what I thought being a soldier was about."

"What do you mean?" Eldad asked, looking unenthusiastically at the food.

"I mean, standing guard on the country's border. With a woman to call at home."

He brightened and began to tell me, once again, how he met Miri.

This month of reserve duty had begun one mid-August day at Camp Yishai, along the Jerusalem–Jericho Road. Ten of us were arrayed as three sides of a square. Two guys from the quartermaster platoon constituted the fourth side. One was large and balding, with a paunch too big for his army shirt. He read out each piece of necessary gear listed on the requisition form we'd already signed and handed in. As the list got called we dug through the drab-colored pile in front of us to ensure that we indeed had it. Duffel bag, check. Helmet, check. *Efod* (an ammunition girdle with pouches for cartridges, grenades, maps, and chocolate-coated wafers), check. Two plastic, olive green canteens, check—wait! "I've only got one!" I yelled to the supply guy's short, dark, curly-haired partner, who was walking the square. He stopped to make sure that I had not overlooked or deliberately concealed my second canteen and, satisfied as to my efficiency and honesty, went over to a heap of the things and threw me one. Work clothes, as the everyday fatigues were called, consisting of two shirts and two pairs of pants, plus a belt and Australian wide-brimmed hat (a lucky few got American-style caps, which were considered cooler)—check again. "The pants are all smalls!" shouted Eiger, who clearly needed larges. "We can't fit you individually, this isn't a boutique. Trade with your friends afterward," snapped the fat guy.

The desert sun had us dying for water even though we'd drunk just before we lined up on the square. It was almost nauseating to pick up the winter equipment we were being issued. But we'd be spending the month sixty-five hundred feet above sea level and would need it. Wool gloves, check. Dark green scratchy sweater with many holes, check.

Stocking cap, check. And every soldier's favorite items—the sleeping bag and the *dubon*, or winter coat with attached hood. Never go anywhere where night might fall without your dubon—even in this parched desert the nights are chilly. Finally, the *tadal*, a small canvas rucksack of 1950s vintage that invariably came with only one of the two straps you needed to carry it on your back. Furthermore, that single strap always got lost before the gear was returned to the quartermaster in another open square at the end of the month's service.

Eldad, Eiger, and I stuffed our gear into the duffel bags and proceeded to the armorer's hut, where we received rifles, rifle slings, and seven magazines to fill with bullets. Eldad and I were disappointed. The rifles were rodlike metal-and-plastic American M-16s rather than the foldable metal-and-wood Israeli-made Galils we had as infantrymen during our mandatory service. M-16s were a pain to dismantle and clean, and in the regular army at that time, they were given to less serious units. But Eiger, a veteran of a year in Company C, told us we'd soon appreciate the fact that an M-16 is half the weight of a Galil. And, anyway, he'd heard that regular infantry units would soon switch to M-16s.

We lugged our rifles and duffel bags back to the open shed the company had been assigned and emptied them again. The first thing we did was write our names on every piece of equipment; we'd have to pay for what we didn't return. In my overstuffed chimidan I had two Magic Markers, black and red. My prescience in bringing them immediately made me sought after by the rest of the guys.

Being back in the army was comforting in a way, even if it felt as though I was starting at the bottom all over again. Eldad and I were two of the four new soldiers to join Company C that year. He and I had discovered each other almost immediately as we sat around our enlistment point, Shneller base in Jerusalem, waiting for the unit's latecomers to arrive. I guess it was a common shyness that made me gravitate toward him rather than either of the other newcomers. One, a broad-backed, loud kid named Hezki, was already bumming cigarettes off the veterans, while the other, a fair-skinned kibbutz boy, seemed to know several of the older guys from somewhere. There were actually two familiar faces: the Platoon Two medic, Shaya, and his best friend, Kobi. They had been part of a Nachal contingent based at Tirat Zvi while I lived there. But they were passing acquaintances, not friends.

My six months as a civilian had been exhilarating but also unsettling. A brief, if concerted, attempt to remake myself as a Hebrew journalist and land a job on one of the local dailies had failed. I started again as a freelance journalist for American publications, but work was slow and I wasn't at all sure it was a realistic career for me. At twenty-eight, I could no longer think of it as a stopgap, a way of getting by until I decided what kind of job I really wanted. On the other hand, there was nothing else in particular that I was qualified to do.

Then there was Ilana. How I should go about loving Ilana was a question I hadn't figured out yet. In the past, I hadn't been adept at falling in love. I could neither fake nor be casual about my emotions, and the result had been a loneliness that left me totally unprepared for the woman—it was obvious despite my delaying tactics—I was going to marry. Unfairly for her, she was playing multiple roles for me—first adolescent infatuation, serious girlfriend, and object of my mature affection—and I kept stumbling over my own feet opposite her. As Yehuda Amichai, another 1948 soldier-poet, writes, I had "to read the past out of the palm of the woman that I love."

In the army, at least, I knew what I had to do. I began to work on my equipment, as I'd done whenever I'd been transferred to a new unit and issued new gear during my mandatory service. Eldad joined me. We adjusted our efods so that they wouldn't joggle on us when we ran—this being accomplished by playing with the straps and inserting pieces of foam rubber (which we'd saved from our regular army gear) into the sides of the girdle. We'd also brought pieces of camouflage netting, which we stretched over our helmets, and slices of inner tube that held the netting in place. We traded tips about adding useful extra pouches to the efod; we had some of those, too.

A few minutes into this we noticed that none of the other guys had done anything at all with their equipment other than lounge against their duffel bags or make Turkish coffee on their camp stoves. A few had even rolled out their sleeping bags for a nap. Eiger grinned.

"What exactly are you doing?" he asked, leaning back on his duffel bag and placing his hands slowly and deliberately behind his head.

"We're getting our gear ready," Eldad said.

"Do you see anyone *else* getting their gear ready?" Eiger asked, doing a long, slow pan of the company with his eyes.

"I *want* my gear to be ready. I *intend* for my gear to be ready," Eldad muttered. His eyes were fixed on the extra smoke-grenade pouch he was attaching to the shoulder strap of his efod with steel wire and a pair of pliers.

I was torn. What Eldad was doing seemed to make a lot more sense than what the rest of the guys were not doing. But if there was one thing I'd learned as an enlisted man, it was that looking too eager and too diligent was not good, at least not for me. It tempted officers to give you extra duties and it made you look ridiculous among your peers.

"Aren't we going to be doing lots of foot patrols on Mount Hermon?" I asked Eiger.

"Probably," Eiger said.

"And tonight won't we be hiking for hours with lots of weight on our backs? In the brigade maneuvers?"

"Most likely," Eiger confirmed.

"And isn't it really uncomfortable to walk long distances with a badly fitting efod? With canteens banging against your butt and the magazines against your hip bone at every step? The weight will be badly distributed and make me walk crooked, all because I haven't adjusted the straps properly."

"You bet!" Eiger agreed.

I glanced at Eldad. "So doesn't it make sense to do what he's doing?"

"Do it later. Anyway, we're only in for a month." Eiger yawned and closed his eyes. "The first thing an infantry reservist should do after putting on his uniform is find a place to sleep. That's my advice."

I had met Eiger earlier that morning on the Number Fifteen bus, a line that meandered slowly, infrequently, and seemingly irrationally from Palmach Street through downtown Jerusalem and then to Shneller base. Ilana sat beside me and we chatted quietly. This was to be our first lengthy separation since we'd met in May, and it would determine whether we remained together. Ilana had made clear that she wanted a decision from me, and that if I was not willing to commit, she would leave. I knew that I wanted to marry Ilana, but making plans for a marriage only three months after I met her seemed hasty. Why not wait a bit longer, I suggested. Is there something you don't know now that you'll know later? she asked. I couldn't imagine that there would be. But only in books and movies did people get married on the basis of a three-month acquaintance. Ilana granted a stay until the end of my reserve duty.

It was this that we were discussing in undertones when the guy in front of us turned and introduced himself.

"I think we're going to be in the same unit," he said.

He was in uniform already, with his chimidan on the seat next to him. A bit chubby, he had a square face and curly, sandy-colored hair. When he threw in an occasional English phrase, it was with a British accent. His name, he said, was Yonatan Eiger and he studied pharmacy at Hebrew University. He'd be marrying Na'ama, a fellow student, later in the year, he told us with familiarity that seemed to stop just short of inviting us to do a double ceremony.

Had I known that this guy would end up being my best friend in Company C, I would have been more friendly. But I wanted to talk to Ilana, not him. He didn't seem offended and turned back to his newspaper. I wasn't sure what to expect from Ilana when we parted. It was the first time I'd ever had to say good-bye to a girlfriend. Would she cry? What was I expected to do if she did?

But she didn't. At the entrance to the camp I presented my call-up order. Ilana and I embraced and kissed. Then, with Eiger, I went through the gate.

After a week and a half at the Lower Ski Lift base, Eldad and I were transferred back to the main part of the company at Astra, and now I was on patrol. We'd been walking for only ten minutes and already my bottom was sore and damp from canteen blows. Under the weight of weapons and whatnot, I was walking like an actor playing the Elephant Man. In addition to seven full ammunition clips containing twenty-nine bullets each (I'd insisted on filling them all even though Eiger urged me not to. "We're crossing the border into Lebanon," I'd exclaimed. "You'll enjoy it more with less weight," he'd said), I had two hand grenades, a red smoke grenade, two first-aid bandages, and a back pouch containing a chocolate spread sandwich and four chocolate-covered wafers of various brands and varieties.

I'd been given the job of radioman, so I had a twenty-kilogram army radio pack on my back, including an extra battery. Also attached to the radio pack was a metal case containing a night vision device built, like everything else on me, to be durable without regard to comfort. It was all meant to be borne by athletic eighteen-year-olds, not by a klutz ten years beyond that age who had been a civilian for six months and was not much of a cart horse even when he was a full-time soldier.

It was as tough a patrol as any I'd done during my regular army service. The battalion maneuvers we'd done on our first night, after signing in and getting our gear, had been on the same level.

"Are you okay?" my NCO, Yoel, asked after I stumbled over a rock. We were on a steep descent on the mountainside at Astra's north face, in somewhat ragged formation.

The radio sputtered: static and some words I didn't catch. I was too busy watching my feet while trying to keep my back straight.

"They're calling us," Yoel noted in a tone of mild interest rather than the reproof I expected. Yoel was very big in all directions; he had a roundish beard, not particularly well trimmed, and a large, dingy white kipah with blue trim. Like my own kipah, it was the knitted type, which meant that he identified with the modern religious Zionist branch of orthodoxy. However, at the size of his outspread hand, it had a diameter half again as big as my own, which meant that he belonged to the right wing of that broader group. He had the gait of a hiker rather than a soldier; every so often he stopped to examine a flower or take in the view.

I ran up to Elnatan, the company commander, and shoved the handset at him.

"Calling us," I mumbled.

"Who?" he asked.

I hesitated. Elnatan gave me a sharp glance and spoke into the handset. The brigade's operations sergeant asked for our location, and Elnatan gave it—a total of three or four words, punctuated by roots and avors. Then he shoved the handset back at me and proceeded to walk. I tried to attach the hook on the back of the handset to the tiny slot on my efod's shoulder strap, where it could hang close enough to my ear for me to hear any future calls. But between the straps of the radio and my rifle I couldn't find the slot and I ended up walking while holding the handset to my ear with my left hand and gripping my weapon with my right.

"Stay right behind me," Elnatan ordered.

That was about as much conversation as I'd had with him.

As far as I could tell by walking behind him, Elnatan operated on several planes of consciousness simultaneously. He could talk on the radio, navigate, and observe an anemone or an eagle, all while keeping track of exactly where the company's men were—not just those on this patrol but also those on other missions. He was dark haired and trim, and I was continually rediscovering that he was of average height, like me. His presence made me assume he was taller.

Elnatan halted, raised his arms at his sides, and flapped his hands three times. We all stopped and knelt. He surveyed the valley with his binoculars, then gestured again, and we rose to continue our descent.

Toward the bottom of the slope we entered an orchard. Olive trees grew on terraces, and farther down, by a stream, were stands of peach and apple trees, the latter with fruit on the branches. The trees seemed pruned with an eye to beauty, not merely utility, and a platoon in dusty green fatigues was about as out of place among them as a garbage crew in a sculpture garden. We passed a heavyset older woman with a plastic basket balanced on her head; she stared at us with hatred and scorn. An older, mustached man with a hoe over his right shoulder smiled and nodded. We were in the midst of the Shaba farms, a cultivated strip of valley around the town of Shaba, caught in a corner where Lebanon, Israel, and Syria meet.

Shaba was a staging ground for Palestinian terrorists who sought to breach the fence that lined the perimeter road up on the mountain. Sometimes they succeeded and found their way into civilian settlements to murder and destroy. We had no specific intelligence about any terrorists lurking there just then. Our purpose was to "show the flag," as Americans say, though we had no flag. In other words, ours was no stealth operation. We intended to be seen by the citizens of Shaba, so they'd know we were watching them.

Although Elnatan told us to remain in formation, with two columns of men guarding the flanks and a vanguard of five spread out beside him, the terraces and the trees made it hard to do so, and we began to feel like we were on a nature walk rather than a patrol. As we entered the village's outskirts, some elementary school boys brazenly called us names, then asked for money. The adults mostly pretended to ignore us. We saw no young men—either they were off working in some far city or they were making themselves scarce until we left. We wended through some streets, then headed out and back toward Astra. The climb up was difficult. Our muscles ached. Some muttered curses; Eiger cracked jokes. At one point he even tried to get everyone singing, but Elnatan silenced him. We trudged past a lonely UN peacekeeping post, where blue-helmeted soldiers sat impassively. I fell behind again, and Yoel pushed me up the final incline to the gate in the fence that led us back home.

"Everybody up!" a voice called brightly, back on our first afternoon at Camp Yishai. A short, round-faced, softly smiling soldier with a spiral notebook and pen in hand walked among the snoozing men, tapping each lightly on the shoulder, like an airline steward handing out hot towels as the sun rises on an international flight. He was, in fact, an El Al bursar and an instructor in the airline's flight attendant school. It was Jacques (don't forget the soft French *J* and that half syllable at the end, *Zhak-eu*) Segev, our Tunisian-born company clerk.

"The company commander would like a word with everyone," Jacques explained as he approached us. "How are you two new boys doing? Are the men helping you out? Are you feeling at home?"

"We're fine," I said. "What's happening?"

"Battalion maneuvers tonight," he announced soothingly and moved on.

The men lethargically arranged themselves in a vaguely semicircular formation, still stretched out on their duffel bags. Elnatan arrived from the battalion commander's tent flanked by his three lieutenants—the wispy-looking commander of Platoon One, Matan; the bearded, tough-looking Platoon Two commander, whose name I hadn't learned; and Yermi, the blond, good-looking Platoon Three sergeant who was acting as its commanding officer. Jacques stationed himself between Elnatan and Yermi and signaled us to pay attention.

"Everyone sit up," Elnatan commanded. Unlike most of the other men, he wore his shirt tucked in. He had his pant legs rolled up under elastic bands, as regulations required. His uniform even looked ironed.

In the regular army, Elnatan had been a company commander in the NCO school of the Golani Brigade, an infantry unit known for its toughness. When it comes to discipline, the Israeli army is to the American army as vaudeville is to opera, but Elnatan's military persona had been molded in one of the few corners of the Israel Defense Forces where officers don't hang out with enlisted men.

In terse, rapid-fire sentences, he outlined the night's exercise, the mission of each of the company's two forces, and the preparations to be made. I was sitting in the rear and couldn't hear well over the snores of the guy next to me. By the end of the short set of commands, I was still very much in the dark about what we were going to do.

There was stuff to get ready. Mostly, this was what we called "*pakalim*," a word formed from a Hebrew acronym for "fixed order for the warrior" that refers generally to any standing order or routine operation and more specifically to the extra weapon or piece of equipment that each soldier is assigned to prepare, care for, and carry. It could be a jerrycan of water, a stretcher, a mortar, a radio, extra ammunition, or anything else that was needed for an exercise or mission. Whatever it was, it was bound to be heavy, awkward, and annoying.

Jacques read off a list of pakal assignments. I'd had a brief introductory interview with Elnatan earlier in the day. He explained to me that Company C was a "superior infantry" reserve unit, and that I should not be misled by the flabbiness and easygoing demeanor of my new comrades. Last year they'd served for a month near Beirut, and these men had proved themselves top-quality soldiers. He asked me what pakal I'd had in the regular army. I chose not to mention the RPG, the Russian-made wood-and-metal rocket launcher tube that had made my life miserable in Lebanon. I said I'd been a radioman, which was my assignment in basic training. I assumed that I'd be given the radio pack that night. But Jacques didn't call my name; thankfully, I would be going on this exercise with no more than my basic gear. Still, I had to help the others prepare.

Eldad was assigned a helicopter landing kit, so we went off in search of discarded Coke cans. We found the required six, cut off their tops, and filled the remainders halfway with sand and the rest of the way with strips we tore from a burlap bag. Eldad signed out a small jerrycan, filled it with diesel oil, and closed it tight; all this he packed into a tadal knapsack, appropriating the strap from my gear to add to the single strap he was issued. To make the Coke cans into beacons for a nighttime helicopter landing, you pour the diesel oil into the cans and light the burlap wicks. There would be helicopters in this exercise.

After these preparations, the sergeants and officers made a quick inspection, finishing half an hour before midnight. We had four hours to sleep before setting out. The day was so warm that our battalion hadn't even bothered to sign out tents from the base; we spread our sleeping bags on the gravel by the shed and slept while we could.

At the time I arrived, Company C had not had a major infusion of new blood for quite some time. The average age of the soldiers, probably a bit above thirty, was relatively high for an infantry unit. When you're new in a group of guys who have worked together for years, you do what you have to do and try to figure out the warp and woof of the fabric of which you're now part. But it takes a long while, and in the meantime, one day doesn't really link to another in any logical way. You observe events around you as if the army base were a play in which you've been told to take a role without benefit of a script, the scenes being rehearsed out of order according to the director's whim.

We are in the dining–commons room of the Astra outpost—really not a room so much as a distension of one of the dark corridors that make up the structure. There is barely enough space for six metal tables with green Formica tops, each flanked by two heavily stained wooden benches. A table with two benches seats four people comfortably, but eight soldiers.

At one of the tables, two men play backgammon. One is short, out of shape, and haggard looking, as if he's been up all night playing poker, which he has. The other is white haired and borderline obese. At another table, three gaunt men drink coffee and read the previous day's newspapers. Through a large pass-through window on the back wall we see into the kitchen, from which we hear a clatter of pots and curses. Jacques and Micha—the latter Company C's deputy first sergeant, an auto mechanic in real life—are preparing supper. Jacques patiently explains to Micha how army-issue orzo and eggs can be presented with first-class flair. To the window's right, Platoon Three NCO Mizrahi and a graying, mop-haired guy whose name I haven't learned yet argue over how to thread the first reel of *The Good, the Bad, and the Ugly* onto the outpost's film projector.

Along the bare, pale yellow left wall, which Mizrahi is planning to use as a screen, lies a long, low bench. On it is a rotary telephone so old that its receiver cord is not even coiled. Watzman is sitting—crouching, really—next to the phone, holding the receiver close to his ear in a desperate attempt to catch the words of his girlfriend, Ilana. Ilana's voice is faint from being filtered through hundreds of kilometers of bad wire and a series of outmoded civilian and military telephone exchanges. What with the clatter in the kitchen and the curses, now alternately and now in unison, of the players, readers, and film technicians, the mission is nearly impossible.

Nearby Watzman are three more of his comrades, standing and waiting for their turns to call home. Since Astra receives an outside line for only two hours in the morning and two in the afternoon, such waits are common. The three are Eiger, whom we've met; Benin, a kinky-haired, dark-skinned NCO; and Meron, graying but trim, who at thirty-seven is, with Jacques, the oldest present.

"You promised!" Watzman shouts into the phone. He strains to catch the reply. "I can't hear you!"

A pot falls in the kitchen.

"We said we'd talk about this when I got home!"

"Oh, just go ahead and tell her you'll marry her," Eiger says, nudging Watzman.

Meron offers sage advice to Eiger. "He shouldn't commit himself until he's ready. That's what I tell my kid."

"You've got a kid getting married?" Eiger asks.

"No, but he's sixteen. In high school. It's already beginning, this kind of stuff."

Watzman is still shouting into the receiver. "Yes, of course. You know I do."

Jacques's voice from the kitchen: "Sauté the chopped onion until it colors." Through the window we see Jacques pouring cooking oil into a pot the size of a bass drum.

"I don't know how to sauté. I'll just fry it," Micha grumbles.

"Will you please get your grubby fingers off the fucking projector and let me do it?" Mizrahi says to his partner.

Watzman is still shouting. "I'm not upset, I'm having a good time."

"He *knows* he wants to marry her. He told me so," Eiger informs Benin and Meron.

"Maybe he's having second thoughts. Happens sometimes when you're away," Benin suggests. Watzman glares at him.

"Of course I miss you. Terribly," he yells into the telephone.

"I sat in front of them on the bus to the induction site. You should have seen how he was looking at her," Eiger says. Meron makes a "T" with his hands to indicate to Watzman that his time is up.

"How long has he known her?"

"Why are you putting bread in the oven?" Micha shouts in the kitchen.

"We will serve the scrambled eggs on croutons, garnished with parsley and radish flowers," Jacques explains.

A reel of Sergio Leone falls on Mizrahi's toes.

"You," he says, pointing for emphasis, "are an asshole."

"No, I'm not getting out again. I asked Elnatan." Watzman's voice is hoarse.

"Poor guy, in for three weeks straight. Elnatan gave him the first weekend off, after the crash, and didn't tell him that that would be his only leave," Eiger says.

Benin's sense of justice is offended. "That's really not fair. Just like Elnatan to screw the new guys."

"I'm going to have a talk with him," Meron declares.

Watzman shouts desperately into the receiver. "Hello! Hello!"

"Must have been cut off," Eiger observes dispassionately to the others. He turns, solicitous, to Watzman. "Were you cut off?"

Watzman is miserable. "It went dead."

Jacques sticks his head through the pass-through. "Watzman, you're supposed to be at the blue guard post in ten minutes. Go make sure that partner of yours is awake."

Yishai camp's gravel turned out to be an acceptably comfortable sleeping surface. It was fine enough to mold itself into a man's shape, and the sleeping bag padded the sharp edges. Jacques woke us, stepping perkily, flashlight in hand, among the olive green mounds of snoring soldiers, calling each man by name. I was up and dressing immediately. Eldad continued to doze. Matan sat up in his sleeping bag and stared uncomprehendingly at the sky until Jacques, coming by on his second pass, gently shook him. There was the roar of a blowtorch; Micha had hooked up a "gas dog," a two-pronged torch, and had a huge pot of syrupy coffee boiling. We passed around plastic cups of the hot drink, along with chocolate-spread sandwiches, before tugging on our efods and pakals and slinging our rifles over our shoulders. Then we trudged, less ordered than Elnatan wanted us to be, to the base's landing pad. Two large transport helicopters—Superferlons, or Wasps, an old model I'd never flown in before—waited for us. Their propellers spun in dissonance and blew the desert chill through our uniforms. We put on our helmets and divided into our two forces: Platoon Three and half of Platoon Two in one helicopter, the other half of Platoon Two and all of Platoon One, my own, in the other. Elnatan rode with us.

The hatch under the Wasp's tail opened, lowering until it touched the ground. One of the crewmen stood to its side and beckoned to us. We ran across the tarmac and up the ramp.

Elnatan established himself at the commander's post at the front of the dimly lit chamber. He alone had a radio helmet that allowed him to listen in on the pilots and the ground command. The rest of us found places on the benches that ran along either side of the craft and sat uncomfortably with our efods still on. We stowed our pakals under the benches and lay our rifles in our laps. The pakals were supposed to be secured with straps, or so I learned during my mandatory service, but the crewman who came to check that our seat belts were fastened didn't check under the seats.

The din was pervasive. The very air was in vertigo and careened from face to face—faces that were variously impassive, tired, and tense. Some men attempted conversation. Shouts from the cockpit. The hatch rose and thudded into place. The propellers picked up speed, and we rose slowly from the ground and headed east.

Barely audible exchanges on the tarmac had given me some information about where we were going. We would land on a hilltop and then charge up and take another hilltop. Our second force would land on a third hilltop; the battalion's other companies would be conquering yet other hilltops. But I had no idea where the hilltops were or how long we'd be aloft. One of the Company C veterans had informed me that our regimental commander's brother was in the air force, so we got helicopters for every exercise.

I sat opposite a window, but at first I could see little—no more than a star here and there. Then we banked to the right and, as we turned, I saw a patch of lights below a line of mountains. I assumed that this was Jericho, the only city in this part of the Jordan Valley. We continued to bank gently and I felt drowsy; after a slow circle I could see Jericho's lights again, and then again. We began to descend.

We seemed to be losing altitude rapidly, more rapidly than anything I'd experienced before. I'd flown in helicopters many times in Lebanon, but mostly on administrative, not operational, missions. So maybe this is how it is in combat, I thought. Elnatan, I could see, was peering into the cockpit. He'd later tell me that he was listening to the pilots panic. They were new at the job, fresh out of flight school, and they were losing power, shouting frantic orders at one another. There was a sudden acceleration downward. We hit the ground and bounced back up into the air. Unsecured pakals slid out of place, I was still under the impression that this was a mock-combat landing. Then we hit the ground again. A side door at the front of the cabin flew open and Elnatan disappeared as the craft rose again, briefly, before hitting the ground a third time. This time it flipped over on its side and slid down a mountain slope. The tail ripped off, we came to a halt, and there was silence.

Men scrambled out of the hole in the fuselage created by the broken tail, and out of the side door that was now above us. Fumes began to fill the cabin. I was lying on my back; I saw Eiger suspended from the ceiling above and to my right. Eldad was gone. I tried to undo my seat belt but I couldn't locate the clasp. The fumes reeked of gasoline, and I realized that the helicopter might be on the verge of exploding. My hands groped desperately for the buckle but couldn't find it. The fumes were now acrid and thick enough that I couldn't see if anyone else was still in the cabin with me. Well, that's it, I thought rather calmly to myself. Good-bye, Ilana.

Suddenly I saw Matan standing above me. He'd come back to make sure that everyone was out. I called out to him, "I can't undo the seat belt." He leaned over, looking into my eyes as if I might be an intruder.

He inserted his hand between my back and the seat. In a second I was free and following him out of the tail hole. As I exited, I saw a body sprawled on the ground, skull smashed.

Singer, the stocky platoon sergeant who earlier in the day had exhibited a largely laissez-faire attitude toward his job, was in charge. He issued orders to the pilots, who were spraying fire extinguishers at the smoky hulk. One moaned over and over again: "What have I done? How did it happen?" Elnatan suddenly appeared, running and stumbling down the slope without his glasses. Singer reported concisely: one apparent casualty, though the medic is still working on him; two with what seem to be no more than abrasions and minor cuts; one with back pains lying on a stretcher.

Singer ordered me to get up the hill, as far as possible from the helicopter. I ran to the peak, panting, in my efod but without, I suddenly realized, my rifle. Where was Eldad? Was he caught inside?

But when I got to the top, Eldad was there, sitting on the edge of the slope, looking down. I collapsed next to him.

He was grinning. "That," he said, "was a real experience."

And despite the fact that I was shaking, that I was still horrified by the sight of my comrade's brains and the thought that they could have been mine, and that my conscience told me it was wrong to label something so deadly an "experience," I realized shamefully that there was something deep inside me that concurred.

Soldiers were milling around behind us, some shouting, some talking in low tones. Eiger was recounting the accident to some guys from Platoon Three, who were half certain he'd made the whole thing up. The deputy regimental commander was barking orders to a group of staff officers. He wanted the exercise to continue while the dead and wounded were evacuated.

I couldn't talk for a minute, but then I said to Eldad, "Do you think that this is how it's going to be? That for the next twenty years we are going to report for reserve duty every year and almost get killed?"

Eiger came over and kicked me lightly in the behind. He knelt beside me and put his hand on my shoulder.

"You okay, Watzman?"

"I think so," I said.

"Well, then, you'd better get up. You look pretty ridiculous here, sitting and watching the action like it's a movie."

"I was just thinking," I said, "that right now I barely know these guys. But they could be the people I'm with when I die."

The deputy regimental commander shouted out a new order. The exercise was canceled. We'd all be evacuated. By helicopter.

"I wish I had my camera with me," Eldad said, shaking his head, still spellbound.

I struggled to my feet. "I don't think I want another helicopter ride just now," I told Eiger.

"What's your alternative?" he asked.

Chapter Two

· RELIGIONS ·

HEBRON, APRIL–MAY 1987

I T IS WHAT MEN DO AT THEIR BEST, WITH GOOD INTENTIONS, AND what normal men and women find they must and will do in spite of their intentions, that really concern us," writes George Bernard Shaw in his introduction to *St. Joan.* Yermi stood in as commander of Platoon Three on Mount Hermon in 1984 because the lieutenant who was supposed to fill that post was under arrest. Amichai was an idealistic, dedicated, and intelligent officer much admired by the guys. Like Eiger and like me, he wore a knitted kipah, the emblem of the religious Zionists. Like Eiger, but unlike me, he'd grown up in a middle-class Ashkenazi family in the heart of the Israeli subculture that combines an observant lifestyle with an acceptance of the modern, secular world. The previous May, just around the time I met Ilana, Amichai and thirty-six other religious Zionist men had been rounded up by the police. They stood charged with membership in a Jewish terrorist organization that was caught booby-trapping buses full of Palestinian civilians.

Previously, the group had planted car bombs that maimed the mayors of three Palestinian cities in the territories and had shot up Palestinian students at a college in Hebron. All this was preparation for their grand plan to blow up the Dome of the Rock and the al-Aqsa Mosque on the Temple Mount, where the Jewish sanctuary had once stood. The conspirators had hoped that the destruction of the mosques, comprising Islam's third-holiest site, would bring on a doomsday war with the entire Muslim world. They were no doubt correct about that. The rest of the scenario was more doubtful: Israel would emerge victorious, annex the rest of the territory between the Nile and the Euphrates, which, they believed, God had promised the Jewish people, and rebuild the Temple where the mosques had once stood.

The religious Zionists, or the national-religious camp, as they are sometimes called, emerged at the end of the nineteenth century as a middle ground between the secular Zionists, who rejected the Jewish religion as antiquated superstition unbefitting an enlightened nation, and the ultra-Orthodox Jews, or *haredim*, who rejected both modernity and the goal of establishing a Jewish state.

When Israel was founded, ultra-Orthodox men refused to serve in its army. Religious Zionists served eagerly, just as they sought to integrate themselves into every aspect of Israeli life. In the country's early years, when secular socialist Zionism was the ruling national ideology, the national-religious camp felt itself an embattled minority. The camp defended itself by making its political incarnation, the National Religious party, a permanent and indispensable coalition partner to the undisputed party of government, Mapai (later the Labor party). Though its faction in the Knesset, Israel's parliament, was never more than a tenth of that body's 120 members, the camp was thus able to gain slices of government budgets for its community and thereby maintain both a system of social services for families and a second public school system, separate from the secular schools, in which general and religious studies were combined. It charged the socialist Zionists with imposing a secular version of Judaism on the hundreds of thousands of traditionally religious Jews who poured into Israel from the Islamic world during the country's first decades. But the national-religious community managed, through political deals, to reserve a certain quota of those immigrants for its own schools.

Another extremely important achievement for the religious Zionists was a deal with Israel's first prime minister, David Ben-Gurion, that guaranteed a minimum standard of religious observance in public life. Friday night and Saturday, the Jewish Sabbath, were made the new country's official day of rest; stores and cultural institutions closed and public transportation largely halted. Marriage, divorce, and burial were left under the purview of an official state Orthodox rabbinate that refused to allow other streams of Judaism to engage in these activities. Food served at public institutions and in public buildings was kosher.

The public observance of the Sabbath and of dietary laws made it possible for religious Zionists to perform military service. Because they were not forced to train on the Sabbath, and because the food served in army mess halls was kosher, Orthodox men and women could serve alongside their nonreligious compatriots. While these rules involved some imposition on nonreligious soldiers, they were nevertheless generally accepted by all as necessary and positive. If religious and nonreligious young people could not serve in the same army, the country could not survive.

Still, the army was a problem. For the religious Zionist teenager, it was often his first venture outside the protection of his community's institutions and his first intimate contact with people who lived, and enjoyed, a secular lifestyle. That, along with the natural rebelliousness of youth, frequently made the army a place that the young religious man entered wearing a kipah and left with his head uncovered. Furthermore, many religious parents wanted their sons to continue their religious studies beyond high school in a yeshiva, and military service stood in the way. The community's solution was to establish the *hesder* yeshivas. Like Nachal soldiers, hesder soldiers signed up for a longer term of duty. Nachal soldiers interspersed periods of kibbutz work with stints of combat service, while hesderniks, as they were called, spent their off-duty periods studying at a yeshiva. The hesder system blossomed in the 1980s and soon became part of the standard life path of young religious Zionists. It wasn't universal—Eiger had not gone that route, nor had any of the handful of religious guys who were serving in Company C when I arrived. But most of the sons of the religious families I knew either served or planned to serve in the army in the hesder program. In the fall of 1987, Company C would absorb a large group of hesder graduates and take on a significantly different character as a result.

Religious Zionism had originally embraced (within the bounds of orthodoxy) a spectrum of religious approaches and philosophies. On political issues outside specifically religious subjects—such as economic, social, military, and foreign policy—there were diverse views, with the National Religious party generally toeing the left-of-center line drawn by Ben-Gurion. But in the 1960s and 1970s, a large portion of the community's younger generation was attracted to a particular religious Zionist theology, one that came together with a political philosophy that had much more affinity with the right-wing nationalism of Menachem Begin and his Likud party than with the Labor party of Ben-Gurion's successors.

The theology emerged from a Jerusalem yeshiva called Merkaz HaRav, the Center of the Rabbi—the rabbi in question being Avraham Yitzhak HaCohen Kook. In 1921, under British rule, Rabbi Kook became the first official Ashkenazi chief rabbi of the Jewish community in Palestine. (His appointment, alongside the extant post of Sephardi chief rabbi, created a two-headed official rabbinate that exists to this day.) A subtle thinker and poet, Rabbi Kook was a pioneer in finding workable solutions, within the framework of Jewish religious law, to the many questions that emerged with the establishment of new Jewish communities, including agricultural communities, in the Holy Land. He also developed a comprehensive theology that viewed the Jewish return to Israel as part of a divine process that would lead inevitably to the arrival of the Messiah. In his view, the ardently secular Zionist settlers were furthering that messianic goal, even if they did not realize it.

Rabbi Kook's son, Rabbi Tzvi Yehuda Kook, took over leadership of Merkaz HaRav after his father's death in 1935. Continuing and developing his father's messianic views, he saw the Six-Day War as another stage in God's plan. Israel occupied vast new territories, including the West Bank, the heartland of the biblical kingdom of Israel. Rabbi Tzvi Yehuda believed that Jews had to settle these lands, which he and his followers insisted on calling by their biblical names—Judea, the southern part of the West Bank centered on Bethlehem and Hebron, and Samaria, the northern part of the West Bank stretching from Ramallah north to Jenin. His students, who became rabbis, community leaders, and educators in the religious Zionist community, were charismatic, powerful influences on religious Zionist youth, and he became the spiritual leader of Gush Emunim (Community of Believers), a movement made up primarily of young religious Zionists dedicated to this goal of settlement. In the years immediately after the Yom Kippur War, Gush Emunim conducted a series of squatting campaigns in key sites in the West Bank, Gaza Strip, and Golan Heights. These campaigns ended with the government—the Labor government headed by Yitzhak Rabin and his defense minister, Shimon Peres—allowing the establishment of a number of Jewish settlements in the territories, some of them in the heart of Palestinian population concentrations.

The young people of Gush Emunim viewed Menachem Begin's election in 1977 as another step along the road to the messianic era. Begin and his government were also committed to a Greater Israel that would include all the occupied territories, and he encouraged Gush Emunim to establish many new settlements.

But then Begin committed a grave sin in their eyes. He signed a treaty giving the Sinai Peninsula back to Egypt in exchange for a peace treaty. Since in Gush Emunim's ideology Sinai was no less part of the Land of Israel than the West Bank and Gaza Strip, the peace treaty with

Egypt precipitated a theological crisis. The messianic process was unaccountably regressing. The plot to blow up the Temple Mount mosques was meant to set it back on track.

I did not deny the profound historic and emotional connections the Jews have to the entire Land of Israel, including the West Bank and Gaza Strip. I opposed the settlement enterprise not because I didn't think the Jewish people had a claim to those lands, but because I understood that the entire Land of Israel was claimed by two peoples. Peace would require compromise. Furthermore, it was not in Israel's interest to annex the territories, with their large Arab populations. Since the Palestinians' rate of natural increase was much higher than our own, in a few decades Jews would lose their majority in their own land. Then Israel would face a choice: either cease being a Jewish state, or cease being a democratic one. Since I believed that the Jews needed and deserved their own state, and that a state that was not democratic was not worthy of being called Jewish, partition of the land between Jews and Palestinians was the only realistic option. Unlike many nonreligious Jews, I wouldn't give up these territories happily. I would hand them over with great sorrow, but with the knowledge that peace, and Israel's long-term viability, was worth this heavy price.

I never met Amichai. By all accounts, he was a good man. His role in the terrorist group had been a small one, and he'd later publicly express contrition for his acts. Eiger and the rest of the Platoon One reservists had a hard time fitting the Amichai they knew into the terror group they read about in the papers. Apparently he'd been swept up by what seemed to him to be the call of God and history. Many years later I came across a newspaper article about him. It said that he considered his disqualification from reserve duty a heavier punishment than the jail term he served.

One of the first squatting operations by Jews inspired by Rabbi Kook's theology took place a year after the Six-Day War in Hebron, a city about an hour's drive south of Jerusalem. Hebron's status as a Jewish holy city is second only to that of Jerusalem. It contains the Tomb of the Patriarchs where, by tradition, Adam and Eve, Abraham and Sarah, Isaac and Rebecca, and Jacob and Leah are interred. Hebron was also David's capital before he won Jerusalem from the Jebusites and had been home to a venerable Jewish community until the early twentieth century. Under Muslim rule, the tomb was for centuries off-limits to Jews. After Israel gained control of Hebron, the government declared the site open to Jews as well as Muslims, and separate prayer chambers were set aside for each faith.

In August 1929, an Arab mob, incited to believe that the Jews planned to rebuild their Temple in place of the holy Muslim mosques in Jerusalem, rampaged through Hebron's Jewish quarter. While some Arabs sheltered Jews, the mob slaughtered sixty-seven men, women, and children and seriously injured many others. The Jews were evacuated, and a brief attempt to reestablish the community a few years later ended with another evacuation in the face of a threatened massacre.

On April 4, 1968, a group of Jews under the leadership of Rabbi Moshe Levinger registered as guests at Hebron's Park Hotel. The next day they announced that they would not leave and intended to reestablish Hebron's Jewish community. The announcement provoked a sharp debate in Israel. Some saw the settlers as religious fanatics who aimed to prevent the Israeli government from giving the West Bank back to Jordan, from which it had been conquered, as part of a peace agreement. Others—including some left-wing secularists—hailed the settlers as pioneers reasserting a Jewish right to live in a city of deep religious and historical significance. In the end, the Israeli government made a deal with the settlers. They'd leave Hebron proper, and the government would build a new Jewish neighborhood, separate from but adjacent to Hebron and within walking distance of the Tomb of the Patriarchs. The new town took in its first residents in 1972 and was called Kiryat Arba, one of the Bible's names for Hebron. It quickly became a center of right-wing nationalist religious activity. The settlers there saw it as a way station on the way to returning to the homes of the old Jewish quarter in the city itself. In 1979, a group of Kiryat Arba women led by Rabbi Levinger's wife, Miriam, set up a squatter settlement in Hadassah House, a central building in the old Jewish Quarter abutting the city's casbah. Menachem Begin's government granted the women's settlement legal status and allowed them to bring their families to live there. Later two other Jewish neighborhoods were established—Avraham Avinu, near the Tomb of the Patriarchs, and Tel Romeida, next to the city's old Jewish cemetery.

As a religious Jew who opposed the entire Jewish settlement enterprise in the territories, I was an anomaly, part of a tiny left-wing minority within the Israeli religious community. I was quite happy that the units I'd served in as a soldier had almost never been stationed in the West Bank or Gaza Strip and that I'd thus never had to enforce a military occupation that I found morally troubling. My two brief stays in the territories during my basic training—a weekend in Gaza and a snowy Christmas in Bethlehem—had been uneventful. We'd manned some guard posts and patrolled some streets. Contact with the local population had been limited to polite, sterile exchanges of greetings with shopkeepers.

But Hebron was different. No Jews lived in the middle of Gaza or Bethlehem. The occupation there was purely military. In Hebron, Jews with extremist religious and political philosophies were imposing themselves on the Palestinian population. So I was not at all happy in April 1987 to find that Company C was being sent to the City of the Patriarchs. A lot of the guys welcomed the change of location. It was so much more convenient to Jerusalem and Tel Aviv than was distant Mount Hermon, where we'd served again in the summer of 1985. I anticipated an unpleasant month.

That didn't mean, though, that I dragged my feet leaving home. I knew I ought to feel bad about leaving Ilana, seven months into her second pregnancy, at home alone with our sixteen-month-old daughter, Mizmor. In fact, I did feel bad. I loved Ilana and was ecstatic about being a father. Still, I knew I could use a little change from the routine of diapers and middle-of-the-night crying fits. In the army I might get only three hours of sleep a night, but at least those three hours would be uninterrupted. I considered myself a feminist through and through, and believed that men should shoulder an equal share of housework and child-rearing duties. I would never dream of doing what fathers had done in these parts not too long ago—abandon the house and kids to my wife and go to chat and play backgammon at the local coffeehouse. However, if the defense of my country required me to drink coffee with my buddies and even allowed me to get in a few games in the process, I would not refuse.

So I embraced Ilana, kissed Mizmor, hoisted my chimidan onto my shoulders, and trotted happily down the stairs to catch the bus to the Jerusalem convention center where I was to meet the rest of the guys. Not all of them, actually. Most of the company would enlist the next day, on Monday. But the company staff was always called up a day early, and I was now an NCO.

The promotion had come a few months ago at Tze'elim, the huge training base in Israel's southern Negev where we usually had our annual maneuvers. As always, the army had done its best to choose the most frigid, damp, miserable week of the year. On the first night there, as I was shivering in my dubon outside my tent, engaged in some now-forgotten task that was absolutely essential and urgent at the time, Elnatan called me aside for a talk. Eiger, with whom he'd been chatting for a few minutes, stepped back but remained close by.

"You've probably noticed," he said, "that the company is changing. I'm moving the older guys out or into support units so that we can make room for younger men. Yoel, your NCO in Platoon One, is going to be a battalion operations sergeant, and Singer, your sergeant, is going to be battalion staff sergeant."

I wasn't sure why Elnatan had singled me out for this personnel report and mumbled something about being sorry to see them go. I also noted that Yoel and Singer were both only two or three years older than I was.

"I've decided to make Eiger Platoon One sergeant," Elnatan said.

"Good choice," I said. "Eiger's an excellent navigator. He knows how to handle people. Has a clear head and a good eye."

"And I want you to be NCO under him."

I stared at Elnatan. "That's bizarre," I said.

"You're a responsible guy," Elanatan said. "I know I can trust you to do the job right."

"You can't possibly believe that I can command these men in war," I protested. "I only did a year and a half in the regular army. Everyone in the platoon is a more experienced soldier than I am."

"In war a lot of things change," Elnatan said enigmatically. Then he walked away, leaving me to wonder whether it was me or the command structure that he expected to metamorphose when crisis came.

I was flattered by Elnatan's confidence in me, even though I knew that one reason I'd gotten the job was that he'd already approached and been turned down by at least one better-qualified candidate, Eldad. The prospect of doing a few extra days of reserve duty each year didn't bother me. In fact, it meant I'd spend more time with Eiger, who over the past couple of years had become my best friend in the unit and a good friend outside it as well. We had a lot in common. We were both new fathers and we were both religious but willing to challenge what we saw as the hidebound conservatism of much of the Orthodox community. Eiger, too, opposed the Greater Israel ideology of the settlers and thought the Palestinian territories should be handed over to Arab control as part of a peace deal. He wasn't as radical about it as I was—he had, after all, grown up in the national religious community and had an emotional loyalty to its institutions that I lacked. He often poked fun at what he saw as my knee-jerk tendency to believe the worst about the settlers and most of what was published in *HaAretz*, the left-liberal intellectual newspaper that I read devotedly every morning.

A minibus was waiting at the convention hall opposite Jerusalem's central bus station. Eiger was there already and gave me a slap on the back that sent my chimidan plummeting to the ground. Matan was already on the minibus, impassively gazing into the distance. Mizrahi, who'd moved up from NCO to sergeant in Platoon Three, paced beside it, edgy at having left his carpentry shop in the hands of his Arab assistant. The minibus took us through Jerusalem and out into the hilly wilderness that began abruptly beyond the city's newest northern neighborhood. After a short drive along a lonely road, we pulled into the dusty, unpaved parking lot of our regiment's home base. Shouldering our chimidans, we trudged through the gate and to the left, down a hill to a row of Quonset huts. There, carefully sealed in plastic and tended by a dedicated band of young soldiers, were our battalion's emergency supplies—rifles, grenades, MAG machine guns, RPGs, rations, and individual duffel bags packed with uniforms of the right size for each reservist. All of these items were carefully arranged alongside the APCs that each man would, in accordance with a prearranged plan, board to go into battle. Or so we had been told.

Company C staff members who had driven their own cars were waiting for us there. Yermi, the Platoon Three sergeant who had now moved up to the post of company first sergeant, had brought Jacques along in his blue Audi. Yermi was now in charge of logistics, equipment, and creature comfort, and, together with Jacques and Micha, comprised the company's technical staff. Zevulun Falk, who'd joined the unit at the previous winter maneuvers and who was also a Platoon One NCO, had arrived in the pickup truck from the curtain store he ran with his brother. Like Eiger and me, he also wore a kipah. He had a warm smile and a special sensitivity for other people's moods, and was able, as I had seen demonstrated during the winter maneuvers, to balance a MAG machine gun by the barrel on the palm of his hand. Falk et Falk of

Jerusalem was part of an informal network of Falk drapery emporia run by numerous Falk brothers in most of the country's major cities. There was a clear division of labor between Zevulun and his fraternal partner, as I had discovered during a visit to his store a month earlier. Zevulun— attentive, personable, and with an instinctive sense of color and design—tended to the customers, while his petulant brother scared them away.

After signing out our gear, we headed to a training base in the foothills between the Hebron plateau and the Israeli coast, where we tried out our guns and got organized. Then we headed to Hebron to be briefed on our duties by the unit we'd be replacing.

There were occasional Arab attacks on Jews in Hebron. The worst had been in 1980, when terrorists ambushed a group of Jews returning from the tomb to Hadassah House and killed six of them. In the year before Company C's arrival, several stabbings had taken place but no one had been killed. In general, Jews felt safe in the city. On the road in, we passed tour buses bringing pious Jews to pray at the Tomb of the Patriarchs. Other buses contained Christian pilgrims and foreign tourists on their way to see the sights and visit Hebron's glassblowers' workshops.

Like other West Bank cities, Hebron sprawled and blended into nearby towns and villages. The old center of the town was cramped, while neighborhoods farther from the center featured larger dwellings faced with marble from nearby quarries. Traveling down the main street into the center of town we passed a boarded-up cinema—the Muslim religious authorities, powerful in this holy city, frowned on films—and an Israeli government vocational training center. I used my largely self-taught Arabic to read a signpost to Eiger: Shar'eh Shuhada, Martyrs' Street. Arab street hawkers wheeled weather-beaten wooden wagons, selling bread, hard-boiled eggs, and sweet semolina cakes drenched in syrup. The stores were doing a brisk business, and as we drew close to Hadassah House, we saw a number of Jewish customers. They were dressed in the entire range of Orthodox fashion. There were ultra-Orthodox men in black hats, long black coats, white shirts, and baggy black pants and women wearing long-sleeved dresses in subdued colors, and thick stockings, their hair carefully hidden under large and elaborate kerchiefs. There were modern Orthodox settler types, the men sporting jeans and flannel or T-shirts and the women in fashionable skirts and blouses and hats that allowed some hair to show. And there were any number of variations in between. Jewish and Arab shoppers mixed freely and, it seemed, without fear on either side, though there was little conversation between them. Jewish children played on the sidewalks; the Arab kids we saw seemed mostly to be helping their parents mind their stores or sell their wares.

Hadassah House stood at an intersection where a street branched off the main road to the left, and led down a short hill to the entrance to the casbah. After that the street veered left again and ran back parallel to the main road, but several meters lower. We spotted two unimposing reservists with shaggy mustaches manning the guard post at the entrance to the square building. Just beyond the intersection was our base, a compound that had until not long before served as Hebron's bus station. Just behind the base, overlooking the Casbah, was a hesder yeshiva.

As we pulled into the base, we spotted one of the outgoing unit's officers ordering his men into a three-row lineup of a type used in regular army inspections. The officer appeared to be in his mid- or late twenties, while the men he commanded were flabby older guys. Some looked like they were in imminent danger of becoming grandfathers. The men lined up silently and stood erect as we disembarked from our minibus.

"What's going on here?" Eiger asked one of them.

"Shhh!" the guy scolded. "Do you want me to get punished?"

Then, with a few clipped orders, the officer marched the men out of the base's gate. It was a good thing that the marching reservists kept their gazes straight ahead, because we were barely able to keep ourselves from laughing out loud.

"I've never seen anything like this," Mizrahi said, shaking his head. "Treating forty-year-olds like grunts?"

"Is that the kind of unit we get shunted off to when we get too old?" I asked.

We were ushered into one of the small rooms that lay off the main courtyard to hear Gadi, the outgoing company commander, explain to us the missions we'd perform in the month to come.

"Look at this filth!" Jacques said sotto-voce to Elnatan. "I'm afraid to see the kitchen."

Soon it wasn't just the filth that had us down. After briefly showing us a map of the city, Gadi took us to see the posts. The first was the one we'd seen at the entrance to Hadassah House. Across the street was another, on the requisitioned roof of an Arab home that had a clock repairman's shop on street level. The third was on a roof next to the base, overlooking the yeshiva and the entrance to the casbah. Then Gadi led us down the hill and around to the back of Hadassah House to show us another post where a row of Arab stores operated out of the building's ground level. There had once been an attempt to bomb the Jewish settlement from here, so a line of barrels and a fence had been set up. The fence and the squad of soldiers who guarded it stood straight in front of the stores, but the establishments seemed to be doing decent business anyway. Guarding these posts and those at the nearby neighborhood of Tel Romeida would be the sum total of our responsibility in Hebron.

The proprietor of what looked to be a metalworking shop stood in his doorway, eyeing us stonily. A stout Arab man with a pencil-thin mustache and an even stouter wife climbed out of a battered pickup truck across the street and hesitated on the far curb. Judging from their dress, they came from one of the small villages outside Hebron. The man wore an old-style Levantine suit, consisting of a faded tie, a dark, stained, and worn pinstripe sports jacket, and a kind of long skirt made of the same material as the jacket. The woman, who squinted in the sunlight, wore a dark, embroidered robe.

I smiled at them while Gadi explained the rules governing this guard post. The Arab couple looked back at me with a fear in their eyes I couldn't understand. Then I remembered that I was in uniform, carrying a gun. They no doubt identified my smile with the one they'd seen time and again on Israeli soldiers they encountered at roadblocks, checkpoints, and in the offices of the Israeli military and civil administrations—a smile of menace and contempt. They probably got the same look from many of the Israeli civilians they encountered. The man most likely worked as a day laborer somewhere in Israel, rising well before dawn to make a two- or three-hour trip to Jerusalem or Tel Aviv to earn a substandard wage.

As a journalist I'd traveled enough in the West Bank to have come into contact with the grinding poverty in which many of the area's Palestinians lived. I'd never been able to square Israel's claim that its occupation of the territories was benign with what seemed to be a deliberate policy of keeping the Palestinians poor so they'd be a source of cheap labor to support growth in the Israeli economy. The fact that they'd been even worse off under the Jordanians, their previous rulers, didn't make Israel's policy excusable.

I turned away from the Arab couple so they'd feel free to cross the street. After some hesitation, they did. Keeping their eyes on me, they approached the metal-shop proprietor, who stood only a few meters from me, and asked a question in Arabic. I couldn't follow the exchange. The proprietor ushered them into the shop.

I stepped back to peer inside. The shop was, in fact, a small factory. One worker cut out large sheets of metal, while another bent them into a box shape and welded the sides together. Another attached rubber hosing and a gas balloon. I couldn't figure out what the resulting object was, so I asked the proprietor in Hebrew, after first making a bumbling attempt to word the question in Arabic.

"They're ovens," he said.

"Ovens?" I asked.

"Yes. For cooking."

"You mean they put this box and a gas balloon in their kitchens?"

"That's right."

"That sounds awfully dangerous."

The proprietor shrugged. "They're villagers. They can't afford a Westinghouse. They can barely afford one of these." I followed his contemptuous gaze and saw the couple listening intently to an explanation from one of the workers, who pointed to different metal boxes. Apparently there were several models.

"It's probably their first oven ever," the proprietor said. "They've probably saved up for it for years."

"The soldiers here are often tempted to get too friendly with the locals," Gadi said loudly. "One of your jobs as commanders is to make sure that doesn't happen." Everyone looked at me.

Gadi led us back to the main road and north, to our right. We took a left turn up a hill and around a bend until we reached a cluster of seven prefab caravan homes set up on blocks next to the old Jewish cemetery. There was no fence or wall separating them from the Arab homes around them.

This was Tel Romeida, the newest nucleus of Jewish settlement in Hebron, established just three years ago as part of the government's policy of expanding the settler community in the city. Two soldiers guarded it by day and four at night. As Gadi explained the routine to us, a woman in a housecoat emerged from one of the prefabs and shouted, "We don't need you here. We don't want to be guarded. We can handle the Arabs ourselves!"

"Your job is to keep the Jews and Arabs apart," Gadi told Elnatan.

"Things look deceptively quiet here. But if there's ever an explosion in the territories, it's going to be Hebron that sets it off. This could be the place where World War III starts. It's a holy city, and that means it attracts the extremists from both sides. You've got the most fanatical Jews and the most fanatical Muslims here, so don't get chummy with either side." He directed his gaze at me, Eiger, and Falk. "It's sometimes a problem if you've got men who have ties to the settlers."

I bristled. I wanted to make sure that Gadi didn't identify me with these fanatics. Why, just last week I had attended a demonstration in Jerusalem condemning the settlements. I opened my mouth to respond, but Eiger nudged me just as Elnatan said sternly, "We can do without your comments, Watzman." Falk stared at me quizzically. There was a Falk brother who lived in Kiryat Arba.

"Our job is to protect them," Elnatan continued. "They are here by decision of the Israeli government and as a result they have every right to be here and we will protect them."

But when, after Gadi's tour, the Company C staff gathered to make its plans, no one could feel much of a sense of purpose in our assignment. "We'll be guard dogs," Mizrahi snorted dismissively. Each of our soldiers would spend four consecutive hours either once or twice a day at one of the guard posts and four more hours at night. No foot or jeep patrols, no special assignments—just guard duty and more guard duty. It wasn't surprising that the job of guarding the Jews had been given to Gadi's band of geriatric cases, but what was Company C doing here?

Yermi and Jacques delivered an even more depressing report on the physical facilities. The rooms were cramped, the kitchen was primitive, and the whole place was grimy and gray. It would take a lot of work to make it into a decent home.

On Wednesday, when we took possession of the grungy bus station and bid Gadi and his golden-agers farewell, we set to work. We had taken in a large crop of young reservists and, under Jacques's direction, we all swept and mopped and scrubbed until the base's floors and walls looked as bright as they could get, given the exhaust stains laid down by years of malfunctioning carburetors. Falk made a short run home to Jerusalem and brought back a television set. He and Amram Achlama, a ponytailed redhead who'd joined Company C a year after I did, commandeered an antenna on the roof of the Arab house next door.

As we feared, guard duty quickly became an oppressive grind, and morale declined precipitously. The unit's veteran members—among whom I now counted myself—were embarrassed that the newcomers were getting the impression that Company C was capable of no more than this. Also, it was hard to develop a sense of cohesion within the company because the battalion had sent a dozen or so older guys from the support units to help us out.

The oldest of these auxiliaries had been enlisted men in the Six-Day War, and while they had no doubt displayed courage and fortitude then, they were tired twenty years later. I found out just how tired the first time I went with one of them to guard on the rooftop over the watchmaker's shop. My partner for the four-hour shift seemed a nice enough guy. He'd moved out of Company C some years ago and had been a truck driver for the battalion ever since. Wiry and nimble, he had a broad smile and a chiseled face. I thought it odd that he was lugging his entire chimidan with him, but it was only a five-minute walk from the base to the post. I myself had a couple of books with me. After we relieved the outgoing guards and settled ourselves on the plastic chairs from which we would keep an eye on Hadassah House, the driver pulled a radio out of his chimidan. Radios were against the rules but helped pass the time, so that was fine with me. So was the coffee kit he took out next. But when he pulled out his sleeping bag, I uttered a cry of disbelief.

"What the hell did you bring *that* for?" I asked.

He looked at me as if I were out of my mind. "To sleep in."

"What do you mean, to sleep in? We're on guard duty!"

"So we'll each do two hours and the other guy can sleep. Do you want the first two hours or the second two?"

I was insulted. He was probably right that one alert soldier was sufficient to keep an eye on things below. But part of our duty was to keep each other company. Sitting on the roof for hours was bad enough; sitting up there for hours without conversation was intolerable. And we hadn't been working hard enough to be short on sleep. So I sharply told him to stow the sleeping bag back in his chimidan. Then I had to put up with a sullen partner for the next four hours, so I didn't get much conversation anyway. Afterward we both told Jacques not to pair us again.

Unlike roof duty, guarding the entrance to Hadassah House was a popular assignment, especially for the religious guys. The families who lived in the building were welcoming and constantly sent cookies and drinks out to the reservists. It seemed pretty transparent to me that the settlers were trying to win my fellow soldiers over to their cause, despite the fact that our orders were to maintain neutrality between them and the Palestinians. One Saturday morning when Eiger was on duty, Rabbi Levinger himself struck up a conversation with him.

"Isn't it great to spend the Sabbath in the holy city of Hebron?" he asked.

"I'd rather be at home with my family," Eiger said.

"So next week bring your family here. We'll put them up and you can have your family *and* Hebron."

Though I thought their cause was wrong, I couldn't help acknowledging these families' commitment and appreciating their generosity, which was genuine even if it was meant to co-opt our men. Furthermore, despite our political and even theological differences, we shared a lifestyle. We observed the Sabbath and holidays in the same way, prayed the same prayers, and studied the same texts.

The guard post in the back of Hadassah House was a mirror image of the one in front. Duty there involved rubbing shoulders with the locals who frequented the shops along the road, and the guys largely ignored the rules forbidding fraternization with Palestinians. The nearby shops did a thriving business with the guards in cigarettes and soft drinks. Keisar, a young member of Platoon One's Yemenite contingent, trumpeted the news that one of the stores was selling high-quality duffel bags at a price far below what the same make cost in Israel, and soon half the company had brand-new, bright blue chimidans. The street's music store, which sold cassette tapes (mostly pirated) of current Levantine stars and classic Arab crooners like Farid al Atrash and Um Kultum, did good business as well.

Israelis have a complex relationship to Arab language and culture. For Company C's Oriental Jews, well over half of our group, Arabic was the language of old-country memories, the language that parents originally from Morocco, Tunisia, Syria, or Iraq spoke to grandparents. Many of these guys could sing popular Arabic songs and understand the gist of the words. An entire genre of Israeli Oriental music, songs sung in Hebrew but with Arabic modalities and themes, had in the preceding decade gained legitimacy in the general culture. I knew this subculture well from home—Ilana's family had come to Israel from Baghdad, and she often tuned the radio to Oriental Jewish or Arabic music. When we spent the weekend with her mother, the Sabbath evening meal couldn't begin until Israeli television's Friday night Arabic-language movie—usually a saccharine romance from Egypt—was over. Once Ilana and I went to see a popular Iraqi-Israeli comedian who had Ilana buckled over in uncontrollable laughter while I remained hanging in the air, feeling like I was watching Robert Klein's Borscht Belt routine with Arabic punch lines substituted for the Yiddish ones.

However, only a small handful of Company C's men could speak Arabic with any fluency. A larger number had a minimal vocabulary they'd picked up working with Arab laborers in Israel. The employer-laborer relationship was the most common link between Jews and Arabs, and while such relations were generally affable, it was always clear who was dominant and who subordinate. For most of the guys, then, the soldier-Palestinian civilian relationship that prevailed at the back of Hadassah House was familiar and comfortable. It was probably more or less comfortable—in the sense that the known is always more comfortable than the unknown—for the Arabs on the street as well.

I had quite different experience with Palestinians than anyone else in the company. One of my journalism beats was covering university studies in Israel for the American academic weekly *The Chronicle of Higher Education*, and part of that beat was Palestinian higher education. During the years of occupation, Palestinians had established several universities in the West Bank that were frequently shut down by the Israeli military government. I occasionally made visits to the larger ones—Bethlehem University, An-Najah University in Nablus, and Bir Zeit University outside Ramallah. At the Palestinian universities I met teachers and students who were much more politically aware and defiant of Israel than was the average Palestinian laborer or shopkeeper. The little Arabic I'd learned was thus on a different level from that of my Company C friends. I could carry on a conversation about politics if it didn't get too complicated. But I disappointed the guys when I was assigned to the post behind Hadassah House and they discovered that my Arabic wasn't much help in the stores along the street.

The guard post most of the other guys and I liked least was Tel Romeida. Kiryat Arba's Jews were hard-core religious nationalists; the Jews living in Hebron at Hadassah House and Avraham Avinu were the nationalist fringe of the Kiryat Arba community. The seven families at Tel Romeida were the ultranationalist fringe of the Hebron Jews. They didn't want the army around because they preferred to defend themselves. They greeted each contingent of soldiers who came to guard them with harangues and cries of "Go home and leave us alone!" Our hours of guard duty were generally demoralizing, but guarding at Tel Romeida was even more so. After a couple of shifts there, even the members of that half of Company C who thought the entire West Bank ought to be annexed by Israel were depressed and angry about the assignment we'd landed.

On the hill above Tel Romeida stood a tarnished black cannon, a relic brought to this part of the world by some conquering nation—perhaps the Ottoman Turks, who arrived at the beginning of the sixteenth century, or the British, who arrived at the beginning of the twentieth. That latter conquest was accomplished without tanks and RPGs and MAGs and M-16s. Cavalry was still important then, and old iron-ball cannons like this one. The British and Turks even fought each other with swords.

Our month in Hebron coincided with the Muslim holy month of Ramadan. During Ramadan, Muslims fast from dawn to sunset. In the mornings they rise before dawn to eat and pray before the fast begins, and at nightfall they eat a festive meal with family and friends.

Our last night watch ran from 2 to 6 a.m., just after sunrise at the end of April, and I did that shift first at Tel Romeida. Sometime around 3:30 the drums began. We heard a beating drum coming from the neighborhood below us, and we saw what looked like a torch flitting through the fragments of street that we could see through the rooftops. Then another drum joined in, and another, and the streets below filled with torches carried in procession and the shouts of young men. Was Hebron rising against us? No, my companions reassured me, this was how people were awakened to pray and eat before the fast began.

Drums brought in the fast and the cannon signaled its end. We had a new Platoon Three lieutenant, a nervous type named Weiner who didn't remain with us long. When the gun went off to announce the end of the fast during his first evening shift at Tel Romeida, he thought it had been aimed at him. He deployed his three soldiers according to the drill he'd learned in officers' course, sending two sniggering men to circle the hill from behind while he and the third guy took cover behind a boulder and prepared to charge straight up the hill at the enemy artillery. It took the guy a good ten minutes behind that boulder to explain to Weiner that the canon went off every night, that the charge was blank, and that this was a quaint local custom.

The Muslims use a lunar calendar, so Ramadan shifts seasons slowly as the years go by. Then, in the late 1980s, the holy month overlapped Israel's national observances. The Sunday after we arrived was Memorial Day. In Israel proper the day's most salient event is the siren that goes off in the morning. The entire country stops and stands at attention (minus a lot of the Arabs and the ultra-Orthodox, each for their own reasons); drivers pull over their cars and get out to honor the memory of the country's fallen soldiers. We couldn't hear a siren that morning in Hebron and went about our duties. In the evening, Memorial Day melds into Independence Day. Jacques insisted on a celebration, so those of us who weren't on guard duty gathered around the flagpole in the base's dingy courtyard and Micha raised the sorry-looking Israeli flag we'd found in the base's storeroom. Jacques said a few words about sacrifice and freedom, and then we had a cookout with meat that Falk and Achlama bought in Kiryat Arba.

Tel Romeida wasn't foreign to all of us. Hezki had friends there. They were okay people, he thought. When he joined Company C with Eldad and me in 1984, he'd had no discernable political, religious, or ideological convictions. In fact, his somewhat puerile ebullience, combined with a macho streak (he always wore a large bowie knife on his belt), would have made him entirely at home at an American college fraternity. Oddly enough, he was thoroughly Americanized despite his Moroccan ancestry and Israeli birth. At the time of our first year in the unit, he worked for a Jerusalem pizza parlor that was a hangout for American teenagers spending a year in Israel. There he picked up a near-perfect New York accent and the ability to banter about TV shows he hadn't grown up watching. When I'd hum a few bars of a popular song from my high school days or even of something from my early childhood, such as the Rice Krispies jingle, Hezki was the only guy in Company C who could complete the tune. I didn't like being identified as the company's American, but sometimes it was comforting to have someone who could share my pre-Israel memories, even if those memories weren't real ones for him.

Hezki had been an adamant and unabashed Sabbath desecrator and an eater of forbidden foods when we first met, but there was something in his way of viewing the world that made me predict back then that he'd become religious in the messianic national-religious mold. It had something to do with the totality of whatever he did. He never seemed to have any doubts or questions. So it wasn't entirely a surprise when he showed up in Hebron in a large kipah with the Torah-mandated fringes swinging out from under his shirt. It turned out that he'd been studying at the yeshiva behind our base, right next to Hadassah House. He'd married a newly religious woman and now lived in Kiryat Arba.

Hezki's rude exuberance and now doctrinaire political and religious views did not make him popular among the guys, nor did his fascination with the various sounds his body could make. He certainly wasn't attuned to any of the subtle signals essential for life in close quarters. He never seemed to know when to lay off or to leave you alone so you could sleep.

One afternoon when we were off duty he offered to take me on a walking tour of the city. I was curious to see the sites outside the small perimeter of our guard posts and figured that if I was spending a month in Hebron I should make at least one visit to the Tomb of the Patriarchs, which was being guarded by another of our battalion's companies.

We took our rifles and made the circle out of the old bus station's gate and around to the entrance to the casbah. The narrow marketplace was packed with shoppers. They picked through huge piles of cabbages, each the size of a cow's head, and crook-necked green summer squashes of a different variety from those generally found in Jewish markets. We passed a meat stand where a white-smocked butcher was spraying insect repellent on freshly slaughtered cuts of mutton, the sheep's head hanging above. Hezki pointed out the spots where Jewish shoppers had been stabbed.

"You weren't always religious, were you?" he asked.

"No," I said. "But I think our experiences are different. I didn't have a sudden revelation. It was a very gradual process with me. I don't feel like there's a sharp dividing line between a former life I reject and a new one that has all the answers."

Hezki mused about this. "What's the point of being religious if it doesn't give you all the answers?"

I shrugged. "I know I'm hardly typical, but what got me interested in Judaism wasn't the answers but the questions. What I like about Judaism, at least the way I see it, is that there are always questions. It never lets you rest."

A Palestinian grandmother in a black robe was screaming what sounded like curses at a spice merchant, who was rallying the owners of neighboring stalls to his position. Was this some ancient family feud, or had a crime been committed by the merchant or the grandmother? "Just the usual price haggling," Hezki assured me.

"There are hundreds of rabbis who say it's God's commandment that we settle the territories and reestablish a Jewish kingdom in the ancient Land of Israel," Hezki said. "Are there any who say we should give away what God gave to us?"

"There are some, though I admit not many," I said. "But that's not the point. I don't need a rabbi to tell me what's right and wrong. Being religious doesn't in and of itself make you a moral person or a good person. You have to make those choices yourself. The talmudic rabbis had a name for it—*naval be-reshut ha-Torah*, a scoundrel with the Torah's sanction. You can observe all the rituals and keep the Sabbath and eat only kosher food and pray three times a day and still be a bastard."

"We're bastards? Don't you think Jews have as much right to live and pray in Hebron as the Palestinians? How can you say that we have a right to Tel Aviv, which is only a few decades old, and not to Hebron, where our people have lived since biblical times? Should this be the only place in the world where Jews aren't allowed to live?"

I laughed.

"What's so funny?" he asked.

"I was out at Bir Zeit last month and I saw a poster on the office door of the deputy press spokeswoman," I explained. "It was put out by some United Nations committee on Palestinian rights. There were four pictures. I don't remember them exactly, but I think one was a picture of a yodeling guy in lederhosen with the caption 'The Swiss have Switzerland.' Next to it was a picture of a dark-skinned guy in a grass skirt and with a bone through his nose captioned, 'The Papua New Guineans have Papua New Guinea.' Below there was one of a dancing Cossack in a fur hat with the caption, 'The Soviets have the Soviet Union.' And then there was a picture of a crying Arab kid with the caption, 'Only the Palestinians don't have Palestine.'"

"I bet you asked for a copy for your own office," Hezki said.

"So I asked the woman, doesn't that mean that the Jews should have Judea?"

Now Hezki laughed.

"She didn't think it was funny," I said.

"So, shouldn't we get Judea?" he asked.

"I think you people here have a blind spot," I said. "You don't see the Arabs as real people. If you did, you'd understand that they also have feelings about their homes and about this land. I don't mean that settlers are evil. In fact, I've got very close friends who come from these circles. They've been tremendous influences on me in my process of becoming more observant. But they honestly, sincerely believe that if we build enough settlements in the territories, the Palestinians will realize that this land is really ours and just pick up and leave. That's blindness. Of course we have a claim to these lands, but that doesn't mean that we can ignore what's in front of our nose. We've got to compromise."

We emerged from the casbah close to the tomb. After chatting with the reservists guarding the gate, we mounted the steps—the closest that Jews were allowed to come to the tomb in the days when the Muslims exercised sole control there—and into the marble building. We heard a Muslim prayer service in progress in one of the rooms and went into a chamber, by the spot marking Abraham's grave, where Jews prayed.

Hezki shook his head. "If God doesn't tell you exactly what to do, I don't see the point."

"Reread Genesis," I suggested. "Even Abraham heard from God only once every decade or two. In between times he had to decide things for himself. And don't forget that even when God told him His plan to wipe out Sodom, Abraham argued with Him. I need a God I can argue with."

In my early years in Israel it seemed as if the kind of Judaism represented by the Hebron settlers was the only way you could be modern and Orthodox. Either you were like them, or you were ultra-Orthodox, or you were secular. None of those categories fit me. But a few months after I settled in Jerusalem in 1980 I discovered I wasn't alone. On Rosh Hashanah, the Jewish new year, I stumbled quite by chance on a community in formation that seemed like it was made for me. These people, mostly young immigrants from the United States and England, were observant but left-wing in their politics. They were committed to Jewish tradition but disturbed by the narrow place that tradition allowed women in public religious life. In their prayer services they sought to allow women to participate much more than was customary in other Orthodox synagogues, while still observing the requirements of Jewish law. Many of them were active in the peace movement, attending demonstrations that called for accommodation with the Palestinians.

Up until that Rosh Hashanah, the group had gathered only occasionally, but the turnout that year was larger than expected, and some of us newcomers were enthusiastic about making the sometime prayer group into a real community. To me, it was not just a solution to a religious dilemma, it was an answer to the question of what I could do to make Israel a country that lived up to Jewish ideals as I saw them. I didn't have the power to change an entire country, but I could be part of a model community, one that would exemplify my most deeply held beliefs. From that point on, Kehilat Yedidya—"Yedidya" means "friend of God"—was central to my life.

At the time, Kehilat Yedidya's practices put it on the very edge of the religious community in Israel and we tried to maintain a balancing act—to be as close to the edge of what orthodoxy could tolerate without falling off. We were often vilified by traditionalists in the larger religious community. Even rabbis and religious leaders who thought we were creating an important and useful alternative to an increasingly ossified and unquestioning orthodoxy were afraid to have their names publicly associated with us.

During the Lebanon War, when I was in the army, a number of the community's members helped found Netivot Shalom, a small religious peace movement that tried to break the stereotypical association of religious Judaism with the hypernationalism of the settlers. In the 1980s it was not easy to be on the left. At demonstrations against the Lebanon War and in favor of negotiations with the Arabs, we were accused of treason by right-wing agitators. It was even harder to be a religious leftist. In the average synagogue, sermons were often devoted to condemning all those who called into question Israel's God-given right to the West Bank and Gaza Strip. At times it looked to us as if the religious right was veering into a Jewish version of fascism. In the 1981 elections, an American-born rabbi, Meir Kahane, who worked crowds in poor and religious neighborhoods into a frenzy by calling Arabs "dogs" and democracy "un-Jewish," won a seat in the Knesset. During the Lebanon War, polls showed his support increasing many times. His party might well have won several seats in the elections of 1984 had Israel's Supreme Court not ruled that his opposition to democracy disqualified him from running for or serving in Israel's parliament.

One of Kahane's chief deputies, Baruch Marzel, lived at Tel Romeida. One day when I was on guard there he showed up to give me and my partner a lecture.

My companion that day was Alon, a newcomer in Company C. Slim and tall, with an oval face and straight jet-black hair over a high forehead, Alon was a quiet type who seemed to accept with equanimity whatever life gave him. Elnatan had singled him out on our first day at the training base before arriving in Hebron and appointed him NCO in Platoon Two. But in Hebron the job of NCO was pretty much meaningless, so instead of commanding others, he and I found ourselves sitting on a boulder together, looking at the prefab homes of Tel Romeida and sipping Turkish coffee we'd bought from the small Arab general store down the road.

A herd appeared above us at the top of the hill. The hill was a tell, a mound created by successive layers of settlement dating back thousands of years. This was the site of ancient Hebron, where Abraham had gone to purchase the Machpela Cave for a family tomb.

A wave of dirty white meandered down the slope toward us, ewes and nanny goats grazing the mound. The shepherd—a wiry, dark-faced boy of eleven or twelve—followed them down. He smiled and waved at us.

I was silent. This had been my first extended conversation with Alon and of course I'd steered the talk to politics. He didn't take my bait but told me a story that made me swallow my words. His mother, he told me, had been born in Hebron. According to family lore, she'd been saved from the massacre of 1929 when her brother tossed her out of a window of Hadassah House as marauders armed with clubs and axes stormed the building.

Marzel, who had a scraggly beard and was extremely overweight, emerged from one of the seven homes and spied on the boulder. He invariably dressed in a white shirt and black suit, making him look like a sumo wrestler moonlighting as a waiter. He came over to us and went through the standard spiel about how we could go home, that he and the rest of the Tel Romeida crowd didn't need us. Then he launched into a harangue against the Israeli left which, he maintained, controlled the country's media, large corporations, and even the government—which at the time was headed by Begin's successor, Yitzhak Shamir.

"Shamir is probably even to Begin's right," I noted.

"Believe me, I know," Marzel said. "It's just a put-on. Don't trust him."

He pointed to the shepherd boy. "He hates you. They all hate you. We've got to kick them out of here before they kill us."

I began to protest, but Marzel cut me off.

"I'm saying out loud what you and every other Jew thinks inside, what you are afraid to say. Don't you realize what you're looking at? The rebirth of the Jewish community in Hebron. You'll see, in a few years these mobile homes will have turned into a huge Jewish neighborhood. The Arabs will be gone."

"The family in that house on the corner," I reminded him, "has a plaque thanking them for hiding Jews in their basement during the massacre of 1929."

"They hate you, too," Marzel laughed. "Believe me, I know the Arabs. I live with them. You guys don't know a thing."

Alon's expression conveyed boredom and disgust. "About time we did a patrol," he told me. We got up and put on our efods.

"Running away from the truth," Marzel jeered, heading for his home.

Alon and I wandered through the old Jewish cemetery on the top of the hill. His reaction to Marzel surprised me. I would have thought that his mother's past would make him sympathetic to the settlers. But it was difficult to read his face. Unlike the other guys, he seldom told tales from his regular army service and seemed to have no residual pride in the brigade he'd served with. Even when he mentioned his upcoming marriage he made it sound like something of little consequence.

Having verified that there were no terrorists lurking in the grave-yard, we headed back to the mobile homes, where we stood watching the boy and his flock. One of the nanny goats seemed to have something sticking out under its tail. We asked the boy what it was, thinking we were viewing some sort of folk-veterinary treatment. The boy followed our gaze and smiled. Walking over to the goat, he grabbed and pulled hard at what turned out to be a pair of hind legs. A breech-birth kid slid out, damp and listless. The nanny goat continued to graze as if nothing had happened.

Alon let out a cry of joy at the birth we had witnessed, but the shep-herd boy just shrugged. He kicked at the motionless mass on the ground.

"It's dead," he told us. Blue-black flies were already buzzing over the stillborn carcass.

Chapter Three

· PREMONITIONS ·

TZE'ELIM, NOVEMBER 1987

MAYBE IF YOU TURNED THE RADIO OFF WE COULD HEAR you," Efi suggested. He wiped his glasses on his shirt and pressed his hand to his forehead as if to hold his eyes open. Eiger raised his eyebrows and turned the volume up.

"Riots in Gaza."

"Just the same garbage every day," said Falk.

"A thousand Arabs storming an army base in Jebalya? That's the same garbage? We didn't have anything like that in Hebron last year," Eiger said. "They kept climbing over the walls while the soldiers shot at them. This is something new."

"It won't last long. The army will knock some sense into them and they'll realize who's boss," Falk insisted.

"They're finally getting fed up with us. It won't be easy to get this kind of anger back into its bottle," I said.

"You sound awfully pleased to have Arabs throwing stones at Jews," said Falk.

"I'm not pleased. I'm just saying that you can't let Israelis shoot

Palestinian kids who are throwing stones and expect that it won't cause riots."

"Hey, guys, our mission now isn't to put down the riots in the territories," Efi said. "It's to conquer the Maya pita."

"Last time we took that pita it was from the west side," said Eiger. He turned off the radio and provided a blow-by-blow account, tracing a line on the map with his finger, his breath steaming in the cold air. His finger swept across a thick purple oval. It marked a typical Syrian stronghold, armored and infantry installations encompassed by an earthwork embankment. The map labeled it "Maya," in keeping with the Israeli army's custom of giving military objectives alphabetized feminine names, as used to be done with hurricanes. The flat disk indeed looked something like a round of pita bread. "We came up through this wadi and put my overwatch contingent on this hill. Platoon Three took the first target and Efi led the rest of you in the charge to the second one while Three covered for you."

I don't want to be here, I thought, huddled in my coat. The dark outside the window was oppressive, draining. Last week's cold had turned into this week's sore throat. It was November 1987, half a year after our stint in Hebron, a month before the great Palestinian uprising began. At least, the bulk of this story takes place then. Some incidents or conversations might have happened during other maneuvers. But how can I distinguish one from the other? They have all merged in my memory. At Tze'elim, the huge field forces training base in the Negev in Israel's south, there was no real before or after. When you were there, you had always been and would always be in those dusty hills, cold and tired, with too much weight on your back.

Perhaps the stark landscape affected me more than most, because I'd been in boot camp there. In 1982, with most of the reserve and regular units in Lebanon, the base was freed up from its usual routine of reserve training, and we Nachal grunts were given the "privilege," as my lieutenant called it then, of learning our fighting skills at a state-of-the-art base abundantly equipped with steep slopes and thorny scrub. "The only place in Israel where there's no view," Stern had said. During basic, Stern was a blunt but exuberant corporal in the next platoon over, with clipped carroty hair and a kipah.

By the time Stern showed up, a year after me, as a new Company C recruit, his kipah had gone the way of his old-country surname. His name was now Achlama, a Yiddish stone replaced by a Hebrew amethyst. But at Tze'elim, the landscape remained the same. It was here that we did our real work as reservists, preparing for the next all-out war we hoped would never come. In a country that had fought five such wars in its thirty-nine years of existence, the odds were that it would anyway. Yet stories from this place, or at least stories that would be comprehensible to anyone outside, were much fewer than the ones from our stints of active duty on Mount Hermon or in the West Bank. Here, at Tze'elim, we turned inward, we worked among ourselves.

We were at the end of the longest consecutive period of maneuvers we'd ever been called up for. First a week for the officers and NCOs, then two more weeks with the entire company—target practice, weapons lessons, capturing imaginary enemy installations on the team, squad, platoon, and company level, parched by day and frozen by night. The final act was a three-day, two-night regimental war game. It would begin in just a few hours.

Efi, who had succeeded Matan as Platoon One commander at our exercises the previous winter but missed our month in Hebron, looked up at Eiger with a mixture of amusement and weariness. He'd begun as a hesder soldier, but his decision to become an officer meant dropping out of the yeshiva part of the program. Now between army stints he was studying software engineering at the Technion in Haifa. His air of quiet competence made everyone in the platoon happy to do as he said, without him needing to say much. I'd grown fond of him, though we ran into silences whenever the two of us tried to have a conversation about anything but army matters. We seemed to need Eiger as a catalyst.

"You actually remember how we attacked Maya last year?"

"Last year and the year before and the year before that, since Maya was born," Falk laughed. "Eiger's overwatches are famous throughout the IDF."

"No big deal. It's always the same. Only the direction changes," said Eiger. "You guys are just jealous."

We were, and not without reason. The overwatch contingent, with its big guns and mortars, was deployed on a hill some distance from the objective, which was invariably on a hill as well. The overwatch commenced heavy fire on the enemy to force them into their bunkers, so they couldn't fire against the attack force. That was the rest of us, who charged up the enemy hillside and filled the cardboard-cutout Arab soldiers with bullet holes. When we got in range of the enemy redoubt, Eiger ceased fire and sat back to watch us slog up the slope and try to aim at the same time.

"Sometimes, instead of Maya we take Daliah or Gila or Rotem," I noted.

"It's all the same shit," Falk said.

Falk was right. They were all the same, as were we soldiers in our damp uniforms, army coats the color and texture of battered Syrian olives, and stubbly faces. It was always winter; it was always cold and wet, and we seemed to have been here all our lives.

We were sitting around a wobbly white metal folding table in the prefab mess hall assigned to our battalion. The large room was unheated and poorly lit and, with walls and roof and floor the thickness of cardboard, would not in any case have retained any heat for long. At the tables adjacent to us, the officers and NCOs of Platoons Two and Three pored over maps and peered through stereoscopes at aerial strip photos of the bleak landscape around us. The staffs of other companies sat at other tables.

Elnatan strode over to us and looked over Efi's shoulder at the map.

"I'm going to follow this channel in the second act, tomorrow night, when I'm on my own," Efi said quietly, tracing the route with a capped Bic. "It's shorter."

"It's harder to navigate," Elnatan pointed out. "You've got fewer markers along the way and there's no moon." But of course he consented; Efi was the best navigator among our lieutenants, and Elnatan was the best among the battalion's captains. We'd never known either to make a wrong turn.

"Why are all the NCOs here? Why isn't anyone back at the tents making sure the men are getting their gear ready?" Elnatan asked, glancing at Eiger, Falk, and me.

"They're okay," Eiger bluffed. "Trust me."

Elnatan didn't. "They're all snoring in their sleeping bags, if I know them. With the possible exception of the hesder guys. Efi can plan the route on his own. You three get over to the tents. My inspection is scheduled for ten p.m. That's an hour from now."

Falk, who had a way with the supply units, went off to finagle some more machine gun ammo and perhaps another mortar round or two to make Eiger's overwatch all the more impressive. Eiger and I headed back to the Company C tents, though not until we made, at his insistence, a stop at the canteen for steak-and-pita sandwiches. Years later, when Elnatan became battalion commander, he'd insist on having all four companies bivouac in the field, far from the base, precisely to prevent such culinary detours.

"Why are you so down?" Eiger needled me as we walked to our tents over sand packed down by the afternoon's drizzle. Away from the streetlamps that illuminated the roads crisscrossing the base's central compound in pools of weary yellow light, the place was ominous. Structures loomed in the shadows—storerooms, latrines, concrete platforms denuded of the tents for which they were made.

I longed to see Ilana and the kids, but it was a longing for something in a story I'd read years ago. The pay phones on the base had been out of order since we'd arrived, and though I'd gone home both weekends, I'd had my head full of the army even then. Ilana had been exasperated when I talked about little else. In the basement room in a neighborhood elementary school that Kehilat Yedidya used as its synagogue, I'd felt apart from my friends and acquaintances, as though they lived a fantasy and only I knew reality.

Reality was this base, the sandy hills out there in the dark where we would be later this night. Eiger, too, was real, as were Falk and Efi and Elnatan and the guys back in the tents. They were points of light in this dark, closer to me than my closest friends. Yet I felt like a stranger among them, too. This was how I wanted to answer Eiger's question, but I couldn't.

"It's freezing. My toes are completely numb," I bitched. "Why do we train in the winter? We only have wars in the summer."

"I'll pass that on to the chief of staff," Eiger said.

We walked another minute in silence.

"This place gives me the creeps," was all I could say.

When we got to the tents we saw that, as expected, some of the soldiers were dozing on their cots and the rest were drinking coffee and chatting. Achlama stepped out of the Platoon Two tent carrying a valise, his long hair and scraggly beard glowing in the dark. He opened the valise, famous for containing anything and everything a soldier might suddenly need, and pulled out a pair of metal buckles.

"Take that, Sheib, and no more excuses," he shouted in through the tent flap. He looked up at me. "I'm going crazy. Everywhere you look there's a kipah. Is this Israel's future?"

On the first day of general maneuvers the battalion had absorbed a large number of hesder soldiers, and about a dozen and a half of them were assigned to Company C. They were very young, technically still in the final stage of their regular army service. Elnatan took them in enthusiastically. While he was not at all religious, he discerned that their religiosity and youth together produced a high level of motivation. This was more important to him than their subpar combat skills. They'd spent less time in active duty than the other guys, and many of them looked more like scholars than soldiers.

Sheib was a good example. At twenty-two, he already had a B.S. degree from Israel's Open University, earned through correspondence courses he'd completed while he was an enlisted man. He was now enrolled as a graduate student at Bar-Ilan, a university outside of Tel Aviv that had an Orthodox Jewish character. There he was able to split his day between advanced religious study and physics. Slight and short, with a thin mustache and glasses, Sheib didn't look like the kind of guy who'd survive in the infantry—but he did, for many years. Still, he was always an outsider. He had an antisocial streak that made him hard to approach, and a lack of concern for what others thought of him that bordered on the eccentric. While he viewed the world in black-and-white terms, his thinking was often unconventional and his reasoning sharp. I liked his rationalist outlook, according to which the commandments were duties in and of themselves rather than a means to reach communion with God. But he lacked any sense of irony and thus could not see when his rationalism led him into absurdities.

Greenberg was his foil in Platoon Two. Round of face and body, with curly hair and freckles, he, too, looked out of place in uniform. Whereas Sheib was curt and confrontational, though, Greenberg was quiet and cooperative. He never asked for special favors or objected to an assignment. It wasn't until years later, when he was working as a computer engineer in a high-tech firm and got married at what in the religious community was considered a late age, that he ever requested an extra day off.

Achlama looked me in the eye. "What are you so glum about?" And then to Eiger: "What's he so glum about? Hey, so we've been living in a trash heap for the last two weeks, eating lousy food and freezing our balls off. Is that any reason to be depressed?"

Eiger yawned and turned toward the two Platoon One tents. "Okay, let's get everyone up." He strode to the nearest tent.

"Okay, everybody up. What's going on here? We've got hills to conquer! Eldad, Fisch, there's ammo in the truck—go get our share over here."

"Someone else can do it," Eldad suggested, his eyes still closed.

"No, you're going to do it," Eiger said, grabbing one of Eldad's ankles and shaking it. "Watzman, go get the guys in the other tent out of their sleeping bags."

"Me? The Yemenites?"

"See, Watzman, the big liberal, won't have anything to do with the black guys," Eiger remarked to Fisch, a new hesder kid with a dense growth of bristles on his face. "By the way, you'll be carrying a MAG machine gun tonight." Fisch had a serious countenance that made him look older than he was. He had an easier time fitting in to Platoon One than Sheib and Greenberg had in Platoon Two—perhaps because Platoon One was more cohesive, or perhaps because he was more outgoing.

"Me? A MAG?" Are you crazy?" The MAG, a twenty-five-pound iron firing machine, was usually given to a platoon's tallest, heftiest guys. But we didn't have enough of those, and we certainly weren't going to unload it on one of the old-timers. Fisch looked good enough.

I trudged over to the next tent as Fisch turned red and charged Eiger with a variety of moral crimes, providing a talmudic reference for each one.

The Yemenites were up, huddled around a camp stove in the center of the tent. Turkish coffee was brewing with the sharp, pungent fragrance of *hawayej*, a powder made of cardamom, pepper, and ginger. The Yemenites' deep brown skin camouflaged them well in the dim light of the tent's forty-watt bulb, and it was hard to tell where one guy ended and the next began. I made out faces vaguely. There was Tzadik, the oldest and most experienced of the group, who counseled us earlier in the day to pack body-sized sheets of plastic in our efods and told Yermi that he could appropriate a roll of the stuff from the base's communications room. There was Shabbetai, a thickset, broad-backed, mustached machine gunner who raised flowers for export, and Shaltiel, the radioman whose accent was so heavy that his speech was practically incomprehensible to members of every other ethnic group. And there was Keisar—skinny, hyperactive, and high-volume—who greeted me with a toothy smile and an enthusiastic offer of coffee. They motioned for me to sit down and join them. I was tempted. The camaraderie of the coffeepot was one of the great things about this army, so much homier and less threatening than that of the beer keg from my college days in the United States. Alcohol broke down inhibitions, but the closeness that flowed from it felt premature, raw. Caffeine encouraged conversation while allowing each man to guard his privacy when he chose.

"Elnatan's inspection is in half an hour. Are you guys ready?"

They made affirmative sounds but did not get up. Shaltiel said something that caught their attention and they turned in on themselves again, forgetting my presence. I plodded back to the first tent.

"They're up," I reported to Eiger.

"Are they ready?"

"They didn't say. Or maybe they did. I'm not sure."

Twenty minutes of intense activity commenced as the men filled their canteens in the latrine's sinks, topped up the bullets in their magazines, adjusted the straps on their pakalim, and stuffed empty pouches and pockets with chocolate-covered wafers and candy bars. A main point of debate was whether to wear your coat during the long march to the objective, in which case you would sweat and then freeze during the long wait before the dawn attack, or not to wear it, in which case you would freeze along the way.

Loaded with coats, rifles, ammunition, pakals, gas and bio warfare shin packs, plastic sheeting, and snacks, we were already heavy and awkward. Added to this was another burden: We had been issued bulky life jackets that we were to carry with us for most of the night. There were various theories about how the jackets might be rolled, folded, or otherwise manipulated so that they could be slipped through the straps of the efods at our backs. None of the theories bore up under experiment, however, so everyone improvised.

"Ten minutes!" Eiger shouted, his cry echoed by Falk and me and, farther down the row of tents, by Alon and Mizrahi. Then Eiger spotted Fisch trying to force an item more or less the size of his head into the back pouch of his efod. Its plastic case rustled and sparkled in the yellowish lamplight.

"The tefillin go in the crate over there," said Eiger. "The truck'll bring them to us in the morning."

"The truck is always late," Fisch complained. "It never ends up coming until after the attack and then the time for the morning service is over. We're all taking our tefillin with us." By "we" he meant himself and the other hesder guys, not the rest of us nonhesder religious guys.

Alon, who'd become Platoon Two sergeant the previous week after his predecessor was in a automobile accident on his way home for the weekend, walked over with a puzzled look.

"The yeshiva guys are all putting their prayer stuff in their efods. I thought it goes on the truck."

Eiger shrugged. "If they want to lug their tefillin all night and get them all sweaty, that's their business."

"Get the platoon together," said Efi, whose arrival had gone unnoticed.

"Why bother? Everything's fine. Perfect," said Eiger.

"Everyone's filled their canteens? Topped up their magazines? Fixed up their pakals?" Efi asked doubtfully.

"They've been ready for an hour already," Eiger assured him, just as Keisar wandered out of the Yemenite tent, bleary-eyed and dressed in his army-issue long underwear. Spotting Eiger, he waved two empty magazines at him.

"Are there any bullets anywhere?" he shouted at the top of his lungs.

As Efi instructed Eiger to round up the platoon for inspection, a voice like a mortar shell detonated at the Platoon Two tents. It was Udi, the new deputy company commander, who was built like a half-size version of a heavyweight boxer. He was staring Sheib in the eye and, since Sheib was no taller and painfully thin, it looked as if the shock wave produced by Udi's voice might send Sheib flying headfirst into the tent.

"You're a fucking clown!" Udi bellowed. Sheib had his efod on, apparently at Udi's order, but it was hanging unevenly, and his canteens were dangling. "How are you going to walk ten kilometers in that? You call yourself a soldier?"

"I'm not a soldier, I'm a theoretical physicist," Sheib said, in a tone that suggested he regarded Udi as being, in the scheme of God's creation, of somewhat less consequence than a muon neutrino.

"What the hell have you been doing for the last two hours?"

Sheib held up a book. "I've been studying Rabbi Yehuda Alfasi's commentary on the Sabbath tractate of the Talmud."

"The what?"

"Never mind."

"And your shirt is filthy. You haven't changed it all week, have you? You stink."

"Cleaning is just moving dirt from one place to another," Sheib muttered.

Alon stepped forward to separate the two as Efi conducted a rapid inspection of Platoon One, except for Keisar, who barely had time to fill his magazines before Elnatan appeared.

Elnatan stood silently by the lamp pole front and center of the two rows of Company C tents as Jacques and Yermi rounded up the men. We formed an open box, a platoon on each of three sides, and Elnatan, Udi,

Jacques, and Yermi on the fourth. The lieutenants stood in front of their platoons, flanked by their NCOs. Elnatan began his inspection at one side, Udi at the other, conducting spot checks of magazines and canteens and paying special attention to the pakals. Elnatan asked Shabbetai how many rounds he had for the MAG and then asked Tzadik, the "second" who carried extra ammunition and equipment for Shabbetai's weapon, how many MAG rounds he was carrying and how he had tied the MAG's extra barrel to his efod. On the Platoon Two side, Udi, Alon, and Alon's new lieutenant, Ben-Ami, inspected Greenberg's 60mm mortar and the pack with the explosive and illuminating charges, as well as the charges in the pack of Sheib, Greenberg's second. Elnatan quizzed Eldad, Platoon One's sniper, about his rifle, and inspected Amzaleg's RPG launcher. Amzaleg was a hesder kid with an uncanny resemblance to Theodor Herzl, even though his family was from Morocco. Already married and a father a couple of times over, he had two two-stage RPG rockets in his pack. Elnatan wanted him to have at least one more and told Yermi to see if he could wheedle another from the battalion command.

Satisfied that all was in order, Elnatan called on Yermi to say a few words about logistics. Yermi pointed to a carton filled with sliced bread and several tubs of jam and containers of chocolate spread. "Everyone should make some sandwiches to take along," he said. The next organized meal wouldn't be until after Maya was taken, probably around noon the next day.

Udi weighed in with some points of his own, and then Elnatan gave us his view of the coming mission.

"I expect all of you to take this exercise with absolute seriousness. I know you're tired. I know it's been a long two weeks. But we have a responsibility to take advantage of every hour we're here. Tonight's exercise is as close as we can get in training to what we will be doing in wartime.

"This is why we're in the reserves," Elnatan emphasized, and we all understood. What we had done the previous May in Hebron was not what we were supposed to do as soldiers. That was police work, not combat—an anomaly not worth a minute of valuable training time.

"As all of you know, in war we will go to the Jordanian front. This exercise simulates the crossing of the Jordan River and the taking of Jordanian and Syrian positions on the hills east. You are all graduates of top combat infantry units, and I expect you to perform tonight and tomorrow with the utmost professionalism."

He then dismissed us to our two hours of sleep.

"What a great speech. It makes me want to pick up a MAG and start running," Achlama yawned. "But not before I have a few wet dreams."

"Why do we need to know how to attack Jordan?" Shabbetai grumbled. "Jordan is innocuous. It's the Arabs over here I'm worried about."

"What, that guy with the oven factory?" Achlama said.

"No, his teenage kids," said Shabbetai.

My Cassio emitted its double beep just as I opened my eyes to check it. I had set the alarm for five minutes earlier than the wake-up call so I'd have time to get my thoughts together before getting out of my sleeping bag. My sleep had been sound but intermittent—every twenty minutes I'd surfaced from deep within my brain to check the time. The army blanket I'd stuffed into the bottom of my sleeping bag an hour and a half ago had not prevented the cold that was assaulting my exposed face from numbing my toes. The very thought of unzipping the sleeping bag and exposing the rest of my body to the air paralyzed me.

I do not want to be here, I thought again. What possible use was it to anyone that I was freezing my feet off in the desert? I had a wife and children and work I ought to be doing, and I wasn't even any good at this army stuff. Five minutes went by.

"Eiger," I said. "Time to get up."

"Who cares?" Eiger said, pulling the dubon he'd been using as a pillow over his head.

I made out the irregular line of another sleeping bag, like an over-stuffed sofa I remembered from my grandmother's old apartment, in the bed beyond Eiger. I tried to remember who slept there. Efi.

"Efi," I said. "Good morning."

Efi immediately sat up, stared at me in the dark, and started hunting for his glasses.

We heard Amzaleg, who'd had the last guard shift, urging the Yemenites out of their beds. He was ineffective until he enlisted Keisar in the job. Keisar had a trademark way of waking people. He shouted "Good morning to all!" at the top of his lungs directly into their ears.

I slowly rolled over to my right side, where Falk lay. Barak, his best friend, was in the next cot over. No, he couldn't be, because Barak hadn't yet joined the unit in 1987. But Falk and Barak always slept in adjacent cots. Anyway, Falk's shadow contours were smooth and puffy, for he abjured army sleeping bags and always brought a feather quilt and fresh bed linen from home.

"Falk, time to get up."

A debate ensued about who would be the first to slide out of his sleeping bag and screw in the lightbulb hanging from the tent's center pole. The issue became moot when Keisar bounded through the tent flap and took care of the bulb, allowing us to see that he was dressed in rubber flip-flops, bikini underwear, his dubon, and a huge, toothy smile.

"Good morning," he shouted.

"My God," we heard Jacques moan from the company staff tent on our other side. "Has he no manners?"

With the light on, the guys began to move. Everyone dressed quickly simply to keep warm. Within a few minutes we were out, standing by the efods and pakals we had left in the square we stood in just two hours before. Yermi had a huge pot of hot and syrupy-sweet coffee boiling over a gas dog and bags of jelly sandwiches for those who wanted them. We sipped the steaming fluid, letting it warm our noses and ears, as Elnatan gave us a final pep talk.

"I want to see everyone walking in formation. Don't bunch up, and nothing but total silence," he ordered.

Then we heaved on our efods and the soldiers their pakals. As an NCO, I was without the latter. Naturally, the guys were jealous and, just as naturally, I felt guilty. Inevitably, Eiger told me I was an idiot for feeling that way.

"They're in their twenties. You're over thirty. You deserve it," he said.

"Still, I'm in better shape than most of them," I pointed out. In civilian life I ran every day. I wasn't fast or graceful, but I was consistent. As others my age had metamorphosed from athleticism to indolence, I had gone from being the worst guy in gym class to an exemplar of fitness, without any change in my habits.

"I don't see them having any trouble. They may not lug around machine guns and mortar shells every day at home, but when they get here and have to do it, they do it, and do it well," Eiger observed.

He was right. I may have had stamina, but I still couldn't do the acrobatics. When it came time to charge an enemy position, guys like Eiger and Shabbetai and Falk hit the ground, shot, rolled into position, and sprang to their feet for another sprint toward the objective with an elegance I could only envy. The instinct seemed to have been imprinted in them during their three years of regular service. Company C stormed a hillside more professionally than had the kids in my NCO course.

We proceeded to a gate in the base's fence, by the lot where the APCs were parked. The rest of the battalion arrived as we did. There was the usual delay as the battalion commander, an easygoing but meticulous religious guy named Akiva, conferred with the company commanders and the commander of the support unit about a logistical problem. Some of the guys jumped up and down in the cold, while others huddled forlornly on the ground. Eiger chatted with Ben-Ami, whom he knew from way back. The two of them had consecutive serial numbers, having met in line for gear and inoculations on their enlistment day. Then a whisper ran among the men, Elnatan called out "Forward," and we set off.

Company C led the battalion, probably because of Akiva's appreciation for Elnatan's navigating skills. We walked in two files representing the forces we would split into when we reached our objective. The left file consisted of Platoon One, with Efi leading, and half of Platoon Two. The right consisted of the rest of Platoon Two and Three, led by Ben-Ami. Eiger and his overwatch contingent walked behind. The battalion commander and his staff followed us, then Company A. The Heavy Weapons Company and its mortars and rockets were mounted on APCs and set off by a different route to the same destination, led by the recon platoon in its jeeps. The support units, medical team, and Company B brought up the rear.

Once we started walking, my mood improved. My body warmed. The moon had not yet risen and, when we got beyond the first line of hills after the fence, thousands of stars that could not be seen from the city appeared in the sky. This is okay, I thought. This is really okay.

Eiger caught up to me, breaking out of formation. "How're you doing?" he whispered.

"Fine," I whispered back.

"Because you look kind of depressed. Is everything okay at home?"

"Everything's fine," I said. And after a pause: "It seems so far away."

"I don't know what you're doing here," Eiger lectured me. "At your age you could easily move into one of the support units. There's an opening for an operations sergeant in the battalion. Why not go for it?"

"You don't want me here?" I shot back, annoyed.

"The question is, what are you trying to prove?"

I sighed. "I was an op sergeant for nine months in Lebanon. I hated it. Too much sitting around."

"I'm sure lots of guys would have given anything for your job," Eiger said.

"I'm sure they would have. But it was torture for me. I felt awful that other guys were in the outposts on the front and I was farther back at brigade headquarters."

"As if being in brigade headquarters in Lebanon isn't plenty dangerous," Eiger noted.

"It's the same here," I said. "I can't let the other guys charge up Maya while I'm sitting by the radio. Even though I know they can all charge up Maya just as well without me. Maybe better."

"Eiger, Watzman, shut up," Udi hissed behind us. Eiger fell back to his position, and we continued on.

Even though Efi had shown us the route on paper, I could only vaguely connect the wadis and paths we were walking with the lines on the map. The terrain didn't have undulating brown contour lines like its representation. I allowed myself to sink into my own thoughts. My legs moved automatically, the weight of my efod and rifle becoming part of my body and, therefore, unnoticed. Only the huge life jacket attached to my back kept returning me to reality. I hadn't fastened it properly and it kept slipping off to one side. We passed a dark hill that blocked the stars and stumbled through a riverbed whose stones were dry and cold.

Wasn't that field the place we had learned trench warfare in basic? And that hill beyond it the one we had run up day and night during that winter week in 1982, taking the enemy positions first with a fire team, then with a squad, then with the entire platoon? And that plateau stretching below to the next row of hills must have been where we did a week of APC training, our upper bodies exposed in the fighter's hatch to an endless freezing rain. And that shape breaking the form of the hilltop over to the left, wasn't it the large acacia tree that marked Chicago, the mock village of bare, bullet-pocked concrete where we had learned combat in built-up areas? But, no, it couldn't all be so close; the training area at Tze'elim was vast. Eiger couldn't help me with his prodigious memory for the details of every attack, because he hadn't been with me then. I reflected that in a year and a half as an enlisted man, I hadn't made a single friend worth keeping.

It strikes me now, when I think back on this, that this was the proof I needed to assure myself that it wasn't being a soldier that held me so solidly in Company C. I had been a soldier during my regular service as well, and hadn't liked it. I served only because it was necessary. Recently, the army instituted a new policy—aimed at promoting cohesion in the reserves—in which friends who served together in the regular army can ask to transfer as a group to the same reserve unit. It's a good idea, but it wouldn't have been of much use to me.

Apparently it was luck of the draw that I landed in a unit whose members enjoyed being together. It wasn't always the case. I knew guys who served in units that never coalesced, where soldiers competed with each other for perks more than they worked together as a team. And others served in units that were nice enough but didn't have any sense of solidarity that went beyond the work itself. Company C seemed to have been that way when I first arrived and, from what I heard later, moved back in that direction in the years after I left. But at this point, in 1987, a nucleus was forming—Efi, Eiger, Falk, Achlama, Mizrahi, and others—around which the rest of the company would cohere in the years to come.

My position was anomalous. In 1987 I'd barely begun to feel at home in the company, yet I already seemed to be on my way out. Like Eiger, Efi, and Falk, I'd finished my mandatory service in the previous five years, and since then I'd met my wife, married, and had my first two children. But the guys in my cohort were in their midtwenties, and I was now thirty-one. After only three and a half years in the company, I was already at the age when guys left combat service entirely or sought a job on the support staff. The support staff offered less strenuous duties plus shorter stints of service and longer vacations. Worth it, I reflected as I felt the life jacket slip down to my thighs. I reached behind to try to shove it back up but got it only partway up my back. I must look ridiculous, I thought. Perhaps, I sighed to myself, I owed it to my family. There was a new child at home, my son, Asor. Was it really fair to leave Ilana on her own with a baby and a toddler for weeks at a time when I had another option?

The growing unrest in the Gaza Strip and the West Bank also had me worried. Our service in Hebron the previous May seemed to have marked the end of twenty years of relative acquiescence to the Israeli occupation. Since then there had been a series of riots, general strikes, and attacks on Israeli civilians and soldiers. In August a military police officer had been shot to death in downtown Gaza by Palestinian terrorists escaped from an Israeli prison. That same month an attack of a radically new kind had been narrowly prevented by the Shin Bet, the secret Israel intelligence force—a young woman from Bethlehem had intended to drive into Jerusalem in a car packed with explosives and blow herself up at a crowded intersection. In September a reservist had been stabbed to death at a bus stop. Many of these attacks were carried out by Palestinians associated with a new fundamentalist Muslim group called Islamic Jihad. Islamic Jihad, and the more established but hardly less militant Hamas, seemed determined to radicalize the Palestinian population in the territories and bring it out to the streets. Even the local cells of the Fatah, the largest of the Palestinian political groups, seemed to be chafing at the established PLO doctrine that liberation would come through military action from the outside, led by the Palestinian leadership and its headquarters in Tunis.

Increasing Palestinian violence had brought with it more counterviolence from the Israeli side. The army, attempting to quell a demonstration at Bethlehem University that had turned violent, shot into a crowd of students, killing one and wounding several others. The university was only a fifteen-minute ride from my home. I visited the campus regularly as part of my newspaper work. Israeli settlers in the territories were turning ever more trigger-happy. Two Palestinian youngsters had been killed by settlers who began shooting after the kids threw stones at their cars.

Now the life jacket was sliding down the other side of my back. Somehow, one of its straps had gotten tangled in my rifle's sights and I couldn't see my gear well enough to get it loose.

If this was indeed a permanent change in Palestinian behavior, then Company C would be doing more and more duty in the territories. The month in Hebron had been distasteful and boring but not scary. Going back there, or to any Palestinian city, would now be a dangerous assignment. Elnatan's certainty that that sort of police work was not our job was encouraging, but did he really know? And if he was wrong, did I have a right to put myself on the front line and give Ilana sleepless nights? Of course, in a support role I'd still be in the territories during reserve duty, but I'd be in the reserves for less time and I wouldn't be out on patrols.

What if I had to put down a riot at Bethlehem University, or at Bir Zeit University near Ramallah, or at An-Najah University in Nablus? How could I visit such places as a journalist one day and be there as a soldier the next? Would the students and teachers stop talking to me if they saw me in uniform? Wouldn't my editor raise legitimate questions about my ability to report objectively on Palestinian higher education if the students I interviewed were the same ones I fought?

Some unthinking journalists (and readers) equate objectivity with not having opinions. If a journalist had to be free of convictions about the people he wrote about, he couldn't cover any beat for more than a few weeks. Some of the best and most incisive reporting about Palestinian affairs is done by Israeli journalists. Since my first trip to Bir Zeit in 1979 I'd had the opportunity to observe this slice of Palestinian society and I'd inevitably developed my own thoughts about it.

I admired the mettle of these students and teachers who braved roadblocks and checkpoints to get to their campuses. A lot of them frankly admitted that the high value Palestinian society placed on education was something it had learned from its Israeli adversaries. Many students came from refugee camps or indigent villages, and a large proportion of them were so poor that they had trouble paying tuition that amounted to a couple hundred dollars a year. Nevertheless, their families were determined to put at least one child through college, and the chosen one was usually supported by brothers who worked in Israel or in the Persian Gulf oil fields. These students proudly defended their colleges and bristled when Israeli officials dismissed the institutions as glorified high schools.

On the other hand, I was disturbed by a closed-mindedness among many of the educated Palestinians I met. A prime example was Saeb Erekat, then the press spokesman for An-Najah University and at this writing a member of the Palestinian cabinet. I once visited the campus after the Israeli army had conducted one of its periodic raids. While most times the raids seemed unjustified and primarily intended to intimidate the institutions, this time the army was able at least to show that it had found something sinister. It put on a display of vile anti-Semitic (not anti-Israeli) posters and literature it had confiscated from the office of an Islamic student organization. The university protested the raid on the grounds that its students should enjoy free speech even if their opinions were deplorable. In principle, I agreed. I went to visit the campus soon after the raid and asked Erekat whether the university was going to hold any educational activities to explain to students the difference between opposing Israel's policy in the territories and hating Jews as a racial group. He said nothing was planned.

"If a group of students were discovered with racist literature at an American university, the institution would probably organize a seminar or a teach-in in response," I noted. "Shouldn't An-Najah deal with anti-Semitism the same way?"

"No one here is an anti-Semite!" Erekat exclaimed. "How can we be anti-Semites? We are Semites ourselves!"

"You know what I mean," I said.

"How can you accuse Semites of anti-Semitism?" he said, aghast, and I soon realized that I wasn't going to get any farther with him.

At some point the double file of soldiers stopped. We went down on one knee and readied our rifles, as standing orders required. There was a muffled roar somewhere up ahead, but I couldn't place it. It wasn't a desert sound. The troops rose and moved again, a wave standing and flowing onward as we rounded a bend by a dark hill.

The roaring grew louder and the ground took on a blue glow. Suddenly I made out Jacques and Yermi standing up ahead, bundled head to foot in the thermal coveralls we wore on Mount Hermon. They stood next to an army truck, and they had a large pot set over a flaming gas dog. They were handing out plastic cups of something to the soldiers who strode by. When it was my turn, I saw that it was hot semolina cereal, heavily sugared in the army style. It warmed you more than coffee because it stuck as it went down. It felt incredibly good. I glanced at my watch—3:30 a.m.

"How are you doing?" Jacques asked me, pulling me lightly by the sleeve out of file. "It's so cold."

"I gotta go," I said, pointing at the receding platoon and hitching the sagging life jacket up my back.

"I wanted to talk to you about something," Jacques said conspiratorially. He looked up at the soldiers going by. "You're not like the rest of them. I saw that the first day you were with us. Isn't it horrible what's going on in the territories now? Another little girl was just killed by these brutal settlers. I heard it on the radio last night. You're the only one with culture. Maybe Eiger, too."

"I really have to go, Jacques. I'll lose the rest of the platoon."

"Listen, I've decided that you should be my replacement as company clerk. What do you think?"

"You're leaving?" I said in astonishment. Jacques was a fixture in the unit, its longest-serving member, having joined it in the Yom Kippur War in 1973.

"Not now, but I'll soon be over age. I can't leave this job in the hands of just anyone. It's so important. You don't realize how important."

"I really don't think I want to spend my time making up duty rosters and doing paperwork. Thanks, but no thanks," I said, turning away.

"Think about it," Jacques called after me. "Don't disappoint me."

I jogged past the guys of Platoon Three, then reached Eiger's overwatch group.

"What was Jacques after?" he queried as I passed.

"He wants me to be company clerk after him," I said, panting.

"And what did you say?"

"No way," I whispered, and trotted forward to retake my place in the file.

Did everyone think I was decrepit? I looked at the guys around me. I'm in good shape, I said to myself. I'm not that old. Okay, so I was ten years older than Sheib and Fisch. But wasn't I more like them than I was like other guys my age?

It was odd that I felt closer to these guys than I did to my friends in civilian life. With the exception of Eiger, I didn't spend time with them outside the army and had little acquaintance with their families. But there was something about sleeping in the same tent and sharing the same burdens that endowed these twice-a-year friendships with greater intimacy.

Yet I was a stranger among them, too. I hadn't gone to their high schools, belonged to their youth groups, grown up in the same milieu. I didn't remember the same songs or TV programs, and while my Hebrew was fluent, my army slang didn't come naturally. Ilana was Israel-born and we spoke Hebrew at home, but most of my social group, centered around Kehilat Yedidya, was English-speaking.

Nor did I fit neatly into any of the subcultures, what Israeli sociologists like to call "tribes," into which Israeli society is divided. My liberal

American middle-class upbringing and liberal arts education meant I shared a lot of the background of guys like Alon, from the secular tribe, but I didn't feel entirely comfortable with them because they drove on the Sabbath and ate bread during Passover. My religious observance placed me with guys like Fisch and Sheib. They were the ones with whom I prayed three times a day in the army, outside in all temperatures and all weathers. I shared my army Sabbaths and discussed commentaries on the weekly Torah reading with them. But this group of young yeshiva students had been educated in institutions where a nationalist and messianic version of Jewish orthodoxy prevailed. For most of them, human rights took second place, at best, to Jewish destiny. The only place I felt really comfortable was at Kehilat Yedidya—but even there, with my army experience and my Israeli wife, I wasn't typical.

We halted again and dropped to our knees. The silence and the darkness were broken simultaneously. An unfamiliar officer—a senior one, his oak-leaf insignia told us—stood before us, a searchlight in his hand. He was apparently from the base's training staff.

"Okay, guys. The Heavy Weapons Company has just laid the pontoon bridge. You are now to put on your life jackets," the officer said crisply.

"Can I ask a question?" We all turned around. It was Achlama, standing up, his hands clasped before him like an obedient schoolboy and his red braid draped casually over his right shoulder. The officer shone the spotlight on him.

"Yes, what is it?" he asked impatiently.

"Are you out of your mind?" Achlama asked. His tone was so innocent that even Elnatan laughed.

"What was that?" the officer said flatly. He wasn't sure whether or not he was being mocked.

Achlama submitted his evidence to the court of Company C. "We're in the middle of the desert. There's no water for miles around. You've taken dozens of men away from their families and jobs to lay a pontoon bridge across a stretch of sand and now you're afraid we're going to fall off it and drown?"

But we had to play the game by the rules. We undid the strings that held, or did not hold, the life jackets in place and we put on the jackets. Some of the heavier weapons, like the MAGs, got their own life jackets. Then we walked down into the wadi and crossed the pontoon bridge. On the other side, a contingent of Heavy Weapons guys stood collecting the life jackets as we discarded them. And we headed on into the night.

Without the life jacket to annoy me, the time went more quickly. I was able to enter into a walking, dreamless trance in which a just-sufficient portion of my brain remained alert. The rest of my mind shut off. It was impossible to say how much later we suddenly halted again and descended, reflexively, to our knees.

A whisper relayed back from Elnatan informed me that this was our staging point. We were behind the hill where Eiger's overwatch contingent would deploy itself just before dawn, as the rest of us looped to the right around another hill toward our objective. But dawn was an hour off, and we had to wait. Tzadik and his cohorts reclined against boulders to doze, wrapped in plastic sheeting to protect against morning dew.

This was the worst moment of any maneuver. You stopped, kneeling or sitting on the cold, damp sand, and the sweat that had soaked your clothing slowly chilled. It seemed to absorb the cold from the night even after you put on your dubon. The rest that you had welcomed as a respite for your feet and shoulders now became your enemy. You would have given anything to move and become warm again, carried any load and climbed any hill. But you had to sit still and freeze.

We fumbled through our pouches for the chocolate bars and jelly sandwiches we'd stuffed in them before leaving and shared them with our neighbors. Last week Platoon One had purchased a communal camp stove, glasses, and other accessories so we would have a coffee kit to take into the field with us, but Elnatan had strictly forbidden bringing it along on this major maneuver. We'd been drinking so much of the stuff these three weeks that four hours without a glass felt like a fast. At such moments I was always frightened by how elemental needs—for warmth, food, and caffeine—became so intense and desperate that I felt rules, manners, and principles slipping away.

Sheib, next to me, stuffed something into his mouth.

"What you got, Sheib?" I whispered.

"Coffee," he mumbled.

"Coffee?" I asked, incredulous but hopeful. Perhaps he'd lit a camp stove secretly, or brought a thermos from home? Would he give me some? I edged closer to him, but he had no glass. He brought his hand to his mouth again.

"Where's the coffee?" I whispered, perplexed.

Sheib pulled a foil package of Turkish coffee powder out of a pouch.

"Want some?"

"You're *eating* coffee?" I hissed.

"Gotta have coffee in the morning," Sheib explained. "Can't do without it."

Fisch, just behind us, suggested, "Let's get some guys together and have morning prayers before the attack."

"You can't pray until dawn, and we're attacking at dawn," I pointed out.

"We can start a little before, and do it fast. And we never attack on time anyway."

"Elnatan won't like it," I said.

"You're not supposed to eat until after morning prayers and I don't intend to wait until after the attack to eat. This is a major operation. We won't be through until ten a.m.," Fisch said.

"My tallit and tefillin are on the truck."

"Told you to bring them with you." Fisch got up and walked down the line, telling the hesder guys that a minyan, a prayer quorum of ten men, was being formed.

Despite his own yeshiva background, Efi opposed the improvised service. Fisch and Sheib prevailed, though, and soon a group of guys stood off to the side, the white of their prayer shawls glinting in the moonlight.

It was a signal for the rest of the formation to break up, and the guys had soon rearranged themselves according to friendships. Eiger and Efi and I watched the guys praying.

"I prefer my synagogue at home," Eiger remarked.

"So do I," I said.

"You know that Watzman belongs to this weird synagogue?" Eiger said to Efi.

"What's weird about it?" Efi asked.

"They let women give sermons and they go to peace demonstrations together," Eiger informed him. Efi shook his head in disbelief.

"Something really odd is going on there now," I laughed.

"I'm scared to ask what it might be," Eiger said.

"You've heard of that guy Mubarak Awad that the army wants to deport? The one who's been trying to get the Palestinians to engage in mass civil disobedience?"

"Yeah, what about him?"

"Well, he's called on religious institutions to offer him refuge, and some of the people in our community want us to shelter him. There's going to be a big meeting about it next Saturday night."

"And you're probably in favor. Don't you realize he's just a front for Arafat and the PLO?"

"I don't know how I'll vote on it. It seems like he might be a positive force. Civil disobedience is nonviolence, and that's good for us. It would be good for all of us if the Palestinians saw that they could make more gains through nonviolent tactics than with violent ones."

"I read about him in the paper. The Shin Bet says he's dangerous," Efi said.

"Maybe. But if they think so, they should tell us why," I said.

Udi suddenly appeared next to us. "What the hell is going on here?"

he demanded. "In five minutes we're hitting the road. Get these clowns back in formation, Efi. Eiger, make sure your overwatch is ready. Helmets on, everyone."

The service wound up and the soldiers quickly stowed their prayer gear and donned their efods and pakals. There was a blue-gray glow in the east, over the hills. We put on our helmets and readied our rifles. Eiger and the overwatch mounted the hill above us and, in response to a radio order from Elnatan, began their bombardment. The morning filled with explosions and machine gun fire. Tanks roared by, and a helicopter beat overhead. Parallel files of soldiers rose and set off north, skirting another hill. As the dawn lit the plain before us, we could see the light splashes of mortar rounds and the red track of machine gun fire arcing through the air toward the pita, now clearly visible. The radio crackled and Elnatan transmitted to Eiger an order to cease fire on the closer targets but to continue to bombard the more distant ones. The tone of the explosions changed, but they did not end.

Chapter Four
· CONFRONTATIONS ·

BANI NA'IM, MAY 1988

IT WAS A THURSDAY IN MARCH 1988 AND I WAS STANDING AT JERU-salem's big downtown intersection, munching on a tuna sub. I was free! But people were staring at me with curiosity and alarm, perhaps because, in my hospital pajamas, I looked like an escapee from an asylum. In fact, I was AWOL from Bikkur Holim, the hospital just up the street, where I'd been sequestered since Monday. The hospital fare, bland and monotonous in the best Polish-Jewish medical tradition, had driven me to disobedience. I sneaked out into the filthy, germ-ridden city and bought unsanitary food. According to my doctors, I was risking death by massive infection. That's why I told the sandwich guy to use every spread and sauce on the menu. Carpe diem.

I'd been hospitalized with a most embarrassing condition. Some weeks before I'd woken up with a large and extremely painful abscess on my bottom. My GP sent me to the emergency room, where a sadistic surgeon drained the abscess and poked around inside it with sharp instruments as I screamed. At a no less excruciating follow-up examination a couple of weeks later, the surgeon poked even sharper instruments into the still gaping cavity left by the abscess. I screamed some more, and he told me that I had not suffered enough. Surgery was required to ensure that the condition did not recur. He ordered five days in the hospital and three weeks of home rest.

Medical contacts in the United States told me that there this operation was a same-day, in-and-out procedure, though they confirmed that modern science didn't know how to anesthetize this part of the body. A friend who worked at the Israeli health ministry explained that the per diem funding structure in Israel encouraged hospitals to maximize hospitalization days. But the system was the system—the operation was Monday, by Tuesday afternoon I was feeling fine, but I could not get discharged until Friday.

I finished the sandwich in the waiting room outside the surgery ward and then walked in. But I couldn't get to my room because a television crew, several newspaper reporters, and a black-suited, bearded young man were crammed into the corridor. I recognized the latter as an aide to one of Jerusalem's numerous deputy mayors, Nissim Ze'ev, the local leader of a new ultra-Orthodox Sephardic ethnic party called Shas.

"What's going on?" I asked the aide.

"Nissim has come to visit the terror victim," he said, referring to a fifteen-year-old kid who'd been stabbed by an Arab earlier in the week. Then he turned to one of my fellow patients who also wore a kipah. "We're going to run all the Arabs out of this city. Their presence here is a desecration of God's name. We let these pagans live in our holy city and look what they do to us. We're going to teach them a lesson."

"You know," I pointed out, "there are two Arab doctors on this ward. They've been treating this kid."

"That's scandalous!" the aide gasped. "I'll get Nissim to look into it. Thanks for telling me."

"What I meant is that not all Arabs are terrorists."

"Believe me, I know the Arabs. They all want to kill us."

"Absolutely right," said the patient.

I'd heard this kind of vicious rhetoric on many occasions, but it had become more common in the months preceding my hospital stay. In December 1987 the Palestinians of the West Bank and Gaza Strip had erupted in a massive uprising against Israeli rule. There had been nothing like it since Israel captured the territories in 1967. For twenty years the Palestinians lived under the occupation with relative complacency, even as Jewish settlements were constructed in their midst. A small number of them committed terrorist attacks—bombs left on buses or in public squares, stabbings, an occasional shooting—but by and large the Palestinian population in the territories went about its business. They put their trust in the Arab countries and in Yasir Arafat's Palestine Liberation Organization. The Arabs beyond Israel's borders would, they hoped, one day defeat the Zionists and establish a Palestinian state. In fact, most of them no doubt hoped that Israel would be utterly defeated and Arab sovereignty restored to the entire territory between the Jordan River and the Mediterranean Sea. But the Arabs with whom I'd had contact in Hebron the previous year seemed mostly concerned with making a living and getting their kids educated. A majority of them worked in Israel or with Israelis, largely as unskilled laborers, even helping to build the very Israeli settlements that were encroaching on their land. Others depended in large part on the tourist trade, Israeli and foreign, for their livelihoods.

But the long-simmering frustration with the impositions and humiliations of Israeli rule had finally boiled over. Mobs of Arabs threw stones and Molotov cocktails at cars and army installations, killing many Israelis. Terrorist bombings in Israel proper increased. Young men formed underground revolutionary committees to direct and coordinate the uprising, issuing leaflets instructing youngsters to hoist Palestinian flags on telephone poles and roofs and to paint nationalist slogans by night on walls in cities and villages.

The Israeli army reacted fiercely. The generals and civilian leadership thought the uprising could be squelched by a massive show of force—Minister of Defense Yitzhak Rabin called on soldiers to "break their arms and legs." The press reported case after case of soldiers, both enlisted men and reservists, unnecessarily beating and humiliating Palestinians and destroying their property.

Not long before entering the hospital I'd gotten call-up orders for our next long stint, in May. We were again being sent to the Hebron district.

When I mentioned it to the surgeon who was treating me, he said to forget about it. "There is no way you will be able to go to the army in May."

"Not even for part of the time?" I asked.

"You'll have an open wound. It has to be kept clean. In the army you'll be getting dirty and dusty and bouncing around in jeeps. It'll get infected. You can't do it. Don't even try," he insisted.

My first reaction was relief. I wasn't at all sure what to expect from my friends in Company C in this new situation. Wouldn't some of them see this assignment as an opportunity to vent their anger against the Arabs? What would I do if I was present when one of them taunted or picked on a Palestinian, or even beat one senseless? How could I stand by and not protest or report such an action? On the other hand, what kind of friend would I be if I reported a comrade? Who would want to serve with me after I did such a thing? What could I expect from those members of Company C whose views I knew to be like those of the deputy mayor's aide? What about Hezki, Company C's own Hebron settler? Would Elnatan order me to beat up Arabs? If so, would I disobey? Disobedience would land me in jail. In fact, there were already some reservists in jail for refusing orders. Some had refused even to report for duty in the occupied territories.

My medical condition provided me with a providential solution to this dilemma. I was free to pass up this stint, retaining both my moral integrity and the fellowship of Company C.

But in the weeks that followed my hospitalization, I grew more and more uncomfortable with this easy way out. For the first time since I'd joined it, Company C would be under attack. How could I let the others risk their lives while I stayed home? As my recovery progressed speedily, I had less and less confidence in the doctor's orders. I couldn't see any medical reason why I shouldn't go, and if I were to stay home knowing that I was fit to serve, I'd feel awful.

Furthermore, as I followed the public debate in the press and discussed the issue of duty versus conscious with my friends in Kehilat Yedidya, I became increasingly convinced that a soldier could not rightly make a blanket refusal to serve in the fight against the Intifada. A small number of soldiers and reservists had indeed announced their refusal to serve in the occupied territories, but most of them came from the far left. Most Israelis who opposed the occupation accepted the principle, laid down in Israeli law in the country's early years, that a soldier could and should refuse to carry out an illegal or immoral order. But that refusal had to come at the point that the specific order was given. It would be easy to stay home and judge any of my friends who might stand accused of improper behavior. But how could I judge them if I had not been there with them, not knowing what challenges and complex choices they'd faced?

Another, more selfish consideration also burdened me. I knew that sometimes men who didn't serve during one of the unit's regular stints were called up for alternative duty, usually as guards at the home base near Jerusalem. If I was going to have to spend a month in the army, I wanted to do it with my friends, not with strangers.

So late one night, after the kids were in bed, I sat down with Ilana at our kitchen table to convince her that I should go. The table, with legs of unvarnished wood and a yellow Formica top, picked up second-hand when I got out of the army, creaked as I laid my hands on it and enumerated my reasons for going.

I expected Ilana to interrupt me and insist that I stay home. She was not one to keep silent, and she never hesitated to tell me to get my pri-

orities straight when anything—the army or work—conflicted with family. But she didn't. I'd already prepared my fall-back position, and I
found myself presenting it even though Ilana had not yet said that I
shouldn't go.

"So what I'll do," I said, "is go in on the first day and present my
medical papers, which say I can't serve at all. And then I'll tell them that
I want to volunteer for the second half of the month. That way they
won't be able to call me up for service with some other unit, and I won't
leave you alone the whole month with the kids."

"That will help," she said. Her acquiescence seemed entirely sincere.
Now I had to raise another possibility.

"You know," I said, "I'm a little worried about how the guys will
act. I don't know what I'll be told to do. I know that there are things I
can't do, even if I'm ordered to. If I refuse orders, I'll go to jail."

"Of course," she said.

"It could be for a month, or two, or three."

"You have to do what's right. Really, don't worry about me. I'll
manage. Remember that life doesn't stop here when you go to the
army," she told me.

I could see a critic—perhaps that assimilated Jew at Duke who refused to sign the petition denying that Zionism is racism, or one of Kehilat Yedidya's radicals, or Saeb Erekat at An-Najah University—saying,
Aha! This is the proof that you've been compromised. You claim to be a
liberal, to advocate human rights and statehood for the Palestinians, but
here you are on your way to becoming an instrument of repression.
Your principles have been in steady erosion since you agreed to become
a soldier. First, your service in Lebanon, when you put aside your opposition to the war in the name of military duty. Then the month in Hebron that got you used to playing the occupier in the West Bank. After
that, the next step wasn't such a large one—volunteering to participate
in the repression of an oppressed nation's popular uprising. If loyalty to

your friends was going to trump your sense of justice, you shouldn't have made those friends in the first place.

My sense of justice hadn't previously had to face up to a complex reality, though. The Intifada was not merely a fight to liberate the occupied territories. Most of the Palestinian partisans considered the entire state of Israel an illegitimate colonial usurper of Palestinian land. Mubarak Awad, the champion of civil disobedience that Kehilat Yedidya had considered sheltering, was virtually a minority of one among his people. The Intifada wasn't a matter of sit-down strikes. It was violent and directed against the people of my country, both soldiers and civilians. I could hardly be a loyal citizen while cheering on the Palestinian rebels and encouraging them to kill more Israelis. That would be no more just than encouraging Israelis to kill Palestinians. Furthermore, it would place me outside the political discourse of my own society. By doing my duty as a soldier, I'd retain my right as a citizen to advocate accommodation with the Palestinians and my right to demand that my fellow citizens listen to me. Was I free to refuse?

While this was the line I took with left-wing friends and acquaintances, I was still ambivalent about my choice to report for duty. My uncertainties came out one day not long before the company enlisted when I ran into Shaya, the Platoon Two medic, on a Jerusalem city bus. When he asked me where I was going, I said I had an appointment with my lawyer to prepare my defense before the impending war crimes tribunal. Shaya was insulted and I had to apologize and assure him that I'd been joking—not that he saw anything funny in this implication that the Israeli soldiers serving in the territories were all criminals. Shaya knew my political opinions well enough to surmise that I might well be speaking seriously.

When I think back on that conversation, I wince, especially since I made my remark to a friend, and on a crowded bus where many people could hear me. I certainly didn't mean to side with those self-righteous radicals who claimed that Israel was the world's leading fascist, repressive state (conveniently ignoring dozens of dark dictatorships that, unlike Israel, keep the media away from their war zones and suppress public dissent). But still, the stories in the press about soldiers beating up Palestinian kids and drumming families out of their homes at night sounded unpleasantly like the stories my grandparents brought with them from Russia. After being the victims of such oppression, how could we Jews do the same to others? How could we even do anything that might be viewed that way by outsiders? It seemed to contradict the very idea of what a Jewish state should be.

On the other hand, my grandparents had not thrown rocks or Molotov cocktails, nor had they taken potshots at the Russians. But wouldn't they have been well within their rights to do so? Wasn't the Jewish right to self-defense one of the founding principles of Zionism?

My eyes were so red and filled with tears when I reached Hebron that the uniformed girl manning the radio at the city's military headquarters asked compassionately whether it had really been so hard to leave my family that morning. Just allergies, I assured her, requesting directions to the rooms occupied by my reserve battalion's headquarters company. It had been a bad idea, I knew now, to frolic on the grass at the park with my eleven-month-old son, Asor, the previous afternoon. An unusually wet winter had turned into a vicious spring. During the fifty days between the Passover and Shavuot holidays, masses of desert air float up from the Arabian Peninsula and crouch over Israel for days at a time. Each mass is yellow with powdery sand that precipitates out, coating cars, trees, and windows. The heat waves break only when a hot spring wind, the khamsin, blows out of Arabia to push the gritty air pocket out into the sea. Breathing is heavy and difficult. Can it be a coincidence that Jewish tradition stipulates that this is a period of mourning? The heat and the dust were not, however, keeping the poppies, anemones, and mustard plants from blooming. I was having my worst allergy attack in years.

I had little knowledge of what Company C had been doing in the preceding two weeks. Eiger had called me during a visit home a few days ago, so I knew that platoons One and Three were stationed east of Hebron in a village called Bani Na'im, and that Ben-Ami's Platoon Two had been sent to a different village to Hebron's west. There, Eiger told me, they were living in miserable conditions and having a hard time with the locals. Up until Eiger's trip home, the Bani Na'im contingent had been bivouacked in the village's elementary school, a stone building that offered reasonably cool shelter from the heat. The day I spoke to him, however, they were moving into a tent camp to the south of the village. Eiger's usual luck had him at home instead of loading gear onto trucks.

As the Palestinian uprising dragged on, both sides became more practical. The Palestinians realized that it was counterproductive for them to keep their kids on strike and out of school indefinitely, while the Israelis realized that Palestinian kids were more liable to cause trouble when they were idle than when they were studying. By tacit consensus, parts of life like the elementary schools were returning to some semblance of normal operation.

But most of my conversation with Eiger had been devoted to more pressing issues, such as the best place to buy disposable diapers, which were a major line in our families' budgets. So on Monday, May 15, 1988, when I arrived in Hebron to get my gear and join my unit in Bani Na'im, I really had only press reports to feed my expectations. And the newspaper accounts I'd read about the army's means of controlling the Intifada only exacerbated my fears.

"Bani Na'im? Hop in," said an officer in a jeep I flagged down at the battalion base's gate. I threw my chimidan into the back and climbed in. The officer was wearing the uniform of the Border Guard, a division of the Israeli military under the command of the police. The

Border Guard had a reputation for treating the Palestinian population with contempt, even brutality. This officer, like many Border Guard soldiers, was a Druze, a member of an Arabic-speaking religious minority that, unlike Muslim and Christian Arabs of Israeli citizenship, is conscripted into the army. While some Israeli Druze identify themselves as Arab and Palestinian, many see themselves as patriotic Israelis, partners of the Jews. Sometimes their loyalty expresses itself in a chauvinism that would shock many a Jewish nationalist.

The Border Guard officer spent the twenty-minute drive telling me how Company C ought to handle the Bani Na'im populace.

"They live like animals and that's how you've got to treat them," he said with fierce earnestness. "These leftist Peace Now types think that if you're nice to Arabs, then they'll be nice to you. That's bullshit. They don't know the Arabs. I do. And I can tell you that the only language they understand is force. Show them who's boss and they'll be sweet and easy to handle. Show them that you're scared, that you're willing to give in, and they'll make your life miserable. Don't trust a thing they say. They're all liars. It's part of their culture."

He looked over to see my reaction. Apparently he sensed my discomfort and my unwillingness to engage him in debate. So he went on.

"You guys are lucky. A village like this is off the radar of the bleeding hearts. It's not like Hebron, where you've got a hundred journalists watching every move you make. You can do the work the way you're supposed to here," he assured me. "There's just one thing you need."

"What's that?" I asked.

"Trust. It means that you guys have to be a team. You've got to be closer than brothers. Because if you think there's just one guy who's going to rat on you, who's going to go running to the newspapers, then your hands are tied."

After this lecture, I was ready to believe that my crack to Shaya on the bus had not been off the mark. I'd better begin planning my courtroom speech of defense and contrition, I thought ruefully. Either I'd be hauled before a military court for refusing to carry out one of Elnatan's orders, or I'd be appearing before an international human rights tribunal for my participation in Company C's campaign of terror. We entered the village. It seemed tranquil enough. Why did the army need to be here at all, I asked my driver as we emerged on the other side and approached Company C's tents.

"Farther down this road there's a Jewish settlement, Pnai Hever," he said. "That's where I'm headed. The road through Bani Na'im has to be kept open for them. Otherwise they'll be isolated. They don't have any other way out."

In other words, I thought, if the settlement hadn't been built on Bani Na'im's far side, the army would have no compelling reason to impose itself on this Palestinian village.

I must not have looked good when I climbed out of the jeep. Or maybe it was my red eyes. In any case, Jacques's usual bright welcoming expression turned into one of concern as he showed me to my cot in the NCO tent.

"It's really not so bad here," he promised. "Not so bad at all."

Eiger would soon come by in his patrol jeep and take me out to show me the village and brief me on my duties, Jacques told me. In the meantime, I could get organized.

I shoved my chimidan under an unoccupied cot and made my bed by unrolling my sleeping bag on the dusty green army foam-rubber mattress. The canvas stretched over the cot's metal frame sagged, as usual, making the bed into more of a hammock. I went looking for a board of some sort to support my back and soon found just the thing. It was a pinewood door, unvarnished, dented, and with scraps of Scotch tape clinging to it, lying in a pile of miscellaneous items to the side of the parking area between the road and the tents. It had probably been appropriated from the elementary school where the company had previously bivouacked, but there was no way for me to return it to its rightful owners now.

Elnatan in particular had me worried. What was he going to expect of me? I knew that his political views were on the extreme right. In the last election he'd voted for Techiya, a party that had opposed Israel's withdrawal from the Sinai Peninsula and the peace treaty with Egypt. He was firmly against territorial compromise in the West Bank and Gaza Strip, enthusiastically supported Jewish settlers of the type we had seen in Hebron, and thought that only an aggressive military policy could keep the Palestinians docile. Too bad, I thought, that Udi, our new deputy company commander, wasn't in charge. In conversations during our maneuvers the previous winter, Udi had voiced a great deal of respect for Islamic society and culture, which he was studying at the Hebrew University in Jerusalem. He'd advocated territorial compromise with the Palestinians and was contemptuous of the settlers. In the past he'd voted Labor and would no doubt do so again in the elections scheduled for the coming November. True, he swaggered like a street tough, but certainly his political views meant that he'd take an enlightened and humane approach to the people of Bani Na'im. At least he would have a moderating influence on Elnatan.

Late afternoon of the day that Company C came to Bani Na'im, a week and a half before I arrived, the company's three patrol jeeps and the commander's jeep were ranged in a circle in the village's central plaza, in front of the mosque. The plaza lay at the top of the hill on which Bani Na'im was founded; the mosque's minaret rose above like a flag planted by those first settlers to stake their claim. Surrounding it, at a respectful distance, were stone fences and within them stone houses, most of them small, some with a second story that looked somewhat newer. The plaza also served as the village's commercial center, so in many of these houses part of the ground floor served as a family shop— fruit and vegetables, dry goods, cloth, agricultural tools and hardware.

From this vantage point at the village's nucleus the soldiers could see how Bani Na'im had grown. From the look of it, it had expanded gradually and slowly over several generations as pieces of the surrounding fields and terraces were taken by the young men of the founding clans to build homes for their own families. Then, the houses were built close together, hugging the hill, signifying the strength of extended familial bonds and the need for self-defense against brigands.

But as the company gazed farther out, it saw a change. A narrow belt of newer but still decades-old houses gave way suddenly to entirely new neighborhoods on the hills to the north and west. Again, there was a progression: houses that were merely more spacious versions of the ones near the mosque, followed by homes with larger yards and even small groves of fruit trees within their walls, followed finally by an outer belt containing an architectural exuberance virtually unknown in Israel—all rococo turrets, filigree, and broad, Cinderella-style staircases.

Udi told the men that the village's increasing prosperity had several causes. First, after Israel's capture of the West Bank from Jordan in the Six-Day War, the Israeli economy welcomed the manual labor that the region's residents were willing to provide. Israeli Jews abandoned unskilled and low-skilled jobs as quickly as the Palestinians could fill them, the Israelis moving into higher-paid supervisory positions. The Palestinian laborers never made anywhere near as much as Israelis. Furthermore, many of them received no social benefits or health insurance because they were employed—with the state conveniently looking the other way—on the black market, outside the purview of Israel's advanced labor and social welfare laws. Yet, despite this, they made more money than they ever had when the Turks, British, or Jordanians ruled them.

But Israel was not the only consumer of cheap Palestinian labor. The oil boom in the Persian Gulf had made that region's sparsely populated princedoms hungry for workers, so any West Bank family that could arrange it sent a son or two to work in the oil fields. These sons sent generous remittances back to their parents, enabling their brothers and sisters to attend high school and college, make good marriages, and open businesses.

But the largest, most palatial homes, Udi told the company, owed their fine stone and their stained-glass windows—not to mention the Mercedeses and Audis in their driveways—to more than the labor market. These were the homes of the mukhtars, the Israeli-appointed village chieftains who served as the military government's agents in meting out sanctions to the uncooperative and privileges to the cooperative. Needless to say, the mukhtars' position was dicey in the wave of militant anti-Israeli nationalism sweeping the territories. One of the company's jobs would be to protect Bani Na'im's mukhtars from harm.

Old men hobbled past the soldiers toward the mosque. It was still early afternoon, long before the evening prayer and the funeral. Perhaps they would pass the time reciting the Qur'an or some other holy text. Company C had again been called up to serve during Ramadan.

The soldiers were nervous because the people of Bani Na'im were angry. Just the day before, two young Palestinian men had been shot dead on this very spot. Two reservists from the unit that Company C replaced that morning had been on guard. The crowd that came to pray at the mosque had been larger and rowdier than usual; it had been the day on which Muslims commemorate Allah's gift to Muhammad of the Holy Qur'an, the Muslims' most sacred book. The young men had chanted slogans and waved Palestinian flags. Alarmed, the guards had shouted to the crowd to disperse. In response, the Palestinians had hollered their slogans all the louder and sent a barrage of stones in the direction of the reservists. The reservists were wary and weary from a troubled month in Bani Na'im, whose residents had treated them to jeers and rock showers and even Molotov cocktails. I don't know what went through the soldiers' minds at that moment. Were they afraid that, on their last day of duty, they would be killed or injured instead of heading home to their families? Were they sick and tired of the treatment they'd received from the insolent locals, who should by all rights be servile and obedient? Did they want to teach the Palestinians one final lesson? Perhaps they had not been briefed by their officers about the difference between this day and other days in Ramadan and thought that the larger-than-usual crowd had gathered expressly to lynch them. Either angry or panicked, they fired—in violation of their standing orders—live ammunition. First they fired into the air. But when the crowd did not disperse, they directed their fire at the Arabs in front of them. Some weeks later they would be tried in a military court, expelled from their unit, and given short terms in jail.

Company C thus had the luck to inherit Bani Na'im in its most resentful and explosive mood since the Intifada had begun the previous December. And it had to face down Bani Na'im with a team of reservists who were, on the one hand, scared that the Palestinians would take revenge on Company C for the sins of the previous unit and, on the other hand, scared that if they used their weapons in self-defense they'd end up in jail. Nearly all the men believed that the shootings must have been justified and that it was the standing orders, not the reservists, that were at fault.

Elnatan and Udi were responsible for seeing that the standing orders, and the specific orders relating to this sector, were obeyed. But the orders they had been given by the commander of the Hebron district left considerable leeway on the question of how to handle Bani Na'im. The Israel Defense Forces have a tradition of encouraging initiative in the field. In fact, some of the army's great legends are about commanders—one of the best-known named Ariel Sharon—who took a spirit of independence well past the boundary between initiative and insubordination. The flexibility and resourcefulness of its officers accounted in part for the IDF's high quality, but the consequences were not always positive. In the current Intifada, local initiative—like the previous day's shooting—led to death and an exacerbation of tensions. And they caused Israel considerable damage in international public opinion.

But the orders Elnatan and Udi received were vague for another reason. At this point, five months into the Intifada, the IDF was rethinking its tactics. Defense Minister Rabin and the army command had realized that the uprising could not be quelled quickly by a massive show of force. The top command now understood that the Intifada was an ongoing conflict that had to be managed. Extreme measures would simply make the young leaders of the Intifada decide they had to act even more belligerently. And it would drive the older generation, worried about money, work, and business, even farther into the arms of the younger, which was willing to sacrifice stability on the altar of revolution. So Israeli soldiers were no longer expected to terrorize the rebels into submission. On the other hand, the standing orders said that no act of rebellion, whether a Molotov cocktail or a homemade Palestinian flag flying from a telephone pole, was to go unpunished—even if the army didn't know who the perpetrators were. If an entire family, neighborhood, or village was punished for a sin committed in its midst, so the reasoning went, the silent majority that wanted to be left alone would keep agitators far from their homes.

The instructions for handling the funeral of the two men were similarly open to interpretation. On the one hand, Elnatan and Udi had been told to beware of creating yet another deadly clash. On the other hand, they were to ensure that the crowd did not get out of control.

Elnatan by nature had respect for and confidence in the chain of command. The Hebron regional commander and his staff had long experience in the area and half a year's experience handling the Intifada, and they surely knew what was best. Elnatan had no argument with the mission they'd assigned him. It wasn't clear to him, though, how he was supposed to keep order given that the rules of engagement restricted the use of live ammunition to the situations of desperate self-defense he was supposed to avoid. The meager riot control gear with which the company had been equipped would be all they could use, and it was inadequate. The Palestinians had long ago learned that they could withstand tear gas by rubbing onions on their eyes, and the rules restricted the use of rubber bullets to a limited range of distances and circumstances. How was he going to keep today's funeral from turning into another disaster?

But Udi had no doubts. He quickly persuaded Elnatan to adopt the proactive strategy he was now expounding to Company C before the mosque.

"We're going to be assholes. We're going to be mean," he declared, standing erect in front of his jeep, his hand tight on the grip of his short M-16. "The Arabs are going to know that Company C has arrived. They're going to know that if they behave themselves, we'll have a pleasant month together. But they're also going to know that if they make trouble, we're going to smash their faces in."

He glanced at Elnatan, but there was no conflict of egos here. Elnatan didn't feel his authority was being challenged because his deputy was laying out the strategy. The two men were a team.

"The soldiers who were here before us were scared. The Arabs saw they were scared and made their lives miserable. Well, now we're going to make their lives miserable," Udi continued. "By the time we light our bonfire tonight, Bani Na'im will know who Company C is."

The bonfire was the symbol of the Jewish holiday that fell that night—Lag Ba'Omer, the thirty-third day of the forty-nine-day count from the first day of Passover until the day before Shavuot. The custom of lighting a bonfire was observed by religious and nonreligious Israelis alike. The standard religious explanation for the holiday is that on this day God granted a respite to a deadly plague that had beset the students of Rabbi Akiva, the second-century sage whose teachings are central to the talmudic tradition. The plague was punishment for the students' failure to respect each other's opinions.

Scholars, secularists, and modern Zionist mythology say the day commemorates the Bar-Kokhba revolt of the second century C.E.— hence the bonfires. Bar-Kokhba was a Jewish military leader whom Rabbi Akiva and others thought was the Messiah. They supported his uprising against the foreign military oppressors of that time, the Romans. The rebellion was a failure and the rabbis, along with a good portion of the Jewish population of Palestine, were slaughtered.

Udi's specific instructions were as follows: In the time remaining before the funeral, the patrols were to disperse to their respective sectors. Only a minimum number of guards were left at the school. The rest of the men—a full complement, since the vacation rotation had not yet begun—would be out manning roadblocks and doing foot patrols.

Nothing, but nothing, was to be left without a response, Udi ordered. If a pebble landed in a patrol's vicinity, the patrol was to pursue the offending teenager, catch him, and scare the wits out of him. If a patrol discovered a makeshift Palestinian flag tied to an old shoe and flung over a telephone wire or a tree branch, they were to nab the nearest kid or young adult and force him to remove it. If they discovered PLO graffiti scrawled on a wall, they were to haul the men out of every nearby house and store and confiscate their ID cards until the men painted over the offending words. However, there was to be no shooting, not in the air and not at anyone. We can be plenty mean without shooting, Udi instructed the men.

"That's awful," I shouted to Eiger. The tailwind, hot as a blast from a blow-dryer, shot my words out to our rear. I sat in the backseat of Eiger's patrol jeep, facing aft. Eiger was in the commander's seat, and Shabbetai drove. The road was bumpy, and I could feel each smack of the hard leather seat cover on my still tender behind. We were in Bani Na'im's northern neighborhood. Eiger was showing me the way around and where the tough spots were so that I could command this patrol the next day.

Being in a jeep with Eiger was great fun. He made wisecracks that had me laughing helplessly even though I could never remember when I got back to camp, or home to Ilana, what it was that had been so hilarious. We were free of supervision from officers. We could go where we wanted and do as we wished. Eiger, like Falk and the other NCOs, assured me that there had never been a stint of duty so enjoyable. But I, of course, told myself that I should not be pleased.

"Awful," Shabbetai grunted dismissively. "Thank God we've got officers who know how to put the Arabs in their place."

"I'm not going to say that Udi didn't go overboard with some of it," Eiger said. "I don't think you need to slap people around or humiliate them. But you know what? It worked."

"What do you mean, it worked?" I protested. "The best thing we can do, for them and for us, is pick up our gear and get out of these territories. Let them do what they want here and we'll defend ourselves from behind our border. This stuff is just going to make them hate us more." The dissonance between the political views that Udi expressed and his actions in the field had me confused.

"I bet they do hate us more," Eiger said. "But the fact is that since then it's been very quiet here. Sure, we have to deal with flags and graffiti, but we've had very little violence. There's an unwritten understanding. They don't have big demonstrations, they don't let the flags get too big, they keep the loudspeaker in the mosque's minaret disconnected. Here and there some stone throwing, and that's about it. The guys who were here before us said they had it a lot worse.

"And don't think that anything goes in Udi's book. Everyone here knows what the red lines are. Almost everyone, anyway," Eiger continued. "The other day Hezki walked into a bakery, held up his gun, and asked the owner to 'donate' a bag of pita to his patrol. The guys who were with him were really upset. They reported it to Elnatan, and he canceled Hezki's weekend home."

At Eiger's direction, Shabbetai turned down a side street—it was a shortcut out of the neighborhood and onto the terraces of olive trees beyond it. Suddenly Shabbetai put the brakes on hard and the jeep screeched to a halt. I jumped out and readied my rifle.

We stood opposite a tiny neighborhood grocery, operated out of the ground floor of one of the houses. Shabbetai pointed at the concrete wall next to the store's entrance. The wall above the crates of potatoes and onions had several large black splotches on it. Two lines of Arabic had been painted over them in white. I puzzled out the letters. The first line, in large letters, said "Fatah," the name of the largest Palestinian guerrilla movement, headed by Yasir Arafat. Below it, in smaller letters, was the slogan: "With blood and fire we will redeem you, Palestine."

Shabbetai cursed under his breath, but Eiger smiled and hopped out of the commander's seat. The shopkeeper in the doorway raised his hand to greet Eiger.

"Abu-Nimr," Eiger declared, gesturing dramatically in the direction of the graffiti. "What is this?"

Abu-Nimr shuffled out to the street, turned around, and inspected the lettering. He shrugged.

"This is not making a good impression on my friend here," Eiger lamented. "He's like me. He thinks you people really want to live in peace with us. He thinks you've had a raw deal. Frankly, neither of us really cares what you paint on the wall here."

Shabbetai snorted and Abu-Nimr acknowledged Eiger's magnanimity with a nod.

"But it's against the rules and you know it," Eiger continued. "You're familiar with the procedure."

Abu-Nimr grinned and walked back to the entranceway. Pulling out a can of paint and a large brush, he proceeded to expunge the offending slogan, adding yet another black patch to the mosaic there. It was hard to tell what he felt—was he good-humored, resentful, or just anxious to get the whole thing over with? When he finished the job, we resumed our patrol.

Shabbetai's next sighting was a Palestinian flag. It was the size of a large handkerchief and had been thrown over a telephone wire with the aid of the old child-size athletic shoe to which it was tied. Two twelve-year-old boys in jeans, one with a red T-shirt and the other with a white one, tried to disappear as we arrived. But they weren't fast enough. Eiger called them over. The kids obeyed reluctantly, trembling.

"You did that," Eiger said, pointing at the flag.

"We didn't," said the one in the red T-shirt.

"You did."

"I swear we didn't."

"Don't your parents teach you how to behave? Is this how you want your village to look? With garbage on the telephone wires and paint all over the walls? I'm going to talk to the principal at your school about doing a neighborhood beautification project."

Eiger was both firm and facetious. It was his way of doing his job but also placing a distance between himself and the unpleasant work he had to do.

He shouted to me, keeping an eye on the two kids. "Watzman, go bang on that door over there." He nodded at the door of a house across the way.

Was this a point of decision? Was banging on that door an immoral act? It seemed innocuous enough. But I knew that this was part of the collective punishment policy. Could I take part in that? Or, having made the decision to report for reserve duty in Bani Na'im, and having gotten in the jeep with Eiger, was I obliged to do as I was told?

Conscientious objectors to whom I spoke made two arguments for their blanket refusal to serve in the occupied territories. First, they said, once one is serving with one's friends, an act of refusal can put them at risk. So it is more correct to refuse in advance. Second, there are seldom clearly defined transitions from moral into immoral behavior. The individual act of banging on the door, they would say, doesn't seem a turning point. But, collectively, when hundreds of Israeli soldiers are banging on hundreds of doors, it creates intolerable oppression.

Those claims are strong ones. But the first one leads inevitably to the absurdity of pacifism and the paralysis of inaction. One might receive an illegal or immoral order anywhere, not only in the territories. It could happen on Mount Hermon if you were ordered to shoot to kill a suspicious intruder without issuing the required warning first, and it could happen if you were at a training base and ordered to beat up a comrade who had not run up a mountain fast enough. By that logic, you could never be a soldier, your country could have no army, and you must abandon your family and nation to the guns of your enemies. The second argument ignores the necessary division between military and civilian life. The intolerable oppression created by hundreds of soldiers banging on hundreds of doors must be fought in the civil sphere. The individual soldier's refusal to bang on the door will not change the policy. The oppression will continue.

That didn't mean, however, that I didn't hesitate when Eiger instructed me to bang on the door. My gut told me not to do it. But my brain said that to refuse Eiger's order would be to embarrass and perhaps even endanger a close friend. Whatever arguments I might have with Eiger and Shabbetai, the middle of Bani Na'im was certainly not a place to hash them out.

So, trying to make my reluctance evident, I walked over and banged on the door. A stout middle-aged woman opened it. She glanced at the two boys with a worried expression.

"Where's your husband?" I demanded.

"He's at work," she said, but it was obvious that she was lying.

"Really, get your husband," I said.

"If you don't bring your husband to the door we're going to fucking tear your house apart until we find him," Shabbetai shouted from the driver's seat.

The woman retreated into the house and, a few seconds later, a man appeared. He was perhaps ten years older than she was and dressed in striped pajamas. He didn't look particularly well.

"*Hawiyyeh,*" I said. ID card. The word didn't come from my Arabic lessons. It was the one Arabic word that every man in Company C knew.

The man produced a worn orange plastic card holder from his shirt pocket and gave it to me.

"These your kids?" Eiger shouted at him.

"No." The man shook his head. He didn't focus on the boys.

"Go get their parents for me."

"I don't know them," the man said, his words slurred.

"Well, you aren't getting your *hawiyyeh* back until they get that flag down from the wire up there."

Without his *hawiyyeh*, the man wouldn't be able to obtain travel and work permits from the military government. He wouldn't be treated at the local clinic and he wouldn't get his pension. He'd be arrested the next time a soldier at a roadblock or on patrol discovered that he was without papers. If we kept it, we'd hand it over to military headquarters in Hebron. To get it back, he might be required to inform on his neighbors. He gazed forlornly at the boys.

"It's dangerous," the boy in the red shirt said. "We could fall down and get killed."

"He's right," I told Eiger.

"Don't worry, they know how to do it," Eiger said.

The boy in the red shirt walked slowly to the man in the doorway. The man wordlessly produced a wooden broom handle from behind the door. The kid with the white shirt gave his friend a leg up and the kid in the red shirt shimmied with great agility up the telephone pole, broomstick in hand, until he had climbed high enough to knock the flag down. Eiger took the flag and put it in the back of the jeep. The kid slid down and returned the broomstick to the man in the doorway. I returned the ID card to him and he went back to bed. The two kids continued on their way, and Eiger took me to see the lookout point on the east side of the village where the east face of Mount Hebron plunged down to the Dead Sea.

Our ideals are about the way the world ought to be, but we act in the world as it is. My ideals told me that the zero-tolerance policy pursued by Elnatan and Udi in Bani Na'im was wrong and fruitless. Harsh treatment would only drive the Palestinians farther from acceptance of Israel. The kid who'd had to shimmy up the telephone pole to take down the flag would now be more likely to grow up to be a terrorist. We'd humiliated him, so he'd hate us, and through us all Israelis and all Jews. Of course he'd want to kill us when he got old enough to do it.

The Palestinians were human beings just like we were, my ideals told me. They told me to try to imagine myself in Abu-Nimr's shoes. If I were in Abu-Nimr's shoes, I'd be grateful and happy if the foreign occupiers picked themselves up and went home. Then my countrymen and I would be free to run our own lives. In the meantime, before they picked up and went home, I'd want them to be as unobtrusive as possible. If they didn't bother me, I wouldn't bother them. That's what I would do in Abu-Nimr's shoes.

This kind of thinking didn't take me far, however. Because if I were in Abu-Nimr's shoes I wouldn't think like Haim Watzman. Abu-Nimr and Haim Watzman shared a common humanity—that could not be denied. But we had different languages, and different religions, and our peoples had different histories and cultures. Abu-Nimr had not grown up in suburban America and I had not grown up in occupied Bani Na'im. So having Haim Watzman's thoughts in Abu-Nimr's shoes wasn't a very good way of predicting what Abu-Nimr specifically and his community at large were likely to do in response to any given Israeli military policy.

I had ideals, but I also counted myself an empiricist. True, I was not a physicist like Sheib or an engineer like Elnatan and Efi or a pharmacist like Eiger. But I was a humanist of rational bent, a writer who wrote about science and scholarship. So I couldn't deny the evidence I had before my eyes. Most of it corroborated what Elnatan had told me just before I went out to command my first patrol.

"The way I see it, I'm more moral than officers who go easy," he said. "We're acting tough to keep the village quiet. If the village is quiet, there aren't going to be any clashes like the one the day before we got here. I'm tough because I'm determined that, at the end of our month here, there won't be any more dead Arabs."

During my first outings as commander of a jeep patrol, I tried to take a different approach. I deliberately ignored the graffiti and the flags, and kept as much as I reasonably could on the margins of the sectors I was sent to patrol. The third time out I had stones thrown in my direction from alleyways and rooftops. Over the vocal protest of the soldiers under my command, I disregarded those as well. The fourth time out the stones were bigger and they hit us. That I couldn't ignore. We chased our attackers but they got away.

I talked it over with Eiger, and what he said made a lot of sense. The young men of Bani Na'im were well organized. They had us under observation and were certainly capable of identifying individual soldiers and commanders. They'd seen that I was avoiding confrontations that other patrols sought out, and they interpreted it as cowardice. So they singled me out as an easy target, and that's why my patrols were getting stoned. Keep up my hands-off policy and I'd soon be the target of a Molotov cocktail, Eiger warned—and that was dangerous. Two soldiers from another unit had been horribly burned by one when their patrol was attacked a few weeks ago.

It wasn't a question, Eiger said, of the specifics of the current anti-insurgent policy. In fact, he agreed with me that going after the graffiti and the flags made us look foolish and caused unnecessary friction with the locals. What the locals were homing in on was not the fact that I was willing to let PLO graffiti go untouched. Rather, they had noticed that I was reacting differently from the other patrols. I wasn't sticking to the rules that Elnatan had laid down the first day he took over the sector. I stood out. *Mai nafka mina?* he said, using a talmudic phrase— What's the outcome? You're a target.

The change wasn't easy. It went against all my better instincts. And it didn't fit my personality. When Mizrahi talked to his three-year-old daughter on the phone, he'd warn her, "If you don't do what your mother says I'm going to give you such a slap across the face when I get home that you'll see stars for two weeks." So he was entirely convincing when he made the same threat to a Palestinian teenager. I tried that rhetoric, but I didn't have the inner conviction required to make it sound convincing. After all, I wasn't the disciplinarian in my own home—that was Ilana's job. I tried Eiger's tack, combining humor and authority, but I couldn't get the right mix. Efi turned out to be the best role model for me. He had a silent glower that made him look as if he might explode at any minute, though he almost never did. It was mitigated by a slight inclination of the right corner of the lip, conveying a sense of weary exasperation, a you-know-the-rules-so-why-don't-you-keep-them look that provided the smidgen of irony I needed. It wasn't me, but it was as close as I was going to get under the circumstances. It was very effective.

Tuesday, May 17, 1988. The Ramadan fast ended yesterday and today was 'Id al-Fitr, the break-fast feast, one of the major Muslim holidays. We in Company C did not know how the Muslims of Bani Na'im felt on this, their first 'Id al-Fitr of the Intifada. Even those of us who tried to strike up conversations with the locals in Hebrew or broken Arabic sensed that our Palestinian interlocutors were not talking straight. The conversations were little more than exchanges of pleasantries and platitudes.

But it was an asset to have a deputy company commander who was studying Arabic language and culture. At our daily briefing the previous evening, Udi had given us a rundown on the holiday and its customs. Like our own, they centered on praying and eating. The Muslims were more blessed, however, in that their prayers were much shorter.

The major difference between our holidays, Udi explained, was that the Muslim custom was to visit the local cemetery. Jewish religious law forbids entering a cemetery on a holiday, and according to Udi Muslim religious law also frowned on the practice. But folk custom was stronger than the law, and we could expect most of the village's population to head on the holiday morning from mosque to cemetery before going home for their festive meal.

We'd been on special alert since the previous evening. This morning, before dawn, the entire company was mobilized and sent into the village, leaving only a skeleton staff of guards and kitchen crew at the base. In the early hours the jeep patrols drove slowly through their sectors, looking for any signs that a major disturbance threatened. The foot patrol that had responsibility for the area of the mosque split into two teams so as to better cover its territory. The rooftop guards surveyed the village with their binoculars, and the men manning the roadblock at the entrance to the village searched every car that came down the road from Hebron.

It wasn't long before the movement commenced. As the first glow of dawn appeared over the Mountains of Moab, elderly men, mostly from the older neighborhood on the central hill, began to shuffle toward the mosque. A tape-recorded muezzin called the faithful to prayer from the top of the minaret. The old men were joined by young men with short beards and intense eyes, the catechumens of militant Islam. Soon the middle-aged, the older children, and the women were also on their way. The jeep patrols that covered the northern and western neighborhoods moved in closer, to the edge of the old neighborhood, as their sectors emptied of almost everyone except young mothers and toddlers.

We were tense. We thought of the riot of the day of the Qur'an's revelation, just before our arrival in the village. Two soldiers might have been killed instead of two Palestinians. We had our own holiday coming up this weekend, Shavuot, the day that God gave the Torah to Moses on Mount Sinai. If all went well, some of us would go home for the holiday. If there was a major riot, home leaves would certainly be canceled.

Some of the men griped that the whole village should have been put under curfew, to prevent so many Palestinians from gathering together in a small space where they'd no doubt be inflamed with tales of the perfidy of the Jews.

But Elnatan and Udi gave unambiguous orders. Anything amounting to a direct attack on us, with stones or Molotov cocktails, was to be met firmly with tear-gas canisters and rubber bullets, all in line with the standing orders. But in the absence of a physical provocation, we were to leave the worshippers alone.

The prayers began. Elnatan called all the jeeps in toward the mosque, to be prepared for any disturbance when the crowd emerged. Three jeeps—his and Udi's and Eiger's—stood by the mosque, ready for action. I was number three in Eiger's team, on the backseat. My rear end was getting sore again and I'd hoped to get my own jeep and thus get to sit in the commander's seat, which had springs. But there weren't enough jeeps for every NCO, and this at least gave me a chance to be with Eiger.

Falk's jeep, with Shabbetai as driver and Achlama as number three, was farther down the road leading to the western neighborhood. Efi's jeep waited on the road to the south, the one that led to the cemetery and thence to our camp.

Eiger stood on tiptoe to take a look through one of the mosque's windows. He reported that men were jumping, leaping in the air as the prayer leader recited his verses. Udi said it was a local custom.

The prayers lasted only about twenty minutes. Then the worshippers emerged.

It was immediately clear that they were challenging the tacit agreement under which we'd been operating all month. Young men unfurled huge flags inscribed "Fatah" and "Hamas," and began to chant political slogans through megaphones, with the crowd responding. The throng, perhaps three thousand people, marched in the direction of the cemetery. If this were merely a religious procession it would be within bounds, but the young agitators wanted it to be a political demonstration as well, and we did not tolerate mass political demonstrations.

It was a point of decision. Would Elnatan and Udi order us to disperse the crowd, confiscate the flags, and disconnect the mosque's loudspeaker, to prove that we would not tolerate this challenge to our authority? If we did so, interrupting what was nevertheless the observance of a religious custom, would we rouse passions better left dormant?

Elnatan ordered us to pull our jeeps back to the edge of the square. The crowd flowed onto the southern road, in the direction of the cemetery. As the square emptied, we followed, close enough to watch, far enough to remain detached.

The crowd reached Efi's jeep. Efi stood his ground and the crowd streamed around him as if he and his two men were not there. The two sides watched each other but did not interact. The chants continued, but the Arabs threw no rocks. Efi relaxed. When the crowd passed by we joined him, and the four jeeps proceeded to the road leading to our camp, which stood above and to the west of the cemetery. The villagers practically filled the small field, each paying respects to the departed in its family plot. Gradually, they began to leave the graveyard, family by family, heading home for their holiday feast.

The khamsin came with a vengeance, at the worst possible moment. It began at about 3 p.m. on Friday as a hot southern breeze that broke through the still, sandy air. It was the eve of our last weekend in Bani Na'im. In the usual Friday routine, Shimon the cook was in the kitchen tent preparing the Sabbath meals with the help of Micha, Jacques, the soldier assigned KP for the day, and a couple others who were off duty and offering their help. The kitchen crew blessed the breeze, since the temperature close to the large steel-frame stove and the generator-powered oven was well over 100 degrees Fahrenheit.

Jewish law forbids cooking on the Sabbath and the lighting of fires, even if a nonreligious Jew performs these activities. So the cooking for the Sabbath had to be completed before sundown on Friday, and the food was kept warm on steel plates placed over the stove's gas fire, which was kept burning through the entire night and day. A huge pot of water would also be kept on the fire, just below a simmer, for coffee and tea (preparing these hot drinks with already heated water was not considered cooking). While most of the men in the kitchen tent were not religious, army rules stipulated that when it came to cooking, both the Orthodox dietary restrictions and the laws of the Sabbath must be observed. This enabled an entire unit to eat together, with only some minor inconvenience to the nonreligious.

This Friday was even more frantic than usual because, the way the calendar had worked out, Sabbath would meld on Saturday night into the holiday of Shavuot, feast of the first fruits and of the revelation of the Torah at Mount Sinai. Most of the restrictions that applied on the Sabbath would obtain on Shavuot, but cooking would be allowed, so the Shavuot noon meal, on Sunday, could be cooked on the stove. The condition was that the fire had to be lit on Friday and kept burning continuously. But the Saturday night meal, meant to be a festive one welcoming the holiday, could not be prepared on the Sabbath, so it, too, had to be prepared in advance, on Friday. So there were three meals rather than the usual two to be cooked. Every pot and pan in the kitchen tent was called into service.

The breeze gained force gradually. By 3:30, it was snapping the tent flaps. Not long after, a particularly strong gust managed to blow out one of the stove's four burners, which Jacques quickly lit again under a pot full of beans. Soon the wind was picking up sand and gravel and flinging it into the tents. Shimon covered the pots to keep the food inside them clean.

At about 3:45 the wind began working on the tents themselves. The southernmost tent's ropes strained and began pulling the pins out of the ground. Soon the entire south side was flapping free, allowing the wind to fill it like a balloon. The soldiers who were asleep there woke up in panic, bounded out of bed, and tried to stabilize the tent. But within minutes the wind cast it up in the air and against the next tent in line, whose poles groaned and then collapsed. The pins in the kitchen tent, and in the tent where the ammunition was stored, also began coming out of the ground.

Just after four, Yermi returned in the company truck with additional supplies from battalion headquarters in Hebron to find the camp half destroyed. He immediately radioed Elnatan, who was out on patrol, and began helping the kitchen crew save the food. The fires were all out and, fearing an explosion, Yermi disconnected the gas balloon. The Sabbath would begin at 7:20 p.m.

When Elnatan arrived a few minutes later, he told Yermi and the men in the camp to try to re-erect the tents, but Yermi said it was hopeless; the wind continued to wax and was now blowing at gale force. The camp would have to be moved, and quickly, Yermi insisted.

Elnatan radioed battalion headquarters. He demanded to speak directly to Akiva, to whom he reported that his camp was being blown away. Akiva laughed in disbelief. Elnatan requested permission to move the company back into the elementary school it had evacuated a week and a half before. But Akiva said that shutting down the school would send the wrong kind of message and would most likely provoke severe protests from the villagers.

At that moment a pickup truck drove into what remained of the camp. Yehuda, a gruff building contractor with a bushy mustache who occasionally stopped by to bring us gifts of cake and soft drinks from Pnai Hever, jumped out. He asked no questions, just walked straight over to Elnatan and said that there was an empty warehouse in the settlement we could use.

Elnatan hesitated. Moving into the warehouse would make him beholden to the settlers, and Elnatan, despite his sympathies, did not want to owe them anything. He radioed Akiva, who didn't like the idea either. But with the two-day weekend coming on fast, any further delay would mean we'd have to celebrate the holiday with canned rations. The battalion commander asked and received permission from the Hebron regiment. We began the job of packing up, the kitchen first.

The warehouse was clean, cool, and expansive. By the time we were setting up our cots, the food was back on the fire, with every free hand helping out. Amazingly, Shimon and his crew managed to get the cooking done and even some extras, like fried eggplant salad and stuffed peppers, and we—religious and nonreligious men together—brought in the Sabbath with a feast.

The problem came on Saturday night. We observant guys were desperate for a decent cup of coffee. The nonobservant had, of course, made their own Turkish coffee on their camp stoves throughout the Sabbath, but we'd been able to drink only the water that had been kept warm from Friday. It wasn't hot enough, and the coffee made from it was barely drinkable. In any case, it had run out early Saturday morning. We set our sights on Saturday night, when new water could be boiled on the flame kept burning since before the Sabbath.

But just as we were assembling for the Shavuot night prayers, prior to the holiday meal, Fisch reported that a gust of wind had come through the warehouse door and put out the flames on the stove. Jacques had taken a box of matches and relit the flames. When Fisch protested, Jacques apologized but said that the whole company shouldn't have to eat cold food just because of the religious strictures of some of us. And he'd prepared an excellent meal, he said. It would be worth it for us to bend our rules just a little bit to enjoy it. If Fisch hadn't come by at just the wrong moment, he noted, we'd be none the wiser.

Faces fell. The caffeine headaches had been repressed for hours by acts of will, but now the will was broken and our foreheads throbbed. There seemed no way out. Not only would we not have coffee, but we wouldn't be able to eat any of the food cooked with this forbidden fire.

Hezki was furious at Fisch for telling us. He should have kept this dangerous knowledge to himself, so that the rest of us could eat and drink without culpability.

A legal discussion ensued. Was there room here for a lenient interpretation of the facts that would allow us to have our coffee? We turned the matter over and over and could not find a loophole.

As we were debating the point, something scuttled across the warehouse floor in front of us. The whole group of us stepped back because at first glance it looked like a scorpion. My memory seems to have made too much of the creature—I recall it being very large, the size of my hand, with long, spindly, spidery legs. I also remember a snakelike tail that stuck straight back, not curved up and over like a scorpion's. But a local expert tells me that what I'm describing is a whip scorpion, and one larger than any in nature. There are no whip scorpions in Israel. Apparently it was a camel spider, a large arachnid, but still only three inches or so in length. Whatever it was, it was a species unknown to us.

"What the hell is it?" Fisch muttered.

Hezki stepped forward nonchalantly and identified the monster, using a Hebrew word that translates as "scorpion spider." There is indeed a creature by that name, but my expert tells me that it doesn't match my description at all.

"I've never seen anything like that," I said.

"They're very rare," Hezki explained, stepping on it.

Fisch noticed that Sheib wasn't among us. We hadn't been able to wake him up, but Fisch made another try, and the prospect of discussing an intriguing case of Jewish law was enough to get him out of bed. Sheib wandered over, in shorts and the same sweat-stained, dusty undershirt he'd been wearing for several days now, and listened to Fisch's exposition of the problem. He put one arm into a shirt sleeve and considered.

Finally he said, "It's okay."

"What do you mean, okay?" Hezki shot back angrily.

"The actual cooking will be done on the holiday, when it's permitted, as soon as the stars come out. It's the cooking, the boiling of the water, that's at issue here, and that is clearly permitted. The fact that the fire was lit in violation of the Sabbath makes no difference once the Sabbath is over," he explained. And then he provided references, including quotations recited by heart, to the several rabbinical opinions on which he was basing his ruling.

Smiles returned to our faces. Sheib, not the kind of guy who usually got his back slapped, got enough slaps now to last him several years. When we looked at the problem his way, the solution was obvious. Had we not asked a person of authority, we would have gone a day without coffee for no real reason at all.

"Some people think that you shouldn't ask too many questions, because the more you ask, the more things you'll be told you're not allowed to do," Fisch observed. "But the opposite is true. The more you know, the more freedom you have."

I nodded and shifted uncomfortably on my sore rear end. I knew a whole lot more about the Intifada and the army now than I had just two weeks ago. I no longer believed that being nice to the Palestinians was in their interest or ours. The Palestinians were a determined enemy, and they wouldn't sit by quietly and leave us in peace. The young, intense Islamic radicals of Bani Na'im wouldn't be content for us to redeploy on the Green Line, either. They'd pursue us even afterward. We'd have to negotiate an agreement with the Palestinians before we could get out. And until then we'd have to defend ourselves here in Bani Na'im and throughout the territories.

Chapter Five

· WIMPS ·

I SLEPT LITTLE THAT SUMMER. BUT, FRANKLY, IT WASN'T THE MORAL dilemma of my involvement in repressing the Intifada that was keeping me awake. It was Asor, now a year old and teething. With reckless disregard for my heavy workload and for the financial damage that sleep deprivation brings on the self-employed, he'd wake me up two or three times a night, hysterical with gum pain. And the punishment went beyond those fitful hours spent trying to concentrate on the novel I was translating. I could no longer take time out of what little sleep I got to get up for my early-morning run.

In the rare moments when children and work were not imposing on my schedule, I was angry at myself for being so politically inert. I had done my military duty in Bani Na'im on the principle that I had an obligation to help and defend my comrades. Wasn't now the time to do my duty as a civilian?

How could I justify my next stint in the West Bank if in the interval I did not take action to oppose Prime Minister Shamir? He intended to hold on to the West Bank and Gaza Strip forever and to fill them with

Jewish settlements. Elections were coming up in November. I plunged briefly into the Labor party's local branch. But I quit after a few weeks, disgusted by the hacks and hangers-on I found there. I had no time for intraparty intrigue. Disillusioned with the big party, I organized an evening at our home with a representative of a small liberal party that I liked. I invited everyone I knew, but no one came. Eiger had become enthusiastic about a new religious party, Meimad, that opposed both the occupation and the legislative religious coercion that the established religious parties had pursued since Israel's founding. But I didn't like the idea of a party confined to the religious community. Anyway, I was exhausted. The previous fall I'd accepted the post of president of Kehilat Yedidya. This in and of itself was more public activity than I could handle.

Friends from the synagogue and from the religious peace movement were organizing demonstrations and sponsoring letter-writing campaigns. Some had initiated dialogue groups in which Jews and West Bank Palestinians exchanged perspectives about the conflict. This in particular appealed to me, because it seemed to me that participating in ongoing conversations with people on the other side was a way of preparing the ground for a future peace, even if at present there was no agreement as to how the peace would look. But the meetings were generally in the afternoon, when I had to pick up the kids from day care. Also, they usually took place in the West Bank, since army roadblocks often prevented the Palestinians from reaching Jerusalem. Ilana insisted that it was too risky for me to travel into the territories. She didn't even want me going to the West Bank universities anymore. I was, she pointed out, a father of small children, and any harm I incurred would harm them as well. In any case, she did not consider the promotion of dialogue with Palestinians an adequate reason for leaving her alone with two toddlers. Certainly not after she'd just put up with that for two weeks at the army's behest. So I did little more than attend an occasional peace demonstration with kids in tow.

Even if I had had the time to get more involved, my experience in Bani Na'im had set me apart from many of my left-wing friends. Most of them were, like me, immigrants from the United States or other Western countries. But the men had generally been older when they moved to Israel, or were already married by the time they were drafted. Thus, they'd served a much briefer time in the regular army and in less intense activity. Some of them served in combat reserve units, but ones made up of older, less well-trained men. They didn't draw assignments of the same order that Company C did. I had seen the Intifada from the army's side in a way that few of my friends had, and I was much more aware than they of the dilemmas that individual soldiers and officers faced. If, before my time in Bani Na'im, I'd had some sympathy for dovish reservists who refused to serve in the occupied territories on principle, I now was certain that I opposed this form of conscientious objection. I even drafted an essay arguing that while a soldier could and should refuse to obey an immoral order, he could not rightly refuse to serve in a particular location.

I wrote: "An army charged with defending its country may often find itself on some other country's territory . . . Clearly, specific actions carried out on that territory may be judged moral or immoral, but it would be difficult to say that a soldier's simple presence there was illegal unless it was manifestly clear that the army was there for no other reason than to conquer and oppress the local population. The West Bank and Gaza were occupied during a legitimate war of national defense and there is a legitimate debate as to whether these territories are crucial to Israel's military security. The Israeli soldier should, therefore, be constantly examining whether what he is doing, rather than where he is, is moral . . . The petty humiliations and collective punishments I was ordered to inflict on the Palestinians in whose village I served not long ago were unpleasant and difficult to carry out . . . But preserving order in the territories is, like it or not, necessary for Israel's security so long as it occupies them.

"I have the luck to serve with men who, despite their widely differing political opinions, are disciplined enough to carry out their tasks without overstepping the orders they receive, and wise enough to understand that it is the orders that prevent us from disintegrating into a bickering and powerless rabble. The standing orders on how to handle the Intifada are not harsh enough in the opinion of some of them, not lenient enough in the opinions of others. These opinions were set aside when orders were given."

I had planned to send the piece to a newspaper or magazine, but I filed it away instead. I no longer remember precisely why, but I probably thought that no one in the United States would be particularly interested in the opinions of a sergeant. Also, mailing it out to editors would require time that came at the expense of my moneymaking writing and translation work—and even when I worked every available minute, I wasn't making enough money to support our modest standard of living.

I was indeed convinced that the vast majority of the men in Company C had acted honorably and admirably during our month in the Palestinian village, even if they were enforcing a policy that I disliked. Since then, I'd become less quick to accept at face value media reports of cruelties and crimes committed by Israeli forces. I had no illusions—I knew that some units and individuals acted reprehensibly, whether out of thoughtlessness or malice. But I also knew that the media seldom told the story from the soldier's perspective. Now, when I heard such reports, I asked myself how the situation had looked to the soldier. What danger did he think he was in? What had his adversaries done to provoke him?

There was no consolation in the peace demonstrations, which were having little effect. While the Labor side of the national unity government had tried to open channels to the local Palestinian leadership in the West Bank, Prime Minister Yitzhak Shamir and his Likud party were adamantly opposed to any negotiations so long as the rebellion continued. They were in any case opposed to territorial compromise under all circumstances. As far as I could tell from talking to my Company C friends—the best cross section of Israeli society that I had available to me—the Intifada had not produced any major change in Israeli public opinion. The public remained more or less evenly divided between those who wanted to keep the territories and those who were willing to give up some or all of them in exchange for peace. It seemed unlikely that a government committed to negotiations and withdrawal, and politically strong enough to execute such a policy, would be elected in November.

On the Palestinian side, the uprising had passed, after its spontaneous initial stage, into the control of a network of underground activist cells. These consisted of operatives belonging to the Palestinian resistance organizations, including Yasir Arafat's own Fatah, the Marxist factions, and the Islamic movements. Local control was the strongest, but there was also a central leadership, which had varying amounts of success in coordinating activities throughout the territories. The cells used clandestinely printed leaflets to rally the public and to inform it when to strike and to demonstrate. To counter this coordinated resistance, the army began to police the territories much more heavily than it ever had before. This burden fell primarily on reserve units like mine.

As the Palestinians became more professional about running their uprising, so did the army become more professional about quelling it. It purchased new riot-control equipment—both the mundane, such as police helmets with Plexiglas visors, and the sophisticated, such as a vehicle that sprayed gravel at demonstrators. And there was more innovative ammunition—it seemed a new kind was added to our gear each time we reported for duty. Of course, these came in addition to the conventional rounds and tracer rounds we carried in our efods. Though we were acting primarily as policemen, the army command wanted us fitted out for war as well.

In Bani Na'im, we'd been introduced to rubber bullets. These were cylindrical lumps of hard rubber (not the rubber-coated metal rounds that came into use in later years) that looked like thick, short cigarette filters. A cellophane-wrapped roll of three was fired—in the packaging—from a special attachment at the end of our rifle barrels that made our M-16s look like Elizabethan blunderbusses. The roll would rocket several dozen meters before the wrapper disintegrated. The three rubber bullets would then scatter indiscriminately, inflicting painful but superficial wounds on rioters. The army's General Staff issued strict rules about the use of this ammunition. We could fire it only if the demonstrators were beyond a minimum distance. If fired at closer range, the projectiles would pack enough power to cause serious injury or even death.

Similarly, the rules explicitly forbade us, under any circumstances, to dismantle the package of three and shoot individual rubber bullets. We'd all heard friends and acquaintances in other units brag about doing just this. A single rubber bullet, launched with the force meant for a package of three, would have triple the momentum and thus triple the impact—with potentially fatal results. The press, both Israeli and foreign, published exposés about this practice, and human rights groups protested it. Yet my soldier's perspective cast it in a different light. While Hollywood movies give the impression that soldiers most often set their rifles on automatic and spray bullets in the direction of their enemy, real combat soldiers are in fact taught to shoot one bullet at a time, with an emphasis on accuracy. The infantrymen with whom I served found this new ammunition unsettling. Shooting bullets designed to scatter randomly in a crowd, rather than carefully aiming through rifle sights at a specific enemy, clashed with every instinct that our training had instilled in us. While there were no doubt soldiers who fired single rubber bullets because they wanted to kill Palestinians, I knew from talking to my comrades and to guys I knew in similar outfits that a lot of the men who engaged in this forbidden practice were simply trying to aim accurately, which is what they thought a soldier ought to do.

Company C's regiment was under the purview of the IDF's Central Command, which was responsible for the West Bank. Apparently the command had high regard for us, because in August, less than three months after we left Bani Na'im, we received call-up orders for October.

When October came, I packed my chimidan and found myself sitting with the Company C staff at a training base's firing range. There, the training officers assigned to prepare us for the West Bank introduced this season's new flavor of ammunition—the plastic bullet.

"A plastic bullet?" Keisar asked under his breath, meaning that everyone in a fifty-meter radius could hear him.

"My uncle told me to go into plastics," I said, making an American joke that no one around me got.

"Why not? Half your M-16 is made out of plastic," said Achlama.

"I'm just waiting for them to give us a plastic hand grenade," said Eiger.

"Can I have some quiet over there?" Elnatan barked.

"Your commander is speaking," Jacques reprimanded us.

It turned out that the bullets weren't really plastic. They were metal bullets with a plastic tip. If used properly they would, the training officers assured us, disable but not kill. As with rubber bullets, there was a specific permitted range. Unlike rubber bullets, they could be aimed accurately, and they were to be aimed only below the waist. The bullets were designed for the ringleaders of a riot. The theory was that if the ringleaders were disabled, the rioters would quickly disperse. Because of the severe restrictions on their use, the bullets would be issued only to NCOs and officers, three apiece. They were to be loaded into a separate magazine that contained no regular ammunition, and they could be fired only on the order of the commanding officer on the scene.

Thus equipped, we headed to Jenin, the northernmost Palestinian city in the West Bank, a dozen miles due south of the Israeli city of Afula. Only the ridge of Mount Gilboa to the east kept me from having a view of Tirat Zvi, the kibbutz in the Jordan River Valley where I'd lived during my regular army service.

One of the brigade's four companies was stationed in Jenin itself. Two others were in large villages to the city's south, manning road-blocks and doing patrols much as we had in Bani Na'im. Company C, however, was to be the brigade's special task force. We were virtually free of routine activity, but we were on constant alert. At a few moments' notice we might be sent in jeeps and trucks to set up a roadblock or to squelch a major demonstration in a village. At night we went on silent sorties to round up the uprising's commanders.

Our base, which we shared with the battalion command and service units, was an outpost off the main road, on a low hill just east of Jenin. At the top, where our tents stood, was a parking lot, a number of small prefab buildings, a basketball court, and a small grove of trees. At the north end was a group of cages and pens ranged around a graveled walkway—this had been the petting zoo of the original inhabitants, a coed contingent of Nachal soldiers who were preparing the site to be a new settlement. There was a fine view of the Jenin Valley to our north and of the foothills leading eastward to Mount Gilboa, already green from the fall's first rains. It was the time of the olive harvest, and we could see entire families out banging trees and branches with long sticks, catching the falling fruit in blankets spread on the ground. The village olive presses were operating around the clock.

Once we settled in and got through our ritual bitching, the guys were largely happy in Jenin. At first I had trouble understanding why. There seemed to be a lot of reasons to feel out of sorts. This was our second round of duty in a single calendar year, and to make it worse, the army had lengthened the standard stint from three and a half to four and a half weeks. We'd be in for a full month, until after the November elections.

Of course, it helped that the entire company was stationed together, the first time we had served as a single, integral unit since I'd become a member. The previous spring, while we'd been in Bani Na'im, Platoon Two had been stationed in a different village. In Hebron the year before, we had been reinforced with a large number of adjuncts seconded to us from the battalion staff, so we weren't on our own. And our command team was now stable and strong. Our officers and support staff worked unusually well together, Elnatan's cool head complemented by Udi's exuberance and genius for logistics, Yermi's reserve a foil for Jacques's ebullience. After a period of frequent turnover, we now had a solid team of platoon lieutenants as well—understated, capable Efi in Platoon One; sharp, unpretentious Ben-Ami in Platoon Two; and Shammai of Platoon Three, an earnest med student who was, by odd coincidence, married to Efi's wife's closest childhood friend. The three sergeants, Eiger, Alon, and Mizrahi, were both dedicated and laid-back. We NCOs felt we could handle any challenge the army or the Palestinians flung at us. Some other key members of the company, such as Keisar and Achlama, contributed to an easygoing competence that made service together both pleasant and satisfying. There was a sense of cohesion, mutual respect, and common purpose that broke down the usual dividing lines of religion, politics, and ethnicity, not to mention our widely varying civilian lives.

However, another factor contributed to the general good mood, one that I only gradually comprehended. In Jenin, the guys felt more like soldiers than they had in our last two rounds of duty. Acting as guard dogs in Hebron and petty disciplinarians in Bani Na'im had been the antithesis of my comrades' idea of manhood as instilled in them in school, youth groups, and yeshiva, and during their regular army service. In Hebron and Bani Na'im we had been on the defensive; here in Jenin we were taking the initiative.

True, we were not storming Jordanian outposts or Syrian armored positions. That kind of military action had been drilled into us in basic and advanced training and, as we saw it, was our real work as soldiers. It was also the stuff of army legend, the stories of heroism that the Israeli-born guys had grown up on. But we were acting out another part of the same legend. In Jenin we were the foot soldiers for the Shin Bet, the secret security service whose exploits were, despite all the mystery surrounding them, part of the Israeli military mythos. The Shin Bet's role in the Intifada was tracking, infiltrating, and breaking the Intifada's command structure, and we were helping them do it.

Personally, my spirits were high because I was able to run nearly every day. Of all the changes that fatherhood had brought into my life, not being able to run each morning was the one I'd had the most trouble accepting with equanimity. On days when I didn't run I felt flaccid and slothful. I was not a particularly graceful or fast runner, but I was consistent, and the habit had become an inseparable part of the way I felt.

In basic training and my NCO course, I'd been forced to run more frequently for longer distances and with heavier loads than I could possibly enjoy. But this rigorous training somehow got running into my blood. I even ran outside the cramped regimental outpost on the leeward slope of the Lebanon mountain range where I'd been sent after completing the NCO course. Running laps inside the outpost's fence didn't give me the high I was after, so I found a route through the adjacent village, down the mountainside, and along the main road, which I ran with rifle in hand. In retrospect, this was a habit so dangerous and foolish that I don't understand why my superiors didn't stop me. But after braving Lebanon, where Israeli soldiers had frequently been attacked by Lebanese irregulars, the possibility of an Intifada terrorist in Jenin taking a potshot at me seemed hardly worth considering. Still, Elnatan insisted I run with my rifle over my shoulder—there had been a few incidents of Palestinian snipers firing on the base from passing cars. Eiger would often join me on my route down to the main road and back. We seldom had other takers.

It was after an afternoon run that Jacques found me lying on my back in gym shorts, drying off from a shower.

Alon was dozing. Falk was playing backgammon with Barak, a friend of his from his regular army days who'd just joined Company C. Barak wasn't an NCO, but his status as Falk's alter ego got him a place in our tent. The two of them were lying on their sides on the quilts they'd brought from home, elbows on their neatly cased pillows, with the game set up on an ammunition crate between their cots. Jacques had come to give me a new assignment, and I'd refused.

"I thought you'd thank me," he pouted, sitting on my bed.

"I'd jump at the chance," observed Barak. Trim and crew-cut, he still looked like a soldier in regular service. But he claimed that the hair-style wasn't motivated by a desire to look young. His hair had begun to fall out and he figured that the less it weighed the longer it would stay in place.

"Look at the advantages." Falk ticked them off on his fingers. "Regular hours, no nights. You've got two privates under you who do the dirty work."

Jacques had assigned me to command of the lockup at military government headquarters in Jenin. This was where we and other units dumped Palestinians we'd rounded up. The prisoners were mostly young men caught throwing stones, but some were Fatah or Hamas agents we'd flushed out during our nighttime raids. The pen's guards were military government staff soldiers, but the NCO who commanded them had to be a responsible man with combat credentials. The post had been filled by one of the hesder guys, but now he was being discharged for some personal reason and Jacques needed a replacement.

I'd seen the lockup; it was an open-air cage about the size of the tent we were sitting in, generally occupied by ten or twelve blindfolded prisoners. Each one spent several days there until he was brought before a military judge and sent to the regional military prison just to the north, on the Green Line that marked the border between the West Bank and Israel. There was little shade, no furniture, and no toilet—the guards made prisoners wait until they were bursting, then escorted them to latrines that had been dug nearby. The prisoners were not allowed to speak to each other or to anyone else. It was a nauseating sight.

I wanted no part of it, nor did I want to be separated from the rest of the company. I had friends here and some standing; people knew me and accepted me as I was. At the pen I would have to earn the respect of those serving under me and the confidence of the military government's staff officers.

So I made Jacques an offer he had to refuse.

"Okay," I said with a show of resignation. "Tell Elnatan I'll do it. But tell him that I'll do it my own way. I'll put a tarp over the cage so they'll have some shade, I'll take off the blindfolds, and I'll give them a radio. And I'll tell the military prosecutor that I'll release any prisoner who isn't brought before a judge within forty-eight hours."

"You know I respect your sentiments, but you can't do that," Jacques protested. "They'll tell us to take you back."

"Two points for Watzman," Barak laughed.

"Oh, all right, I'll think of someone else," Jacques said, walking back to the officers' tent. "But this means you'll be going out on the raid tonight. Make sure your gear is ready. Orders are being given at the military government building at five p.m."

There was an exchange of smirks after he left.

"He likes you a little *too* much," Barak needled me. "Good thing you were lying on your back."

That Jacques was gay was common knowledge in Company C. New members hardly needed to be told—Jacques fit nearly every stereotype in the book. He minced, his voice lilted, he fussed over table settings. He smiled even when angry and made no attempt to assume the stony look that is the natural resting state of the Israeli male face.

Yet in my six years of service with him, I never heard Jacques make any reference to his sexuality, even an oblique one. Indeed, when I raised the subject with him explicitly for the first time many years later, he raised his eyebrows.

"Did people really know I was homosexual?" he asked. By his account, the subject had come up, whether out of rancor or curiosity, less than a handful of times during all his years in Company C.

I had come to see him at his top-floor walkup in a fashionable neighborhood. It was located near the small Tel Aviv port, where the buildings look seedy on the outside but are well tended and luxurious on the inside. Jacques's was a long, narrow two-story affair, dense with objets d'art and coffee-table books picked up on his travels.

He'd recently taken early retirement from El Al, where he'd trained a generation of flight attendants and served the rich and famous in first and business class. He was planning, he told me, to buy a small place in Paris and spend much of his time there.

As we sat sipping lemonade at the kitchen table on the enclosed balcony that constituted the apartment's upper level, he told again the stories I'd heard him tell many times in the army—stories I'd never known whether to believe or not.

He grew up in Tunis, one of the few places in the Arab world in which a significant Jewish community remained after the mass emigration that followed Israel's founding. As a teenager he joined the Communist party's youth movement, where he so excelled that he won a prize: a free trip to visit comrades in either of two socialist paradises, Czechoslovakia or Israel. A sister of his already lived in Tel Aviv, so he had no hesitation about which country to choose.

In Tunis, his primary language and cultural affiliation had been French, and so it remained when he decided to stay in Israel. He was drafted into the paratroopers, an elite combat force, where he first served in the ranks. But his commanders soon decided that his skills could best be put to use by making him a liaison with the French paratroopers who then, in an age when relations between the two countries were close, came to Israel for joint maneuvers.

Jacques disliked the army, and by the time he completed his service he disliked Israel as well. As far as he was concerned, its people were uncouth, uncultured, and uneducated. His language skills, not to mention his flair for organization and style, qualified him to be an airline steward, and he spent most of the next few years traveling, stopping in Israel only for brief family visits. He was on such a visit on October 18, 1973, when the Yom Kippur War broke out.

He hadn't served in the reserves until then, but in the general call-up he was assigned to the Jerusalem Brigade, then the name of the regiment of which Company C was a part. During the War of Independence in 1948, Arab forces had laid siege to Jerusalem, and after the war the capital lay at the tip of a narrow corridor of Israeli territory that projected into the Jordanian-controlled West Bank. The army decided that the city needed its own resident infantry brigade. Most of the soldiers came from the city's underclass. While many of them were, like Jacques, natives of North Africa, that hardly gave them a common outlook on life.

"I took a look at the guys and, well, I'm from a different background. I don't belong with them in any way. And then I said to myself, you will now lock Jacques up in a safe. Otherwise, Jacques will die. And that helped me become one of the guys," he recalled. His self-discipline and dedication—"I never missed a day of reserve duty"—made him popular with his officers, and with the men, too.

At war's end, Company C was not discharged. During the tense watch that followed, it spent six months in rudimentary outposts along the Suez Canal. There was little to do, so Jacques took it upon himself to teach the brigade's men etiquette. He'd hitch a ride to a lonely outpost, balance a door on a pair of barrels, and seat the soldiers around the impromptu table. He taught them "please pass the salt" and "I'm much obliged," how to refuse a second helping politely, and which topics were appropriate for conversation at a formal dinner. He explained to them how to excuse themselves from the table and how to order wine in a fine restaurant. A few years later the company commander appointed him to the post of company clerk.

When I first met Jacques in the summer of 1984, he was already a

Company C institution. His homosexuality was an occasional subject of conversation when he was not around, and there were men, like Shabbetai, who wouldn't go to the shower if he was there. But most of us, the religious men included, accepted Jacques matter-of-factly. No one doubted that he was an asset to the unit. Elnatan often praised him for being available on short notice. He'd cancel flights and vacation plans to join the company wherever we served.

Newcomers to Company C were surprised, however, when they learned that Yermi, too, was gay. He was the antithesis of Jacques— blond, muscular, handsome in a rugged way, soft-spoken but firm. The Yom Kippur War had erupted toward the end of his regular service, which he'd performed in the Golani Brigade, the tough infantry unit that was assigned to retake Mount Hermon from the Syrians. During our patrols on the mountain during stints of reserve duty there, we'd frequently ride past sections of the Golani ascent, the route taken by Yermi's unit on its way to combat with the Syrians. The steep, rocky path was a tough climb for a hiker, and it was hard to imagine how soldiers in full battle gear had made it up and still had strength to beat back the enemy.

Meticulous and professional, Yermi had proved himself to Elnatan by functioning for two years as Platoon Three's commanding officer after Amichai was arrested and permanently discharged. But Yermi seemed to take no joy in his stamina and agility. His motivation came out of a simple, quiet determination to do everything well. He never spoke of his private life, though he certainly knew that we all knew he was gay. He lacked the extroverted self-confidence that enabled Jacques to be insouciant about what he was. Did the men with whom he served in Golani suspect him, and did they taunt or ostracize him? Or was it a secret that kept him from ever being open and comfortable with his comrades? Either way, his regular army service could not have been an easy experience, making his devotion to his reserve unit all the more remarkable.

Like Jacques, Yermi worked for an airline, but in an administrative position. As a result, he and Jacques both flew for free, and at times they'd tell us of trips they'd taken to Brazil and Mexico and Spain. They showed up for reserve duty together, usually in Yermi's Audi, and generally took coordinated time off as well—Jacques would say there was a party being thrown by a top fashion model that they just couldn't miss, or a gallery opening that everyone who was anyone had to attend. We all assumed that they were a couple. Not that anyone ever saw them hold hands or exchange a loving glance. Of course they slept in separate cots, in the staff room or tent along with Elnatan and Udi and Micha. But they seemed very much a domestic pair.

At the end of December 1990, as the world waited for war against Saddam Hussein, Company C reported for a month of duty on Mount Hermon. Yermi didn't show up, but no one knew why.

It was only a year later, when we reported for another round of Intifada duty, that we had word. Achlama reported that he'd run into the two of them on the Tel Aviv beach promenade. Shaking his head sadly, he related that Yermi had been leaning on Jacques, emaciated and so weak he could barely walk. At the maneuvers that followed a few months later, Benin, the Company C old-timer who was now on the quartermaster staff, told us that he'd attended Yermi's funeral.

Jacques had been a presence in the company, but none of us had developed a close friendship with him, so we had no contact with him in civilian life. I imagined him lonely and widowed, and felt a little guilty for not seeking him out to offer my condolences. On the other hand, I couldn't imagine what I'd say to comfort him. For a while someone or other would report having flown with Jacques on an El Al flight, but then those stories ceased. We assumed that the disease that had defeated Yermi had attacked Jacques as well. By the time I began putting together this account, I presumed that Jacques was dead.

It was Falk who called that assumption into doubt. He was the most astute observer of men in Company C. I met with him, Barak, and

Achlama, who by then were close to finishing several years as the company's three first sergeants, at a mall outside Jerusalem. When the subject of Jacques and Yermi came up, we listened to each other's accounts and agreed that the company's respect for these two men was a mark of how close-knit Company C had been and how accepting of the often radical differences in the lives and histories of its individual soldiers.

"But I don't think they were a couple," Falk commented.

Having long ago learned to credit Falk's impressions, I decided to see if I could find Jacques.

At his apartment, Jacques confirmed Falk's hunch. He and Yermi had never been romantically attached, had never even had a fling. But, Jacques related, Yermi had indeed spent much time here. After discovering what they had in common, Jacques had offered Yermi the use of his spare room. Yermi was still living at home, in a small apartment with his parents and two brothers, and had nowhere to tryst when he met a man he liked. In return, he did some cleaning and looked after Jacques's place when Jacques was out of the country.

"It was very sad when he got sick," Jacques told me. "But I never even knew what he had. All in all, he was only hospitalized twice. The doctor said something about tumors in his brain. Back then," he shrugged, "you didn't talk about it."

That the men of Company C accepted its two gay members more or less with equanimity was not entirely a surprise to me. Early in my regular army service I took note of some differences between the ways Israeli and American young men define their masculinity. One of the most salient of those differences was that straight young men in America seemed obsessed with the fear that someone might think they were homosexual. They'd go to tremendous lengths to avoid incurring such suspicion. Young Israeli men, on the other hand, did not seem to be anywhere near as preoccupied with this issue.

Israeli men freely exchange touches, embraces, and even kisses on the cheek. They even dance together—after all, the circle dances of both the secular Zionist folk dance tradition and the religious tradition in which mixed dancing is prohibited mean that a young man may often find himself holding hands with another young man.

I don't mean to say that the men of Company C, or Israeli men in general, have a liberal attitude toward homosexuality. They don't. The guys in the company cracked the usual jokes and made the standard crude remarks. The religious guys could not view homosexuality as other than a sin, given that it is prohibited explicitly and in strong terms by the Torah. What was notable was that they kept these attitudes separate from their working relationship with the two men. I never heard from anyone a suggestion that Jacques and Yermi should be expelled from the unit, or that homosexuals should be kept out of the army. Many of the men may not have approved of Jacques and Yermi's sexual habits, but none of them seemed to feel that their own masculinity was threatened by spending a month or more a year living in close quarters with two gay men.

Back in the tent, Barak's rude comment went unanswered, the subject returning to the wisdom of my refusal to take up the jailer's job that Jacques had so generously offered me.

"I admire your principles, but you're an idiot!" Falk settled back on his feather pillow. "Another game, Barak?"

"I'm going to get some sleep," Barak replied, turning over so that his face was in his pillow, his arms hanging over the sides of his cot. "We're going to be up all fucking night. Efi says this is a no-holds-barred operation. Everyone and their mother is in on it. Border guard, the battalion in the next sector, Shin Bet. Probably the air force, too."

"Udi says it's the Intifada commandant for the whole Jenin region," Falk said.

"Must be why the phone is out. They're afraid that someone will brag to his girlfriend about what he'll be up to tonight. You know those

Arab bastards have the phones tapped. They're not as stupid as they look."

"So we'll get some sleep," Falk sighed. "You, too, Watzman. And no complaining. You cooked your own stew this time."

We were roused from our nap a half hour later by a curse emanating from the center of our tent.

"*Merde!*" Marcel Levy followed this with a long string of lesser-known French expletives. He was standing between Falk's bed and mine with an M-203 grenade launcher dangling from one shoulder, holding a tadal knapsack by the corner as if it were a newly fixed, still wet photo print. The three explosive and five flare grenades inside were preparing to slide out and crash to the floor.

Marcel was a newcomer to the unit. He'd arrived in Jenin several days after the rest of us, making a grand entrance into our lives when Udi brought him to an improvised roadblock that some of us were manning outside the village of Burkin, just to the west of Jenin.

When a Palestinian car or truck came by we'd stop it, ask for the *hawiyyeh* of the driver and adult male passengers, search the vehicle, and send it on its way. There wasn't a lot of traffic, and we'd run into virtually no problems. As in Bani Na'im, Elnatan had made a show of force and discipline during our first few days in the sector, and apparently the locals had gotten the message that we were not to be fooled with. It also helped that they had the olive harvest to get in. An extended family including adults, grandparents, and a dozen children of all ages was at work in the grove alongside the road, moving from tree to tree, filling up blanket bundles of hard green olives and loading them onto an ancient pickup truck. They were no more than a hundred meters from our roadblock but studiously ignored us.

Shabbetai and Shaltiel were making coffee when we heard Udi's siren. Udi loved the siren on his jeep and never went anywhere without turning it on. Swerving off the main road onto the Burkin access road, he screeched to a stop at our roadblock as if he were testing the jeep for stunts in a Hollywood action movie. He jumped out of the commander's seat in full battle gear, took a look at Shabbetai, and turned to Eiger.

"Why isn't the coffee ready?" he demanded, only half joking.

"You should have radioed ahead," Eiger said.

"Kusemak!" came a shout from the jeep. This Arabic curse is perhaps the most common one in the Israeli soldier's vocabulary. It's an all-purpose expletive expressive of frustration or anger. Years of use have virtually detached it in military consciousness from its literal reference to the genitalia of the mother of the curser's interlocutor. But the throaty French accent in which it was now pronounced seemed to restore to the tired expression all its original connotations. We turned to see a skinny soldier with a mop of black hair and a wild look in his eyes trying to extricate himself from the back of the jeep. He was tottering precariously on one foot, entangled in one of the many straps of indeterminate use with which the jeep was equipped. Udi stepped back to support him, and the newcomer angrily slipped off the offending strap and stood at attention, which is something reservists never do. Even so, he seemed to be in permanent motion. Indeed, as we'd soon learn, he was unable to keep his body, mouth included, still for more than a few seconds at a time. In addition to his efod, helmet, and M-16, he had a Pentax with a telescopic lens dangling from his neck.

"This is Marcel Levy," Udi informed us. "He's new in the company and in Platoon One. I brought him here to learn the ropes. Give him a good orientation in our mission and in how we do things in Company C."

"Hi, Marcel," Eiger said.

Marcel surveyed our surroundings suspiciously.

"Dangerous spot, hmm?" He whistled ominously through his teeth. "But I've seen worse."

Udi gulped down a small glass of coffee and zoomed off. I refilled the glass from Shabbetai's pot and gave Marcel a rundown on our location and our duties at the roadblock. Shabbetai and Shaltiel took glasses of their own and stationed themselves on either side of the road, next to the collapsible accordion of spikes and the propped-up stop sign that constituted the roadblock. Eiger sat on a boulder.

I had turned to point out and name some of the villages we could see to the south across the Dotan Valley when I heard the smack of a body hitting the asphalt.

"Enemy fire from the right! Everybody hit the ground!"

I turned to see Marcel flat on his belly on the road, training his gun on the family in the olive grove.

"What happened, Marcel?" Eiger asked. I'd grabbed my rifle, but when I saw that Eiger was unperturbed, I released it.

"They're shooting at us! Hit the ground!" Marcel commanded.

Eiger and I turned to look at the harvesters, who were now murmuring among themselves and pointing at Marcel. Shabbetai and Shaltiel had their hands over their mouths. Marcel looked from Eiger to me to Shabbetai and Shaltiel, and then at the olive pickers, who were now laughing audibly. He slowly got up, brushed himself off, and said, "You can't be too careful. That's what I learned in Lebanon."

Shabbetai and Shaltiel shook their heads and from that moment on treated Marcel as Platoon One's resident lunatic. He never seemed to notice.

Like me, Marcel was in the news business. He was, he said, a photographer who regularly sold pictures to popular French newspapers and magazines. But while I considered myself a serious reporter on my small part-time higher education and science beat, the closest Marcel had come to actual news was selling to a major French glossy photoweekly a photo of one of the standard green garbage bins that the Jerusalem municipality supplies to apartment buildings and shopping centers. How had he made the sale? Apparently it was the caption he attached to the picture: "High-tech bomb detector deployed in Israel's capital."

But this sort of investigative work was not his true calling. No, he was a paparazzo in body and soul, devoting his professional life to chasing down European supermodels and Hollywood actors who happened to be visiting Israel. He was unmatched in catching them in ambiguous positions that could be salaciously interpreted by editors and readers. His accounts of these celebrity ambushes were accompanied by tales of sexual conquest. He claimed to have screwed every woman in the showbiz and fashion worlds who had set foot in Israel during the last two years, and their sisters and secretaries as well. Since Marcel was a talented performer—he acted in an amateur theater group in Jerusalem—his stories could be highly entertaining in small doses. But you had to be in the mood.

For the most part, the guys viewed his self-professed promiscuity as an eccentricity. The fact was that you got no points in Company C for sleeping around. Indeed, after the exit of the older guys who dominated the unit when I first joined it, I never heard a man other than Levy boast about cheating on his wife. I seldom heard any of the single guys brag about, or even admit to, a casual sexual encounter. Perhaps they avoided talking about such things in my presence because I was religious, but I doubt it. Certainly they were not reticent about providing me with mouthwatering descriptions of shellfish repasts or Saturday cookouts, both forbidden to me because of my beliefs.

"*Merde!*" Marcel shouted again in the NCOs' tent, as if the first time hadn't been enough to wake us all.

"Shut up," Barak muttered into his feather quilt.

"I am going to go get my camera immediately," Marcel declared. "I will show the world how Israeli soldiers lie around on their asses at their taxpayers' expense."

"Who let him in here?" Alon called out from his bed.

"Ah, there is Alon," Marcel said brightly. "Maybe you would like to hear how I photographed Sharon Stone in her shower at the Tel Aviv

Hilton and then acceded to her request that I make love to her several times, even though my pager was ringing and my editor was urging me to get over to the Sheraton to catch Bo Derek at the swimming pool."

Alon rolled his eyes and didn't reply.

"What's your problem, Marcel?" asked a grinning, if impatient, Falk.

"Being a dedicated soldier, I have been preparing for tonight's action," he declaimed, adopting an attitude that somehow made me picture him in the role of Inspector Clouseau's obnoxious little brother. "And I come to seek the help of my NCOs and I find that they are sleeping, sleeping as their soldiers slave away, perspiring profusely in the heat of the day, to ensure that on this night the evil minions of our Palestinian enemies will not escape us. Apparently our NCOs do not care if we succeed or not. It is of no concern to them, it is more important for them to sleep."

"So what do you need?" Falk asked Marcel quietly, propping his head up on one hand.

But Marcel was not to be deterred. "Now I could understand it if *Watzman* was to sleep rather than prepare for the raid. Watzman is a well-known Arab lover and he wants the raid to fail. He wants the Fatah warlord to walk free and plot the murder of yet more innocent Israelis. But Falk? Why is he sleeping at such a critical time?"

"Lay off, Marcel," Falk said firmly, sitting up in his bed. I also sat up, with a grimace. I had no patience to deal with Marcel and no talent for it, either, so I left the job of handling him to Falk.

"Just tell me what the problem is," Falk said.

"The problem? The problem?" Marcel perorated. "The problem is that our army, its finances ravaged by left-wing, unpatriotic governments, has been unable to provide me with a second strap for this knapsack!"

He swung the tadal dramatically in the air as I lunged to grab it before the bombs inside cascaded onto the cement floor.

"We haven't had a left-wing government since 1977," I said, gingerly placing the knapsack on my bed.

"More subversive obfuscation," Marcel declared.

"Marcel, ask one of the other guys for a strap. Everyone gets issued just one," Falk said.

"This is scandalous," said Marcel, as he grabbed the tadal and stalked out of the tent. "I intend to expose it in *Paris-Match*."

The orders for the Tamoun operation were given later that afternoon at the military government building in Jenin. The Jenin regional commander and our own brigade commander stood at the top of an open square formed by Company C and the other two units that would be participating in the action—another reserve unit and a Border Guard contingent. Alongside the two commanders was a guy in jeans and a blue button-down shirt. He was an inch shorter than me and had a fit, sturdy frame, short-cropped black hair, and an intense look in his eyes. This was the Shin Bet agent responsible for Tamoun.

The goal of the mission was to capture one of the top Palestinian operatives in the Jenin region. The Shin Bet had learned the location of safe house where he would be spending the coming night. Tamoun was a hotspot of anti-Israeli activity, its residents well organized—hence the need for a large force and a complex plan. We would set out on foot two and a half hours before dawn from a point several kilometers distant from the village, so as to enter without noisy vehicles signaling our presence. Platoon Three would take up positions in the center of the village and, with an additional team led by Eiger and including Shabbetai, Shaltiel, and Marcel Levy, enter the mosque and disable the loudspeaker in the minaret so that it could not be used to sound an alarm and rally the villagers as we made our arrest. Platoon Two would take up commanding positions in the neighborhood where the safe house was located, while Efi and Platoon One surrounded the safe house, sealed off escape routes, entered, and made the arrest. The other reserve unit's job was to secure the roads and flight paths out of the village. The Border Guard would arrive in their jeeps as we entered the house to quell the disturbances expected to erupt once our presence was known.

The square broke up into its three component units for individual briefings about the details of the plan. Elnatan was called into the headquarters building to receive some aerial photos of Tamoun. As we sat waiting for him in the parking lot, we listened to the other two commanders give orders to their men. The contrast with Elnatan's style was palpable and disturbing. The other reserve company's commander spoke to his soldiers contemptuously, as if they had no right or need to know what the other units were doing.

The Border Guard soldiers looked young, wiry, and eager. Their commander, a dark-complexioned man with a potbelly, explained the positions that each platoon and team would take up in Tamoun. He proceeded to read out the rules of engagement, the standing orders stating how soldiers were to treat civilians and when and under what conditions they could open fire. The officer flourished the printed pamphlet containing the rules—we were all supposed to carry copies in our breast pockets—and recited them theatrically with a smirk on his face.

I nudged Alon. "If you were one of his soldiers, how would you interpret that?" I asked.

"That real men ignore these orders," Alon said.

At 3 a.m. we met the other reserve force at the intersection of a dirt road and a wadi that headed toward the hill on which Tamoun perched. The other guys were unshaven. Their shirts hung out, and their efods sat on them sloppily. Some of them smelled as if they'd recently been drinking beer. One standing next to me, an overweight guy with glasses, cursed under his breath as the officers gave final instructions.

"This has been the worst round of duty I've ever had," he complained. "Every single day they've been pelting us with stones, even shooting at us. We beat 'em up but they just keep at it. I'm never doing this again—I'm going to get myself out of this unit."

"Is this how you guys look when you patrol a village?" I asked, noticing that his shirt was missing two buttons and he was wearing tattered cloth commando shoes rather than the regulation army boots.

I added, "Maybe if you'd straighten yourself up, you'd be a little more imposing."

"Hey, what is this, basic training? We're in the reserves," he guffawed.

We walked for a short distance alongside the groaning guys from the other unit before going our own way. Once we left them, the silence was broken only by the scraping of the stones in the wadi between our feet, and once by Marcel Levy inexplicably shouting, "You're breaking rank!" at Shabbetai before Efi shushed him.

At the edge of the village we divided into our constituent forces as planned. Efi and Elnatan led Platoon One through dark alleys. Within minutes we had identified the safe house. Each soldier silently took up his preassigned position—two at each corner of the house, two clambering up to the roof, and six of us with Elnatan, Efi, and the Shin Bet agent at the foot of the stairway leading up to the house's front door.

The agent whispered final instructions. "Elnatan bangs on the door and, when they open it, you charge in and take positions in the corner of the main room. My guess is that our man is sleeping there. I'll identify him and you will grab him. If there's any sign of resistance by him or the others, use reasonable force. If you see him reach for a weapon, kill him. But our objective is to take him alive. He has information we want. We've got every window and door covered and he can't get away. If he's not in the living room, we'll search the other rooms."

A light went on.

"They've already heard us—go to it," the agent ordered.

I was more nervous than I had been on any previous reserve mission. The man we were after was an experienced guerrilla fighter, most likely armed, and I was going through the front door in the direct line of fire. What if the Shin Bet had messed up and this was the wrong house?

Maybe the man had gotten word that we were after him and had changed his plans. Then we'd be terrorizing this family for nothing.

But there was little time for these doubts. Elnatan was already banging on the door. A frightened young woman opened it, and he ordered her to step aside. She fell back into the room, and Efi led the rest of us in. A toddler was bawling in one of the bedrooms. Before I could even think, I found myself in my assigned position, at the entrance to the hallway that led to the rest of the rooms. In the dim light, I made out a groggy, unshaven figure rising slowly from a mattress on the floor. I glanced around the room. This seemed to be the home of a fairly well-off family. There was a couch and a loveseat and two armchairs, all in the baroque, overstuffed style that many Arabs seemed to like. One wall of the living room was painted or wallpapered—I couldn't make out which—with a full-scale picture, in flat, unmodulated colors, of the Dome of the Rock, the Muslim shrine on the Temple Mount in Jerusalem. To the left of the door was a set of freestanding wooden shelves that served as a showcase for some china pieces, olive wood gewgaws, and elaborate glass vases.

The groggy figure was raising his hands. The Shin Bet agent nodded to Elnatan, who ordered two of the guys to handcuff, search, and blindfold the prisoner. A matronly woman dressed in an elaborate housecoat entered the room. She shouted at us in fluent, slightly accented English, ordering us to release our prisoner, calling the arrest illegal, and threatening to notify the American consul in Jerusalem. "We are American citizens," the woman declared. She was scornful of us and undeterred by our guns. Her eyes searched mine, but I avoided her gaze.

The guys led the prisoner out, and Elnatan motioned for me to follow him. As I passed the shelves by the door I heard the sound of running feet. As I turned sharply to see who was coming up behind me, the butt of my rifle swung around and shattered an intricate maroon vase on one of the lower shelves. The younger woman who had opened the door screamed. The older woman reprimanded me.

"This was totally uncalled for," she said. "You have caught your man. Must you also destroy our property? But we have learned what to expect from the soldiers of Israel." The little boy whose running feet had alarmed me clung to her housecoat, looking up at me in fear and in awe.

"What was that for?" Elnatan snapped as I came out the front door. "Keep your cool."

"It was a mistake," I said miserably.

"Okay, it was a mistake," Elnatan said dismissively, ordering me and the others to get into the truck that was waiting for us.

"What's wrong?" Falk asked as I climbed in the bed of the tarpaulin-covered truck. I just shrugged.

No doubt the vase had been a family heirloom, I brooded, something of worth far beyond its monetary value. That must be why the young woman screamed. The little boy would remember my carelessness as an act of gratuitous vandalism by an evil enemy.

I was no less agitated over the fact that Elnatan clearly believed I had acted out of rage. How could he think that of me? Had all my talk of tolerance and restraint seemed so shallow? After four years of serving together, didn't he realize that I seldom got angry, and that on the rare occasions when I did, I never lost control of myself?

Or was he discerning something that was hidden from me? Had my carelessness really come of resentment? Was I mad at these women for harboring a terrorist, for forcing me to walk half the night, for making me into an oppressor, for condescending to me?

My self-interrogation was interrupted by the impact of a very large rock on the truck's tarpaulin cover. The driver swerved and brought the truck to a halt; Efi, sitting in the cab, ordered us out, and quick. Elnatan was also shouting orders from his jeep as we scrambled down. It took us a few seconds to orient ourselves in the barrage of stones coming from somewhere above us. Elnatan ordered us to lower the visors on our riot helmets, but most of us had done that already, just as a hiker instinctively pulls down the brim of his hat to block the glare of the sun. At a further order from Elnatan, we lined up on either side of the road. Then he ordered me, Falk, and the other NCOs to remove the magazines of regular bullets in our rifles and insert the ones with plastic bullets.

We now saw that we were at the bottom of the street leading out of the village and toward the main road, at the last line of houses before the olive groves and fields began. The street bisected the village, which sprawled horizontally over the slope of the hill on which it was built, running straight up to the mosque at the top. Our attackers were a gaggle of teenage boys on the incline, no more than 150 meters from us.

One of them seemed slightly older than the rest—maybe eighteen or nineteen—and was leading the chants, his right arm raised above his head and a red kerchief in his hand. He drew a circle in the sky to mark off each slogan. He'd shout a slogan as he made one circle, and the boys around him would repeat it at the top of their voices as the kerchief circled again. I couldn't make out the words, but we recognized the chant by the rhythm: "With blood and fire we will redeem you, Palestine."

We were at a topographic disadvantage, and the red-kerchief kid had the initiative. He was forcing us to engage him and his teenage brigade. In the best guerrilla tradition—if he was a cadet of the Marxist fronts, as perhaps the red kerchief indicated, he'd no doubt read Mao and Che—he meant to draw us into his home territory, the village where he and his boys knew every alley and tree and where every house belonged to a cousin. He could be sure that his boys would be at their fiercest here, because they knew that at every window a girl watched.

Was this a spontaneous response to our raid, or a well-thought-out contingency plan being put into action? I suspected that the kid's objectives in this skirmish were well defined. The secondary goal was to galvanize his troops, test them in battle, and observe the natural leaders who might be solicited in a year or two's time to join an active cell of his resistance organization.

His primary goal, however, was to embarrass and frighten the enemy force that had invaded his village. He certainly knew, from intelligence and from our appearance, that we were reservists here on short-term duty in the Jenin sector. He meant to show us that Tamoun was a liberated territory, not merely in word but in action, and that if we wanted a quiet and safe month we would keep our distance from this stronghold of Palestinian nationalism.

The red-kerchief kid's cell commander may well have told him that the ideal outcome of the battle would be forcing the Israelis to overreact. If these alarmed, apprehensive reservists could be provoked to open fire, there might be a martyr among the boys, or a stray bullet might pierce the wall of a house and hit a child or mother. The Palestinian cause would score a victory on the propaganda front. The Israelis would investigate the reserve officers and maybe try, convict, and punish them. The unit's soldiers would be demoralized and thus less effective, not only here in Jenin but also in future rounds of duty in the territories.

The strategy was as follows: Catch the enemy in an inferior position, at the bottom of the hill, hemmed in on both sides by houses. Have the main rebel force stationed at the top of the road unleash a barrage of light weapons fire (in this instance, stones) on the regulars. When the reservists commence pursuit, out-of-shape family men chasing agile fifteen-year-olds, have the main rebel force disperse into the village's byways while an overwatch contingent stationed on nearby roofs continues to assail the invaders.

A rock the size of my fist hit the barrel of my rifle, forcing the cloth strap into the skin of my neck. Another rock hit Falk in the helmet, eliciting an uncharacteristic curse.

Elnatan began advancing slowly up the hill toward the attackers, and we followed. The boys fell back—were they afraid of our guns, or was this a strategic retreat toward a better position? The hail of stones continued unabated.

But the red-kerchief kid darted toward us, still waving his standard above his head. Was this an attempt to rally his retreating troops, or was he so caught up in his chanting that he forgot his own plan? Whatever the explanation, he was now within the permitted range of the plastic bullets.

Elnatan ordered Efi, Falk, and me to raise our rifles and keep the kid in our sights. "If we can disable him, the rest of them will disappear," he said in an even voice. "I'm going to shoot as soon as I can be sure I'll hit his legs. But if I don't shoot and he seems about to get closer than the permitted range, any of you is authorized to fire." We halted and aimed. The red-kerchief kid took another step forward; Elnatan dropped to one knee and we heard the crack of his rifle. The kid fell to the ground, clutching his left thigh. The hail of stones ceased and the boys vanished. Border Guard jeeps appeared out of nowhere and began pursuing the fleeing teenagers.

We ran to the fallen commander as Elnatan summoned Shaya, the medic. The red-kerchief kid was grimacing and bleeding fast. The wound seemed no less serious for having been inflicted by plastic. Shaya bandaged the thigh.

"He's got to get to a hospital," Shaya said dispassionately. He'd done his job well but had no sympathy for his patient. "He's lost a lot of blood."

"Get Barak up here with his jeep," Elnatan ordered, and within seconds Barak appeared. Elnatan's gaze fell on me.

"Watzman, get this guy in the jeep and take him out to the main road. Flag down a Palestinian car and tell the driver to take him to the hospital in Jenin."

"Shouldn't we take him ourselves?" I asked. "Maybe he needs a medic with him."

Elnatan looked at the houses around us. "By now fifty people here have called Jenin and told the people there what happened. If I send a jeep alone into the city, its crew will be lynched by a mob."

We heard screams and the sound of blows from one of the nearby alleys.

"The Border Guard's taking care of them now," Elnatan said impassively.

I began to help the red-kerchief kid climb into the backseat of the jeep, but Elnatan stopped me.

"Are you crazy? Put him here where you can keep your rifle on him." Elnatan pointed to the hood. I helped the kid settle as best he could on the front of the jeep. He was surprisingly cooperative. By now his grimace had been replaced by a stoic stare. I kept my rifle trained on him as Barak slowly turned the jeep around and trundled over the potholed asphalt down to the main road.

A Palestinian cab appeared, coming from the south. I waved my hand, but he showed no sign of slowing until I raised my rifle. He stopped short at the intersection.

"He need to go hospital Jenin," I said to the driver in Arabic, my grammar, not good to begin with, getting lost in the emotion of the moment.

The driver nodded silently and I opened the back door of the cab, helping the youth climb in. Instinctively, I drew my wallet from my pocket and offered the driver a ten-shekel note. He looked at me as if I were from another planet.

"It's okay," he said in Hebrew, waving my hand away. "It's really okay." And he sped off toward Jenin.

"I admit it, I vote Labor because I'm a wimp," Udi declared. Given his wrestler's physique, the term seemed hilariously inappropriate, and we all smiled.

We were standing by the improvised polling booth the army had set up at our base. There was a line. Nearly everyone was voting. Eiger was collaring the hesder guys and trying, without much success, to get them to vote for Meimad, the new moderate and modern religious party.

Jacques and Marcel were arguing loudly in French—that is, Marcel was shouting and gesticulating while Jacques, his arms crossed, nodded like a schoolteacher waiting for an unruly pupil to reach the end of an outburst so that discipline could be applied.

"If we had balls," Udi continued, "we'd do to the Arabs what they do to themselves in their own countries. What did President Assad do in Syria when the Hamas guys there pulled an Intifada on him? He went in and slaughtered twenty thousand of them and leveled an entire city. That's what we'd do if we had balls. But we don't have balls. We're wimps. Watzman's a wimp, Mizrahi's a wimp, I'm a wimp. We vote for Labor. We think that if we're nice to the Palestinians, they'll like us and make peace with us. If we give them land, they'll give us peace. We're wimps."

"So why not be a real man and vote right-wing?" I asked. "If Elnatan's more of a man than you are, why not be like him?"

Udi shrugged. "That's the way my parents raised me. To be a wimp. You ought to know. It's a Jewish thing."

He looked around. "You know," he said, "when you think about it, this is pretty amazing. My great-grandfather and your great-grandfather wouldn't believe it if they could see it. All these Jewish guys in uniforms, with rifles and mortars and jeeps, voting in elections to choose a parliament and a prime minister of a Jewish state."

I nodded.

"But in the end, you know what, they would believe it," Udi corrected himself. "Because what's these guys' biggest problem, the one that decides who they vote for? It's that they're worried about the goyim, the non-Jews, these Palestinians. Half of the guys in the company are scared stiff of them, and they vote for the right. The other half want the Palestinians to like them, and they vote for the left. So you know what? We're all wimps. So your great-grandfather and my great-grandfather would be very, very pleased. Because they'd see that despite the rifles and tanks and an air force full of F-15s and F-16s, we're still Jewish just like they were. We're still wimps."

Chapter Six

· CONVERSATIONS ·

HEBRON/BEIT SAHOUR, NOVEMBER 1989

M Y PASTA SALAD LOOKED FORLORN AND OUT OF PLACE ON THE
table amid the hummus, tehinna, and *zhug*, the paste of hot peppers, garlic, and coriander that is a Yemenite staple.

"Why aren't you talking to anyone?" Ilana asked. "From the way
you describe it when you come home from the army, these are your closest friends."

"It's strange," I admitted. "When we're in the army, we never seem
to stop talking. Now it's hard to get started. Everyone looks so different."

Take this guy in the crisply pressed cotton shirt and jeans, the one
with the neat part in his hair—he just didn't look the way Mizrahi was
supposed to look. Could the woman with the purple eye shadow and intense eyes really be his wife? I couldn't remember her name. And what
about *his* name, for God's sake? If I called him "Mizrahi," wouldn't it
seem rude to his wife? Yet how could I call him anything else?

It was strangely quiet around the swimming pool. A couple arrived
at the gate to the usual enthusiastic shouts, just as when we gathered for

a round of duty. Some of the guys would stride over, their wives in tow, and slap the newcomer on the back. They'd introduce the wives deferentially, exchange pleasantries and some personal news—yes, I bought that Subaru I told you about in Jenin; the baby was a girl; the bastard still hasn't paid and my lawyer says I'll be lucky if I see half of it—and then lapse into an awkward silence. Only the most outgoing of the guys, like Falk, Achlama, and Eiger, seemed able to sustain a conversation. Yet even with the best efforts the women were left feeling like foreigners as they listened politely, if in secret horror, to recitations of the classic Company C stories. Eiger recounted the helicopter crash, Achlama told how he'd gotten pinned under a jeep in Bani Na'im, Falk recalled the crepes Eiger had concocted the time we received an unaccountably large supply of flour and eggs. But once the stories were finished, even they fell silent.

"Actually, now that I think about it," I told Ilana, "when we talk in the army, I don't say that much. I mostly listen."

"I never thought of you as the quiet type. You always seem to have something to say," she said.

"When the subject is politics, or preschools, I have things to say," I said. "But a lot of times the conversation is about things I don't have. Like cars. Like an employer. Or about television shows I don't have time to watch and wouldn't like even if I did."

The good feelings generated by the month in Jenin had given Falk and Barak an idea that I'd been mulling for a couple of years but had never had the courage to voice. They'd decided we should have a company party. We'll meet the wives, they said, and have a chance to enjoy each other's companionship without the pressure of the army. Achlama, who was in the sign business, could make up some plaques and we'd hand them out to the old-timers who'd left the unit recently. Keisar was the director of the community center in Rosh Ha'Ayin, a town northeast of Tel Aviv inhabited almost entirely by Yemenites, and he said we could have the party there, around the swimming pool.

Like everything that Falk and Barak organized, the evening was impeccably planned. There was abundant food, a ceremony for the old-timers with brief but sincere words of appreciation, and an Israeli folk song sing-along with Elnatan on the accordion.

"But it really didn't work, did it?" I said to Eiger as his newly bought used Seat slowly ascended the road back to Jerusalem. "Or was it just me?"

"It's a problem when half the people there don't know anyone else," Na'ama noted.

"Did you hear?" I added. "Jacques said he heard that we've got maneuvers in the summer and that we're back to Jenin in the fall."

"Eiger, tell them you have other plans," Na'ama ordered.

My pessimism about the election had been borne out. The right-wing parties that opposed a territorial compromise with the Palestinians won a majority in the Knesset. It seemed as if the Intifada would go on and on.

But the Americans didn't want to accept a stalemate, and the Americans couldn't be ignored. The outgoing Reagan and the incoming Bush administrations continued to pressure both sides to find a way to talk, and the result soon made headlines. Prime Minister Yitzhak Shamir of Likud, who could have easily formed a government with the other parties of the right, gave his ideological partners the cold shoulder and made overtures to Labor. A season of postelection bargaining—byzantine even by the standards of Israel's deal-crunching, vote-buying system—ended with Shimon Peres leading Labor into yet another national unity government. His party colleague Yitzhak Rabin would continue as defense minister. Labor would at least try to push the government toward negotiations (though it, too, officially opposed any contact with the PLO), and Rabin, though he was no bleeding heart, could be counted on to keep the military response to the Intifada on an even keel. The extreme rightists, some of whom were calling for the physical expulsion of the Palestinians from the territories, remained outside the government.

On the Palestinian side there was a more dramatic development. In exchange for America recognizing the PLO's claim to represent the Palestinians in the territories, Arafat issued a statement accepting UN resolutions that implied Israel's right to exist. This seemed to mean that the PLO was no longer intent on destroying Israel.

Of course, like all things diplomatic, the PLO statement was hardly unambiguous, and the United States had extracted it only under considerable pressure. Furthermore, the PLO's move didn't represent new thinking about Israel as much as it did a sober evaluation of the geopolitical balance of power. The Palestinian leadership watched with trepidation as the empire ruled by its main sponsor, the Soviet Union, began to disintegrate. But the fact that Arafat and his associates had assessed their position realistically was encouraging. It seemed they were getting over their reactionary dream of the Palestinian people fighting their way back into a pre-Zionist paradise. Perhaps their leaders had realized that they might achieve more by reaching an accommodation with Israel. I hoped so.

While the months that followed were full of political machinations, everyday life didn't change much on either side. For our part, Ilana and I were mostly concerned with bringing up Mizmor and Asor, who demanded an incredible amount of attention and stimulation. We gave it gladly, but we were exhausted.

They were old enough now to have a relationship with each other, and I was fascinated by their distinct characters. Mizmor was the humanist and dreamer. She sang, she danced, she played with words, she challenged convention. Asor was the hardheaded empiricist and man of principle. One of his principles, for example, was that any open door should be closed forthwith. Another was that pots and pans should be out on the kitchen floor rather than hidden away where they could not be observed.

They also cost a lot of money. My freelance income couldn't keep up with a growing family's expenses, especially when family, country, and God kept demanding so much of my time.

In the summer I was called up for a week and a half of maneuvers at Tze'elim. This was the first time Company C had conducted lengthy maneuvers at that time of year. It seemed that someone in the army's training division had decided we needed to be shown that August could be just as miserable as January. After a few days of infernal heat and afternoon dust storms that filled our bodily orifices, our food, and our gear with sand, we longed for the damp, freezing winter we'd so maligned in previous years.

When we came home it was still August, a month when virtually all of Israel goes on vacation, so I had nothing to report for the newspapers and no new translation clients knocking at my door. Mizmor and Asor were home, making it difficult to do what work I had. In September they went back to their preschools, but on the two days a week that Ilana worked round-the-clock shifts at the Jerusalem airport meteorological station, I had to care for them in the afternoon. Then came the autumnal month of Jewish holidays, from Rosh Hashanah through Yom Kippur and on to Sukkot and Simkhat Torah, on which, like the Sabbath, work was forbidden. Almost all the holidays fell midweek, with no respect for economic realities.

The holidays had no sooner ended than I found myself in the army for another month. Jacques had said at the pool party that we'd be back in Jenin, and Elnatan had confirmed that the sector commander there had been so pleased with us the previous year that he was determined to have us assigned to him again. But we were no less popular with the other regional commander who'd seen us in action in the Intifada, and he, apparently, pulled more weight in the army's higher echelons. In November 1989, as Germans stormed the Berlin Wall, we found ourselves back in Hebron.

———

I was pissed at Eiger, though I tried not to show it. He hadn't reported for duty on enlistment day. When I called him, he told me that he was the beneficiary of a spot-inspection at our battalion's permanent office. Army regulations stipulated that reservists receive at least two months' advance notice of every call-up, and Eiger's orders had been mailed a few days after the cutoff date. The woman who was our liaison officer phoned Eiger to inform him that his summons was null and void. Since he'd just moved to Haifa and was about to begin a new job, Eiger accepted the reprieve gladly and, it seemed, with none of the pangs of conscience that would have plagued me.

I felt more than a little lost without him. Eiger had always served as an intermediary between me and Company C. I had other friends in the unit, but with my American upbringing, my intuitions were not always in line with theirs. Eiger could explain the things that passed me by, and he could interpret me to the others. Now I was on my own.

This time we were operating out of a base just to the south of Hebron, sending jeep and foot patrols into the section of the city for which we were responsible. The other NCOs preferred the jeep patrols, but I liked to walk. I'd never been interested in anything mechanical, and I tended to get antsy sitting in the commander's seat for hours on end. Given that I preferred the least popular assignment, Jacques had no problem scheduling me for a foot patrol most days.

Our principal sector was Abu Sneineh, a large neighborhood located on Hebron's western hill. It overlooked the cluster of Jewish homes centered around Hadassah House and the old bus station we'd bivouacked in two and a half years previously, as well as the Avraham Avinu neighborhood next to the Tomb of the Patriarchs.

The strategic advantage of high land was something the army had taught me to appreciate. Before I was a soldier it seemed easy enough to draw a line on a map that would separate Israel from the West Bank. I dismissed military analysts who claimed that the topography of the Green Line—the cease-fire border that had separated Israel from the

West Bank between 1948 and 1967—put Israel at a disadvantage. How much difference could it make whether you were at the top of a hill or the bottom?

I was disabused of that indifference the first time I had to run up a hill to take an enemy position. It didn't matter that I was on maneuvers and no one was shooting back. There was enough gunfire to make it feel very real, since the Israeli army uses live ammunition in most exercises. The enemy above me could sit in his defensive position and take careful aim while I panted and searched desperately for the next rock or trench to dive behind. It would be much easier for him to blow me away than it would be for me to hit him.

Some writers on the Israel-Arab conflict argue that cruise missiles, high-speed combat aircraft, and other long-range weaponry obviate Israel's need to control topographically important positions. Statesmen and diplomats might well decide that such points should be ceded in the framework of a larger peace accord, but they would have a hard time convincing the average infantryman who has been shot at from above. This doesn't mean that the foot soldier's perspective is the correct one—he must control and conquer the enemy, whereas a diplomat might see the advantages of compromise and a military balance of power. But the fact that nearly all of Israel's top military officers since the army's founding have begun their careers as infantry privates, running up hills against enemy positions, might well explain their reluctance to return to the old borders.

The importance of controlling Abu Sneineh was thus obvious to all of us. A sniper deployed on one of the neighborhood's rooftops could easily pick off anyone who walked down the main road, and Israeli civilians had indeed been killed in such attacks. Even those who opposed Jewish settlement in the heart of this Arab city, as I did, thought that Jews had the right to visit and pray at the Tomb of the Patriarchs—a right that the Muslim religious authorities stubbornly refused to recognize.

Inevitably, however, we weren't securing the road only so that Jews could pray at the tomb. We were also battling the Intifada. This time the army gave us a somewhat different set of standing orders. We were no longer overly concerned with nationalist Arabic graffiti and Palestinian flags on telephone poles. Army strategists were now more worried about countering the power of Palestinian civil disobedience. The line given to us soldiers in our briefings was that thugs were forcing Hebron's shopkeepers to close their stores in accordance with commercial strikes declared by the Intifada leadership and the PLO. The same thugs were also enforcing a Palestinian boycott of the Israeli civil administration, threatening Palestinians who applied for permits for travel, work, health care, and study. Our job was to protect the innocent Palestinian in the street. The average Palestinian, the officers of the Hebron command assured us, only wanted to conduct his life normally and earn a living for his family. He had no interest in nationalist agitation, which was carried out by a small band of terrorists whose funding was funneled in from PLO headquarters in Tunis.

This was clearly nonsense and bore a disturbing resemblance to the Southern segregationist rhetoric I remembered from my childhood in the early 1960s. At that time, conservative white opponents of integration had claimed that most blacks were content living under white suzerainty and that it was only a small group of agitators—funded by the Communists, of course—who were stirring up trouble. In truth, Palestinians had not been living normal lives before the Intifada—the Israeli government had strictly circumscribed their freedom in the interest of the Jewish polity's security and economic interests.

"Your problem is that you believe what you read in the newspapers," said Shaya. We had turned left off the road that climbed to the top of Abu Sneineh and onto the broad but muddy avenue that ran along the top of the ridge and served as the neighborhood's main street. "The newspapers report that Arafat said this and the local Intifada leaders said that, and you think that that's what the guy buying pitas at the corner grocery store thinks, too."

It was early morning, a bit before 7 a.m.; the sun hovered above Kiryat Arba to the east and was heating the moisture left by the previous night's drizzle. A fine mist rose from the road to the level of our rifle barrels. The neighborhood had been awake for some time already, but it was quiet. The Intifada leadership had declared a commercial strike for the day. The stores along the street were closed, their metal shutters pulled down and padlocked.

"Let's turn here." I pointed to a small side street, almost an alley, to our left.

"What's wrong with the main drag?" complained Kobi. "We'll walk down to the end and take a rest."

"The jeeps cover the main roads just fine," I said. "Our job is to cover the side streets."

Shaya and Kobi were always together. They knew each other from their regular army days, when they'd served in an infantry brigade. They were both religious, but they didn't have the ideological fervor of the hesder crowd. Both had dark, North African complexions, but Shaya was wiry, hot-tempered, and impulsive, whereas Kobi was mild-mannered and imperturbable to the point of indifference. After several years of marriage, he had developed a noticeable paunch and looked just right for his job as a bank clerk. Shaya worked as a salesman in a toy store only a short walk from my apartment in Jerusalem and seemed steady in the job after being fired from several previous ones. He was by now Company C's senior medic, but I wasn't sure I'd want him to treat me on the battlefield. He was quite capable of abandoning an uncompleted tourniquet because the soldier he was treating got on his case. Kobi's job in the company was keeping Shaya on an even keel.

"These guys aren't interested in whether or not they have their own country," Shaya said loudly, waving his free left hand expansively to indicate the houses and shops around us. He pointed at the one establishment that was open, a small grocery and dry goods store operating out of the ground floor of a three-story house. The store's shutter was pulled down to shoulder height. The proprietor ducked out, looking anxiously at us, as a five-year-old kid skittered out and down the street with a package of Noblesse cigarettes in a translucent pink plastic bag. The shopkeeper was old, grizzled, and slightly stooped, dressed in a *jalabiyyeh* that reached below his knees. The long shirtlike garment is common at-home dress for Arab men. Perhaps he meant to signal to the strike's enforcers that he was "at home" rather than "at work," or perhaps his generation had been accustomed to dressing this way before Western styles became current in the West Bank. He was certainly of the generation that had found it prudent to be diffident rather than defiant when confronted with force. His dilemma these days was presumably that it was no longer clear whom he was supposed to be diffident to.

"See, he's got his shutter half down so he can close up fast if any Fatah goons come by to enforce the strike," Shaya declared.

"No, he's got his shutter half open because he knows the army's around and expects him to be open," I countered. One of the ways the army encouraged shopkeepers to keep their establishments open was to weld shut the entrances to stores that participated in strikes. Like a lot of what the army did to fight Palestinian civil disobedience, it wasn't very effective.

The old man turned to the east and raised his hands in what looked like supplication. But it was not clear whom he was supplicating. Was he asking the help of God by praying in the direction of the city's holy site, or was he signaling his helplessness and despair to a neighbor he had spied in an upstairs window? Was he calling for help?

"Maybe grocery stores are exempt from the strike," Kobi suggested. "After all, the people have to buy milk and bread in the morning."

"Go away," Shaya said.

"Why don't we ask him?" Kobi suggested.

"Great idea," Shaya said. "Let's show Watzman some facts." He walked up to the shopkeeper and stood very close. The man glanced nervously to either side, avoiding the soldier's gaze. This seemed natural enough, given that Shaya was a head taller and decked out in an efod that contained seven magazines of bullets, two hand grenades, a smoke grenade, and medical gear that made the pack look even bigger and more imposing.

"Tell me, Ahmed," Shaya said in a voice that he no doubt meant to be friendly but that came out patronizing. The use of the common name "Ahmed" as a generic form of address certainly didn't help. It was something like calling a black man in America "boy." "The shutter on your store here. Is it half open or half closed?"

"I don't understand," the shopkeeper said, as he glanced from Shaya to me. He was army-wise enough to see that I was the commander of this detachment. What marked me as such was not my imposing presence or a natural aura of authority, but the shorter, lighter model of M-16 I carried. Shaya and Kobi had the standard long model.

"I mean," Shaya said, "are you afraid that Fatah goons are going to come and force you to close your store, or are you afraid that the army is going to come by and force you to open it?"

The shopkeeper considered for a minute and then said, "We want peace."

"See!" said Shaya, turning to me triumphantly. "He just wants to be left alone."

"He wants *us* to leave him alone," I said. "For heaven's sake, Shaya, he'll tell you that he fought on our side in the War of Independence as long as you stand over him like that with your hand on your rifle."

"I'm not touching him," said Shaya. He turned back to the shopkeeper. "Do you feel threatened?"

Two men had stopped to watch. One was clean-shaven and trim, dressed neatly in a blue shirt and white pants; the other was bearded and stouter, in a *jalabiyyeh*. They both appeared to be in their midthirties. They looked angry; they clearly thought Shaya was bullying the shopkeeper. I was worried that Shaya's harangue was about to attract a crowd and that the crowd could get violent.

I turned to the two men. "Move on over there," I called out to them.

"Let's ask them, too," Kobi suggested, ambling over to the pair. "Tell me honestly, guys, do you like living in this garbage heap? Not knowing when you can work, with us bursting into your houses at night? Wouldn't you rather go back to the way it was before the Intifada?"

"Before the Intifada, it wasn't any different," the clean-shaven one said in precise, almost unaccented Hebrew. "Then we worked at your pleasure and you also invaded our houses. We just didn't do anything about it. At least now we can look each other in the eye and not be ashamed."

Two teenage boys and a forty-something man with a mustache stopped to watch.

"A commercial strike is a completely legitimate form of protest," I said to Kobi. "We used to complain that the PLO was using terrorism and killing Israelis. Now, when the Palestinians here use nonviolent tactics, we force them to open their stores."

The two men looked at each other in surprise.

The guy with the mustache said something in Arabic to them. I couldn't make out the words, but presumably it was something like, "You guys are about to get into a lot of trouble—get out of here!"

But I understood the clean-shaven man's reply. "No, no, these are soldiers we can talk to!"

The shopkeeper had vanished into his store, but the two men engaged us in a discussion of the issues of the day. The clean-shaven one, who turned out to be a high school math teacher, did most of the talking. The bearded one was a functionary of some sort at the neighborhood mosque; apparently he spoke little Hebrew. The schoolteacher said that Israel's continued insistence that it could construct settlements wherever it wanted and its refusal to recognize the PLO were signs that our government did not really want to compromise with the Palestinians. Kobi said he doubted that Arafat's recent talk about recognizing Israel was sincere. After all, wasn't the PLO still demanding that a million or so Palestinian refugees return to their original homes in what was now Israel? Those places were now inhabited by Jews who—"like our parents and his in-laws," he said, pointing to himself and Shaya and then at me—had fled Arab countries. What was the PLO proposing to do with them? A boy of about ten—apparently the shopkeeper's grandson—appeared and passed around a tray bearing several tiny glasses of Turkish coffee. We were so involved in our conversation that I didn't notice Udi's jeep until it practically touched me.

"Watzman, brother," Udi said in total exasperation, leaning out of the commander's seat to observe the scene, "what the hell is going on here?"

"Um, we were just talking," I said as my face went red. "They're okay."

"How do you *know* they're okay? How do you know that they're not keeping you busy while a sniper positions himself in that window and aims at your brain? I know it's the size of a pea, but you've given him plenty of time to get it precisely in his sights." He pointed at a third-story window above the store.

He turned to the small crowd surrounding the schoolteacher. "Scatter," he commanded. "Get away from here as fast as your scrawny legs can take you. And don't let me catch you fraternizing with any of my soldiers again." Within seconds, they were gone.

Udi leaned back in his seat. "Watzman." He sighed. "Continue with your patrol."

Two weeks into our tour of duty in Hebron, there was a sudden change in plans. On a Thursday we were told to pack up our duffel bags and chimidans, and were sent to a school building on the northern edge of the city. The entire brigade was bivouacked there. The word was that a special operation was being planned for Saturday morning, a major raid to capture a top terrorist in one of the nearby villages. Vacations were canceled. Then, just as suddenly, Elnatan told us on Friday that our orders had been revised again. The other three companies would carry out the Saturday raid. Company C was being sent to Beit Sahour.

"I've got a problem," I whispered to Jacques as Elnatan explained the new mission to us.

"Don't we all?" Jacques hissed.

"Beit Sahour is the village where my friends from Kehilat Yedidya have their Israeli-Palestinian dialogues," I said.

"So?"

"What if a bunch of people I know show up in the village while we're there?"

"It's not going to be a problem. The army's declared the whole village a closed military area. No one can get in or out."

"They might find a way in anyway."

"Then you'll have to kick them out," said Jacques.

Beit Sahour had been in the news for the last month. Built on the side of a valley just east of Bethlehem, it had shared in that city's tourism-based prosperity. According to tradition, it was the site of the field where the shepherds of the nativity tale had received word of Christ's birth. Although a small, outlying Muslim neighborhood was less well-off, the village's core population was Christian, well educated, politically aware, and middle class. As was characteristic of the Palestinian Christian community, the Marxist factions were strong there. These groups rejected reconciliation with Israel and the entire concept of a Palestinian state that would coexist alongside a Jewish state. So while the village was a center for dialogue with Israelis, this did not necessarily mean that the Palestinians who lived there were moderates.

The military didn't like Beit Sahour. They were unnerved by the political savvy of the residents. Whenever the army wanted to do something there, the locals called in the press and the television crews. They were good at staging media stunts and maintained contact with Christian groups in the United States and Europe. The army was also suspicious of the Israeli-Palestinian dialogue groups that had become a hallmark of the village during the Intifada. Earlier in the year the Popular Front and the Democratic Front, the two major Palestinian Marxist factions, had categorically rejected Arafat's acceptance of the UN resolutions that implied Israel's right to exist. The army and the Shin Bet claimed that the cells of the Popular Front for the Liberation of Palestine and the Democratic Front for the Liberation of Palestine in Beit Sahour were dangerous, and that soft-hearted Israeli leftists were being co-opted by these extreme rejectionist Palestinian factions. Many of the Beit Sahour residents who participated in the dialogue groups were subject to harassment and even arrest.

The previous summer, the town's leaders had decided as an act of civil disobedience to stop paying Israeli taxes. (International law allows an occupying power to collect taxes from residents of an occupied territory for the purpose of funding local administration and development.) Aware that this tactic would play well in the international press—after all, why should people pay to be oppressed?—and worried that the phenomenon would spread throughout the West Bank and Gaza Strip, the army decided to come down hard on Beit Sahour. It blockaded the town, closed it off to the press, and broke into houses and stores to confiscate property. Beit Sahour responded with stones and Molotov cocktails. The reservists stationed there weren't handling it well, apparently, and the army planned to move in a tough regular army unit to impose order. But the regular unit wouldn't be available for a week and half, and somebody in the Central Command had decided that one of our battalion's companies would be perfect for the job. Akiva had decided that Company C was the one.

I had even less sympathy for what the army was doing in Beit Sahour than I had for its general policy in the territories. Had I known of the assignment before enlisting for this stint in the army, the question of whether I could in good conscience serve in the occupied territories would have come up with friends at Kehilat Yedidya who were involved in the dialogue groups. While I would not have made a public display of refusing to serve in Beit Suhour, my standing with Elnatan and Udi was such that, had I pestered them, I could probably have arranged for an alternate assignment as a guard at the emergency warehouse at our home base. Again, I was pissed at Eiger—this time for his luck.

So why didn't I take Elnatan and Udi aside that Friday and tell them how I felt? For one thing, they didn't have a second to spare now that plans had changed so suddenly. Furthermore, I was already there with the guys, and a million things had to be done to get us equipped and bivouacked in Beit Sahour. Raising a matter of principle while my comrades frantically loaded duffel bags and gear onto the rickety bus we'd been assigned seemed selfish. How could I walk out on them at such a moment? And, anyway, what could Elnatan and Udi do? They needed every man they had for the assignment.

When I talked in later years to guys who had refused to serve anywhere in the territories, they pointed to situations precisely like this one to justify their decision. Once you're in with your comrades, they pointed out, refusing a particular order becomes a betrayal of your friends. Better not to put yourself in that position, because the logic of the moment will always be that your first responsibility is to your buddies.

Suppose my order had been canceled as Eiger's was, though, and then I learned that Company C had been sent to Beit Sahour. I would have felt all the worse for not being with the guys when the unit faced its biggest challenge since the Intifada began. For better or worse I was an NCO in Company C and this was my duty.

But the most important factor that kept me with the guys was that they had, I felt, proved themselves during our stints in Bani Na'im and Jenin, as well as the previous two weeks in Hebron. My comrades and officers had been consistently disciplined and responsible, and I had no reason to doubt that the same would be true in Beit Sahour.

Not that I really had time to think this through. Everything happened very quickly that Friday. The unit we were replacing had been stationed at a camp along the road leading from Beit Sahour to Bethlehem. But the army wanted our presence to be felt, so it decided to house us in the center of the village, in the shell of a half-finished two-story villa. We had to set up a camp from scratch, and the word from the Bethlehem sector headquarters was that we'd have the most primitive of conditions with which to work—no beds, no mattresses, no kitchen, and only canned rations.

But Udi, who as deputy company commander was in charge of logistics, would have none of that. At the headquarters camp in Bethlehem, blond, square-jawed Yermi made eyes at the unsuspecting girls in the quartermaster's office and Jacques lectured the base commander on his patriotic, Zionist obligation to the hardworking reservists of Company C. Udi banged on every table he could find and threatened to bang a couple of heads, too. Within half an hour he'd commandeered a large truck and set us to work loading it with gear, some of which was supplied through regular channels and some of which appeared out of nowhere with Jacques sitting pretty on top. An hour later we left for Beit Sahour with a pile of cots, mattresses, and a complete set of kitchen equipment—including a cast-iron range and oven—tied down on the truck bed. Jacques had even found party napkins for the Sabbath meal. We formed a convoy with jeeps fore and aft. Securely in the middle, like an army ant queen on the march, was the truck, distended with the supplies that were now our most valuable possessions.

Beit Sahour greeted us with a hail of stones, but we let the jaded soldiers of the outgoing unit take care of it. As soon as we had unloaded our personal and combat gear, Elnatan dispatched jeep patrols to replace the other unit, and the rest of us set up camp. The villa's upper floor was converted into our dormitory while the ground floor became the kitchen and commons room. In the Company C tradition, the table had been laid and a feast prepared by the time the Sabbath began.

Neither in Bani Na'im nor in the Jenin villages nor in Hebron had we encountered the uniform hostility we found in Beit Sahour. No one smiled at us, no one responded to my attempts at conversation. Despite the villagers' reputation for nonviolent civil disobedience, nonviolence was hardly their sole strategy. Youths threw Molotov cocktails at our patrols daily, and we seldom succeeded in catching or even identifying our attackers. It was rare for a patrol not to find itself the target of expertly thrown stones.

The Bethlehem command had given us special instructions for dealing with this town. Beit Sahour was on the radar of the international media, the Bethlehem commander told us just before we headed out, so forget the petty police work that preoccupied us before. Leave graffiti and Palestinian flags untouched. Under no circumstances confiscate any Arab's ID card. None of the funny stuff the guys who preceded us had liked—no harassing or insulting any resident of the village, even as a joke. The commander went so far as to say that soldiers who violated these rules would be prosecuted and punished. This was no empty threat—as we all knew, there had been an increasing number of investigations and court-martials of soldiers who had committed such violations in the territories. As usual, my perspective was different from almost everyone else's. I applauded the army's willingness to punish its own disobedient soldiers and thought that too many such violators were still going free. Nearly everyone else thought that many of the soldiers who had been charged had merely been doing their best in tough situations and should be given the benefit of the doubt. The guys sarcastically said that we were getting to the point that we'd have to assign a lawyer to every patrol, to provide on-the-spot certification that our actions did not violate army regulations or the Geneva Conventions.

Despite the limitations the Bethlehem commander placed on us, we were hardly passive. To put it bluntly, we were active simply when and where we were less likely to create bad publicity. For example, a Molotov cocktail provoked a standing response: In the middle of the night

following the attack, we'd cordon off the street where the attack had occurred and bang on doors. We'd order all the men out into the road and
then force them to sit cross-legged on the ground for an hour while Udi
lectured them on good behavior. Next time a bomb gets thrown from
this street, he'd admonish them menacingly, the results will be very
unpleasant.

The idea was to give kids the message that their parents would suffer if they threw a bomb, but it seemed like an idiotic policy to me. Obviously, no kid was going to throw a Molotov cocktail near his own
home. He'd do it somewhere else, most likely by the home of someone
his parents disliked. Furthermore, the tactic took no account of the special profile of Beit Sahour's population. It might have worked in some of
the other villages in which we'd been stationed, where most of the
adults were day laborers with little knowledge of the world outside. But
the men we flushed out of their homes in Beit Sahour weren't dressed in
jalabiyyehs, and they weren't cowed. Some of them had studied overseas
and had subscriptions to *Newsweek* or *L'Express*. It just didn't make
sense to treat them like peons.

During the first two or three days in Beit Sahour, I made a point of
performing my duties with visible reluctance. I didn't stop passersby to
make spot checks of their IDs, and I took long and frequent breaks. On
several occasions I kept the men with me from chasing kids who threw
stones at us, earning my men's ire. Since Elnatan's explicit instructions
were that we must respond actively to every attack, this was the closest
I'd come to disobeying orders. Then, one afternoon as my jeep meandered along a road that followed the spur of a hill down toward our
camp with Barak at the wheel and Hezki in the back, something hit the
vehicle's roof and then smashed on the asphalt with a loud bang. Barak
swerved and almost lost control of the jeep. Looking behind us we saw
a huge block of masonry shattered on the road. Something vanished on
the rooftop above us, a human face staring down on his handiwork.
He'd waited a second too long. Instead of hitting us squarely, his simple

but effective ballistic weapon had careened off the back right corner of the jeep's top.

"Of course you're not going to let us raid the house and find the attacker," Hezki said cynically.

"He's long gone," I said. "Let's get this jeep back to camp."

This was the first time that a Palestinian had deliberately tried to kill me. I'd been a target a few times in Lebanon. At the end of our week in Beirut at the beginning of my NCO course, some gunners, invisible behind a hill, had opened fire on the bus taking us back to Israel. Through a combination of distance and luck, the bus wasn't hit. During my later sojourn in Lebanon there had been occasional ineffective sniper fire on our base or on jeeps in which I rode. Unreasonably, perhaps, I hadn't felt as though my life was in real danger. The only time I'd felt an inch away from death was when a crazy truck driver with whom I'd hitched a ride on my long trip from Israel to my forward base took a turn too quickly and jumped out of the cabin as the truck flipped over. I was glad he'd jumped, because it left room for the force of my inertia to slide me into his place. The impact smashed the cabin roof into the passenger seat and, had I remained there, I would have been reduced to two dimensions.

The masonry block was something different. It had been aimed at me and at the two men for whom I was responsible. It wasn't a stone. It wasn't an act of civil disobedience. It didn't have any purpose but to kill.

I took the patrol back to the base. Presumably we assessed the damage to the jeep and went out again to finish our allotted time. Obviously, I reported the incident to Udi, who was in command that day, and he must have ordered some sort of response. But I don't remember what it was. If someone had asked me at the time whether I was dazed or upset by the attack, I'm sure I would have denied it. My only two thoughts, as far as I can remember, were that I intended to watch rooftops much more carefully from here on out, and that I wasn't going to mention a word of this to Ilana. But something must have shown on my face.

That evening I checked Jacques's duty roster and saw to my surprise that he hadn't assigned me to any patrols or guard duty during the next twenty-four-hour period. When I asked him why, he shrugged. He said that we had more manpower than we needed and that I should enjoy a day off. At the time I thought Jacques was simply trying to play favorites, but looking back, I suspect that Udi had told him to give me a day's rest. Barak and Hezki had been in the same jeep, so why didn't they deserve a day off? For them the attack merely confirmed their expectations of Beit Sahour. Jacques perhaps realized that I'd come to the village believing that its residents were partners in dialogue and, therefore, not dangerous. I think he and Udi wanted to give me some time to digest the experience.

I read a book, helped out in the kitchen, wrote a letter to my parents and to a friend in the United States. Nothing in the letters hints at any reevaluation of my role as a soldier. But there was a change, even if it took me some time to realize that it had happened. When I resumed my job as patrol commander the following day, I no longer pretended that I could serve in Beit Sahour but remain detached from the work we were doing there. So there were people in Beit Sahour who were engaging in dialogue with Israelis. There were also people in Beit Sahour who were trying to kill Israelis, specifically me and my friends. They might be two different groups of people, or they might be the very same group. It didn't really matter. My actions and reactions as a soldier had to be based on the fact that our lives were on the line. I could participate in dialogue as a civilian. As a soldier I had, first and foremost, to protect myself and my comrades.

We had barely gotten used to Beit Sahour when the end of our month of duty approached. As always, the company's unofficial social committee—Jacques, Yermi, Keisar, Falk, Barak, and Achlama—began planning the party that we had on the penultimate night of every tour of duty. One day Jacques returned beaming from a trip to the Bethlehem regimental base. He'd gotten something even better than party napkins—the Central Command's entertainment troupe was going to perform for us.

I returned from my patrol late that afternoon to find the troupe's crew setting up a pair of thirteen-foot-high loudspeakers that would have done a soccer stadium proud. When the performance began after we'd enjoyed the four-course dinner prepared under Jacques's direction, the volume was so loud that it was nearly impossible to figure out what melody the troupe was singing. I went up to the sound technician, thinking that maybe he was professionally deaf and hadn't noticed.

"You know, we could enjoy the music more if you turned the volume down," I suggested at the top of my lungs.

"What?" he shouted impatiently.

"I said, we could enjoy the music more if you turned the volume down. Also, you know, this is a residential neighborhood."

The sound man sized me up. "You just don't understand music," he said and returned to his buttons and levers.

Eiger would have been more successful—he'd have exchanged some banter with the sound man, slapped him on the back, and in the end the volume would have been reduced to a reasonable level. I wasn't able to get the same results, and none of the other guys seemed to be bothered by the noise.

I felt very much alone, and very tired. I wandered out of the house to the spigot and aluminum trough where we did our washing. The party dishes were piled high; once the performance was over the guys would attack the dishes before either going to bed or heading out for the night patrols. I'd do my share now and then go upstairs to bed, I decided, and picked up a sponge.

Falk appeared beside me a few minutes later. "Are you feeling okay? You look kind of down," he asked.

"I just want to go to sleep," I said quietly.

He took the plate from my hand. "Go on up. Don't worry, no one will notice you're gone."

"I feel bad. I want to do my share."

"You've done your share. It's plenty. Go to sleep," he insisted.

I obeyed.

Beit Sahour looked entirely different in the spring. The mud had dried into rich soil covered with grass and exuberant patches of wild-flowers. The minibus drove past the old Company C camp and up to a large house at the lower bottom end of the village. We climbed the out-side stairs to the second, main floor and were welcomed into a spacious living room where upholstered wooden chairs were arranged opposite a couch and armchair covered in a floral pattern. Glasses and pitchers of cold drinks were on a coffee table in the middle.

I'd convinced Ilana that I should go back to Beit Sahour for a meeting held by one of the dialogue groups. Having been there as a soldier, I had to see it as a civilian, I told her. Maybe it was an attempt at expiation, but more than that I simply wanted to talk to the people of Beit Sahour the same way I had talked to that schoolteacher in Hebron.

Our group numbered nine or ten Israelis, a majority of them women. Only one was from my synagogue. A blond American Jewish girl who studied at Hebrew University looked around the room and murmured, "Oh, it's so beautiful, it's so beautiful." A guy of forty-five with wire-rim glasses seated himself in the armchair and gazed firmly at nothing in particular in front of him. There was a woman with curly hair and a dark sleeveless dress who kept sighing, and a blond guy with a beard and a heavy Dutch accent. Elazar, the organizer of the group, was a tall, thin American-Israeli with a clipped white beard. I knew him by sight—he was one of the few other fitness fanatics I'd see on my early morning runs in Jerusalem.

Our Palestinian counterparts were four men in their late thirties or early forties, who appeared both earnest and uncertain. Elazar suggested—in English, the neutral language used by such dialogue groups—that we begin by introducing ourselves. We should also add a sentence about what we saw as the goal of this meeting. The four Palestinians gave their names and professions, and said something to the effect that they sought peace and justice. All four seemed sincere, but there was a boilerplate quality to their words.

Then it was the Israelis' turn.

The guy with the wire-rimmed glasses was the first. "I just want to begin by saying how proud I am to be sitting in the same room as Palestinian freedom fighters," he declared, searching our host's face for approbation. "All power to you. If I were younger I'd be out on the streets with a Molotov cocktail, too."

The blond Hebrew University student was next. "My name is Jessica and I'm studying at the Hebrew University in Israel," she said, sounding oddly like one of those disembodied voices that make announcements in department stores. "I mean in Jerusalem. I didn't mean to say in Israel, since I believe that Jerusalem should be an international city of peace."

I leaned over to my synagogue friend, a veteran of these dialogue groups. "Are these people for real?" I whispered.

"Well, you know, you advertise a dialogue group and you get all kinds," she smiled wanly.

The woman in the sleeveless dress was blushing and relating in a soap-opera voice how she had, earlier this week, at last decided to join the Communist party, as if this were a group therapy session and she were confessing that she had finally surrendered her body to a man who had long stalked her. Then the guy with the blond ponytail produced a set of blueprints and began a lengthy presentation of how the construction of a subway system would bring peace to Jerusalem.

The Jews present seemed to bend over backward to agree with everything the Palestinians said. As best I could read the Palestinians'

faces, they weren't impressed. When it was my turn I mentioned my recent service as a soldier in Beit Sahour; the Palestinians were stony-faced
while most of the Jews shook their heads in dismay.

"I'm one of the guys you want to throw a Molotov cocktail at," I
said to the man in the wire-rimmed glasses. He drummed his fingers on
the armrest of his chair but didn't answer.

The ensuing discussion seemed stilted at first. The Palestinians recounted human rights violations committed by Israeli soldiers—home
searches, administrative detention, curfews. The Israelis expressed shock
and sympathy. I noted that the Palestinians were eager to portray themselves as representatives of a peaceseeking mainstream. The Israelis,
in contrast, presented themselves as members of a small, righteous,
and embattled minority. Both sides used a lot of Marxist code words—
"colonialism," "hegemony," "imperialism," and the favorite all-purpose
aspersion, "fascist"—discordant at a time when the Soviet Union was
the imperialist, colonialist, hegemonic, totalitarian power that the people of Eastern Europe were rising up against.

It reminded me of a conversation I'd had a few months before with
some students from Bethlehem University. It was one of the last trips I
made to the West Bank as a journalist before Ilana put her foot down.
The army had sealed off the campus at the beginning of the uprising,
but like the other Palestinian universities, the school was holding off-
campus classes for those students who lived close by. Roadblocks and
travel restrictions made it nearly impossible for students and faculty
who lived in other parts of the West Bank or in the Gaza Strip to reach
Bethlehem.

I came across the three young men at a café, a student hangout
halfway between the campus and the casbah, the broad market street
lined with souvenir stores that led to Manger Square and the Church of
the Nativity. We chatted about their studies and about politics. The
three identified themselves as members of the student cell of the Popular

Front for the Liberation of Palestine, a radical Marxist faction that had carried out many terrorist attacks in Israel.

"If the uprising were successful and the Palestinians received their state," I asked, "what kind of government would it have?"

"A democracy," they assured me.

"All the signs are that if elections were held today, Arafat's Fatah faction would win," I pointed out.

"That's fine, if that's what the people decide," they said together.

"Okay," I said. "Fatah wins. A few years later, there's another election, and you guys win. What happens then?"

"If that is what the people decide, welcome," they said.

"Then a few years later, you have another election," I continued.

"Oh, no," one of the students corrected me. "Then there won't be any more elections."

"Why not?

"Because once the people have chosen correctly, you don't need elections anymore."

I had none of the sentimentality for Marxism that some of my friends on the left had. The totalitarianism of the left was no better than that of the right, as far as I was concerned. So the Marxism in the air in Beit Sahour disturbed me. On the other hand, I reminded myself, there had been quite a few Marxist ideologues among Israel's founding fathers and mothers. Indeed, our right-wing prime minister, Yitzhak Shamir, had long ago advocated that Israel align itself with the Soviet Union. Most Israeli Marxists had eventually been disabused of their Soviet romance, and the Palestinians might well undergo the same process once they had their own country.

In fact, once the conversation warmed up and the Palestinians spoke about their everyday lives and how the Intifada affected their families and their jobs and their household finances, I couldn't help admiring their standing up to the adversity in which they found themselves. Even if we disagreed about the right way to resolve the conflict, the conversation itself was important. It was a way to keep both sides from forgetting that their adversaries were human beings.

The problem, as I saw it, was that the only Israelis the Palestinians were talking to were the ones who agreed with everything they said. It wasn't a true dialogue if there wasn't disagreement. The people in Beit Sahour shouldn't have been talking to the handful of Israelis who were off in left field. They needed to talk to mainstream Israelis, and mainstream Israelis needed to talk to them. Mainstream Israelis like the men of Company C.

Why not? The idea grabbed me. Over the next few days I suggested it to a few of the guys. Some were doubtful, others sounded interested. I sought out Udi at the university and asked him to help me. He listened to the idea politely and said he thought it might be interesting to try, but he demurred when I asked for his help. He had decided to leave Company C and enlist in the Shin Bet, he told me. Perhaps he figured that his new bosses wouldn't consider such activity appropriate for a new recruit. I made a couple of attempts to set a date for a contingent of Company C men to visit Beit Sahour, but problems kept coming up. One was that most of the guys I wanted to invite couldn't converse comfortably in English and none of them was capable of carrying on this kind of conversation in Arabic. According to Elazar, the Palestinians were unable, or unwilling, to form a group that could speak in Hebrew. Pretty soon I was caught up in my civilian schedule of work and family duties. The Company C–Beit Sahour dialogue never took place.

Ilana was working one of her twenty-four-hour shifts, so I was giving Mizmor and Asor supper. It was their favorite, pasta with my homemade tomato sauce and cheese. They sat at the table as I spooned the shell macaroni into their Mickey Mouse dishes, shredded some cheese on top, and then poured a few spoonfuls of steaming sauce over it. They ate quietly at first, until Mizmor suddenly held up her spoon.

"Asor, do you know what a dialogue is?" she asked in her teacher mode.

Asor stopped shoveling food into his mouth long enough to look down at his plate. "It's not dialogue! It's macaroni!"

Mizmor looked exasperated. "No, Asor, I asked, do you know what a dialogue *is*?"

"It's not dialogue. It's macaroni," said Asor stubbornly.

"A dialogue is two people talking," Mizmor explained.

"Macaroni," Asor mumbled, his mouth full.

Mizmor smiled condescendingly and appealed to authority. "Daddy, isn't a dialogue two people talking?"

"That's right," I said.

Asor glared at me and waved his spoon in the direction of his bowl, spraying tomato sauce every which way. "Daddy, isn't this macaroni?"

"It certainly is," I said.

Asor turned triumphantly to his big sister. "See, it's macaroni!"

Chapter Seven

· DEFENDERS ·

MOUNT HERMON, DECEMBER 1990–JANUARY 1991

THE RAIN BEATING RHYTHMICALLY ON THE BUS'S ROOF COULD
easily have lulled me to sleep, had we not been inching up a narrow
mountain road through a cloud so dense it might have been a forsaken
patch of the primeval waters, never separated into sea and sky. The
driver could barely see two feet in front of him. We all knew this road.
It led from the Lower Ski Lift to the Upper Ski Lift, and then to the outposts on the mountain ridge. We could not see the gorge to our right,
but we knew it was there. The driver had the heat on too high and we'd
shed our coats, but an icy chill penetrated the floorboards and numbed
our feet even as the rest of our bodies sweated. The bus slid on some ice
and I transferred my grip from the worn and battered bus seat to Eiger's
knee.

"It's worse than a helicopter," I muttered.

"Oh, this is nothing," said Eiger, though there was a tremor in his
voice. "When I was in the regular army and we came up here to man the
Yisraeli outpost, it was snowing so hard that—"

"Shut up."

"Don't be so tense. Ilana's not going to have the baby for at least two weeks."

"The way things are looking, I'm never going to see the baby."

It wasn't just the fog. If the army intended to give us a breather from policing the Palestinian territories, it had chosen a bad time to send us back to Mount Hermon. In August, while we'd been on maneuvers, Saddam Hussein had overrun Kuwait. America and its allies deployed forces in the Arabian desert and issued an ultimatum: He was to withdraw unconditionally from Kuwait by January 15, 1991. If he didn't, the United States–led coalition would oust him. Israel was not officially part of the anti-Saddam coalition because the alliance included a number of Arab countries that refused to fight alongside Israel. Israeli and American analysts believed that Saddam would try to divide the alliance by sucking Israel into the war. He would attack with his long-range Scud missiles, perhaps arming them with deadly chemical and biological warheads. Israel would retaliate with its air force, driving the Arab countries out of the coalition. The Americans would then have to change their deployment and strategy. That was the theory.

So the army was on alert, and we were part of it. We'd been assigned to man the Mount Hermon outposts for the period leading up to and past the ultimatum date. Syria, the country we faced on the mountain, was officially aligned with the United States against Iraq, its traditional inter-Arab adversary. But if the Scud scenario played out, Syria might switch sides. Even if it didn't, Israeli leaders worried that this most radical and bellicose of our neighbors would take advantage of the war to harass or even attack us. If the Syrians were to lash out, Mount Hermon, the highest point under Israeli control, would be a key battleground, just as it had been in 1967 and 1973.

"Anyway, you're an idiot to have come," Eiger lectured me. "If my wife were in her ninth month you wouldn't find me anywhere near the army."

"Ben-Ami promised to let me out halfway through. Ilana's fine. The kibbutz is taking good care of her. And at least it's a shorter trip back than it was last time we were up here."

Ben-Ami was crouched tensely next to the bus driver, peering into the fog. As acting company commander, he felt he ought to be up front taking responsibility, even though there was nothing he could do.

"How the hell did headquarters give us clearance to go up this road?" he asked the driver. "This is insane. We're all going to die."

"You think that Golani is going to stay up here another day just because of some fog?" Mizrahi said. Golani was the infantry unit to which Ben-Ami, Eiger, Mizrahi, and many of the guys had belonged during their regular service. It had a reputation as the kind of outfit that would chop down a tree standing in its way rather than walk around it.

As if on cue, the radio leaning against my feet sputtered to life.

"Zach to Yonatan!" "Zach" was the codename for the Golani contingent at the Yisraeli outpost. "Yonatan" was Company C.

"Root, avor," I said into the handset.

"Apex Zach requests to know where the fuck in the world you are, avor." "Apex" was radio talk for "commander."

I queried Ben-Ami with a glance, but before I could transmit his reply, Eiger grabbed the handset.

"From Apex Yonatan. We stopped along the road to work on our tans. Everyone's naked. We'll be on our way in an hour or so. Avor."

Zach's radioman fell silent, pondering this reply.

"Repeat, avor," he requested.

"I repeat, we're working on our tans, avor," Eiger said.

More silence.

"Location, avor."

Eiger shook his head. "Golani," he said.

"Tell him to tell Apex Zach that his men need a course in sarcasm comprehension," Ben-Ami said. He wiped his glasses on the bottom of his undershirt, as if that would help him see through the fog.

The bus halted for a few minutes and then rolled slowly forward.

The raindrops sounded like bullets ricocheting off the bus's roof and windows. The bus stopped again. The driver opened the door.

"What's going on?" Alon asked.

"We're here," Ben-Ami announced.

"We're where?" Falk asked.

A soldier in a dripping green poncho peered into the bus. "Grab your chimidans and make a run for it," he suggested.

"Where to?" I asked. As far as I could see we were alone on a snow-swept crag, too far off to call for help. We had no doubt taken a wrong turn into some sinister world beyond nature where demons in battle dress sought to lead us to our deaths. Or perhaps the driver was in the pay of the enemy and had taken us into hostile territory.

The soldier waved his hand. "Just head in that general direction. Someone will pull you in."

We found ourselves in a small, grimy common room lit by tired yellow fluorescent tubes. It was furnished haphazardly with a shabby couch, an imitation leather office chair on wheels, patched with many shades of duct tape, and several metal chairs, none of which had four legs of identical length. A television was tuned to the education station's fourth-grade English program. Young soldiers dressed in hermonits, the thermal coveralls named for the mountain, sprawled in the chairs. Except for the fact that some of them were smoking, they seemed vegetative. "It's the natural resting state of the Golani man," Mizrahi remarked. "But don't be fooled—there's an enormous amount of energy saved up there for when it's needed."

We rearranged the chairs into a semicircle and the Golani captain briefed us on our duties—guard posts, mostly, and a few patrols. Then he took us on a tour.

Unlike the other outposts we had manned, the Yisraeli was not ours alone. The infantry unit here was not even the primary tenant. The Yisraeli was really a fortress, not an outpost. The Israeli army's center of operations on the upper reaches of Mount Hermon, it perched on the lowest of the mountain's four pinnacles, the only one held by Israel. Its huge network of tunnels and largely subterranean corridors housed intelligence, communications, and command units with secret functions, many locked behind steel doors bearing ominous NO ENTRANCE signs. We would be the sentries protecting the uniformed cognoscenti of the hush-hush. The few we were permitted to see made it abundantly clear that we were but minions in an aerie of military technology far beyond the ken of the foot soldier.

Even Eiger admitted he was having trouble keeping track of the twists and turns and stairways. The base had expanded and metamorphosed beyond what he'd known when he was in the Golani Brigade. By the time we found ourselves back in the common room, we felt completely overwhelmed.

Ben-Ami gathered the company command in a corner.

"Look, guys," he said, his hands clasped on his knees, "this is about as serious an assignment as we've ever had. Saddam is probably going to send some missiles this way and we don't know how our government will react. Syria might well attack. And if it does, it'll be here and we'll be holding the line. And we've got to do that at a time when we've just lost a big chunk of our company command. So we've got to restructure quickly. Everyone's got to pitch in and help out."

Quiet and self-effacing, Ben-Ami always looked as if he were surprised to see the officer's stripes on his shoulders. But when, as Platoon Two's lieutenant, he had to lead his men on a mission, his characteristic attitude of easygoing bemusement fell by the wayside. A year ago, after much urging from Elnatan, he'd enrolled in the army's company commander's course. Upon graduation, Elnatan had appointed him to replace the recently departed Udi as deputy commander of Company C. And it was no secret that Elnatan saw Ben-Ami as his successor.

After six years in the job, Elnatan was the battalion's longest-serving company commander, and the round-robin of high-level exercises, con-

ferences, and site visits the position required, on top of the standard six
weeks of reserve duty, was wearing him out—not to mention the constant paperwork, planning, and phone calls from reservists asking to
have their stints postponed, shortened, or canceled. The battalion commander, Akiva, had no intention of letting Elnatan go and had in fact
been pressuring him to sign up for battalion commander's course. But
first Elnatan needed a little break.

Ben-Ami had adamantly refused to consider the top job. He had a
wife and two babies, a new house in the Galilee, and a high-tech job.
The last thing he needed to do was work overtime for the army. But
Akiva dragged his feet in searching for another candidate, perhaps hoping that a taste of the job would stimulate Ben-Ami's sense of duty.
When we were called up toward the end of December, Ben-Ami found
himself company commander by default. And having refused to move
out of the deputy post, he now had no deputy of his own to help him
out.

Elnatan and Udi weren't the only ones to leave. At our summer maneuvers, Jacques and Yermi had transferred into jobs on the battalion
staff. Soft-spoken Jacques had, incongruously, taken the post of master
sergeant, the official responsible for discipline. It was hard to conceive
of how the unit could function without them.

"We're all with you, Ben-Ami," Falk assured him.

"First, as you know, the whole company isn't staying here," Ben-
Ami continued. "One platoon goes to man the two subsidiary outposts
at 2072 and the Upper Ski Lift. I've decided that it's going to be Platoon
One. Efi and Falk and the bulk of the platoon will go to 2072. Eiger will
take command of the Upper Ski Lift and have five other men with him."

"Which one do I—?" I asked.

"I'll get to you in a minute," Ben-Ami said. "I've asked Mizrahi to
take over Yermi's job as first sergeant." That was the obvious appointment—Mizrahi was the most senior of the platoon sergeants. "Vanunu
will be Platoon Three sergeant." That, too, was obvious—Vanunu, lithe

and agile, had been a newcomer to the company the previous year and had made his mark from the beginning as a dedicated and responsible NCO.

Ben-Ami went on. "Micha is back at the training base getting things ready for the rest of the company. He was supposed to move to the quartermaster unit this year but I asked him to stay with us. But Keisar is going to learn the ropes from him and become deputy first sergeant." Micha was the last of the company's Yom Kippur War veterans, and Keisar's contribution to the organization of the previous year's company party had made this another obvious transfer of duties.

Now he turned to me. "Watzman, I need your help, too."

"Sure," I said nervously. I knew what was coming.

"I know the last thing you want is to be clerk. Well, the last thing I wanted was to be company commander. What I can tell you is that I've seen what Jacques's responsibilities were and I know I can't do my job if I don't have a serious and hardworking company clerk beside me. So I'm asking for your help, Watzman. If you want, it can be for just this time around. But please take it and help me out."

All eyes were on me. I cleared my throat. "Okay," I said. "But three conditions: First, it's just this time. Second, I continue to function as an NCO. I'll go crazy if all I do is push papers. Three, I get no special perks. I get the same conditions and vacations as all the NCOs."

"All that's fine," Ben-Ami said. "Now find the Golani clerk and learn what your duties are."

The perks of the company clerk position were precisely the things I didn't like about the job. I needed to be busy and challenged, a requirement my Golani-trained friends thought perverse at best. A good infantryman rests whenever possible and never volunteers for extra assignments. There were plenty of long hikes and sleepless nights and special missions to go around, so it was best to save energy when you could. A running army joke has it that the minute you put an infantry-man in a uniform he falls asleep.

My inability to subscribe to that wisdom in my regular service eventually became a personal crisis. I finished NCO school with a very low overall grade. My high marks in self-discipline and camaraderie didn't make up for my general klutziness and inability to bark out orders instinctively during command exercises. When we were assigned to active units at the end of the course, it was clear to me that I'd be a failure as an NCO in a forward post. But the course instructors assigned me to the field regiment of my infantry unit, Nachal, which was then, in the spring of 1983, holding the front line in the Beka'a Valley in eastern Lebanon.

The deputy regimental commander sat with two colleagues in an office on the NCO school base. When I was summoned into the room, I saw them looking impassively at my file.

"So," said the commander, laying down the papers in front of him. "Welcome to our regiment. Maybe you can say a few words about how you see your service with us."

I swallowed hard and proceeded with the speech I'd prepared in my head.

"I'm going to be totally honest," I said. "First, I realize that there's a war on and that you need everyone you can get. I know you're desperate for corporals and sergeants for the front-line outposts, and if you assign me to serve there, I won't try to get out of it."

"Very good," the deputy commander said, folding his hands in front of him. "So we'll assign you to—"

"But," I interrupted, "you've seen my file. You see that I'm not very good at this stuff. In a front-line outpost, the lives of other soldiers will be in my hands. A bad move or misjudgment by me can have awful consequences. I've got serious doubts about whether I'm the right person for that kind of responsibility. I'm not trying to make excuses. I just want everything to be on the table. I'll accept any decision you make."

The deputy commander looked me in the eye. "I've got no doubt that when you're on patrol with your platoon and are attacked you will know exactly what to do. You're right, we need you in the outposts. You'll be just fine."

But the officer to the deputy commander's left turned to him. "There's an opening in the regimental intelligence office for an operations sergeant. Maybe that's the place for him."

The three of them conferred for a few seconds and rendered their decision: I would go to the regimental base's intelligence office, just behind the front line.

The job turned out to be all too easy. The main duty of the intelligence sergeants was to man the radio set, keeping a log of intelligence alerts and notifications. Other than that, we pasted up maps needed for missions and staff conferences and tended to the armored personnel carrier we would man if a hot war resumed. With our section as overstaffed as a government office in Israel's old socialist era, each of us was assigned only a few hours of duty a day. We were still a far forward base, close to the Syrians and Lebanese, and there was plenty of danger. But I had more free hours than I could fill by reading or shooting the bull with other soldiers, or even with the correspondence course in the history of the biblical period in which I had enrolled. I quickly became depressed, and I was plagued with guilt for not having gone to an outpost. On a couple of occasions I notified my superior, the regimental intelligence officer, that I wanted to be reassigned. Each time he talked me out of it. I ended up serving out my mandatory time as an intelligence sergeant and hating it. I vowed that in the reserves I would never, under any circumstances, accept another headquarters or paper-pushing job. And that's exactly what Jacques's job looked like to me.

But when I reported for duty and saw Ben-Ami alone at the top, I knew what he was going to ask of me and I knew that I couldn't turn him down. So in December 1990, at the age of thirty-four, I became company clerk.

Because of my previous intransigence, I'd had no opportunity to be trained on the job by Jacques. But I learned my basic responsibilities quickly. I had to make the daily duty roster, help Ben-Ami work out the vacation schedule, and file a daily report about the number and locations of Company C's men with both the outpost's and our battalion's personnel division. All of this turned out to be very simple. Because we were on alert, the general command had jacked up the number of infantrymen required at each base, and there were more men than I needed for our routine assignments. When the level of alert was boosted again in early January, home leaves were canceled and I didn't have the comings and goings of my soldiers to track. I was able to divide guard duty into two-hour stints instead of the usual three or four. The guys had plenty of time to rest, play backgammon, and watch television, so everyone thought I was doing a great job. Of course, there was still plenty to bitch about. We did not have our own kitchen and cook as we usually did, and the base's central mess hall was cramped and unpleasant, serving the worst of institutional and military fare. As for our accommodations, most of the men slept in rooms that were little more than corridors lined, submarine-style, with three-story bunks.

I sometimes assigned myself to a guard post to show the guys I didn't think my new position got me special privileges. I also regularly scheduled myself to lead the "necklace," the break-of-dawn patrol circling the outpost. After that first stormy day, the weather had cleared and most mornings were sunny, if chilly. Occasional rain and some mild snowfall kept the necklace path muddy, but the view of the Syrian plateau beneath us, hazy in the early light, was worth the muck on our boots. We could see villages and make out the outlines of army camps

and the "pita" earthworks of Syrian outposts of the kind we endlessly
practiced taking in our maneuvers. Beyond them, some thirty kilometers
away, lay the sprawling streets of Damascus, the enemy capital. To the
north, on the peak on the other side of the saddle formed by an intervening wadi, was Snowview, the Yisraeli's smaller companion outpost—
where, we had heard, accommodations were far superior to our own.
Towering above Snowview was the nearest of the three Syrian peaks of
Mount Hermon. At dawn we could still see the searchlight of the UN
post on its slope, a rather sorry-looking attempt to keep Israeli and Syrian troops separated, dating from the Six-Day War. Above it, on the
pinnacle, was a ring of light marking a Syrian outpost. In the mud below us we could find, with the help of the bedouin scout who accompanied us, the tracks of foxes, mountain deer, and wild pigs.

I could get an even better view of the sunrise from the other assignment I took for myself. On our first day at the base, a cocky-looking
young blond guy with sergeant's stripes and a slight American accent
had shown up in our common room and grabbed my shoulder.

"You will send three NCOs to the command post to be trained to
man it at night," he ordered me.

"Who says?" I asked.

"The base operations officer and me."

"Who are you?"

"I'm Paul, chief operations sergeant, and I expect your coopera-
tion," he said. He then turned on his heel and walked away.

I made a few inquiries and discovered that this was indeed one of
the duties of the infantry unit manning the Yisraeli. That night Alon
Mizrahi, and I followed mysterious corridors and climbed stairways and
a ladder to reach the command post. It was a spacious room in army
terms, filled with radio equipment, two large desks, a comfortable exec-
utive chair, and the obligatory coffee corner. Its south, east, and north
walls were Plexiglas windows providing a sweeping view of Syria and,
to the south, the Golan Heights. The room seemed to be perched on top

of the world, like the fortress of an evil genius thirsting for global domination in a superhero movie.

"The Syrians have built up their forces down there in recent weeks," Paul informed us, pointing out specific outposts that had been converted from platoon to company or from company to battalion strength.

"If they begin to go into attack formation," he said, "we'll be the first to see them. You'll be the man responsible for relaying the news to the commanders here and then to the general staff in Tel Aviv. It's an incredible responsibility."

"If the Syrians are planning to attack, the general staff is going to have intelligence about it long before we see anything," Alon said.

"Right. Just like in 1973," Paul scoffed. He was referring to the Yom Kippur War, when the Israeli army was caught unprepared by an Egyptian-Syrian joint offensive.

Sitting there, well supplied with coffee and cookies, I'd wait for the classic hour of the surprise attack. But each dawn was quiet. Syria looked peaceful and sleepy under my watchful eye.

I headed out at a good clip. It was downhill from the Yisraeli to the Upper Ski Lift base; the steep climb back was the hard part. Other guys complained about being short of breath when they ran at this elevation, but it didn't seem to bother me.

My responsibilities as company clerk tied me to the company commander. I was no longer part of Platoon One, whose members were the guys to whom I was closest in the unit. So most days, like this one—Thursday, January 10—I took a noontime run to visit them at the two bases where they were stationed. I'd heard the news just before I'd set out that day. The UN secretary-general was on his way to Baghdad in a last-ditch effort to prevent war. The Americans were expected to complete the evacuation of their diplomats and nationals from Iraq by Saturday, meaning that the war could begin as early as Sunday. But the United States would more likely wait for the ultimatum to run out next Tuesday.

There was snow along the roadside but the sun shone overhead. The air was crisp. It was perfect running weather—too chilly to stand for long outside in shorts and a T-shirt but just right when you're on the move. My short M-16 felt light and comfortable in my right hand. As I took the incline to the Upper Ski Lift base I was hailed by Marcel Levy, who was sitting in the crow's nest guard post on the roof of the base's main building, huddled in his hermonit.

"It is the company clerk!" he announced to no one in particular. "When am I going home?"

"No one's going home, Marcel."

"No one, of course. But what about me?"

I found Achlama in the kitchen, carefully placing orange slices on a plate piled high with steaming fried chicken schnitzel. Achlama wasn't in Platoon One, but he'd wrangled a reassignment to Eiger's base from me and Ben-Ami.

"I hope you haven't come for lunch," he frowned. "We've barely got enough for the people here." The shelves around us sagged under the weight of emergency supplies of flour, eggs, and canned goods.

"I won't eat. But I'll remember it next time you want a weekend home."

Achlama drew his hand thoughtfully over his glowing orange beard. "You know what I don't like about you, Watzman?" he asked.

"No, what?"

"Everything," he said, aiming an orange slice at my nose.

There was a shout from above. "Watzman! Is he out yet?"

Eiger ambled down the steps from the base's command post. He'd gained weight over the years and seemed to have packed on another kilogram or two in the last week.

"As of last night, when I talked to Ilana, no, he's not out yet."

Eiger gestured toward the stainless-steel institutional refrigerator. "We don't know what to do with all the food. They're sending us supplies for an entire brigade. Even with the reinforcements we can't eat it all. We're considering export."

"To the Arabs," Achlama said.

"You must be getting our supplies. Yesterday they gave us warmed-over goulash from cans of field rations. I can't stand it anymore," I said. "If I'm going to have to inhale nerve gas, don't I at least deserve some decent meals first?"

"Last night we got orders to break out the gas masks," Eiger said. "Na'ama had to seal up a safe room at home all by herself. Sounds like she bought enough plastic sheeting to cover the entire building."

"You should have seen the show we had to watch," I said. "No points for guessing who's the Yisraeli's biological and chemical defense warden. The whole company got called down to the bomb shelter and that arrogant schmuck Paul lectured us like we were kindergarten kids. How to put on the mask, how to take it off, how to inject ourselves with atropine, the works."

"I just told the guys: Put one of these on if you smell something funny," Eiger said.

"The problem is that everywhere Eiger goes, something smells funny," Achlama observed. Eiger smacked him in the back of the head.

"The weird thing is the drill. If there's a missile attack, we're all sup-posed to run for the shelter," I said. "It makes no sense."

"Watzman would prefer to die a painful, heroic death," Achlama said to Eiger.

"Not just now, thanks. I want to see the baby first."

"How can the army take a man away from his wife in her ninth month of pregnancy? I don't understand it," Eiger said. "Anyway, it's your fault. You should have made a scene. Ben-Ami would have can-celed your orders."

"When there's about to be a war? Leave me alone."

"She'll probably manage much better without him," Achlama

said. "Watzman's the type to go into sympathetic labor. The nurses will all take care of him and leave poor Ilana to push the baby out herself."

"My luck is that we're living at a kibbutz now," I said. "Communal life can be a pain, but there're two situations in which it gives you a kind of support you don't get anywhere else. Having a baby and having a war. Now we're having both."

"Lucky bastard," Achlama agreed, munching on a schnitzel. "Eiger, call everyone for lunch."

I'd returned to Tirat Zvi, the kibbutz that had adopted me for the duration of my regular army service—this time with my family. On our occasional visits to the kibbutz our friends always tried to convince us to settle there, but we were happy in Jerusalem. During 1990, though, we began to reconsider. Ilana was sick of her job as an airport meteorologist and was looking for an excuse to take a year off. My work was slow and I was feeling unsure of my ability to support my family as a writer and translator. When Ilana became pregnant again, we were also faced with the fact that our small apartment would soon be cramped. There seemed no way we could afford a larger apartment in our neighborhood, Baka, where gentrification was driving up housing prices. We wanted to remain part of Kehilat Yedidya, but perhaps we just couldn't afford to live in Jerusalem.

We had a hard time picturing ourselves eating meals in a public dining room and adjusting to the other intrusions on private life that a communal framework involved. But, on the other hand, if we made Tirat Zvi our home, we wouldn't have to worry about our day-to-day income, and the kibbutz had an active cultural schedule that included reading groups and religious study. After putting in a few years of work, most young members were allowed to take a year or two off for university or other study, paid for by the kibbutz. And we liked and admired a number of people there, among them Doron and Ruth, a couple our age who already had seven children. In my eyes at least, Doron, with his mussy blond curls, was the kibbutz ideal—he worked the cotton fields by day and read serious literature at night.

We indicated our interest, the kibbutz sent a delegation to visit us in Jerusalem, and in August we moved to Tirat Zvi for a trial year, at the end of which we were free to stay or to leave, no hard feelings. The kibbutz assigned Ilana to the staff of the communal kitchen and me to the turkey run, allowing me a couple hours off each day to continue to operate, in a limited way, as a writer and translator.

During Israel's early decades, the kibbutzim were the strongholds of the military service ethos. A high proportion of army officers and top soldiers came from this tiny sector of the population. By the time of the Gulf War, the military tradition had waned somewhat, but it was still strong. Nearly the first question I was asked by every new male acquaintance at the kibbutz was, "And where are you in the army?" At Kehilat Yedidya I was exceptional because I served as a soldier in a combat military unit. At Tirat Zvi I was exceptional because I wasn't an officer and belonged "merely" to the infantry, rather than to a commando, air force, or other superelite unit.

While we worked much harder than we'd expected and had a difficult time with many aspects of communal life, Ilana and I loved to see Mizmor and Asor running free in a way we could never have allowed in the city. And it was hard to see how Ilana, nine months pregnant, could have managed alone in our Jerusalem apartment while I was in the army. On the kibbutz, our neighbors had sealed up a room for her and the kids, and the kibbutz ambulance would get her to the hospital in Afula if anything happened suddenly.

A stiff breeze unsettled the graying hair of Uzi, the Yisraeli outpost's commander. It was Saturday morning and a dozen Company C men were gathered around the soft-featured, avuncular colonel on a rocky outcropping a short walk from the base's iron gate. He had come by the common room the previous night and offered to give us a talk on the battle for Mount Hermon in the Yom Kippur War. It would be a first-hand account—Uzi had helped retake the mountain as deputy commander of one of the Paratrooper Brigade's battalions. Now in his late forties, he would be retiring in a few months.

The Yom Kippur War remains an open wound in the Israeli body politic. It was a war for survival that Israel almost lost. The debate over which failings, and whose mistakes, brought the country to the brink continues to this day. But it is generally acknowledged that a major factor was the hubris that Israelis, and in particular their military leaders, developed after the stunning victory of the Six-Day War, when the IDF had seemed invincible and Arab armies comically incompetent. Officers, soldiers, reservists, politicians, and civilians all believed that if the enemy were ever so foolish as to attack again, Israel's victory would come swiftly and at little cost. Now Uzi, nearing the end of his own military service, and with his country facing both an uprising in the occupied territories and the possibility of a general Middle Eastern war, had a message he wanted to convey to us.

"The Yisraeli as you see it now is much larger than it was then," he began. "Over the years we've added annexes and facilities. But even then it was the largest outpost on the Mount Hermon peak.

"Like now, it was, as we like to say, the country's ears. The base's main purpose was to gather intelligence, and most of the sixty soldiers who were here on the day the war began were connected to that mission in one way or another. Even though it was on the Syrian border, it was considered a routine and not particularly dangerous assignment. So much so that only every other soldier had a rifle—half the soldiers here were totally unarmed! It's hard to believe, given what happened, but that's how confident the army was then. The standing orders about issuing rifles didn't change even in the days leading up to the attack, when Syria massed forces on the plain below. Everyone believed they were just holding large-scale maneuvers. Maybe you remember that the previous spring the army had called up reserves because of similar force movements that turned out to be just maneuvers.

"The northern command put forces here on alert on October sixth, Yom Kippur morning, but nothing really changed. Then the Syrian artillery bombardment began at two p.m. and there was panic. The base's electricity went out. You can imagine how hard it was to see in those tunnels with no lights. Four Syrian helicopters landed commando forces here, not far from where we're standing. Two more Syrian companies attacked from the Syrian peak up there. The commandos advanced on the Yisraeli. Some of our soldiers ran for the bunker, which they thought the Syrians could never penetrate. In the tunnels they couldn't tell who was friend and who was foe, and some fought their own comrades in the dark. Another group of soldiers hid in the air-conditioning ducts. The Syrians discovered the bunker's emergency exit and blew it in. They slaughtered most of the men inside and took the rest prisoner. A force under the base commander managed to escape from the outpost and tried to get down the mountain, but near the Upper Ski Lift they ran into a Syrian ambush. Five of them were killed and two taken prisoner. Only ten managed to get safely behind Israeli lines. Out of the entire force at the base, thirteen of our men were killed and thirty-one taken prisoner. The whole thing took just an hour or so, and the Syrians ruled the Mount Hermon peak. In the meantime, our forces below on the Golan Heights were desperately trying to hold the Syrians back. By the way, Iraq sent a division to fight alongside the Syrians.

"Fast-forward two weeks. It's Saturday, October twentieth. Israel has retaken the Golan and pushed into Syria, halting along the road to Damascus at the insistence of the Americans. But Mount Hermon remains in Syrian hands. The Northern Command issues orders to retake the mountain. At the foot of the slope there is chaos. Supplies we need aren't there, the plans aren't clear, the commanders of the different brigades waste time bickering over who will take what route and what objectives. Everyone wants glory.

"It's a two-pronged strategy. The paratroopers will be landed on the slope of the Syrian peak there to our north. They'll take the Syrian posts up there to keep them from shooting down at Golani, who will climb the mountain along three routes to retake the Yisraeli.

"Saturday night at two a.m. the paratrooper forces are landed on the Syrian slope. You can see the spot if you follow my finger—there, the bare ledge just to the right of the green patch about three-quarters of the way up, near the UN post. As deputy brigade commander, I stay below, to manage the logistics.

"The Syrians quickly detect the paratroops and begin strafing them with airplanes and artillery. The paratroops have night-vision binoculars but it's hazy and they don't help much. There's a strong, freezing wind. Rain and snow begin to fall. The paratroops aren't adequately equipped. No hermonits, no way. You guys know those American coats the army used to issue, the ones with the removable linings. You guys all avoid them when they turn up in the supplies because they're nowhere near as warm as our dubons. That's all they had. You know how the wind slices right through them. Wool gloves, the kind that make your fingers freeze the minute they get wet. Regular, standard-issue army boots that seem to conduct the cold if you're standing on a rocky ledge in a snowdrift. The men are freezing and they can't find their way in the storm. They radio us for reinforcements and supplies. I'm down at base, I have the supplies ready, but I can't get a helicopter. Too risky to fly there, the pilots say. I keep radioing back that we're on the way, we're on the way. But we aren't.

"The force tries to use that outcropping there as cover from the wind and the shelling, but it's really no protection. Some guys are fainting, others can't move anymore. One soldier takes the initiative and decides to lead a party to find a safer spot. He navigates as best he can, but it's like that painting that I'm sure some of you have seen, *The Blind Leading the Blind*. After an hour, he finds that he's made a big circle and come back to the rest of the force.

"The storm lasts only until dawn, but it seems like forever to the men and to me down below. Finally we're able to get choppers to them with supplies and reinforcements. They take the Syrian positions. Golani has reached the top by now and the Syrians retreat. Mount Hermon is ours again."

Uzi was staring at the ground. He kicked a rock over the ledge, and after a few seconds we heard it bounce off the slope below.

"Some of the guys who were up there on the Syrian peak never spoke to me again. I'd run into them sometimes in the city and they'd look the other way, cross the street to avoid me. I left the army. I hadn't been a good commander. I hadn't been there when my men needed me. I should have prepared them better. I should have found some way to get them help.

"But then, after some time went by, I decided I was wrong. I'd run away. The way to make it up to those men—even if they continued to think, for the rest of their lives, that I'd failed them—was to go back to the army and make sure that the next time we were more prepared. So I came back, and eventually they made me commander of the Yisraeli."

He gazed at the base, rising on the hill beside us like a medieval fortress with antennae.

"We're as ready for an attack as we can be. I don't think it's going to happen in this war, but if it does, we're ready. What I'm asking you guys to do is to be ready, too. I know all the jokes about the infantry. But don't be too relaxed. Don't be too cool. Don't be overconfident. And never underestimate your enemies. You are the guys who are going to be the outpost's first line of defense if it's attacked. Take that seriously."

On Tuesday the ultimatum deadline arrived and we went on high alert—though this had little effect on our routine. As expected, Iraq refused to withdraw from Kuwait. We gathered around the television, waiting for the United States to attack. Thursday morning at 2 a.m. the guards woke us up. The allied air offensive had begun. We dressed quickly. We were on call and ready for action. The television broadcast news reports interspersed with comedy skits and musical numbers. A lot of us tried to call home, but very few got through on the country's overloaded phone lines. At dawn we did the standard daily defensive drill that we knew from every border outpost where we'd ever served. Dawn was generally considered the most likely time of day for a Syrian assault, but we assumed that if Saddam fired missiles, he'd do so at night. So after the drill, we began to sleep in shifts, leaving a large contingent of men dressed and ready at any given time.

Saddam fired his first Scuds the next night. American satellites identified flashes in western Iraq soon after 2 a.m. Israel time. The coalition command quickly relayed the information to Israel, and air raid sirens throughout the country sounded. Those of us who were sleeping—with our boots on—jumped out of bed and grabbed our rifles and gas mask kits. The guards remained at their posts while the rest of us headed into the corridors and down to the bomb shelter. The crowd included many faces we recognized from the base's corridors but also the pale faces of soldiers we had never seen, guys who'd emerged from secret wings like cicadas surfacing after larval years underground. We put on our gas masks, as the drill required. Some guys had brought transistor radios, but reception was bad through the concrete and metal surrounding us, and the echoes in the sealed bunker made it hard to discern the words that did come through. After a few minutes, when it was clear that there had been but a single barrage, guys began talking off their gas masks. We waited for news.

Rumors passed from one cluster of soldiers to another. Missiles had fallen on Tel Aviv, on Jerusalem, on Haifa. In Holon, where Ilana's mother and sister lived, one had hit a hospital. Micha panicked when he heard that—he lived not far away. The warheads had been chemical, or biological, or inert, depending on which rumor you believed. A cloud of poison gas had engulfed Hadera, the site of Israel's largest electricity plant.

A sense of helplessness permeated the room. Why were we putting up with the cold and the damp and the uncomfortable beds and the bad food if not to protect our families and the civilian population as a whole? Yet we weren't where the missiles were falling. We weren't even keeping an eye on the Syrians or patrolling the border to detect infiltrators. We were doing exactly what our wives and children were doing at home—sitting in a sealed room, listening to the radio, waiting for the all-clear signal.

Unlike many of the other guys, I had no real fears for my own family. Outlying settlements were unlikely targets in this war. Saddam would presumably aim his missiles at densely populated areas and important infrastructure. Tirat Zvi, on the border with Jordan, was, ironically, one of the safest places in the country.

After half an hour we were given the all-clear and returned to the common area. From the television we learned which rumors were true and which fiction. Two missiles had indeed hit Haifa and six more had come down in the Tel Aviv area. None had been armed with chemical warheads. We assumed that they'd been aimed at the army's general staff headquarters.

They had caused considerable property damage—the television news soon broadcast pictures of gutted apartments—but they had not killed anyone directly. However, three elderly Jewish women and one Arab child were reported to have suffocated when they put on gas masks improperly.

Everyone wanted to call home, of course, and we agreed that each conversation would be limited to three minutes, just enough time to check that all was well. When it was my turn, there was no answer at our house. I dialed the number of our next-door neighbors. They answered cheerily and put Ilana on the line. It sounded like a party was going on in the background.

"I gather that everything's okay," I said.

"The kids are having a great time," said Ilana. "When the siren went off they were scared, so we came over here instead of staying at home. Mizmor and Asor put on their gas masks like professionals. Now they're having some ice cream."

"No baby?"

"No baby. Are they going to let you out?"

"They promised, but who knows?"

The situation felt totally incongruous, especially after Uzi's talk. In this new kind of war, border outposts like this one, and settlements, originally built as bulwarks on the country's vulnerable frontier, were the safest places to be, while far from us, in the country's interior, civilians were in danger. Whatever security weapons could confer was being provided by the Patriot antimissile batteries deployed and manned in Israel by Americans, and by the coalition air forces seeking out and destroying Iraqi mobile missile launchers. While some of the guys talked tough about the need for Israel to send its own air force to punish Iraq, most of us were relieved when Prime Minister Shamir ordered no response. He'd been bellicose in previous weeks, warning the United States that Israel could not sit on its hands if attacked. But in the end he seemed to reach the same conclusion as the rest of us—that Israel could not afford to interfere with the battle plan of the American-led coalition. This was one war others would have to fight for us.

I was supposed to have gone home that day. Ilana's due date was the following Tuesday, and Ben-Ami had originally promised to let me go home a week early. But no one was getting discharged as long as we were on alert. Another missile attack occurred the next morning. But while the Scuds were causing a lot of damage, none of them bore chemical or biological warheads. Apparently the army's worst fears were eased. On Sunday, battalion headquarters notified Ben-Ami that a handful of urgent requests for discharge had been approved. Mine was one of them. I telephoned the news to Ilana, who felt as though labor might commence at any minute.

After packing my chimidan and my army equipment, I hitched a ride to the battalion at the Lower Ski Lift base. I returned my gear and signed out at the personnel office. Under normal circumstances that would have freed me, but because of the alert I needed the battalion commander or his surrogate to approve my discharge form. The surrogate on duty was Reuven, the operations officer. He took the form from me and was about to sign it when he gave me a look.

"Where's your gas mask?"

"I returned it," I said, assuming that he was worried about a shortfall in the supply room.

"I have orders from high up that we can't release anyone without a gas mask. There might still be a chemical attack," he said.

"So give me a gas mask."

"I can't," Reuven replied. "You've signed out. You're a civilian now. You can't take army gear with you. Where's your civilian gas mask?"

"It's at home, of course. They didn't issue them to civilians until after our call-up."

"I can't let you go unless someone brings you your civilian mask," Reuven said, putting his pen down.

"Reuven, my wife is going to go into labor any minute. I've got to get home."

"Those are the orders. Where do you live?"

"At Tirat Zvi."

"Great. It's a kibbutz. Call them and tell them to send someone with your gas mask."

I realized that Reuven was serious. I called home, and Ilana, after a flurry of consultations with neighbors and friends, found a solution. The kibbutz would give Doron a car and he'd drive up with my gas mask and take me home.

There was a problem, though. The car was needed back at the kibbutz in three hours. That was enough time for Doron to get to Kiryat Shmonah, the town in the valley below us, and to bring me back, but not to make the trip up the mountain to the Lower Ski Lift. I'd have to meet him in Kiryat Shmonah. Reuven balked even at that until, finally, I put him on the phone with the kibbutz manager, who assured him that Doron was already setting out. Reuven agreed to let me go on the reasonable assumption that Saddam would not aim a chemical warhead at the Mount Hermon–Kiryat Shmonah road during the coming hour.

Heaving my chimidan onto my shoulder, I walked out of the base and down to the road to hitch a ride into Kiryat Shmonah. Then I realized I had another problem. Because of the alert there was none of the usual civilian traffic, and even military traffic was severely curtailed. I waited half an hour before a car showed up. It was the soldier who ran the canteen at the Mount Hermon regiment base. He had to get to Kiryat Shmonah to buy supplies. Alert or no alert, the regiment's men and women needed their Turkish coffee and chocolate wafers. I was lucky that he'd circled up to the Lower Ski Lift base for no good reason at all, rather than heading straight down into the valley.

An amused Doron was waiting for me at the Kiryat Shmonah bus station. He handed me my civilian chemical/biological warfare kit, its seal still unbroken.

"Now I feel safe," I sighed. "Any news?"

"As of an hour and a half ago, no baby," he said.

At Tirat Zvi the war was in many ways more palpable than it had been on Mount Hermon. No one left home without a cardboard gas mask box hanging from his shoulder. The kibbutz used its closed-circuit television network to broadcast updates and defense information. The forces manning the nearby outposts along the Jordan River had been beefed up, and uniformed reservists showed up at the kibbutz store to buy snacks and toothpaste. The factory outlet store at the kibbutz's meat-processing plant did a brisk business in hot dogs and steaks.

There were two more missile attacks before Ilana's contractions began, the following Wednesday afternoon, the day Company C was discharged from Mount Hermon. Falk went back to Jerusalem, where

American-manned Patriots fired at the Iraqi rockets. Wagner got home to his apartment in Haifa at 7 p.m., and at 9:30 an Iraqi missile landed a quarter of a mile away in the wadi below his building. The windows on that side of his home shattered.

Ilana and I were driven in a kibbutz car to the hospital in Afula. It was on combat footing. Maternity stays were limited to twenty-four hours—beds had to be kept open in case of a major emergency. Cartons of medicine, bandages, and IVs were stacked in the corridors. All elective surgery had been canceled and noncritical patients sent home, leaving the building eerily quiet and empty. We had our gas masks with us, of course, and the midwife briefed Ilana on how her mask would be placed on her face if Saddam dropped gas on Afula while she was giving birth.

Niot was born on Thursday morning.

"But we can't send him home without a *mamat*," the head nurse told me. The *mamat* was the plastic tent that the civil defense authorities issued for babies in lieu of a mask. So I had to go back to Tirat Zvi with Niot's birth certificate, sign out a *mamat* for him, and show it to the hospital staff before I could bring my son home. Fitted out with our defensive gear, Ilana and Niot and I headed back to Tirat Zvi.

A war was on, and we were home, and home was where the war was.

Chapter Eight

· AMBUSHES ·

TUBAS, JUNE–JULY 1992

THREE YEARS AFTER WE'D LEFT THE HALF-BUILT HOUSE IN BEIT Sahour we were back in the West Bank. My mental state was *shavuz*, an army slang acronym that designates a mood of weariness and despair. The occupation, and Palestinian resistance to it, dragged on. Israel's new leadership promised to bargain seriously with the Palestinians, but in the meantime we had to serve a month in Tubas, a large village between Jenin and Nablus.

The Palestinians' popular uprising had petered out. We now seldom faced demonstrations or large groups of attackers. Instead, we faced individual snipers and bomb throwers waiting in ambush. They struck only intermittently, but their weapons were deadlier than the rocks of the Intifada's first years. "The Intifada has changed," I wrote to a friend in the United States. "We get very few stones thrown at us and ignore the slogans painted on the walls (of which there are very few new ones), and generally the locals and we try to have only the minimum necessary contact with each other. But then, once a week or so, someone tries to kill us."

Ten years later I'd find the words that expressed how I felt. "In a tactical sense, you have become nothing / But flanks," writes the poet David Wagoner, under the title "What to Do When Surrounded":

> To such fundamental questions
> As *Where Is the Enemy?* and *Where*
> *Should I Direct my Fire?* your answers
> Have been reduced to a simple minimum:
> *Anywhere and Everywhere.*

Wagoner, being a poet, certainly knew that he wrote not only of the enemy but also of friends.

For loyalties, too, can encircle you. If you train your eye on one, the others can sneak up behind you. If you try to watch them all, you end up firing at the gaps between them. I was confused and tired. Was my first obligation to my family or to my comrades? To the present occupation or the future coexistence that it now seemed might turn from dream to reality after so many years of waiting? To higher principles or to the gray, quotidian, imperfect choices that the village of Tubas forced on me?

The army began our tour in Tubas with an election. The soldiers were to enlist on election day itself, Tuesday, June 23, and to vote at the training base where we'd get organized. As usual, officers and NCOs were called up a day early. I'd assumed that we'd also vote on Tuesday, but when we arrived in Tubas to be briefed by the unit we were replacing, the regional command told us that we had to vote a day early, as active army units in the field do. We lined up at the improvised polling station.

The Israeli public's mood had changed since the election of 1988, toward the end of our service in Jenin, when it elected the Likud's Yitzhak Shamir to another term as prime minister. Despite Israel's best efforts to suppress the uprising, the Palestinians had won an important victory. They'd demonstrated to the Israeli public that the occupation came at a cost. Before the winter of 1987, most Israelis could ignore the occupied territories while enjoying the open spaces and cheap labor they provided. The Jewish settlers in the territories seemed like a contemporary incarnation of the Zionist settlers of the early twentieth century— brave and resourceful pioneers civilizing a backward and largely unpopulated wilderness.

The Intifada shattered that myth. It forced Israel's citizens—Company C's men included—to face up to the existence among them of a nation with its own language, history, and culture that did not want to be ruled by the Jewish state. This nation would not agree to be exploited for the convenience of the Israeli economy. More and more Israelis began to acknowledge that the Palestinians had a legitimate claim to the same right the Jews demanded for themselves: self-determination. In the public eye, the settlers were no longer self-sacrificing patriots. Tentatively, Israelis began to understand that the settlements, at least those deliberately established in the midst of large concentrations of Palestinians, were an obstacle to reaching an accommodation with the Arabs.

The Israeli right had misread the new world order that emerged in the early 1990s. Leaders like Prime Minister Shamir and Ariel Sharon believed that the collapse of the Soviet empire and the American-led victory over Iraq were the beginning of the end of the Palestinian national movement. Bereft of a superpower sponsor's financial and institutional support, the flag bearer of Palestinian nationalism, Yasir Arafat's Palestine Liberation Organization, would wither away. With major Arab countries now allied with the United States against the Arab expansionism of Iraq, the Palestinian people would realize that their hopes for a state of their own were in vain, and the local Palestinian leadership in the West Bank and Gaza Strip would reconcile itself to Israeli suzerainty. But the rest of the world didn't see it that way. The United

States, Western Europe, and the Western-aligned Arab countries, as well as the Israeli left, saw an opportunity to find a solution to the Israel-Arab conflict that would answer the needs of both peoples.

We on the left believed that the Intifada had proved that holding on to the territories, even were it militarily and politically possible, would be a huge mistake for Israel. With Palestinian population growth in the West Bank and Gaza Strip far outstripping that of Israeli Jews, Jews would soon be a minority in the land between the Jordan River and the Mediterranean Sea. Zionism had always been a democratic movement and as such was predicated on achieving a Jewish state with a sizable Jewish majority. If the Jews were to become a minority, the state would either cease to be Jewish or cease to be democratic. Both those possibilities were catastrophic in their implications. We hoped that, with the Soviet Union in pieces and Iraq defeated, the Palestinian leadership, Arafat included, would realize that Israel was here to stay and that the Palestinians would have to fulfill their national destiny in a state composed of the West Bank and Gaza Strip.

Immediately after the Gulf War, the United States commenced efforts to convene a Middle East peace conference. Shamir didn't like the idea and issued a number of conditions. In keeping with his hope that he could eventually cut a deal with tractable local leaders in the territories, he vetoed PLO involvement in the conference and even said no to a separate Palestinian delegation. After arduous negotiations, Shamir agreed—over the objections of colleagues to his right—that the Jordanian delegation could include Palestinian representatives from the West Bank and Gaza Strip who were not officially associated with the PLO. The conference opened on October 19, 1991, in Madrid with a framework that included both bilateral negotiations between Israel and its neighbors and multilateral negotiations over regional issues.

Israelis like me were happy to see our country talking with the Palestinians and our Arab neighbors. It was clear from Shamir's statements, however, that he was playing a waiting game. He planned to drag out the negotiations as he continued to build settlements, creating an Israeli presence in the territories so large and ensconced that it could never be evacuated. Under such conditions, he believed, the territories would remain Israel's forever. The people with whom I sided argued that our government could not dictate to the Palestinians who their negotiating representatives would be. To achieve peace, we would have to talk to those whom the Palestinians saw as their leaders—Arafat and his associates. We might not like them, but only they could lead their people into an accommodation based on the establishment of a demilitarized Palestinian state that would accept Israel.

As the 1992 elections neared, three small pro-peace parties on the left united into a faction called Meretz to promote this approach. The much larger Labor party was not yet ready to support a Palestinian state or negotiations with the PLO, but a significant proportion of its members in the Knesset advocated moving the party in that direction. Furthermore, Labor had ousted its longtime chief, Shimon Peres, in favor of Yitzhak Rabin. In my opinion, Peres had been an ineffectual leader. More pointedly, Labor had not won any of the four elections in which Peres had stood at the party's helm. While Rabin said he opposed a Palestinian state and rejected negotiations with the PLO, he was also critical of Shamir's intransigence and of the settlements. He believed Israel must reach an accommodation with the Palestinians so that it could focus on the real military threats—Iraq and Iran. Most important, as a military hero, former chief of staff, and the defense minister who had taken a hard line against Palestinian terrorism in the Intifada, Rabin looked to me like a man who could convince the public that Israel would be stronger and more secure if it ended the settlement enterprise, reached a compromise with the Arabs, and evacuated the territories. And, indeed, the polls showed Rabin leading Shamir, though it was not clear whether he could win a victory large enough to enable him to move the country decisively toward accommodation.

For two months I'd agonized over whether to vote for Meretz or Labor. Meretz's position on the peace process was closer to my own. On the other hand, a policy of negotiation and evacuation would never be adopted if its only advocate was a small radical faction whose support came primarily from middle-class intellectuals. Labor's line might be more equivocal, but it seemed like the only party that could bring the Israeli public around to accepting a Palestinian state. If Rabin ended up endorsing such a policy, most Israelis would probably trust and follow him.

Something else bothered me about Meretz. While many members of Kehilat Yedidya supported the party, they were the exception among religious Israelis. Most Meretz activists were strident left-wingers, alienated from Jewish heritage and religion and all too happy to abandon lands with deep historical and religious significance. Much of Meretz's public abjured any spiritual connection to Hebron, the site of the Tomb of the Patriarchs and Matriarchs, and to Shiloh in Samaria, where Samuel, the boy prophet, heard God speak to him as he slept beside the Ark of the Covenant. Even Tubas was part of Jewish history. According to the Book of Judges, a local woman killed Avimelech, son of Gideon, as he sought to reassert his hold on the village in the face of rebellion. She cast a millstone from a tower onto his head, ending his attempt to establish an Israelite kingdom. We had to leave Tubas and Shiloh and Hebron, I believed, but we should not deny our connection to these places.

Had I voted at home as a civilian, these arguments would no doubt have convinced me to choose Labor. But standing in Tubas, I could see the petty injustices of the occupation playing out before my eyes.

The base was one of the many police stations throughout Palestine that the British built in the 1920s along a "Mickey Mouse" model. It was a large structure flanked by two smaller rooms that constituted the mouse's ears. Then, native policemen kept order under the command of foreign officers. Now the base doubled as headquarters for what Israel euphemistically called the "civil administration." One ear served as the civil administration office. Palestinians who needed work or travel permits or some other document or stamp from the Israeli government lined up in the street in front of a small, barred window. As we were briefed by the commander of the unit we were replacing, I watched a dozen Palestinians, among them elderly men as well as mothers with children, standing in the hot sun as the window remained closed. The soldier on duty sat in his office, sipping coffee and watching television. With one eye on the captain briefing us, I walked over to the office door.

"There's a line of people waiting for you to open," I told him. Perhaps he just hadn't seen.

He looked up at me. "So what?"

"The sign outside says you were supposed to open half an hour ago."

He turned back to the television and took a bite out of a sandwich he held in his lap. "I'll open when the program's over."

"But why should they have to wait for your program to end?"

"What's wrong with you?" He glared at me. "We *never* open on time. We make them wait on purpose. So they'll know who's boss here."

Company C voted last, after the men from the outgoing unit. I put myself at the end of the line. It soon became clear that, were the Company C staff any indication, Rabin was on his way to a major victory. Eiger even came close to persuading Efi to vote Labor before losing him to the National Religious party, the party of the religious Zionists and many of the settlers. But Efi declared that he, too, thought it was time to cut a deal with the Palestinians, though he had one major reservation: "My problem is that it's irreversible. What if we give them the territories and they continue to fight us? What do we do then?"

Alon surprised me by telling me he was voting for Meretz. He said that he'd voted for the left in 1988 as well, attributing his political orientation to our conversations back in 1987 at Tel Romeida in Hebron.

"It's not fair," I said to Eiger. "I planned to decide tomorrow."

"Get in there and vote," Eiger ordered. "We have work to do."

I accepted an envelope from the election wardens, one young man and two women, and entered the cardboard booth. It was so small I could barely move. Before me was a compartmentalized wooden tray containing piles of paper slips printed with the names and symbols of the different parties. I picked out a Labor slip and put it in my envelope. Then I hesitated. Here I am, I thought, stuck in the West Bank again. In the month to come I will once again impose Israeli rule on Palestinians. Labor is too wishy-washy. It's time to make a statement. I took the Labor slip out and inserted a Meretz one.

But before leaving for the army I'd convinced Ilana that, for the first time in her life, she should vote Labor rather than Likud. She'd be upset if I voted Meretz, a party she considered—not without cause—virulently antireligious. If they were in power, they'd slash the budget for the religious schools our kids attended. They'd already set their sights on the education ministry. I took the Meretz slip out and put the Labor one back in.

"What's taking so long, Watzman?" Alon asked from beyond the cardboard. Shouldn't I make the same firm statement he'd made under my influence? I took out the Labor slip and put in a Meretz one.

"Hey, Watzman, are you asleep?"

It was Eiger. I respected his judgment. He'd voted Labor. I took out the Meretz slip and slid the Labor one back in.

Then I heard the soldier in the civil administration office shouting abuse at an Arab who had challenged one of his arbitrary decisions. This has to stop, I seethed. I took out the Labor slip and reinserted Meretz.

"What the hell is going on with you?" the head election warden yelled. "We've got to get the ballot box back to Jenin!"

"I can't decide," I said.

"You've got ten seconds to decide or I close up the ballot box and you don't vote," came the reply.

I took a deep breath, stepped out of the booth, and slipped my envelope into the ballot box.

"So what was it?" Eiger asked.

"Meretz," I said.

"Idiot," he said, shaking his head.

"Good job," said Alon. He slapped me on the shoulder.

"Just don't tell Ilana," I told Eiger. "It's one of those things that happen in the army. Better that she not know."

The next evening in our tent at the training base where we'd received the rest of our soldiers, Alon and I listened to the election results on his transistor radio. I had cause for optimism. Alon was not the only one of my army friends who'd told me that they'd come around to my way of thinking. The guys had always complained that I was constantly talking politics. I was surprised to find that they'd listened to my arguments.

When the voting stations closed, the newscasters announced the results of a national exit poll. It showed Labor far ahead of Likud, and Meretz showing strongly. The right had lost, and Rabin would be able to form a coalition with a solid majority. Suddenly the road to peace seemed much shorter. But we still had to get through a month in Tubas.

It was a Wednesday afternoon and I had just returned from three days of leave. The fading-empire ambience of the musty Mickey Mouse base reinforced my dejection. Its whitewashed walls crumbled to the touch and were splattered with graffiti, including a large "shavuz chart" in red Magic Marker left by a Golani unit that had been stationed here some months before. Drawn in each square of the ninety-day calendar was the literal depiction of the acronym, which stands for *shavur zayin*, busted dick. Eighty-nine broken members flung off drops of desperate perspiration behind the X's that had counted them one by one, up to the triumphantly erect organ of day ninety, the time of freedom.

Because I restricted myself to the number of vacation days that the NCOs got, my trip home had been all too brief. Before, I'd almost always begun my leave on a Thursday, so that the mandatory relaxation of the Sabbath would refresh me for the rest of my service. But this time I had work to do and couldn't award myself a restful weekend. There was a breaking news story to report, a feature to write, and a translation to begin.

Ilana also needed me to babysit. The previous August we'd returned to Jerusalem from Tirat Zvi. We'd enjoyed our year on the kibbutz but still felt strongly committed to Kehilat Yedidya's people and ideals. The community was important enough to us that we were willing to give up Tirat Zvi's open spaces to squeeze ourselves and our three kids into our small two-bedroom apartment in Baka. Ilana did not, however, want to return to her twenty-four-hour shifts at the meteorological station. She signed up for a course, sponsored by the municipal government and our neighborhood community center, that would qualify her to open a small preschool, a *mishpahton*, in our apartment. The course had turned out to be quite demanding, and she was having trouble finding arrangements for our own kids so she could attend its afternoon and evening sessions.

Between my work, Ilana's course, and the kids, we'd barely had time to talk to each other. One morning she insisted I take a break from my computer and go for a walk on the promenade, a public garden on the edge of a valley between our neighborhood in south Jerusalem and the Old City. Mizmor and Asor were at day camp. We had only Niot in a stroller to distract us from each other. But my mind was on my work, and even more so on Company C. How were the guys managing in my absence? No doubt there was a crisis over the duty roster. Mizrahi, who was filling in for me on top of everything else he had to do, had already called twice with urgent issues he was unable to resolve.

Just past a lookout point offering a magnificent view of the city walls, a young couple sitting on a bench caught my eye. The dark-haired girl wore a chartreuse summer dress. Her companion had closely

cropped hair and sported a stained olive green Velcro wristwatch pro-
tector. Even though he wasn't in uniform, I could tell he was a combat
officer. He leaned close to his girlfriend and spoke intently. She, however, looked bored and impatient. As we passed by, I heard, ". . . and
then, at the last minute, I had to hunt up enough ammunition for thirty
new soldiers and get them all squared away on base. It's incredibly hard
to suddenly bring thirty strangers into a functioning unit of guys who've
been together for a year already. Can you imagine . . ."

I smiled, but Ilana waited to react until we were out of earshot.
"That's exactly the way you are when you come home. Your body
comes home but your head stays in the army." I was miffed and we had
an argument.

I considered this unsatisfactory visit home an anomaly, but it
marked a change that had already taken place. Reserve duty was fitting
into my life less well. Bringing up three small children was more than a
full-time occupation for Ilana and me, and I had taken on more and
more work to meet expenses. My army job was more demanding than
in previous years. During my first stint as clerk, the job had been deceptively simple. Only a year later, when we returned to Mount Hermon
for another month, did I comprehend its scope. As an NCO I'd been
busy, but I'd still found time to catch up on my reading. As clerk, I
seemed to work around the clock. An NCO could leave the army behind between stints. A clerk had homework. During the month leading
up to a round of duty, I'd spend unpaid hours keeping track of who
had confirmed his call-up orders, updating my list of phone numbers
and addresses, and fielding petitions for cancellations or abbreviations
of service. The final decisions were made by Eran, our new company commander, but he felt awkward dealing with the men's personal
problems and was eager to hear my advice on each case. No wonder
I had trouble focusing on Ilana and the kids. Wagoner the poet knew
the feeling:

Only one

Question will have a recreational value:
Where Is the Enemy's Weakness?

But now that I was back in Tubas, my head was at home. I tried to be businesslike and efficient. Upon my return, I scanned the operations log and got briefed by Azoulai, the NCO manning the radio set. I seated myself at one of the tables in the large central room that tripled as a mess hall commons and command post (or war room, as we called the place with the radio set and the maps of our sector posted on the walls). Then, placing my rifle at my feet, I unpacked the cloth shoulder bag with multiple pockets that served as my mobile company clerk's office. I laid out my gear—blue, black, red, and green pens, a set of highlighters, a stapler, a roll of Scotch tape and, most necessary, two bottles of Wite-Out. Although Mizrahi had already made up the duty roster for the twenty-four hours that would begin at 6 p.m., I could expect that he'd made a hash of it and that I'd soon face a torrent of appeals.

I heard Eran's jeep pull up, and a minute later he walked in. Over six feet tall, thickset, fair skinned, with thinning, straight blond hair, Eran looked more like an Iowa farm boy than an Israeli officer. Had he grown up in the United States, he might have been the quarterback on his high school football team. In Israel, where the national sport was soccer and the national physique Levantine—compact, slender, and dark, like Elnatan and Ben-Ami—he looked almost alien. His rifle, efod, and helmet were slung over his shoulder, and sweat stains showed under his arms and on his back.

"There was a Molotov cocktail. Just missed Vanunu's patrol," he said by way of explaining his absence.

"So I heard. Everyone's okay?"

"Everyone's okay. Marcel Levy went ballistic. Vanunu nearly had to slap him to shut him up."

He settled his large frame on the bench opposite me.

"Good thing you're here," he said flatly.

"It's that bad?" I asked. Since I'd already returned from a vacation once, I knew what the answer would be.

"Chaos." Eran rested his forehead on his hands and closed his eyes. "I've got to get some sleep. Wake me up at five p.m. By then I want a complete personnel report. I want to know who is where now and where they'll be over the next twenty-four hours. Make up a raid force of twelve under Efi's command that'll be available from tomorrow afternoon through all of the following night. The bulk of the raid force will return sometime after midnight, but Efi and three others will continue on until morning in an ambush."

He got up heavily and walked to the door of the small room that served as his office and bedroom.

"Maybe before I sleep I'll try to hit the books. I've got a pile of articles to read," he mumbled. Eran studied geology at Hebrew University.

"You gotta go home for a break," I said.

"I can't. How can I?" he asked, closing the door behind him.

Eran had yet to take a vacation. His brief phone calls to Rakefet, his med-student fiancée, sounded like the content-free conversations adolescents have with their parents. For Rakefet, they could hardly have been a substitute for his physical presence. Some of us worried that the army would abort their relationship before it was formalized. Normally, the company commander and his deputy switched off, one at home and one on duty. But there was no deputy company commander this time. Mizrahi had fired him.

When the officers, first sergeants, and NCOs reported for duty at Mount Hermon the previous August, we found that Company C had a new commander and deputy. It was unusual for a company commander to be brought in from outside and almost unheard of for outsiders to take over the top two positions at once. These slots were generally filled from among the company's platoon commanders, who already had an authority based not only on rank but also on their friendship with the men. But Ben-Ami, working long hours at his high-tech company and busy with his small children, refused to continue as company commander, and Efi, the only other platoon commander with the experience to move up the ladder, turned down the top posts for much the same reasons.

The newcomers introduced themselves as Eran and Stitch. Eran stood as if trying to fold his frame into a smaller size and I at first assumed that the brash Stitch was the higher ranking of the two. In the event, Eran departed after the first few days of the stint, with the odd excuse that he had to tour Germany with his grandmother. We were left with Stitch.

Using what he claimed was an infallible mathematical model, Stitch drew up a duty schedule that had soldiers heading from guard duty to patrols and ambushes with only one- or two-hour breaks in between. When he found a flaw in the duty roster he dressed me down in front of half a dozen soldiers with language so vicious and scatological it left the guys openmouthed in astonishment. He charged Mizrahi and Keisar with not keeping the base orderly, and when they put together a cleanup operation, he screamed at them for using too much water to mop the floor. At night he watched pornographic movies on the VCR in the common room. Should we act, or wait for him to self-destruct?

> You may dig in
> And hope incompetent or lunatic
> Enfilading fire, brought on by hubris,
> Will cause your enemy to decimate
> His opposite numbers firing the opposite way.

After a week of Stitch's nonsense, Mizrahi called together the NCOs.

"I've had it," he told us. "He's got to go. I'm taking the truck and going to the Lower Ski Lift. It won't take long."

Mizrahi knew that the battalion commander would attend to his counsel—he was a veteran in the battalion and Stitch a novice.

The next day Stitch was called to the Lower Ski Lift station. He returned angry but impotent, and after he completed his month on Mount Hermon we never saw him again. When Eran took up his command in earnest at our winter maneuvers, he proved militarily thorough and, perhaps more important in a reserve unit, fair-minded and considerate of others. But he was so shy and soft-spoken that he had a hard time giving direct orders. Only when he was angry did he look anyone in the eye. Some of the guys misinterpreted his reserve as a lack of will. He needed help handling people, and he was unassuming enough to have no embarrassment about taking it.

A group of seniors from Wilberforce University, a historically black institution in Ohio, were spending the summer in a disadvantaged neighborhood in Holon, the Tel Aviv suburb where Ilana had grown up. I was surprised that students with no Jewish connection had decided to volunteer in Israel and proposed a story to my editor at *The Chronicle of Higher Education*. I was to visit Holon and write the article during my leave.

But what about my kids? Ilana would have to leave for her course before I got back. Mizmor and Niot could stay with friends, but I hadn't managed to arrange anything for Asor, who had just turned five.

"It would be wonderful if you took him with you," Ilana said. "He's been missing you a lot. Last Friday night, when I lit the Sabbath candles, he broke out in tears. 'It's not the same without Abba,' he said."

"This is work," I objected. "I need to interview people."

"It's at a summer camp, isn't it? They must have games or balls that will keep him occupied."

"Ilana, it's totally inappropriate."

Ilana glared with her black eyes. "Do what you want to do."

Asor enthusiastically accepted Ilana's suggestion. When it was time to leave, he reported at our front door with his plastic M-16 slung over his shoulder.

"No," I said.

"Hey, Abba, take yours, too!" My rifle was hidden high up in our closet, where it could be neither seen nor reached by children.

"Asor, if you want to come with me, it's without the gun."

"But it's my *new* rifle. Just like yours!" he said.

I had refused to buy him toy weapons of any kind from the time he was born until two weeks earlier. No son of mine is going to run around shooting people as if it's fun, I'd insisted to a puzzled Ilana. Seeing my kid with a gun would remind me of too many evils. Two years earlier a young man named Ami Popper had taken a rifle and opened fire on Arab laborers waiting at an intersection. And just two days ago, an insurance agent in a middle-class suburb of the southern city of Beersheba had risen in the middle of the night, lit five memorial candles in his kitchen, and put bullets through the heads of his dog, his son, his two daughters, his wife, and himself.

My ban on toy guns did not, however, prevent Asor from becoming obsessed with the military. He and his friends played war incessantly, and he'd grab any long cylindrical object to use as a rifle. He peppered me with questions about how to aim, how to throw a grenade, how to drive a tank. Every other day he'd ask how many Arabs I'd killed, and each time he was disappointed when I told him I hadn't killed any—a response I always followed with a lecture on how soldiers shoot only to protect themselves, their buddies, and their country. Killing is not fun, I told him, but he refused to believe me. A month before I'd left for the army we'd been in a toy store and he'd seen a basket of plastic replicas of the same short M-16 I was issued in the army. His birthday was coming up. He wouldn't consider any other present.

"I'm not taking him if he carries that gun," I declared.

Ilana thought I was joking. She'd grown up in a country where soldiers were ubiquitous and rifles omnipresent. It wasn't like the United

States, where they marked you as a member of the gun lobby. So kids played with toy rifles. That didn't mean they'd grow up to be killers. They were just playing. That was how Ilana saw it. But not me. I didn't have a problem with Asor being a soldier when the time came. I'd even be proud of him. But that was duty, not a game.

"I mean it."

"You can't disappoint him," she said.

"He'll learn that playing with guns is a moral issue."

"Disappointing your son is a moral issue, too," she said. "Don't you see that he identifies with you?"

"But why this way?" I asked. "He could identify with me by running every morning or reading books. He could identify with me by going to a peace march."

At the bus station, we stood in line behind a gentle-faced grandmother with a light complexion. She gave Asor a big smile.

"A day out with Daddy. How exciting!" Her accent marked her as one of the hundreds of thousands of Soviet Jews who had immigrated to Israel over the previous three years. I'd already met enough of this community's senior citizens to discern two characteristics. Many of them revered the military, which was hardly surprising among a group that had battled the Nazis and endured the sieges and hardships of World War II. Furthermore, no small number thought that the problem with the Soviet Union had not been that it oppressed people. The problem with the Bolsheviks, some of these new Israelis believed, was that they had oppressed the *wrong* people.

"We're going to shoot some Arabs," Asor said, waving his rifle.

"How wonderful!" she beamed. "Such a little hero."

"Asor!"

This was definitely not what I had wanted to hear from my son. Was my army service having the wrong effect on him? Did bringing up a child in the midst of armed conflict mean he'd inevitably be an ordnance enthusiast?

We had a talk on the bus.

"We don't shoot Arabs just because they're Arabs. If we do that we'll be just like the Germans and the Russians and all the people throughout history who've killed Jews just because we're Jews," I explained.

"But the Arabs are bad," Asor said. "They want to kill us."

"Not all Arabs want to kill us. You know some Arabs who don't want to kill us." I cast around for examples. "There's Jamal who cleans the stairwell for us. There's those families from Beit Sahour we invited to our synagogue. There are even Arabs who serve in our army and help protect Jews."

Asor considered this. "Okay, so I'll only shoot bad Arabs."

"Even bad Arabs we don't shoot unless we don't have any choice. We'd rather make peace with them. You know, we've got a new prime minister named Yitzhak Rabin who wants to make peace with the Palestinians. We're going to talk to them and try to compromise. Compromise means that we give up some things, like land where they can have their own country, and they give up some things, like wanting to get rid of Israel."

"Isn't it easier to shoot them? Then we can keep the land."

"When people are mad at each other, they talk and make up, they don't shoot each other. When you have an argument with your friend Maor, you don't shoot him. When you're mad at me, you don't kill me. We talk and we try to understand each other."

Asor thought for a moment. "But I like you and Maor. I hate the Arabs."

I was a failure as a father. But what could I expect from a boy his age? He couldn't grasp subtleties. Either the Arabs were our friends, or we hated them.

I echoed a line that had become a platitude in the peace camp by then. "Making peace isn't something you do with your friends. It's something you do with your enemies."

I laid out my pens and then walked over to the room I shared with Mizrahi and Aviel, the Platoon Two lieutenant. I needed Mizrahi to brief me on the changes that had taken place in my absence, but he was fast asleep. Sheets of paper were scattered over the small metal table between his bed and mine, and among them I found the essential tools of my clerkship. First, there was a plastic sleeve containing the daily duty rosters from our arrival through today, including the ones Mizrahi had drawn up during my leave. Second, there was the Justice Chart, a grid covering four sheets of paper taped together to poster size. The columns represented the days of our service and the rows were labeled with the names of Company C's soldiers. A color-and-shape coding system I'd devised showed when each soldier was on vacation and, when each was on duty, which assignment he had received and at which base he'd served. I could thus determine that both vacation days and the less desirable jobs, such as the middle-of-the-night guard shift and KP, were handed out equitably.

In addition to the main base in Tubas, we had two subsidiary ones. A detachment made up mostly of members of Platoon One was stationed, under Efi's command, at the Fara prison camp a few miles to our north. They had little to do but guard duty, and every time I stopped by to see how they were faring, they were in the middle of a cookout. To our west, Alon commanded a small detachment on a pastoral hilltop designated to be a new settlement. These men had to guard themselves but were otherwise free to play basketball. The guys in Tubas, where we had a heavy workload, were constantly badgering me to transfer them to one of the other two groups.

I glanced at the duty roster Mizrahi had made for the next day and was pleased to see that he'd assigned me to command the early morning patrol up to Alon's base. I'd get a nice walk and have a chance to drink coffee with Alon. It wasn't merely a nice walk, though. Just before my trip home, Harizi, a meticulous Platoon Two NCO, had led the patrol.

Striding in front of his jeep, he suddenly, two-thirds of the way up the hill, motioned the driver to halt. A faint glint in the gravel had caught his eye, and he knelt down to examine the ground before him, taking care not to slide his foot even a centimeter past where he'd set it down a few seconds before. With his finger held just above the ground, he traced the line of a copper wire, so thin that it was barely visible. Ordering his men to fall back, Harizi radioed Eran and battalion headquarters. The sapper who dismantled the bomb, hidden in a hollow alongside the road, said it would have blown the jeep all the way to Jenin.

I also noticed that Mizrahi had not entered the last three days' duty rosters on the Justice Chart. I'd have to do that before I could assign anyone to the next night's raid and ambush. Because our routine duties determined the manpower we were assigned, any special operation such as this raid came on top of the ten hours of guard, roadblock, and patrol duty that the guys did each day. At least a couple of the detail's members would have to go straight from guard duty into preparations for the operation.

I took the papers back to the table in the war room, examining the duty roster on the way to see who needed to be woken for the 6 p.m. guard shift. Sheib and Greenberg had the post on the roof, but I didn't need to rouse them—here they were, already dressed.

"Watzman! Back just in time for minhah," Greenberg said, holding out his hands as if he were going to embrace me. Minhah was the afternoon prayer, a short service that could be over in ten minutes if you rushed it. Like the morning and evening prayers, you could recite it alone, but if at all possible you were supposed to join a public service, which required a quorum of ten men.

"I've got to get things in order. Mizrahi's left me a mess, as usual," I said.

"You've got to pray your afternoon prayers also," said Greenberg, "and I think we might just have a quorum." Getting ten religious Company C men together at one time was always a challenge, but the hesder guys never stopped trying.

Greenberg looked at the duty roster. "Here, Fisch and Shaya have to get up anyway. Let me see who else is around."

"How's it going, Sheib?" I asked, somewhat apprehensive of the answer I'd get. He didn't look like he was in a good mood.

"Crappy," he said. "Every time you leave, Mizrahi screws me. He hates me. I was at the roadblock yesterday from noon to seven, and then he put me on guard duty from ten p.m. to two a.m., and then the patrol up to Alon first thing in the morning. When am I supposed to sleep?"

Mizrahi emerged, unshaven and barefoot, from his room. "Stop whining, Sheib," he said. "All you do is whine."

Sheib glared at him.

"Watzman, you've got to send one of the guys here over to Efi at Fara by sundown," Mizrahi informed me, scratching his crotch.

"What do you mean?" I said. "I don't have anyone to spare. What happened?"

"Achlama's wife called him this morning and told him not to bother coming home anymore. Seems some other guy moved in with her."

"Achlama?" I said. "He's such a great guy. How could she find someone better?"

"Women," Mizrahi said. "Who knows what goes on in their heads. Maybe she decided she doesn't like redheads. Anyway, Achlama took his Volkswagen and headed straight home, and now Efi's down one man."

"He'll have to manage somehow. I've got guys here working eighteen hours a day."

Greenberg returned with five guys and told us Shaya was putting on his boots. "That's nine. Mizrahi, if you join us you make the quorum. It's a great privilege."

"No thanks," Mizrahi said, turning into his room.

"God will bring prosperity upon your carpentry shop," Shaya shouted as he came out of his room, his shoelaces still untied. "Your saws will never dull."

Mizrahi stopped in the doorway. "God and I have been observing a cease-fire for a few years now," he said. "He doesn't bother me, and I don't bother him."

"Who else can we get?" Greenberg asked. "We've gotten this far. Just one more."

"That's bad news about Achlama," Shaya said, shaking his head.

"These days you've got to thank God for small favors," I said. "At least she just left him. She didn't shoot him like that guy in Beersheba did with his family."

Sheib's face went red. "Did you see in the paper yesterday? They buried him with the rest of the family. It's a crime—a desecration of the cemetery. They should have thrown his body into a garbage dump."

"Where else could they bury him?" Shaya shrugged. "The guy was out of his mind."

"He wasn't out of his mind. He knew exactly what he was doing. He had some problems, his business was collapsing. He decided to kill himself. But, no, that's not enough. How can his family go on living without him? They've got to die, too." I'd never seen Sheib so upset.

"He was crazy," Shaya insisted.

"He wasn't crazy. He was a man who thought his family was his personal property. He could dispose of them as he saw fit. Their lives were in his hands. He knew exactly what he was doing."

"Hey, Sheib, that's against the Torah," Greenberg said. "You've got to give him a proper Jewish burial."

"That's a Jew?" Sheib hissed. "That's no Jew."

It was Eran's daily briefing, the next evening. Over the course of the day, with much agony and many quiet and not so quiet talks with my fellow soldiers, I'd managed to put together the raid team. Standing orders required an officer at the Fara prison, but Eran insisted that Efi lead the ambush. So Aviel had to go to Fara for the night, wreaking havoc on the duty rotation and forcing me to make a number of adjustments that roused the ire of the guys. Some would guard both first and third shifts that night. Shaya would guard the third shift that night and at dawn become the medic in Eran's jeep. If there was an accident or attack, he'd have to go out without any sleep.

I had assigned myself to the raid force, but Eran vetoed it. He wanted me to remain as commander of the base and also to manage any problems with the duty roster. I'd broken the night into two rather than three radio shifts by stretching the shifts from four hours to six, and I put myself down for war room duty from midnight through 6 a.m. An NCO or senior soldier always manned the command post. The job was more comfortable than guard duty outside, but it bore more responsibility. If something went wrong on an ambush or raid and the force team called for help, the soldier on duty there would be the one to receive the message and notify Eran and the battalion. If reinforcements went out, I'd be responsible for keeping them informed of our other forces' locations and for updating the soldiers in Tubas and the other bases.

I thought everything was finalized, but half an hour before Eran's briefing, Greenberg pointed out that I'd scheduled him for the same shift at two different posts. An amiable guy who seldom complained, he said he'd really like to help me out but didn't think he could manage this particular tour de force. I had to find a creative solution to fill the hole.

The soldiers sat on three rows of benches facing a cardboard easel. On it was a map of the Jenin sector, the list of radio frequencies we used, a glossary of code names, and other operational information. Eran had gone through the routine stuff. He now asked Greenberg to help him tack up an aerial photograph of Tamoun, the same village whose resistance we'd tried to quell back in 1988. Eran pointed out the house that was the raid's target. But this was no ordinary raid—it was a stealth operation planned by the army's Central Command.

"The Shin Bet has information that a major terrorist commander, one responsible for the deaths of several civilians during the last year, is going to be in Tamoun tonight," Eran said in his quiet monotone. He tapped the photograph with the snapped-off radio antenna he used as a pointer. "Efi, give us the details."

Efi rose and faced the men, his face slightly flushed, as it always was when he had to speak officially.

"The idea behind the raid is to catch our quarry unawares, making a visit home when he thinks it's safe. Here's the trick. We'll surround the house at eleven-thirty p.m., even though he's not going to be there, and break in according to protocol. We'll make more of a ruckus than usual, but of course no one does any damage and no one roughs up any of the family members unless they resist. During all that fuss I, Eiger, and the two other members of the ambush contingent will enter this structure, which is a toolshed or something of that sort." He pointed to a small square next to the rectangle that represented the house.

"The rest of the raiders then leave. The family and neighbors will think that we've all gone, and that our intelligence was bad—that we came, looked for our man, and decided he wasn't there and wouldn't arrive. The four of us wait there. The shed has two windows, one on either side. We keep an eye on the house. He'll think the coast is clear and risk a visit to his family. The minute we see movement inside, or a light go on, we know he's arrived. He'll almost certainly be alone. At that moment we radio for our reinforcements, enter the house, and seize our prey."

Eran added, "If he doesn't show up during the night, the ambush will stay in place until five-thirty or six a.m. and be evacuated at my order."

"Right," Efi said. "I think that's it."

"The evacuation protocol," Eran reminded him.

"If there are any unexpected problems," Efi began—but this was standard stuff. I knew that our company truck would be the evacuation vehicle, and that Sharabi, a doe-faced Yemenite, would drive it under Mizrahi's command. They'd sleep at the base and I'd wake them up if anything happened. The night's rapid alert force—the rest of the raid contingent plus two others—would also sleep here, in the rooms off the commons. I shuffled through my papers, looking for a solution to the empty guard slot. Whoever got assigned to it in addition to his other duties would be furious. My thoughts wandered to Ilana. I felt bad for not having been attentive to her. I'd call her later tonight, I decided, even if there was a long wait for the phone. I'd get less sleep, but I wanted to hear her voice.

When I'd taken the clerk job, I'd resolved to sit and listen to the daily briefings just like everyone else. Jacques and Yermi had often busied themselves with other tasks, as if they were above being told our main radio frequency for the umpteenth time. They felt no need to listen again to our rules of engagement. True, they did not go on patrols or other missions, but I thought they should have set an example for the other guys. Since I still served as an NCO, it was even more important that I participate. But I often found myself swamped with last-minute duty roster changes, or manning the radio. In this case, I was trying to handle both. So I didn't really pay attention to Eran. Anyway, I knew the routine.

Ambushes followed a master plan. A year ago, on Mount Hermon, they'd been a major element in our work. Deployed in wadis that could serve as infiltration routes for terrorists, they required a detachment of soldiers to lie motionless in star formation—a circle with the soldiers' feet in the center and heads, rifles, and mortars on the outside—for hours on end in the bitter cold. With our eyes surveying 360 degrees, a team of terrorists could be spotted and attacked before they realized any soldiers were there.

No matter what you wore—long underwear, sweater, hermonit—you slowly froze, beginning at the extremities. It was worse if it rained. When I manned the war room at night I'd be pelted with entreaties to authorize ambush teams to pack up and head back to base. But authorization required permission from the operations officers sitting in a warm office with a coffeepot and a television at the Hermon regimental headquarters, and they were in no hurry to end Company C's misery.

Efi and his detachment wouldn't freeze in this ambush, though they would have to remain silent in a cramped space for hours. Compared to what we'd been through on the mountain, it did not seem like an onerous assignment.

At the end of the briefing, I announced the changes in the duty roster to a chorus of groans and curses. Eran dismissed the men.

"Who's in the war room the second half of the night?" he asked me.

"I am."

"Are you up on the ambush? You know all the details?"

"Sure," I said. "I'll be fine."

"Good. I've got a meeting at battalion headquarters now. I'll be back around eleven and I'll try to get to sleep. Don't bother me with anything stupid, but wake me up right away if there's an emergency."

"Will do. I'm going to try to get some sleep, too."

Of course, I didn't get to sleep until much later. There was supper and coffee and fielding a phone call from the battalion personnel officer, who wanted to know why I was understaffed by two men and why I hadn't cut short the vacations of others to make up for it. I'd meant to call Ilana, but around 10 o'clock I dozed off. When Harizi woke me at a quarter to midnight to replace him at the war room post, Efi, Eiger, and the others had already gone.

I made myself a cup of coffee and munched on the peanut butter cookies Ilana had sent with me. I had a lot because no one else would eat them. Peanut butter seemed to be an exclusively American taste. As protocol required, I made a round of calls to our guard posts, to Alon's crew, to Fara, to the battalion, to the regiment, and to Efi's ambush contingent to make sure we were all in contact. No one had anything unusual to report. Eiger responded for the ambush team with a barely perceptible whisper.

"What's the book?" Harizi asked as he gathered his gear.

I held up my copy of Tom Wolfe's *The Right Stuff*. "It's about the first astronauts."

"Interesting?"

"Actually, it's getting me mad. These test pilots fly ridiculously dangerous missions even though they have wives and children. Doesn't that sound self-centered?"

I stopped short, remembering that Harizi's hobby was riding a dune buggy over the lonely hills of Samaria, around the settlement in which he lived. Everyone thought he was crazy—a small band of terrorists could easily ambush him. He dismissed the worries not because he thought they were nonsense but because one of the things he liked about riding his dune buggy over the lonely hills of Samaria was the possibility that terrorists would attack him. He didn't live with his wife and baby girl in the West Bank because he thought the area ought to be part of Israel. He lived there because housing was cheap and the danger stimulating.

"I guess someone had to do it," he said and walked off to bed.

I perused the horizontal grid of the operations log that Harizi had aligned with the radio set, a blue ballpoint providing vertical emphasis alongside. His small, precise handwriting, so different from my own, recorded only routine tests and position reports from Vanunu's night patrol. The one exception was the notation "2328 raptor diamond," which signified the hour at which Efi's force had departed from the base. As if on cue I heard the rattle-roar of the company truck pulling into the parking area outside the common room, tires scattering gravel against cans of machine oil as the engine sputtered to a stop. The six guys from the raid contingent who hadn't stayed behind with Efi trudged in silently. They'd now have the pleasure of sleeping in their uniforms and boots, ready to head back out if Efi needed help. Mizrahi and Sharabi followed them, efods slung over their shoulders, helmets unbuckled and askew on their heads. Mizrahi glared at me and the world at large, and stomped into his room. Sharabi, who looked high even when he was sober, raised a palm in greeting and ambled into the Platoon Three room.

I turned a page in the operations log, inscribed the postmidnight date at the top, and did another round of calls. I also confirmed that the ambush team—"alligator" in radio talk—was in contact.

"Ratush to alligator."

"Root, receiving," came Eiger's whisper.

The astronauts held my attention until 1 a.m., when Eran returned, bleary-eyed, from his meeting. As usual, it had lasted much longer than planned. He collapsed into bed in his uniform and boots, the way he invariably slept. At 1:40 I woke up the third guard shift.

The next three hours were uneventful. I read, drank coffee, listened to seventies rock on the army radio station, contacted the guard posts, the bases, and the ambush team every hour, and dozed for a few minutes here and there despite my best efforts to stay awake. I was in a temporary stupor when Eiger's voice came over the radio.

"Alligator to Ratush. Alligator to Ratush." How long had he been calling? I reached slowly for the receiver. No doubt a routine test.

"Root, avor."

"Request evacuation, avor."

I looked at my watch. Really, Eiger, I thought, this kind of whining does not become you! You're supposed to be out there until after dawn. Why are you trying to cut corners?

> Meanwhile, you may stand indifferently
> > And casually upright in the midst of battle
> > > Through shot and shell, facing at every turn
> A circular firing squad, may brandish the banner
> > With the strange device of your country
> > > Right or wrong at the heart
> Of this debacle,

"One more round one, avor," I said, "round one" being radio talk for an hour. I settled back in my chair and opened my book.

A few minutes later his voice came through again. "Alligator to Ratush, *request evacuation!*"

"Request denied, avor," I said emphatically into the handset. Eiger was all too accustomed to having me do what he told me to do.

There was a pause.

"Request to know reason denied, avor."

Why couldn't he let me finish my shift quietly? Didn't he trust me to know when to send Mizrahi and Sharabi to pick them up?

"Because you are to be evacuated only on orders of Apex," I said.

There was silence for perhaps ten minutes. I read how one of the astronaut's wives took their four sons and went back to her parents. She wasn't going to put up with a husband who made her into the sole caregiver.

Then it was Efi's voice. He sounded upset. "Request Apex to this instrument."

"Apex is horizontal," I snapped, "and I don't have any intention of waking him up. He needs his sleep."

Another silence.

"Via you to Apex. We are under attack."

I sat upright in my chair.

"Repeat?"

"We have been discovered. We are on the roof of the target house. I repeat, we are under attack."

My head cleared instantly. I had fucked up. My friends had been in danger for more than twenty minutes and I hadn't caught on. I remembered that my mind had wandered when Efi explained the evacuation protocol at the briefing. It hadn't been the boilerplate I usually heard. There were specific instructions and I hadn't listened to them. I had really fucked up.

"Rapid alert force on the way, avor," I told Efi. Then I ran to the room I shared with Eran and Mizrahi and woke them up. Eran was on his feet immediately, as though he had not been asleep.

"Efi's under attack," I said. Mizrahi was heading for the truck.

"Wake up the rapid alert force," Eran commanded. But I was in the soldiers' rooms on the other side of the common room already, turning on the lights. Within five minutes the men were in the truck.

"Rapid alert force diamond," I transmitted to Efi before passing on a terse report to the battalion. My stomach churned with shame, but the urgency of the moment kept me focused and functioning.

Efi was already reporting to Eran, who was in his jeep racing to the house. I listened and scribbled the information in the operations log. It wasn't as bad as I'd feared, it seemed, but if I'd remained in my stupor any longer it could have gotten much more serious. At first light the Arab family had stirred, and soon after a man tried to open the door to the storage shed. Since it was locked from the inside and he couldn't get in, he peered through a window. Efi didn't know whether the early riser had seen him, but he decided not to take a chance. He ordered Eiger to radio for evacuation and told the rest of the men to move out of the shed, which could easily be surrounded and torched. They emerged to find two men standing on the house's doorstep, looking directly at them. *Jeish!* they shouted. Army! Heads appeared at nearby windows and the cry was taken up by the neighbors. *Jeish!* Efi, Eiger, and the others elbowed their way past the men into the house, where they ran up the stairs to the second story and from there to the flat, enclosed roof. A dozen men and teenagers had gathered below, shouting and throwing stones and bottles; more were coming all the time. Eiger radioed again for evacuation and was again turned down. The crowd grew larger and angrier.

Efi took the handset. "Via you to Apex. We are under attack."

When the team returned to Tubas half an hour later, Efi's expression was more one of regret than of anger. I stood a meter from the radio set, one ear stubbornly cocked for any sound it might emit. I was still on duty, but at the end of my shift I intended to tell Eran that I was no longer fit to serve in a combat unit. Having made that decision, I felt calm—or so I thought. My face told a different story.

Eiger walked over to me, his shirt half unbuttoned, a crooked smile on his unshaven face. "Look, it's okay. Nothing happened. We're all fine."

"I fucked up. I shouldn't be here. You could have been killed."

"Bullshit. We weren't in any real danger. We just wanted to wake you up." Eiger placed a hand on my shoulder and shook me.

"I didn't listen to the briefing. This clerk job makes me slack off. I should never have taken it."

Efi joined us. "You're doing a fine job. Everybody says so. You should have seen how crazy things were when you weren't here," he said quietly.

Eran appeared in the doorway. He took off his helmet, glanced around the room, and came over.

"I'm no good at this, Eran," I said. "I'm quitting this job. I'm a disaster as a soldier. I'll transfer to the battalion headquarters, to some boring desk job where I don't put anyone's life at risk."

"No, you won't." There was just the slightest change of pitch in his usual monotone.

"Why not?" I asked.

"Because I need you. When do you finish this shift?"

"At six."

He spoke quietly, with the same bashful expression he used with everyone. "Okay. At six you do your prayers or whatever it is you have to do and then you go to sleep. At eleven I want a personnel report and a recommendation about how we do the work here when we're understaffed by two men."

He turned and walked away.

"Don't take it so hard," Eiger said. "This isn't your real life."

unless those colors seem
  In the end less subtle
    Than the shades of your uniform

"You should give Ilana a call," Eiger said.

"She's asleep."

"So what? What will she do, hang up?"

Mizrahi appeared in the doorway. "Hey, where are you?" he shouted at Efi. "I need to take you back to Fara. I don't have all night."

"Fucking up is part of life," Eiger said. "We all do it. It doesn't mean that you're by nature fucked up." He gave me another slap on the shoulder and went to his room.

I looked around. The guys from the rapid alert force who had time to sleep had headed back to bed. The ones who had to work the first guard shift were making coffee. No one was paying any attention to me.

And your skin, which were intended
  To blend with the earth, to form a useful part
    Of your more natural surroundings.

I looked at the glaring red shavuz chart, scrawled on the wall by another despairing soldier. I would be in Tubas to the end, and peace was still a long way off. Next year we'd be back in another village just like this one. I would just have to try to do better.

There was a little more than half an hour till the end of my shift. Then I'd call Ilana.

Chapter Nine

· BOUNDARIES ·

MOUNT HERMON, OCTOBER 1994

*K*USEMAK! YOU'VE GONE OVER THE LINE! PATROL FROM SIX until midnight and then guard duty from two to six a.m.? I won't do it!"

This throaty baritone could belong only to Platoon One's power-lifting, hard-drinking, fist-fighting machine gunner, Aryeh Nasi. He emulated Rambo but beat him on two counts. He was a couple of inches taller than Sylvester Stallone, and he had a real gun.

I opened one eye and took in the clenched fists, the bulging biceps, the chest puffed up like that of an amorous peacock, straining at a black tank top several sizes too small. This was not what I wanted to deal with. I closed the eye and tried to sleep.

"Asshole. Not even man enough to face me," Aryeh growled. "You got on my case one time too many. Stand up before I drag you out of bed."

"Hey, what's all the noise about? Cut it out, Aryeh." I opened the eye again. My savior had materialized, blond, grinning, and calm. It was Yishai, the new Platoon Three commander. He put a hand on Aryeh's shoulder. "Watzman deserves to sleep some."

"Watzman!" A banshee cry from the yard heralded the arrival of Keisar, his skinny limbs shooting out at all angles like one of the stick figures Niot drew in preschool. "Give me a soldier immediately!"

I pushed myself up on my arms and swung painfully into a sitting position. My shoulders ached from the radio pack I'd lugged on yesterday's foot patrol over the mountains.

"What's the problem, Keisar?"

"I've got to go to the Lower Ski Lift to draw out our food supplies or we're not going to have anything for supper. I need a soldier right now to go with me." He gesticulated to emphasize the important words.

"Oh. Okay, let me check my charts and see who's free." With a dramatic flourish, I drew my personal copy of the day's duty roster from my shirt pocket, unfolded it, and held it at arm's length.

"Well, what do you know," I said. "No one is available."

"I've told you a million times that every day you need to assign one soldier as my assistant," Keisar fumed.

"Indeed you have. The problem is that I can't. We don't have enough men. I can't free up anyone for the job."

"So we won't eat!" our first sergeant declared. "You know that I'm not allowed to take the truck out on the road without a soldier accompanying me."

"There's really no one who can go with him?" Yishai asked.

"Oh," I said brightly. "You can take Aryeh Nasi!"

"Great. Come on, Aryeh."

"Hey, wait a minute! I can't go! I'm guarding at the red post," Aryeh snarled.

"Well, Aryeh," I said pleasantly, "then what the hell are you doing here?"

"You're on guard duty?" Yishai said. "You've abandoned your post? Why don't you have a shirt on? And where's your efod?"

"My efod's in the guard post. I went to get some cigarettes. I saw tomorrow's duty roster posted on the door, so I came here to smash Watzman's face in."

"You're in serious trouble," Yishai snapped. "Leaving your guard? Do you know that there are Hezbollah guerrillas just waiting for a chance to get past this base into Israel? Get back on the double. I'm reporting this to Eran."

"Now you're after me, too? I've had enough of this fucking unit," Aryeh said as he stormed out.

"Go back to sleep," Yishai told me. "I'll make sure he's where he's supposed to be."

"No point. I'm on the mountain patrol again in forty-five minutes."

"So put someone else on it."

"There isn't anyone else. Anyway, it's one of the things I actually enjoy. At least I'll get some exercise."

We'd never had a round of duty like this one. We were at Gladiola, an outpost on Bear Mountain, Mount Hermon's western spur. A decade of army budget cuts and efficiency measures seemed to hit us all at once. Supplies, both food and gear, were miserly, and our manpower inadequate. The guys were on duty sixteen hours a day, not including cleaning and maintenance details. We had hardly any time to enjoy each other's company. On top of it all, we were getting less home leave than ever before. Soldiers who were in for the entire month received the regulation minimum, three days; NCOs and officers got only a day more. Since Mount Hermon was in Israel's far north, most of the guys spent the first of those three days off getting home and the third getting back. Within a week the company was thoroughly demoralized.

An army or finance ministry economist might think it was reasonable for a soldier to work sixteen out of twenty-four hours. That left him six hours to sleep—the official army allowance—and another two hours to eat, shower, and clean his rifle. But in my years in the army I'd learned that only half of a unit's ability to fight depended on training and discipline. The other half hinged on the guys' mutual loyalty, fostered by the backgammon board and the coffeepot. Take away the downtime and a unit would become less cohesive and battle ready. The army didn't seem to understand that.

Attempting to control the hyperinflation that plagued Israel in the early 1980s, a series of governments had slashed the national budget. The once-sacred military was not spared. Many of the effects were positive—in the past there had been wasteful use of both equipment and time. The army now scheduled our annual maneuvers for three or four intensive days rather than one or two drawn-out weeks. With better planning, we managed to accomplish as much as, sometimes more than, we had in the longer periods. Likewise, the army replaced the battalion-scale exercise that had traditionally opened every stint of active duty with two intensive days of target practice and small-scale field exercises. I was of two minds about this change. The battalion maneuvers had been tough and unpleasant, and it was true that such a huge operation was not a good way to hone the skills of individual soldiers. But it did force us to work together and to endure a trial by fire prior to service on the northern border or in the occupied territories. It made us feel like real soldiers and quickly reestablished strong bonds of mutual responsibility and comradeship.

Other changes were problematic. The guys in Company C would have put up with the heavy workload and inadequate supplies at Gladiola had there been no other option. What frustrated them was a powerful feeling that the army was taking them for granted. They looked around at their colleagues at work, at their friends from high school, at their extended families, and saw that very few of their peers were serving in combat reserve units.

At Israel's birth, Prime Minister David Ben-Gurion decreed that the IDF would be a citizens' army in which every able-bodied man and woman would serve. Reserve service was mandatory for men. Over the years, though, it became much less universal in practice. Entire classes of people were essentially exempt, most prominently the men of the ultra-Orthodox community. Under a deal their leaders cut with Ben-Gurion, the army did not call up full-time yeshiva students as long as they remained students past military age. At the time, this exemption applied to only a few hundred men. But Prime Minister Menachem Begin, his parliamentary majority dependent on ultra-Orthodox support, vastly expanded the exemption in the late seventies and early eighties. By 1994, it applied to tens of thousands of young men each year. Not all of them were really full-time students. Some enrolled in a yeshiva but actually worked or just hung out.

In the country's early years, the rest of Israeli society saw military service as a patriotic obligation. Not having borne arms to defend the country was a stain on a man's record that could make it difficult for him to find employment. But by the 1990s such social strictures were weakening. As Israeli society became more Americanized, more individualistic, less collectivist, the Israeli sense of duty to country grew more tenuous. The majority of Israelis did their part, and many young men—including those of the religious Zionist community—still aspired to combat service. But men who weren't in the army were no longer ostracized, and if this was true of regular army service it was all the more true of the reserves. Many had no compunctions about applying for medical or psychiatric discharges for minor ailments. Others made it a point to plan business trips overseas for precisely when reserve duty came around. Still more showed so much reluctance and created so many problems that the army stopped calling them. As budgets were cut, the army spent less of its scarce resources trying to force men to report. It was a vicious circle. As more and more men wriggled out of reserve duty, it became more socially acceptable to do so, and as it became more acceptable, more men tried.

Company C's men had been taught as youngsters that reserve duty was a universal obligation, and the mythic image of reserve duty was service in a combat unit. But in the 1990s the percentage of men who performed such service declined steadily. According to army statistics, about one hundred thousand men served four or more days of reserve duty in 2000. This amounts to 12 percent of the Jewish male population between the ages of twenty-one and forty-five. Two-thirds of eligible men served just a few days, in support roles or desk jobs close to home. Only about 4 percent served for twenty-six days or more—and that figure includes support personnel, as well as combat units made up of older and less trained men that drew less rigorous assignments than did Company C. While elite reserve units with tougher training and missions existed, Company C was near the top of the pyramid, a tiny minority.

When a guy in Company C saw that he was spending forty days a year in the army while most of the men with whom he worked, studied, and prayed did much less or nothing at all, he could hardly avoid feeling that the system was fundamentally unfair. If the burden were distributed more equitably, he'd serve fewer days. So why didn't the army force the ultra-Orthodox and the malingerers to serve?

From my vantage point as company clerk it looked a little different. In principle, I favored enforcing mandatory service for all eighteen-year-olds. When it came to the reserves, I was cognizant of the logic in the army's decision not to go after the dodgers and slackers. With a company brought together for a month of active service or a week of maneuvers, officers and NCOs had too much to worry about to spend time disciplining the recalcitrant. Military law allowed a company commander to mete out prison terms of several weeks, but it was almost unheard of for a reserve captain to do so. It was much more cost-efficient to drop a chronically uncooperative soldier than to try to coerce him to serve. Rather than fortifying our ranks, forcing ultra-Orthodox men into our unit would burden us with social and psychological problems that we had neither the time nor the expertise to resolve.

Aryeh Nasi might throw a tantrum, but his problem was not motivation. After our Gladiola service, still furious about his assignments, he refused to attend a week of maneuvers. Eran sent him to the battalion commander for a formal hearing and the latter sentenced him to a few days in a military prison. But he came back, because the bottom line was that he wanted to serve, wanted to be in a combat unit, and wanted to be in Company C. He'd never try to get a psychiatric exemption—even if there were times when I thought one ought to be forced on him.

Sefi, on the other hand, had lost his will to serve. He'd joined us the previous year when we'd spent a month policing Kabatiyeh, a village not far from Tubas in the Jenin district. Like many young Israelis, he'd spent the year after his discharge from his mandatory service trekking in the Far East. He was diligent, hardworking, and always willing to help out in the kitchen or the ammunition tent. At our staff meeting at the end of the month, the company command agreed that he was one of the most promising of the new soldiers and a probable future NCO.

An aspiring photographer, he was taking a course at a Tel Aviv art school. He frequently consulted Marcel Levy about equipment and technique, but his real interest lay in the artistic composition of landscapes, still lifes, and portraits. He brought his portfolio with him. His black-and-white photographs displayed an instinctive sensibility to line and contrast, even if they were still technically rough.

He desperately wanted to be an artist and talked little of friends or family. While he shared Keisar's characteristic wiry Yemenite physique, the contrast between the two men was striking. The tight black curls that Keisar cut short hung to below Sefi's shoulders. While Keisar dressed neatly, Sefi's off-duty style was loose and deliberately shabby, and he wore an earring. Keisar was frantic; Sefi was laid back. True, Sefi's eagerness to please seemed to come packaged with a certain lack of self-confidence, a trace of anxiety, a suppressed fear that his life was not going to turn out as he wanted it to. But I attributed this to the liminality felt by any rookie in a long-established unit. It would pass. I cultivated Sefi. I talked to him at length about his photographs and tried to pair him on assignments with guys who had similar interests.

When he reported for duty a year later, Sefi was not the same. He responded apathetically to my greeting at the battalion sign-in table and exchanged few words with the other guys as he signed out his gear and lugged it to our cluster of tents. When his tent mates left for the firing range, he remained there, motionless, on his bed.

After a few minutes I approached him. "What's up, Sefi?"

He folded his arms across his chest and didn't answer.

"Anything I can do?"

He turned away as if I were an annoyance. "I guess you can. I want you to put me on KP. Today and every day." Then the request turned into a demand. "I'm not going to do anything else."

Kitchen duty was by far the most unpopular assignment in the company. It meant dawn-to-night dishwashing, onion cutting, and potato peeling under the critical eye of a surly cook. The only compensation was that the KP was allowed a full night of sleep after finishing the supper dishes. Sefi was demanding what I was more than willing to give. The other guys would rejoice at being relieved of kitchen duty, as Sefi must have known. So why the vehemence?

"I think I can work that out as long as Eran okays it," I said. "But are you sure? It means you won't be spending much time with the other guys."

"Doesn't matter."

"You seemed to get along with everyone last time."

He shrugged. "I've decided not to be a soldier anymore."

What did that mean?

"You know we're going to be on Mount Hermon this time. No confrontations with Palestinians, if that's what's bothering you."

"It's not that. I've just decided that I can't do the army."

"Did something happen that I don't know about?" I asked.

He didn't answer.

"Because you didn't say anything like that in Kabatiyeh."

"This is my last time in the reserves. I want an appointment with the MHO. Do we have one in the battalion?" The MHO was the Mental Health Officer.

"No. I think the procedure is that you go to the battalion doctor and ask for a referral."

"He knows about this stuff?" Sefi looked at me for the first time since I'd walked in.

"Well, it kind of depends on what your problem is. He's a gynecologist."

Eran walked into the tent. "Watzman, I've been looking all over for you. I want a report on who hasn't signed in yet." His eyes wandered to Sefi. "Why isn't he at the firing range?"

"He's got a problem," I explained. "Sefi, maybe you should talk to Eran about it. I can leave if you want."

"It's okay. You can tell him."

I summarized our conversation.

"I don't understand," Eran said. "Why is this year different from last year?"

Sefi stretched out his arms and leaned back with his hands clasped behind his head. "I guess it's because of that kid who shot himself," he said.

In Kabatiyeh, an Arab house had been commandeered as an observation center for the intelligence corps. Several enlisted men served there under the command of an ambitious young sergeant. They were involved in some sort of secret work, and one of our duties had been to provide an NCO and a small detail to defend the outpost. Eiger was the first to get the assignment, and Sefi was under his command.

I'd spent my first few days in Kabatiyeh preparing the company vacation schedule. The hours of advance planning I'd done at home had turned out to be in vain when the battalion suddenly changed our assignments. By Sunday I'd finished the task and asked Eran for a couple of days off so I could get some sleep. I had just finished packing my chimidan when the alert siren sounded—the guys at the intelligence out-post had reported gunfire.

Like Tubas the year before, Kabatiyeh was largely quiet, but every few days a Palestinian would open fire on one of our patrols. Perhaps the enemy had decided to launch an all-out attack on this small contingent of soldiers. Eran sped out with our special alert force.

But the single gunshot—we soon learned from Eiger that this was all there had been—was not repeated. A local youngster might have taken a potshot at the outpost as part of his initiation into a guerrilla cell. Or maybe an armed Palestinian had found a chink in the defenses and infiltrated the base. He could be hiding, waiting to murder any soldier who happened by. Eiger ordered his men to conduct a thorough search of the house and its yard. He and Sefi descended to the base's lower level. There they found the intelligence sergeant with a bullet through his head, his rifle at his side. A note explained that he'd killed himself because he'd been rejected from a special course he thought essential to his advancement.

That was at the beginning of our month in Kabatiyeh. It was a shock to us all, and Sefi had been the second person to see the body. He was clearly shaken by the experience, but he seemed to get past it as well as the rest did. There'd been no crisis.

"I'll talk it over with Watzman," Eran said to Sefi. "But even if you're permanent KP, you've got to be able to shoot. Get down to the firing range and train with the rest of the guys."

"I want to see the MHO," Sefi muttered, but he picked up his rifle, efod, and helmet and trudged out of the tent.

Eran was uneasy. "I think it's a put-on. It's not the suicide. That's just an excuse. He just doesn't want to do reserve duty anymore."

"Maybe we should go along with him," I said.

"What? Let him drop out?"

"I mean the kitchen job."

"Don't like it. Duties should be evenly distributed."

"Look, the other guys won't mind at all. He seems to be in a crisis of some sort. I don't know what it is, but it might be something temporary. He's a good kid, worth investing in. Let's try to help him. Let him be KP this time. Maybe after a week or two he'll get over it."

"And if he doesn't?"

"You know what? Even if it's not until next year, it's worth it. What are you going to do, court-martial him? You heard him, he wants to go to the MHO. These days the MHOs aren't hot on forcing unmotivated guys to serve, and he's got that suicide story that any psychologist will love. If we force him in that direction, we'll never see him again and neither will the army. Let's go along."

Eran traced a line on the tent floor with the toe of his boot.

"Okay. But I don't like it."

The way from Jerusalem to Mount Hermon runs through the Jordan River Valley. It's an arid strip of land between highlands wrenched apart by continental convulsions, the northern reach of a rip in the earth's fabric that stretches from the East African Rift Valley through the long arm of the Red Sea and up to the Beka'a Valley in Lebanon. The sundering of the earth began twenty million years ago, and some anthropologists think that the physical and climactic changes it caused were instrumental in starting a group of East African apes on the process of evolving into the human race.

The road that runs through the valley on the Israeli side of the river marks the path of my life in Israel. Close to its northern end lies Kiryat Shmonah, my first home in my new country. Tirat Zvi, where I lived during my regular army service, is just off the road, halfway between Kiryat Shmonah and the two-lane highway that climbs west to Jerusalem, where I finally settled. In 1994, I had traveled the Jordan Valley road for fourteen years, first as an immigrant, then as a soldier, and for the previous ten years as a reservist, commuting between home and my posts on Mount Hermon. The age of the valley and the cataclysmic forces that tore it open always made the battles I was fighting seem paltry and ridiculous by comparison. But I was a human being, a descendant of those creatures who, on the edge of the rift, had begun to fashion weapons to use against one another. Sharpened stones in hand, they pondered and dreaded their own mortality while a great chasm opened slowly, imperceptibly, at their feet.

In the two years since Yitzhak Rabin's election at the beginning of our tour in Tubas, the eastern, Jordanian side of the valley had shifted to the north by no more than five millimeters. There had, however, been seismic political developments.

Rabin had been elected on a platform of pursuing serious talks with the Palestinians and the Arab countries on Israel's borders. Unlike his predecessor Shamir, he declared that, in principle, he would accept a territorial compromise in the West Bank and Gaza Strip in exchange for peace. He was cagier about his willingness to give up the Golan Heights and Mount Hermon, which had also been occupied in the Six-Day War. Their military value as high ground overlooking the Galilee was undeniable, but it was clear that Syria would not make peace with Israel so long as its land was occupied. Bilateral talks with both Syria and the Palestinians had been underway since the Madrid conference of 1991 but, marking time, Shamir had allowed the talks to get bogged down in procedural issues. Rabin wanted peace on both fronts and signaled the Syrians that he was ready to talk seriously, showing more flexibility on procedure as well as substance. However, Rabin continued his tough fight against Palestinian terrorism, aiming particularly at Hamas, the fundamentalist Islamic faction that had carried out a series of deadly attacks on Israeli soldiers and civilians. Hamas was strong in Kabatiyeh and launched several assaults on Company C. The closest call was a Friday night ambush of one of our jeep patrols in which bullets whistled between the heads of the jeep's driver and Falk, the commander. Fisch, in the back-facing seat, instantly fired a volley of his own and the attacker fled. Fisch had had his rifle illegally cocked. With his hand on the trigger, an unexpected bump in the road could have sent the bullet in his barrel flying into an innocent bystander, or into one of Fisch's buddies. But he was able to respond a fraction of a second sooner than he could have had he needed to pull back the bolt on his gun, and this very likely saved the patrol's lives. Elnatan, now deputy battalion commander, reprimanded Fisch but didn't punish him. Neither did the rules change.

This kind of war didn't trouble my conscience much. The people who were shooting at us didn't want to make peace; there was no reason to go easy on them. Israeli rule in the territories was still causing manifold injustices to the Palestinians, but we now had a government that clearly wanted to let the Palestinians rule themselves. If we were still waking up children at night when we raided a home in search of terrorists, if we were still delaying Palestinian families at roadblocks, these were temporary measures. The occupation was going to end.

The talks with the Syrians had soon stalled because President Hafez al-Assad was not prepared to compromise. He wanted all of the Golan Heights and Mount Hermon—not only the territory captured by Israel in the Six-Day War but also some small but important patches of Israeli land that Syria had occupied in the period between the 1948 armistice and the 1967 war. In exchange, he offered "nonbelligerence," but no more. No normalization of relations, no joint economic development, no opening up of the prison society he ran. It hardly seemed a good trade for the strategic assets we'd surrender. Furthermore, the moral issue in the Golan Heights was much less acute. There were many Israeli settlements on the plateau, but only a few thousand former Syrians, the great majority of them members of the Druze sect. While many of them claimed they'd rather be under Syrian rule (though it was hard to understand why), they were well integrated into the local economy and suffered few of the indignities that Israeli rule had imposed on the Palestinians in the West Bank and Gaza Strip. The prospect of them living indefinitely under occupation did not bother me all that much. Were they to accept Israeli citizenship (as a small number had done), they were so few in number they wouldn't affect Israel's Jewish majority.

I had greater hope for the talks with the Palestinians, which proceeded in Washington. Yet these negotiations, too, kept limping from stalemate to deadlock. Despite his promises of flexibility, Rabin had stuck to the long-held Israeli government position of not negotiating with the PLO and its leader, Yasir Arafat. The Palestinian delegation in Washington was composed of residents of the West Bank and Gaza Strip who had no official ties to the PLO. I favored a direct line to the PLO and could understand why the Palestinians were affronted by Rabin's refusal to talk with the organization they saw as their sole legitimate representative. But in practical terms, that was a procedural matter—everyone knew that the Palestinian delegation in Washington reported to Arafat and acted on his instructions. I was disappointed that the Palestinians were not responding in kind to Rabin's interest in making a deal. On the contrary, their positions seemed to be getting more rigid. Didn't they realize that they were missing an opportunity to work with the most amenable Israeli government that could ever get elected?

It was only at the end of the summer of 1993 that we learned why the talks in Washington weren't going anywhere. They were merely a cover. Rabin had been talking secretly to the PLO, through a back channel run by Israeli and PLO representatives in Oslo. The news came over the radio just as I walked into a friend's apartment for an Israeli-Palestinian dialogue group meeting. At first I didn't believe it. According to the reports, Israel and the PLO had made a deal that would soon be signed by Arafat and Rabin. The PLO would receive control of the Gaza Strip and Jericho. Then, in accordance with a detailed treaty still to be negotiated, Israel would withdraw from more of the West Bank. Israel would build no new settlements for five years, but neither would it evacuate any. During this five-year transition period, the two sides would negotiate a permanent agreement in which the fate of the settlements would be determined. It all seemed too good to be true.

But it was true, and on September 13, 1993, Rabin and Arafat met at the White House and signed the accord. (Six days later, Ilana gave birth to our younger daughter, Misgav.) We seemed to be heading into the future for which I had always hoped.

A series of events quickly punctured my euphoria, though. Soon after he signed the agreement, Arafat seemed to have second thoughts. Both in the territories and throughout the Palestinian diaspora, radical Palestinians, and even some of Arafat's close associates, opposed the deal. They accused him of giving away too much. Arafat began to gnaw at the edges of the agreement, demanding control of the border with Jordan and a larger police force than the agreement specified. He seemed to be pressuring Israel for concessions on the assumption that Rabin would not give up on an agreement he had already presented to the Israeli public. Even more disconcerting was Arafat's rhetoric, which continued to glorify armed struggle.

On the Israeli side, the right, and especially the religious right, opposed the agreement utterly. Settler leaders accused Rabin of treason and some talked darkly of civil war. On February 25, 1994, on the Jewish holiday of Purim, a young physician from Kiryat Arba, a husband and father named Baruch Goldstein, put on his reserve officer's uniform and went to the Tomb of the Patriarchs in Hebron. He entered a chamber reserved for Muslim prayer. There he sprayed automatic rifle fire on the prostrate Muslim worshippers, murdering twenty-nine before the survivors beat him to death. That this horror had been perpetrated by a man who ostensibly shared my faith sickened me. Hardly less alarming was the unwillingness of large swaths of the Israeli religious community to condemn the murderer unambiguously. Mizmor's second-grade teacher—who had impressed us with her warmth and her ability to engage Mizmor in her studies—told her class that the massacre was a crime. But she also told the children that she felt she could not judge Goldstein because, as a doctor, he had treated the victims of Palestinian terrorism, as if that could excuse mass murder in a house of God.

Goldstein did not, as he had hoped, prevent the withdrawal. Israel handed over the city of Jericho and nearly all of the Gaza Strip to the Palestinians on May 18. The road from Jerusalem to Mount Hermon now passed through Palestinian territory.

In October I reported for duty at the training base near Haifa, and when I went home on leave the ride I caught with another soldier took me through Tel Aviv. It wasn't until my return to Mount Hermon that I experienced firsthand the new political geography of the Jordan Valley. I'd arranged to ride back with some friends, and when we gathered in Jerusalem, no one discussed which route to travel. We'd always taken the road that descended east into the valley and turned north at the tip of the Dead Sea, riding through Jericho to the Sea of Galilee and Kiryat Shmonah. We'd go the same way this time.

I remember the trip vividly, but apparently not accurately. I can take comfort in the fact that Achlama, another in that party of four, recalls like me that our driver was Falk and that the vehicle was Falk's red van with the "Falk et Falk Designs" logo on its side. Barak, of course, completed the foursome. But Falk tells me that he missed our stint in Gladiola—he was on a long-planned European vacation with his wife. Barak confirms Falk's alibi. Barak served with us that year but has no memory of the ride through Jericho. Who was in the car? I'm not sure. But Falk and Barak and Achlama were so constantly together that even Achlama shares my false memory. So I will tell the story as I remember it.

We set out from Jerusalem in the late morning, and as we descended into the valley, the city's autumnal cool gave way to desert heat. By noon the sun glared through date palms standing sentry along the road in front of the Jericho military government building. The Palestinian forces had affixed a new sign crookedly to the yellow plaster of the old British police station.

"They'll be wanting new curtains," I said to Falk, who was driving, uncharacteristically, only slightly over the speed limit. "Maybe you can get the contract. And Achlama can do the signs."

"No chance. They probably want loud floral patterns and arabesques on turquoise. I don't stock that kind of fabric. Can't stand it," Falk said, grinning.

"Can you imagine what it would be like to submit a bid in Arabic?" Achlama said. "Israeli government tenders are a hundred pages long, and I can't understand them even though they're supposedly written in my language."

"Look at that," Barak said. We'd reached the intersection in the middle of the city where we had to make a left turn to stay on the road north. A chubby middle-aged man with an impressive mustache directed traffic. With his precisely placed beret, camouflage fatigues, and burnished black boots, he seemed a parody of the four of us in our shabby olive green work uniforms. My shirttails were comfortably out and I had many buttons open. Achlama looked worse in a torn yellow T-shirt, and he hadn't shaved even those parts of his face that he was in the habit of occasionally shaving.

The man's uniform sported a sleeve braid, medals, and a unit tag. He was a member of the PLO military that, under the Oslo accords, had been allowed into Jericho and the Gaza Strip to constitute the police force of the newly created autonomous Palestinian Authority. With all that regalia, he looked a lot more like the professional soldier he was than a policeman—especially since, in addition to the pistol on his broad military belt, he had a Kalashnikov slung over his shoulder. We instinctively placed our hands on our own M-16s, though we kept them out of sight.

"Maybe this wasn't such a great idea," I muttered as the policeman's gaze rested on the Hebrew lettering on Falk's van, then on the van's occupants. But he gave us a friendly wave and signaled us to make our left turn.

We drove past the tourist restaurants with their eternal baskets of oranges hanging from their awnings. Falk sped up to take the turn that led us out of the Palestinian city, past the tell where previous Jerichos had been built and destroyed, one on top of the other, for the last ten thousand years. We slowed at the Israeli roadblock that marked our return to home territory and halted for a minute at the passage between the barriers.

"Are they giving you any trouble?" Falk asked, his thumb pointing back at Jericho.

The sandy-haired nineteen-year-old who came to the car grinned. "Their patrol came up here half an hour ago. They didn't like our coffee. We thought there'd be an international incident, but then we conceded. We agreed that next time they visit, they'll do the cooking."

As we pulled out of the roadblock, Barak said, "Everything's changed so much in the last two years. I can't keep up with it."

"The whole world's rearranging itself," Achlama agreed. "They pick up a border from one place and throw it down in another place. You never know where you are anymore. You're driving along peacefully in your car and, whop, there's a border. You're in another country. Then, before you get used to it, another border."

"I might be able to keep up with the changes if I could keep my mind on them," I mused. "But the rest of my life keeps changing, too. The Serbs slaughter the Bosnians, and my office gets burgled. Rabin negotiates with the Palestinians and the Syrians, and my kid has a hernia operation. Syria says they want all of the Golan Heights and Mount Hermon before they even start to talk, and my daughter's first-grade teacher calls to say she isn't doing her homework. Hamas terrorists attack Israeli soldiers, and my two-year-old is beating up the other kids in his nursery school class."

We drove slowly through another roadblock, back into Palestinian territory. Low-lying, worn plaster huts lined the streets, homes converted into storefronts to take advantage of the roadside trade. Their yards were full of carved limestone lawn ornaments, ranging from small and cartoonish dog effigies to humongous stone coffeepots. This was Uja, a village that had been gerrymandered into Jericho to fulfill the

Palestinian demand that the West Bank withdrawal include something more than the oasis city itself.

"Who buys this stuff?" I asked Achlama. "Even if I had a lawn, I wouldn't put one of these things on it."

"You would indeed," Achlama chided me. "You'd do it for peace."

"Even I have my limits," I insisted.

"By the way, now that I think of it," Falk said as he scanned the limestone sculptures with a professional eye, "didn't you say when you called me yesterday that Teitelbaum was driving up with us?"

"He was supposed to. But he called me this morning. Really apologetic. His wife was hysterical. She gets incredibly anxious every time he goes to the army, ever since."

Ever since he'd discovered his baby girl dead in her crib the morning he was to set out for a one-day training session a year ago. A couple of times he had decided that he couldn't leave his wife alone, and who were we to question his judgment?

It meant I was down one more man. How was I going to manage? I considered pleading with the battalion to send us someone from the headquarters company, where the guys served less time than we did. But we already had two loaners and headquarters was feeling the strain. The battalion personnel officer would tell me to give fewer vacations and to call men back before their allotted time was up. But most of the men were getting the minimum days mandated. If I cut their vacation short, they could lodge a complaint and would be right to do so. A few of the guys had gotten extra days off for special reasons, but neither Eran nor I was willing to break a promise. We'd approved those days only when we were certain they were badly needed and deserved.

Some things were out of my control. Policemen, like Eldad, served only a week. A new regulation decreed that university students called up while classes were in session could not serve more than twenty-one days. Another exempted men whose wives were in their ninth month of pregnancy. My only real option was to remain understaffed and schedule the work as best I could with the men we had. Even that was problematic, as regulations demanded that I man the base with the requisite number of soldiers.

We reached the roadblock on the other side of Uja, waved at the soldiers, and passed through. The Jordan Valley road stretched straight before us, the sand and desert scrub on each side broken here and there by an irrigated orchard or field. Some belonged to local Palestinians, others to Jewish settlements.

Falk drove his van like a go-cart on the rolling terrain. He gestured with his right hand toward the Jordan River, Israel's border with the Kingdom of Jordan. It was not a river but a narrow stream, barely more than a glorified creek wending its way through a gully with some greenery on either side.

"I still don't understand," he said, turning his head to look at me, "how people like you can be prepared to let Palestinian soldiers control our eastern frontier."

"The Jordan River isn't much of a natural barrier," I observed. "It's not going to delay an Iraqi armored division very long." I waved my left hand at the hills to our west. "If you want to control the valley, you can do it better from the highlands."

"But you want to give those to the Palestinians, too," Barak said.

"Just think of it," Falk said. "A Palestinian sniper could sit on that hill and get me in his sights with no problem at all."

"Falk, ever since Kabatiyeh you think every Arab sniper wants you for a target," Achlama scoffed. "So someone shot at you. We know. It's great. Just shut up about it already."

The road grew hillier as it drew away from the river. The October sun beat down as if it were August. I made out a clutch of low, white houses and towering date palms in the distance.

"Tirat Tzvi." I pointed it out to my companions. We were still a good ten kilometers south of the turnoff to the kibbutz, but it was nearly due east. The access road followed the Green Line, curving east and then south off the main road.

"You can really see how they used to be hemmed in on three sides by the Arabs," I said.

"And that's how you want them to be again?" Falk asked.

I fell silent.

"I hope it will be different this time," I said.

"I hope you're right," said Barak. "I think you are wrong, but I hope you are right."

We stopped at the army canteen in Kiryat Shmonah to pick up chocolate wafers, candy bars, coffee, and soft drinks—supplies for our own company canteen. North of town we took a road heading east. We again drove along a border, this time with Lebanon. At the foot of Mount Hermon we took a left onto the back road that wound up Bear Mountain. Army outposts appeared at intervals along the north side of the road. We passed a trail on the right that led to the site where, so it was said, God promised Abraham that his descendants would inherit this land. There was also a sculpture garden, an incongruous artistic re-sponse to the barbed wire on the opposite side of the road. Gladiola came up on the left. It had the look of a squatters' village with struc-tures standing at random on and inside earthwork embankments. Mar-cel Levy, the guard at the gate, saluted us before pulling the rope that opened the barrier. He was being facetious. No one in this army salutes.

"Oh-ho!" came a shout from the direction of the war room, a nichelike chamber at the foot of the guard post on the base's northeast-ern corner. Aviel, the Platoon Two commander, descended the steps and strode over, his arms outstretched. He was as much of a contrast with Eran as could be—frenetic, loquacious, haphazard, impetuous, and thin. His shirt was out, his hair was uncombed, and the laces of his boots flapped behind him as he approached.

"What a surprise! If they let me out of here, you wouldn't see me coming back."

Eran emerged from the war room. He walked wearily down the steps and joined us.

"We brought supplies for the canteen," Achlama said by way of encouragement. Eran waved him off.

"Did you guys see Keisar by any chance? He took the truck this morning to get food from the Lower Ski Lift and we haven't heard from him since."

"If you haven't heard from Keisar he must be far, far away." Achlama stroked his beard. "That might not be such a bad thing. The question is, would you rather have peace and quiet, or supper?"

"We just had it out with the Mount Hermon regiment commander," Eran told us. "He's given us another assignment. We have to send two soldiers every day from six a.m. to six p.m. to guard the civilians who are working on the road to Astra."

"Bastard," said Barak.

"Is he crazy?" I asked. "Where will we find two more soldiers? Did you hear from Teitelbaum?"

Eran nodded. "I told him to come as soon as he could. What could I do? He sounded desperate. And he's a good guy. You know he's not playing games."

He looked at me doubtfully.

"I asked Elnatan what he thought about our manpower problems. He said that the math works. You take the number of guys we're supposed to have here times an average of twelve hours of work a day and we're okay. So why doesn't it work?"

Elnatan's analysis was technically accurate but unrealistic. Our missions weren't evenly distributed—there was far more work at night. A soldier could guard at night for six hours and then go out on a six-hour patrol, and he'd be free to sleep all day. The math worked. But the question was what kind of soldier he would be in his fifth hour of guard duty. And he wouldn't be of much use on the patrol if he napped in his seat most of the time.

The Mount Hermon command found an original solution to our problem. They told us to put one soldier, instead of the regulation two, in one of the guard posts at night. We did as we were told, but under protest. I thought it was irresponsible to have a man work alone at night. Even the most motivated guy will doze off in the dark if he's got no one to talk to.

We walked to the dining room to confer over a cup of coffee. Sefi was cutting onions in the kitchen while the grungy cook the battalion had assigned us stared sullenly at a large pot of water that was not boiling. He looked up at us.

"Where the fuck is Keisar?" he barked. "How am I supposed to cook supper if I don't have supplies?"

"Sefi, can we have a pot of coffee for a staff meeting?" Aviel asked. Sefi set down his knife, washed his hands, and took a coffeepot off the shelf.

"You should also know that the battalion personnel officer is waiting for a chance to scream at you. He says we're over budget in reserve days and wants an explanation," Aviel said, pulling out a bench. "I told him to shove it."

"I don't understand." Eran shook his head slowly. "How can it be that we don't have enough men for our missions and yet we're over budget in reserve days?"

I lifted my hands in supplication. "I never claimed to understand the system," I said. A reserve day was a day of service by a single reservist, the unit by which our manpower was measured. Service included both time at base and time on leave, which was paid.

Until the second half of the 1980s—soon after I joined Company C—a reservist didn't cost the army much and men were called up freely. But as part of the economic reforms of the 1980s, the government made a deal with the army: Use reserve manpower more efficiently, and the savings will be credited to the army, to be used on other projects. With this incentive, the army began economizing. Each battalion called up for duty was awarded a budget of reserve days based on the missions and posts it was assigned. The battalion then gave each company a quota. In the old days the allotment had been generous enough to allow a "man in the air." If a base required twenty-five men, the company commander and clerk planned to have twenty-six. If something happened—Teitelbaum's no-show, or an unexpected mission—there was still sufficient manpower. In the 1990s the budgets became tighter and the battalion no longer allowed us to keep an extra man. Whereas it had once been possible to give men an extra day of vacation, the battalion personnel officer now took us to task if we exceeded the minimum.

Sefi brought us the coffee and some blue plastic cups.

"What gets me mad," I said, pouring for Eran and Aviel, "is that on the one hand they say we're combat soldiers and we get the toughest assignments, and on the other they tell us to guard these road workers as if we were some sort of rear unit. They've got more than enough supply and canteen guys at the regiment. Let them stand guard over the tractors."

"They're not going to," Aviel said. "The regimental commander looks after his own. He won't give them more work."

"What are we going to do?" Eran asked.

"I thought about this on the way up," I said slowly. "I think we'll have to manage without KP. We'll tell the guys that each person's responsible for washing his own dishes after each meal. Anyone who has a spare half hour will come and help the cook."

"They won't do it. They'd rather sleep," Aviel scoffed.

"If they prefer to sleep, then we won't have meals. We'll eat rations," I said.

"He's right," Eran nodded.

"I think everyone will pitch in. I think they understand that we're in an impossible situation and that it's not our fault."

"I want to see the MHO," Sefi said evenly but firmly.

"We'll get you an appointment," Aviel said. "But it will take a couple of weeks. In the meantime, you guard and do patrols."

"Sefi," I said, "be reasonable."

He shook his head. "I've decided it's time to look out for myself."

Harizi came in at a run.

"Eran, the patrol reports suspicious footprints by the fence at point 345. You should get over there."

Eran ran to his jeep, and Aviel and I ran back to the war room with Harizi to hear the report.

"Fuck it," Aviel panted. "We need everyone on alert. Where the hell is Keisar?"

The radio was alive with reports and orders. "Full-size shoe prints, leading in the direction of the canyon," Vanunu, the patrol commander, reported. "Can you identify a break in the fence?" Elnatan demanded to know. "I want all battalion forces ready to move out at my order."

In the midst of the reports and orders and static we heard a distant voice. "Keisar to base, Keisar to base."

"Keisar? Your location, avor," Harizi said.

"I'm at Snowview, avor."

"Snowview?" Aviel said. "What is he doing there?" Snowview was all the way up the mountain, past the Upper Ski Lift and the Yisraeli.

"Request to know the reason you are at Snowview," Aviel said, grabbing the handset from Harizi.

"Paprika," Keisar's voice said faintly.

"Paprika?"

"We're all out and they didn't have any at Lower Ski Lift. But they said that Snowview had spices to spare, so I came up here to get some."

"Clear the airwaves immediately," Elnatan's voice commanded. "We have a possible terrorist in the sector."

"Receive cancellation of track report, avor." It was Vanunu's voice again.

"Did you say cancellation, avor?" said Elnatan's voice.

"Root. Cancellation. The tracks are Shaya's. He went to pee."
Silence.

"Via you to Shaya," came Elnatan's voice. "He'd better keep away from me for the duration of this stint because if I see him I will tie a tourniquet around his neck."

"Root. Message received and conveyed."

The commander of the Mount Hermon regiment entered our dining room in a sour mood. Amzaleg, the guard at the gate, had been unimpressed by the career officer's antenna-studded jeep. He'd insisted on checking the commander's ID as regulations required.

Since Brigadier General Hermon had decided to visit at 6:30 p.m., after the night guard shift had begun, not many guys were free to meet with him. Flanked by two junior officers from his staff, he stood before the tables with his hands behind his back.

"Okay," he said. "I'm busy and I don't have much time. I want to hear what all the whining is about."

The guys recited the litany of sleepless nights, of going straight from guard duty to patrol, of working eight or even ten hours with no rest. They expressed outrage that the regiment had supplied them with insufficient food and inferior gear, including jeeps that were constantly out of commission. They pointed out that the shortage of leave days made it nearly impossible for Eran to accommodate special circumstances—the student who needed to get out for an exam, the small businessman who had an important meeting, the father with a sick child. Such situations could easily make a good soldier decide that the cost of serving in the reserves was just too high. The company would lose valued men and morale would decline.

"Okay, I've heard enough," the commander said. "Stop being god-damned crybabies. You're here for a month and then you go home. The army has a right to expect you to work hard while you're here."

I stood up. "I think what bothers the guys more than not getting any sleep or not having enough to eat is that they feel they're being taken for granted. You can't take them for granted. If you do, you won't have any soldiers left."

"That," barked the commander, "is nonsense. We have a reserve army law and you men will do as you are told. Now get back to work." He turned on his heel and stalked out, his attachés running after him.

After that we were on the Hermon commander's shit list. His deputy began to hit us with spot inspections, trying to catch our guards asleep or our patrols unprepared. The climax came on our next to last day in Gladiola.

Elnatan called Eran in a fury. "The deputy Hermon commander says he's lodging a complaint against Company C. One of your patrols was out and lacked the most fundamental knowledge of their gear and weaponry, he says. Your sergeant is incompetent and ignorant and ought to be kicked out of the army. What the hell is going on over there, Eran?"

"Which patrol?" Eran spoke on the field phone in the war room, where I was on duty.

"The eastern patrol that was out this morning at eight a.m.," Elnatan said.

"Who was on the eastern patrol at eight a.m.?" Eran asked me, holding the phone away from his ear.

I looked at the duty roster. "It was Vanunu," I said pointedly, leaning back in my chair.

"It was Vanunu," Eran said into the receiver.

A stunned silence.

"*Vanunu?*" said Elnatan.

Vanunu was the most meticulous of our three sergeants. Unlike

Alon, who found rules annoying, or Eiger, who found in them flexibilities never imagined by their authors, Vanunu went by the book. He didn't do it in a pedantic way, but he had a thoughtful respect for order and procedure. Thus, as rules required, he inspected his patrol car thoroughly each time he set out on patrol, making sure that the guns were in good order and that all the requisite maps and emergency equipment were in place. He briefed his soldiers on the mission and put them through a few drills before setting out, routines with which the other NCOs had dispensed after the first week.

"Call him in," Elnatan ordered. "I want to talk to him myself."

I radioed Vanunu's patrol and told them to come back to base for a break. In fifteen minutes Vanunu stood by me and Eran, phone in hand.

". . . so the deputy Hermon commander signaled us to stop," Vanunu related into the receiver, "and then he got out of his car and walked up and stood close, very close, by my driver. He shot a few questions at me—where's this wadi, how high is that peak, what's the range of a MAG machine gun—and I answered him. He didn't like it that I knew the stuff. Suddenly he turned to the driver and said, 'How many bolts are in the wheel of this jeep?'"

"How many *what*?"

"Bolts in the wheel of the jeep. The driver just shrugged. So he turned to me and said, 'So, Sergeant, your driver doesn't know his equipment. What about you? How many bolts are in the wheel of this jeep?' And I couldn't fucking remember if there are five or eight."

"*I* don't know how many bolts there are in the wheel of a jeep," Elnatan fumed. "What an asshole. He'll hear some things from me now that he'll remember for a long time."

I spent the afternoon drafting a petition, and during the course of the evening I got all the guys to sign. It was a concise indictment of the way the army, and the Hermon command in particular, had treated a dedicated infantry company like dirt.

I took it to the kitchen to get Sefi to sign, too. Our experiment with cutting KP had not been a success. The meals got worse and that only amplified the sense of oppression we were all feeling. Once Teitelbaum returned we had a bit more breathing space and didn't need Sefi as a guard.

"I don't know if I should sign," he said after he read the declaration. "I mean, I don't intend to be in the company anymore."

"The more signatures we have, the better it looks," I said. "And who knows where any of us will be next year."

"You'll be here." He picked up a stack of still-damp blue plates and began to set the tables for the next morning's breakfast.

"You might not believe this," I said, "but I really hope that you will be, too."

"Oh, sure," he snorted.

"I hope you appreciate that we've tried to give you some space this time. There are guys we wouldn't do that for."

Sefi began to put out cups. He didn't reply.

"How's the photography going?" I asked.

He shrugged. "I've done a couple of weddings."

His voice was bitter.

"I guess it helps pay the tuition," I said.

"Oh, I dropped out of the course."

"Dropped out? Why?"

He looked me in the eye. "Look, I'm just not good enough. I don't have it. What's the use?"

"I thought your stuff was pretty good."

"Then either you don't know anything or you're lying."

He was with us briefly the following year and then he had his appointment with the MHO. We never saw him again after that. Perhaps it was unreasonable for me to blame myself, but I couldn't help but see his departure as a personal failure. This made no sense. The army was a small part of his experience. I could not know what forces acted on him and what thoughts he had during the other eleven months of the year. Yet I felt a kinship here, for his compulsion to get out of the army was a mirror image of my compulsion to remain. Both went beyond any rational calculus of what we could contribute to the army and how we might otherwise use the time and energies that the army claimed. There was something deep inside Sefi that told him to get out, and something deep inside me that told me to stay.

When I got home I mailed the petition to the army's chief personnel officer in Tel Aviv. Three or four days later I got a call from a young man who identified himself as the secretary to the chief reserve officer. I hadn't even known there was a chief reserve officer. "He wants to meet with you about the petition," the secretary said. The following week I took a bus to Tel Aviv and was ushered into a small office with white walls. A bearded man with a colonel's insignia asked me to sit.

"I want you to convey my concern to your buddies," he told me. "I'd like to be able to say that combat reservists don't get treated that way in our army, but I know that it does happen. You should tell them that we're going to do all we can to make sure that next time you serve you feel wanted and appreciated."

"The problem," I said, "is that you guys here at the top don't realize that the reserve army is, for all intents and purposes, made up of volunteers."

"I'm very aware of that," he said. "I also know that there's just one thing that keeps guys like you in units like this when you've got families and jobs at home. It's your buddies. If you don't have a good time together—in addition to the work you do—you won't come back."

"So what will you do?"

He raised his hands helplessly. "I'm ashamed to say, not much. I've already spoken to the Hermon command and told them to treat their reservists better. But I can't promise any big changes. Budgets are tight and we're not able to ease up on the reserve day budgets or give longer vacations."

"So I don't have anything to report to the guys."

"There is one thing they'll be glad to hear. Partly because of our efforts to make it easier for the reservists, and partly because of the new situation in the territories, the army has decided that it can cut the regular term of active duty from four and a half to three and a half weeks. So next time, at least, you won't be in for as long." He smiled. "Think of it as Company C's peace dividend."

Chapter Ten
·WITHDRAWALS·

E RAN WAS ON THE PHONE. "THERE MUST HAVE BEEN TEN STUDENTS who complained that the stint is a disaster for them, but I told them they'll just have to live with it," he said.

"Absolutely. They'll miss only a week of classes," I pointed out.

Eran had returned from petition day, an event before each round of duty at which soldiers who wanted an abbreviated tour or a deferral could make their case before the company commander.

"After what happened last year I'm not letting anyone off if it's not an emergency," Eran declared. "First we'll get settled in and see how many people we need. Then, if we can afford it, we'll let them off early."

"If we're giving territory to the Palestinians," I said, "I assume we'll need fewer people toward the end than we do at the beginning."

"Don't be so sure. It takes a lot more soldiers to get out of a place than it does to get in. Anyway, we won't know until we're there."

"I guess that's the one lesson we've learned." I scanned the Company C personnel list. "Sometimes I wonder if there's any point at all in planning."

I hesitated a minute. "Um, Eran, you didn't mention Eiger."

Eiger and I had talked a few days before. His workload was heavy, he said, and the prospect of being a single parent for the coming holidays was making Na'ama frantic.

"Oh, yeah, Eiger called me," Eran said. "He told me he's only coming for the last week and a half."

"Okay," I said. I made a note by Eiger's name.

Now Eran hesitated. "Do you think that's okay?"

"No comment," I said. I had a flagrant conflict of interest when it came to Eiger. It was my responsibility to see that leave time and deferrals were handed out equitably, but Eiger was my best friend. Some guys had already complained that he seemed to get a lot more time off than they did. But Eiger had recently been diagnosed with high blood pressure and was now on medication. All he had to do was hand his medical record to the battalion doctor and he'd be sent home immediately and never called up again. Eran valued Eiger too much to risk that. While I didn't think Eiger would really seek a medical exemption even if Eran told him he'd have to serve the entire twenty-five days, Eran preferred not to press the issue. And if that was Eran's decision, I was not going to intervene.

I changed the subject. "What about Meshulam?"

"I told you. He'll be in for ten days."

"He called me an hour ago," I said. "He sounded really upset."

Meshulam was a thickset guy with clipped hair who'd joined the company the year before at Gladiola. Self-effacing and diligent, he'd stood in as a patrol commander when there weren't enough NCOs, and he'd done the job well. He'd married a few months ago and set up a gardening business, taking out loans to buy equipment and a small pickup truck. Although he employed an Arab laborer, it was essentially a one-man operation that would shut down while he was in the army. It was autumn, and there was a lot of work to be done before the winter rains. He asked Eran to be excused from our entire month of service. When Eran reminded him that the consequence would be a month of deadly boring guard duty at our home base sometime during the winter, with people he didn't know and probably wouldn't like, he wasn't deterred. He'd be less busy then, he said. He maintained that were he to shut down the business now, his clients would find a different gardener.

"It sounds like he really needs a deferral," I said.

"He can do ten days," Eran insisted. "Ten days won't kill his business."

"He was a good guy last time."

"That's why I want to see him with us, not as a guard at the home base," Eran said. "I want to keep him in the loop."

When Company C reconvened at the end of September 1995, a year after its demoralizing stint in Gladiola, the Oslo accords were in high gear. The conventional wisdom around the world—certified by the award of the Nobel Peace Prize to Rabin, Peres, and Arafat the previous December—was that Israel was on the verge of a new era. Foreign businesses had once avoided Israel, either under pressure of the Arab boycott or because they thought investing in a war-torn country too risky. Now money poured in. Efi had his pick of high-paying software development jobs when he decided to move his family from Haifa to Shoham, a former farming village that had metamorphosed into a bedroom community for Tel Aviv commuters. Elnatan, now our battalion commander, was moving rapidly up the ladder of Tower Semiconductor's facility outside of Haifa, and techies like Greenberg, Teitelbaum, and Fisch seemed to switch jobs every few months as better and better offers came their way. The rising tide lifted nearly everyone. Falk, Achlama, and Barak were working overtime to provide, respectively, curtains, signs, and furniture to the office buildings and shopping malls springing up around the country. Shaya's toy store doubled in size and

Eiger quit his day job to work full time at his consulting practice, which helped pharmaceutical and cosmetic firms get Israeli licenses for their products.

Prosperity came with a landscape that looked increasingly American —Dunkin' Donuts and Office Depot made their local debuts. Golden arches popped up everywhere, including—a lot of people thought it sacrilegious—right next to the Golani Brigade war memorial in the Galilee.

I had settled in Israel seventeen years previous to lend my support and my vote to the country's progressive forces. Now came the moment I had waited for. We were on the road to peace with the Palestinians, which would in turn allow Israel to fortify its democracy and devote its resources to social justice. Why wasn't I more enthusiastic? Why did it all seem so much more complicated now? Perhaps it was a matter of time. In July I'd turned thirty-nine, a year short of what the sages called the age of discernment, the stage of maturity when fine distinctions begin to overshadow the hard-and-fast principles of youth. My time as a soldier undoubtedly had a lot to do with it as well. I'd learned about the importance of defensive lines and high ground. I'd learned that a show of strength could be the guarantor of a quiet month, and that a single timely plastic bullet could avert the need to fire many deadly rounds a few minutes later. My faith in peace with the Palestinians had come to resemble my faith in God—both seemed a necessary, fundamental truth that didn't fit easily into the real world, something to be aspired to but also wrestled with. As Jews wiser than I had noted, though, doubting God was one way of affirming Him.

I remained a committed advocate of accommodation, but I was worried. The new wealth was creating much greater inequality than Israel had ever known, with the new upper middle class leaving behind the less skilled and less educated. I was even more apprehensive at what I saw on the Palestinian side, where the lives of the vast majority had changed little. Some of the blame rested on the Palestinian leadership.

Arafat, with the support of his new cabinet, had established a governing system based on cronyism, granting his supporters control of national monopolies on essential commodities such as gasoline. He kept close personal control over all Palestinian Authority funds and handed out money as he saw fit. It hardly seemed like an auspicious beginning for the government that was to be our neighbor.

But the main reason the Palestinian economy declined as Israel's boomed was that Israel continued to restrict the number of Palestinians who could work in Israel proper. This had begun during the Intifada, when terrorist attacks became common. In the two years since Rabin and Arafat had signed the Oslo agreement, however, the frequency and severity of terrorist attacks had increased. Suicide bombing, a tactic inaugurated in the early 1990s, was growing ever more gruesome. In January a bomber had detonated himself at the Beit Lid bus stop, near an army base in central Israel; when soldiers rushed to help their wounded comrades, a second bomber exploded.

It was not surprising that Palestinian opponents of peace, mostly from the Hamas and Islamic Jihad factions, sought to destabilize the process. But as such attacks continued and Arafat refused to take decisive action to dismantle the Islamist militias, it was not easy to convince the Israeli public that tens of thousands of Palestinians should be allowed to circulate in Israeli cities. Instead, Israel began to import labor from the Philippines, Thailand, and Africa. This produced another demographic challenge to the country's Jewish character even before we'd resolved the Palestinian issue. It also created a moral dilemma. The newspapers published reports showing that many foreign workers had been mistreated and exploited by their employers and by the agents who brought them to Israel.

Yes, I had my doubts. But when I was called up once again for reserve duty in the West Bank, I looked forward to a mission different from the ones we'd pursued during the Intifada years. The road might be bumpy, but the direction was clear. This time, I'd be able to serve in the territories with conviction. Instead of repressing the Palestinians, I'd be helping to implement a peace agreement.

After Rosh Hashanah, the two-day Jewish new year, the Company C staff were bused with our battalion's other company commanders to the positions we'd been assigned in the West Bank area of Ramallah, just north of Jerusalem. The Palestinians intended to make Ramallah a temporary seat of government pending the resolution of their demand—adamantly opposed by the vast majority of Israelis—that the eastern, Arab part of Jerusalem become the capital of the Palestinian state to be.

Our company's main base stood alongside Route 443, an old back road that was being widened into an alternative highway linking Jerusalem and the Tel Aviv metropolis. Running north of and more or less parallel to the main freeway, Route 443 originated at the western edge of Ramot, a huge Jerusalem neighborhood sprawling over the eastern face of a ridge that had been Jordanian territory until 1967. Just south of Shoham, where Efi lived, the road linked up with the web of highways surrounding Tel Aviv. Israeli governments of all stripes had promoted development along Route 443. Before the Six-Day War, Jerusalem had been connected to the rest of the country by an easily severed strip of land. A string of settlements built on either side of the road, in between, on top, and largely incognizant of the existing Arab villages, had turned a narrow corridor into a sturdier belt of Jewish habitation.

Some of the settlements were small and peopled by politically motivated, predominantly religious families who viewed themselves as pioneers. But most of the new communities were planned for a diverse, solidly middle class population that eschewed the settler label. These towns were built to be bedroom communities for young families with parents working in high-tech or white-collar jobs in Jerusalem or Tel Aviv.

The linchpin of this residential belt was Modi'in, slated to be a full-fledged city but still largely under construction in 1995. East of it, in the direction of Jerusalem, lay Maccabim and Re'ut, twin communities of duplexes and private homes much like the neighborhood where Eiger lived in Zikhron Ya'akov, south of Haifa. The atmosphere of suburban calm was belied only by the army roadblock just east of the entrance to Re'ut, where suspicious—that is, Arab—cars were searched and their occupants' identity papers inspected. Our base stood above the road-block, on a hill north of the highway, opposite the town.

We also had three smaller outposts to man. Vanunu and Azoulai, with their handpicked crew of guys who liked to talk about cars and soccer, were stationed at a roadblock to the south, on a road linking 443 with the main freeway. Another roadblock, on the road that ran north from the Modi'in junction through a tangled string of Jewish set-tlements and Arab villages, was under Harizi's command. Harizi had assumed the post of Platoon Two sergeant in a company staff shuffle during our previous maneuvers, when Alon moved up to the rather vague position of company communications NCO. The communica-tions position had previously been held by the incomprehensible Yemenite Shaltiel, who, together with Mizrahi and Keisar, transferred to the battalion staff. Falk, Barak, and Achlama took over the first ser-geant position. In the past, this job had been filled by two men, a first sergeant and his deputy, but it now became a triumvirate of equals. Three first sergeants didn't seem too many given the identity of our new deputy company commander, who according to army procedure was the company's chief logistics officer—Aviel. Aviel was warm, easygoing, and fearless, but logistics were about as natural to him as conversation was to Eran. His gut instinct was that the best solution to any contingency was an ad hoc one that ignored all previous plans.

Eran assigned the third outpost to Efi and Platoon One. It was the only base in our sector to be situated inside a Palestinian village. Sitting in the midst of the Arabs had been the norm for us from Bani Na'im through Kabatiyeh. Like Tubas and Kabatiyeh, Harbata housed a regional civil administration office. But the post was temporary. A week and a half into our tour, we would transfer control of that office to the Palestinian Authority. Plans for the evacuation had already been drafted; it awaited only Knesset confirmation of what was called the Oslo II agreement. The agreement stipulated further staged Israeli withdrawals in the West Bank, creating a complex web of zones, some under Palestinian rule, some under Israeli rule, and some in which the Palestinians took charge of civilian functions and local policing but Israel retained overarching responsibility for security. The Knesset would vote on October 6, the day after Yom Kippur. The right was furiously opposing the agreement through a campaign of demonstrations and civil disobedience. Rabin's coalition had only a narrow majority, but it looked as if it would be enough to push through the agreement.

After arriving at the Route 443 tent camp and being briefed by the outgoing unit's captain, Company C's staff dispersed to our respective posts. Along with the new Platoon Two commander, Yoni, I boarded the jeep of an outgoing lieutenant, Oren, to learn the patrol covering the road north to Harbata.

Yoni wore glasses and a knitted kipah. His closely cropped, round head seemed small for his body, and he had a long-limbed, wiry frame that at first made you think he was awkward. In fact, his movements were fluid, precise, and strong, and in the brief conversations we'd had, he exhibited a keen intelligence. The guys who'd attended college had almost all gone into science, engineering, law, or business. That was where the jobs were. Yoni had chosen the humanities—he was about to begin his undergraduate studies in history at the Hebrew University in Jerusalem—and he had a sensitivity for nuance and perspective that I often found lacking in the techies. He also flattered me by taking an interest in my work as a writer and translator.

Yoni lived in Efrat, a large town populated by middle-class religious Zionists. In effect, it was Jerusalem's principal southern suburb. Falk and his family had recently moved there, and Eiger's parents had lived there for some time. But it was located in the West Bank, between Bethlehem and Hebron, over the Green Line. Most Israelis, even those who opposed the settlements, assumed that Efrat and a block of smaller settlements nearby would become part of Israel in any peace treaty with the Palestinians. The same went for those settlements in the Modi'in cluster that also lay in the West Bank. Efrat was close to the old border and could easily be connected to Jerusalem by a road that looped around Bethlehem. Its residents were by and large more moderate than their brethren in the "ideological" settlements that lay in the West Bank's interior, in areas of dense Palestinian habitation. Still, most of them opposed Rabin and his policies.

As quickly as most men steered their first conversation with a newcomer toward cars, sports, and women, I steered mine toward politics. Yoni and I hadn't exchanged more than a few sentences before I'd asked what he thought of the peace process. Given the tensions in Israel, I was worried. Being from Efrat, Yoni was certainly a religious nationalist. He'd just spent a postarmy year working as a farm laborer at one of the most right-wing settlements in the Golan Heights. Could he, as an officer, lead Company C when it handed over territory to the Palestinians?

Though I'd expected Yoni to be an opponent of Rabin and the Oslo accords, the intensity and bitterness in his response took me by surprise. He claimed not to object in principle to the Palestinians controlling parts of the West Bank and Gaza Strip, but he thought the current agreement totally misconceived. Israel was giving power to Arafat while Palestinian violence against Israelis continued unchecked. The agreement created a checkerboard of Israeli and Palestinian land that made it almost impossible to protect Israel's Jews, especially those who lived in the settlements. He was particularly upset that Oslo II gave the Palestinian Authority control of Hebron except for the pockets of Jewish settlement. He wasn't impressed when I noted that the Palestinians were no less incensed by Israel's insistence on retaining a hostile population in the middle of a Palestinian city. But I had to admit that Yoni was right about one thing—while Israel's official position had always been that the Tomb of the Patriarchs should be open to all religions, the Palestinian Authority and the Muslim religious authorities under its purview refused to acknowledge any Jewish claim to the site. They accepted Jewish worshippers there only because they had no choice.

But what made Yoni furious was Rabin's attitude toward the religious community.

"Rabin's stereotyped us all," he declared. "All religious people are primitive extremist fanatics. As far as he's concerned, the religious public's sentiments are of no importance. He'll do what he wants even if there's an entire sector of the population that opposes it. If he can engage in dialogue with Arafat, why can't he do it with us? He demonizes the settlers, makes them all out to be pariahs. I've got a problem with that attitude. It's going to tear our society apart."

I searched for some way to sympathize.

"You know," I said, "you sound the way I did in the eighties. Back then, Begin branded the peace camp unpatriotic. And he pursued a policy of building settlements even though a large part of the population opposed it."

"It's not the same," Yoni insisted. "He didn't put the country in mortal danger by withdrawing from strategic territory and limiting the army's freedom of action."

"No, but by building the settlements he was trying to make it impossible for any future government to reach a territorial compromise with the Palestinians," I said.

"It's not the same," he repeated.

Oren took the commander's seat in the jeep and Yoni and I clambered into the back. Pinhasi, a dark-skinned driver from the outgoing unit whose heavy eyebrows made him look perpetually angry, pulled the vehicle out of the base.

"The only reason for this patrol," said Oren as we took a right turn onto Route 443, "is so the operations officer at division head-quarters can check a box on his missions list. If a sniper shoots up a Jew-ish family's car at the Modi'in junction, or if a suicide bomber who blows himself up in Jerusalem turns out to be from one of the villages here, it won't be his fault. 'The road was patrolled twenty-four hours a day,' he'll tell the investigators, 'but, somehow, the terrorist slipped through.'"

"It's the most fucking asinine thing you've ever done in uniform," Pinhasi concurred. "And that's saying a lot."

"Here's the Modi'in junction," Oren said, pointing it out for me both in the field and on the map he was trying to hold open in the wind. "Note the traffic light. I bet it's the first traffic light you've ever had to wait at during a patrol. No funny stuff. You might be on active duty, but you can still get a ticket."

"Hey, lady, get a move on!" Pinhasi shouted at the car in front of us, half a second before the light turned yellow. The line of cars moved slowly and the light turned red a second time before we could make the turn.

"Good thing we don't have anything important to do," Pinhasi muttered.

"Those houses down there, on the far side of the intersection, are Shilat. Agricultural, just like Kfar Ruth up here on the hill to our right. Kfar Ruth is mixed. Shilat," Oren said, with an eye on the kipahs Yoni and I wore, "is your kind of people. They think we've gone soft on the Arabs."

"Damn right we have," Pinhasi said. "They do whatever they want now, not scared of us at all. It's Rabin's fault. He's kissing Arafat's ass. Giving him the whole store."

Yoni shrugged. "I don't represent anyone in particular," he said. But Pinhasi had revved the engine and screeched into a right turn that he completed, as far as I could tell, before the green photons from the traf-fic light had a chance to reach his eyes.

"Asshole. I don't want to die the day before I go home," Oren said, glaring at Pinhasi. Then, to Yoni, "Sorry, I didn't hear that."

"I said, I don't represent anyone in particular," Yoni said, raising his voice.

"Now look to your left," Oren said.

We saw an American-style suburb plunked down on the hills where, centuries ago, the Maccabees had trained their irregulars for raids on Seleucid strongholds.

"That town is called Hashmona'im. Some amazing houses. Mostly young families, quiet. There's a pizza place and a coffee shop if you get hungry. You should take the jeep through there a couple times a day. Your guys will probably want to spend half the patrol at the pizza parlor, but don't let them," Oren told me.

"*We* spend our patrols eating pizza?" Pinhasi exclaimed, as if offended.

"Of course not Pinhasi personally." Oren winked. "Except when the other guys applied unreasonable physical force. Here on the right is Matitiyahu. Those guys are a little blacker, you know, more religious than you."

"I prefer to say religious in a different way," I said.

"Whatever. I can never figure out what the different hats mean. Farther up there is Kiryat Sefer. They're religious in a *really* different way, if that's how you want me to say it. The men dress in black, the girls wear stockings in the summer, the men and women even sit separately on the bus. And here's our roadblock."

We pulled up at a concrete barrier and Pinhasi switched off the engine. A reservist with a fleshy face and streaks of gray in his hair waved at us as he checked the blue identification cards of two men with mustaches sitting sullenly in a Citroen. He waved them on.

"From East Jerusalem," the soldier called to Oren. "If all the people passing through here with blue Jerusalem ID cards really lived there, there wouldn't be room for the Jews."

Oren motioned him over. "Ben-Shushan, this is Yoni, one of the platoon commanders from the unit that's replacing us, and this is Watzman, their clerk, who does patrols, too. I'm showing them the ropes."

"A clerk who does patrols," Ben-Shushan said, nonplussed. "Well, if that's what gets you off."

The roadblock consisted of a metal booth in the center of the road, a refuge in rain, cold, and dark but primarily used to house coffee, snacks, and a transistor radio. Two concrete barricades staggered on either side of the road forced drivers to slow down, allowing the soldiers to stop and inspect any suspicious cars. A guard stood at a sandbagged position on a low hill on the west side. Behind the position was a tent where the soldiers who manned the roadblock in rotation slept and ate, a latrine, and a field shower fed by a large black plastic tank perched on a metal tower about ten meters high.

"The purpose of this roadblock," Oren deadpanned, "is to keep Palestinian terrorists out of Israel proper and to ensure that no illegal Palestinian workers cross this line."

Ben-Shushan referred us to a chart hanging from a nail inside the booth. Someone had stapled a protective plastic sheet over it, but the sheeting was so yellowed and grimy from time, exhaust fumes, and dust that I could barely make out the text and illustrations underneath.

"This is what a valid work permit looks like, and this document, which has to have a picture on it, indicates that its bearer is a collaborator who's on our side," Ben-Shushan explained. "You have to inspect the permits to make sure that the dates are right and that the information matches that on the identity card. Of course, a guy with a collaborator card will show it to you privately and you don't wave it around because you don't want all the other Arabs to know that he's an informant. Though they probably know anyway."

"You have to inspect every occupant of every car," Oren noted, "even if traffic backs up and it takes them hours to get through. Of course, settlers and other Jews get waved through."

Pinhasi snorted.

"That lasts for the first couple days," Ben-Shushan said. He eyed Oren with a smile. "Until you realize that pretty much every single Palestinian who comes through this roadblock has a permit. If they don't have permits they don't show up."

"They just stay home?" I asked.

"You wish," Pinhasi laughed. "They need to get to work in Israel. You think this will stop them?"

"Come over here," Ben-Shushan waved, already heading up the slope toward the tent. Oren, Yoni, and I followed; Pinhasi stayed at the roadblock to sip coffee and guard the jeep. When we reached the top, Ben-Shushan pointed down into the wadi on the other side of the hill. Scores of Arabs, mostly young men but also women, children, and old people, trudged over what had long since become a broad, beaten path through fields of melons and peppers. The trail began on the road's shoulder three hundred meters before the roadblock and connected back up with the road about the same distance beyond it. Both ends were in full view of the soldiers manning the position—as were the improvised parking lots. Buses, cabs, and private cars let people off at the Palestinian end of the path, and another set of vehicles waited to pick them up at the Israeli end. Some particularly enterprising drivers were navigating cars through the fields. A scratched and dented Peugeot that looked like it had once been painted a metallic maroon had gotten stuck in a muddy patch. Its passengers were trying to push it out. One of them motioned to us, as if asking us to lend a hand.

"Anyone who doesn't have a permit goes this way," Ben-Shushan said.

"A couple times a day we send a squad over and arrest a few of them," Oren said. "But it doesn't do much good."

"Why don't you set up another position there?" I asked.

"They'll just move to the next wadi over," Oren responded. "What's the use?"

We headed back down the hill.

"So, basically, the army allows Palestinians without permits to get into Israel. It just makes the trip longer and messier," said Yoni.

"Precisely," Oren said, shaking his head.

"Let's continue the tour," said Pinhasi, getting into the jeep.

"If you go down this road to the left you get to Qibya," Oren said. "They don't exactly like us there and we let the Border Guard deal with them. You know about Qibya?"

"That's the village where Ariel Sharon led a reprisal raid back in the fifties," I said. "It was just over the border in Jordan then. He blew up a bunch of houses, and a lot of civilians who were hiding in them got killed. Ben-Gurion tried to pretend that the army wasn't involved."

"Palestinian terrorists used the houses as a base to attack Israel," Yoni said.

"Damn right. Sharon knew how to teach those bastards a lesson. You know how many Israelis got killed back then by terrorists who sneaked over the border around here?" Pinhasi said angrily.

"You don't just blow up houses without checking to see who's in them," I objected.

"And the Arabs who blew themselves up at the Beit Lid bus stop, did they check first to see who was around? Twenty-one Jews dead, dozens wounded." Pinhasi spit on the road in disgust.

"A lot more got killed at Qibya," I said. "I don't remember the exact number but I think it was over fifty."

"If we're killing more of them than they are of us, we're doing okay. I wouldn't want it to be the opposite," Pinhasi said.

"Maybe they did check. Maybe they thought there were more terrorists among the civilians," Yoni said.

"We have testimony from Palestinian survivors," I said.

"We have testimony from Sharon, too."

"I don't think he tells the truth."

"Why do you think the Palestinians tell the truth?" Yoni asked.

"This village at the intersection is Na'alin, and the one on the other side of the road, up there, is Dir Qadis," Oren said. "We drive through them once or twice a day to show we're around, but we don't do anything. Here, off to the right, is Harbata. We've got a platoon stationed there to guard the civil administration office. But from what I hear, you won't be keeping men there for long."

"Israel is retaining responsibility for security in Zone B," I said. "So shouldn't we patrol the villages like we did during the Intifada?"

"The orders are to lay off. We show our presence and take care of specific problems on an ad hoc basis. But we're supposed to leave the Palestinians to themselves," Oren explained. "Let's take a ride through Dir Qadis."

We halted on the access road at the edge of the village. It was flanked by what looked like two body shops, both thriving. I could see at least a dozen workers on each side combing through piles of auto parts or harvesting assemblies from under hoods. I'd never taken an interest in cars so I didn't notice what was wrong with the picture until Pinhasi pointed it out to me.

"The cars aren't junked," he said.

The cars the workers were dismantling didn't have bashed-in front ends or twisted chassis. They were in fine condition. Some especially fine specimens of expensive models were parked to the side in a neat row.

"These are the Dir Qadis automobile slaughterhouses. It's the major Palestinian growth industry," Oren said, "producing spare parts out of stolen cars."

"The most successful Jewish-Arab cooperative venture that the peace process has produced," Pinhasi noted.

"You've read in the papers that car theft rates have shot up over the last year. Now you see how it works," Oren said.

"You have your Israeli car thieves. They scout out cars, knowing what the guys here are looking for. They especially like Peugeots, but lately they've developed other tastes," Pinhasi explained. "They steal the cars, drive them through the roadblocks, and sell them to the Arabs. Here they can strip a sedan in twenty minutes, like piranhas devouring the flesh of a cow. They blowtorch the chassis, and poof, no evidence. Then they sell the parts back to Israeli garages. Your mechanic ever ask you if you want a secondhand carburetor or transmission, much cheaper than new, in good condition? Where do you think he gets it?"

"I don't own a car," I said.

Pinhasi looked at me in disbelief.

"What about the ones parked on the side?" I asked.

"If your car is an expensive model and in really good condition, you're in luck," Pinhasi said. "You ask around, and you get a phone number. You call and give the guy at the other end, who probably sounds like someone you wouldn't want to meet on an empty street at night, the make and model and serial number. An hour later he calls back. He knows where your car is, and if you hand over one or two or three thousand dollars in cash, you can have it returned."

"Why should you do that?" I asked. "Why wouldn't you just call the police? Or collect on your insurance?"

"Lots of reasons," Oren said. "First, by the time the police find your car it won't be in one piece. Second, you might have to report details that you don't particularly want to report, such as the fact that the car was stolen when it was parked outside the apartment of the woman your wife thinks you stopped seeing. And you know how insurance claims are. They take forever, and then your rates go up. Much easier to hand over the cash and get your car back."

"Why don't you guys arrest them?" I asked.

"Hey, they're no security threat," Oren said. "It's a job for the police."

"So the police."

"Well, our police don't want to get involved because we're pulling out. As of next week it will be the job of the Palestinian police."

"Obviously they'll want to stop this kind of thing and put their house in order," I said.

"I'm not so sure," Oren said. "When you're setting up a country that has no natural resources, high unemployment, and a lot of poverty, you don't shut down the most profitable sector in your economy."

From Dir Qadis we drove to Harbata. The civil administration office was in a small building with a courtyard, a miniature version of the facilities we'd manned in Tubas and Kabatiyeh. Efi and Dani, the new Platoon One NCO, looked thoroughly bored and not particularly enamored of each other's company. They spoke politely, but they didn't seem to have much to say. Part of it was their age. Efi was already a father and a professional, while Dani, short, with a sharp nose and a permanent sarcastic grin, was a law student at an expensive private college in a classy northern suburb of Tel Aviv. But something cultural was also at work. Efi came from the heart of the religious Zionist subculture. Dani came from the opposite pole of Israeli society, the secular, largely left-wing Ashkenazi bourgeoisie that the guys labeled *"tzfoni."* The word means "northern," but the reference was not to the northern part of the country but to northern Tel Aviv and the suburbs beyond—the well-off part of the city where the kids go to nonreligious elementary and high schools and seldom, if ever, see the inside of a synagogue. Despite Company C's diversity, this group had been notably underrepresented over the years. This was ironic, given that the young tzfonim of the 1990s were largely the children and grandchildren of the Sabras, the Socialist-Zionist elite that had set the tone in the Jewish community in Palestine before Israel was founded and had provided the bulk of Israel's political and military leaders during the first four decades after independence. Certainly some others in Company C fit the tzfoni label—Eran, Aviel, and Yishai were all Ashkenazis from middle-class families, even if they weren't from Tel Aviv—but they were quiet about it. Dani was outspoken about his opinions, whether political, cultural, or religious. He and two other young guys with similar backgrounds who had come into Platoon One at around the same time formed a new center of gravity quite different from the Yemenite clique that had given the platoon its character when I first joined.

I took to the three of them immediately, in a way that my old friends in the unit found hard to understand. I was religious and they weren't. I was in my fortieth year and these kids were in their early twenties. They'd been in grade school when I kept watch on that hilltop outside Beirut, and in basic training when Company C faced the Intifada in Bani Na'im and Jenin.

But I knew exactly why I liked them. They reminded me of myself when I was their age. They were democratic secularists with their feet solidly planted in American and European culture. In this, they showed me the alternative path, the one from which I turned when I decided to spend my life trying to keep my balance between Jewish orthodoxy and Western humanism.

By his own admission, Dani had had little previous contact with religious Jews and was still learning that they were not all ultranationalists. He knew from the press that the religious Zionist community opposed the Oslo accords and he had gone to Harbata ready for a battle of principle with Efi. But over the last hour he'd learned that his commanding officer was more moderate than he'd assumed. Efi, like Yoni, agreed that the occupation was morally debilitating to Israeli society and, especially, to the soldiers who had to patrol the villages, man the roadblocks, and raid the homes of Palestinian families. Company C had behaved well during the Intifada years, but we knew that other units had not. And even if soldiers in a disciplined and mature unit did not act with brutality, the very nature of the work fostered a callousness that we all found disturbing, in others and in ourselves. So Efi and Yoni even welcomed the prospect of the army getting out of the business of policing Palestinian villages.

On the other hand, they doubted whether the army could keep terrorists out of Israel if it didn't control the villages, and if—as they feared—the Palestinian Authority proved unwilling or unable to control the extremists in its midst. One of the lessons they drew from their experience as soldiers was that to prevent attacks, keep the Palestinians intimidated and the leaders of their paramilitary cells on the run. They also knew that the work we soldiers did was only half the picture. The intelligence the Shin Bet gathered in the territories was an important tool in countering terrorist operatives, and without a military presence in the villages, the Shin Bet could not operate freely there.

Dani had spent hardly any time in the territories during his regular army service; for him, the principles were still stark. The occupation was wrong. He felt no ambiguity about withdrawing from Harbata. It was something that should have been done a long time ago and could have been done had the religious right not promoted a policy of settlement and annexation.

I still agreed with Dani's principles. But as I rode past the Israeli settlements and the Arab villages, my political and military instincts seemed to wrestle inside my gut, each unable to pin the other down. I'd expected to feel enthusiastic about a patrol that deliberately avoided entering Arab villages. Instead, I felt nervous. How were we going to do our job if we weren't in the villages? How could we guarantee the safety of the Israelis who drove this road if we had no control over the Arabs who used it? How could we keep the suicide bombers out of Israel if they could walk around our roadblocks with impunity? The military pride I'd thought I didn't have was hurt. If this was what we were reduced to—waiting at traffic lights and driving aimlessly up and down a road we could not protect—then what was the point of being a soldier?

Radical rabbis, particularly a number living in the West Bank and Gaza Strip, were calling on religious soldiers to refuse to carry out orders to evacuate Jewish settlements or to hand over land to the Palestinians. I shared Dani's fears that some of Company C's more right-wing religious guys—like a few of the hesder men—would balk at our assignment. Not that there weren't nonreligious men who opposed ceding land. Elnatan was a prime example. Yet his opposition to dealing with Arafat, while deep-seated and resolute, was at bottom a policy disagreement. He thought the Oslo agreements were a foolish security risk that had been sold to the country by a coterie of dreamers. But the agreements didn't threaten to refute his view of God's relationship with the people of Israel. Elnatan didn't believe in God, so Oslo could not run against His plan.

That's exactly what the Oslo process threatened for the religious guys who subscribed to Rabbi Kook's theology. The agreement with the Palestinians confounded the steady march toward the messianic era that had begun with the establishment of the Jewish state in 1948 and progressed through the conquest of more of the biblical Land of Israel in 1967 and the blossoming of Jewish settlement in these areas after the Yom Kippur War. If portions of the land were to be given to foreigners and the Jewish settlements evacuated, it could only be divine punishment. The Messiah's vanguard—the knitted-kipah religious Zionists—had been too weak, too accommodating; they had not moved forward with the alacrity that God required. When the peace treaty with Egypt put this part of the religious public in that position, the outcome had been the Jewish terrorist organization that was arrested in 1984—with a Company C officer among its members.

The sages of the formative period of rabbinic Judaism, in the centuries that followed the destruction of the Jewish Temple in Jerusalem in 70 c.e., disagreed about how the Messiah would arrive. Some said the Jews must reestablish their political independence, rebuild the Temple, and reach the highest possible level of communal sanctity, forcing God to reward His people with the Messiah. Six decades after the Temple's destruction, Rabbi Akiva, one of the most brilliant and original Jewish thinkers of post-Temple Judaism, thought the time had come. He lent his spiritual support to Bar-Kokhba, a military leader who led a disastrous revolt against the Romans.

But another view in the rabbinic sources said the Messiah would come "little by little." The Messiah's arrival was not an event but a process. Every precept you observed, every good deed you did, was one more step—a small but crucial one—along the road. You observed the Sabbath, thanked God for giving you food and life, remembered the Exodus from Egypt, gave charity to the poor, acted as a citizen to make the society you lived in more just. Working to bring the Messiah and his arrival were one and the same.

The salient fact was that the rabbis disagreed. They always disagreed. One cannot open the Torah or the Talmud or any other classic rabbinical work and find the solutions to one's moral and religious dilemmas. God, through the rabbis, always says: That's your question? Here are some answers. Choose the one that seems the most good. Not the one that you most want, or the one that is easiest, but the one that you decide, after careful study and thought and disputation, to be the most good.

There was currently a dispute in Kehilat Yedidya over the prayer for Israel, which is recited after the reading of the Torah in all Jewish communities that support the Jewish state. The text was written by Shmuel Yosef Agnon, the giant of modern Israeli literature. It refers to the state of Israel as *"reishit tzmihat ge'ulateinu,"* "the beginning of the growth [or progress, or evolution] of our redemption." As the Oslo agreements progressed, some of the rabbis of the Rabbi Kook school ruled that the prayer should no longer be recited because the state of Israel, under Yitzhak Rabin's government, was an obstacle to rather than a facilitator of the Messiah's arrival. A few members of our community objected to the prayer for the opposite reason. Kehilat Yedidya should remove the messianic reference from the prayer because it attached religious significance to the state, and that was dangerous. Sanctifying the state inevitably leads people to place the state above the law and to seek the state's territorial expansion.

I knew of no record of Agnon's intentions when he wrote those words, but what impressed me about them was their hesitancy. The state of Israel was not our redemption. It was not even the beginning of our redemption. It was the beginning of the growth of our redemption. In other words, little by little. It was not the state that brought the redemption, but what we, the citizens of Israel, did with the state. Kehilat Yedidya voted to let the prayer stand.

My fears proved unfounded. Though hesder guys like Sheib, Greenberg, Fisch, and Amzaleg adamantly opposed the Rabin government's policies, they reported for duty with the rest of the men on Thursday.

Given that liberation by treaty was on the way, we hoped that the Harbatans would give us a quiet weekend. But, no, they were determined to test this last Israeli change of guard, this last foreign detachment to trouble their lives. Platoon One had no sooner moved in than thick plumes of black smoke began to rise from piles of burning tires. The first foot patrol Efi sent out was greeted by a gaggle of taunting youth throwing stones. Let's not deal with it, Dani thought. Why not walk out right now and leave them without anyone to make miserable. But he didn't say that to Efi, who was on the radio reporting to me.

Aviel was the senior officer at the Route 443 base. "Assholes," he said to me as he held the handset to his ear. "This is the thanks we get? Let's teach them a lesson."

He grabbed Yoni and whoever else was around.

"Wait," I called after him. "I'll tell you who you can take. You'll disrupt the duty roster."

"I'm taking everyone, and you deal with it afterward," he ordered.

Arriving at the civil administration building, he held a two-minute conference with Efi and Yoni. "Bang on every door in this town and round up all the men and boys. Bring them to the yard here. I want to give them a lecture they'll never forget," Aviel ordered.

Similar actions had begun our stints in Bani Na'im and Beit Sahour and all the other villages that had been our homes for a month during the last seven years. To many of the experienced guys it all seemed mechanical now, going through the motions of a moribund occupation. But some of the hesder guys seemed more intense about the work than they ever had before, as if they might halt the impending retreat by demonstrating how diligent they could be. Dani interpreted the men's determination as enjoyment. He was thus surprised when his path crossed Yoni's and he saw in the new officer's face an expression of extreme distaste.

"I hate this stuff," Yoni said in response to Dani's surprised look. "I'm glad we won't have to do it much longer."

"But you told me yesterday that you think Oslo is the stupidest thing any Israeli government has ever done," Dani exclaimed. "You're a settler yourself."

"Yeah, but I still hate this stuff," Yoni said. "Who needs it?"

After that first evening in Harbata, we settled into the routine that Oren and Pinhasi had described. We all felt that the work on and around Route 443 was not serious. On the other hand, after the Intifada, the Gulf War, and Gladiola there was something to be said for a stint during which we weren't pressured or shot at. Furthermore, the base's location—just a twenty-minute drive to Jerusalem and twice that to Tel Aviv—allowed many of the guys to make unofficial visits home or to their workplaces. Yet this only amplified the feeling that we weren't functioning as soldiers, certainly not as infantrymen. The work could easily have been done by kids in basic training. Why did we have to be there at all?

This was certainly Ilana's view. She made it clear that she expected me home for Yom Kippur, the holiest day on the Jewish calendar, even though it fell a few days after we reached the Route 443 base. She did not intend to fast and manage four children at the same time. I worked like crazy to get the duty roster going and the leave schedule organized and then told Eran that I had to head home for the holiday. It wasn't in Eran's nature to put his foot down, but his displeasure was enough to make me feel plenty guilty for the Day of Atonement. When I returned to the Route 443 base the morning after Yom Kippur, a Thursday, Meshulam was outside a tent, trying on his efod. There was anger in his eyes when I went over to greet him, and he rejected my expressions of sympathy.

"If you'd really wanted to help, you could have," he said, adjusting his straps.

I was sorry that I hadn't argued his case more forcefully with Eran. The care he was taking in positioning his efod made it clear that, despite his anger, he intended to do his job properly while he was with us. But I couldn't tell Meshulam that I disagreed with Eran's decision.

"It might not be so bad," I said. "You can probably get back to Jerusalem here and there to do some work."

"Won't help me. I already canceled all my jobs for the next week."

"Maybe you can make some phone calls and salvage some of them."

"No," he said, shaking his head. "Too late."

I looked at the duty roster I'd prepared before leaving. "You're supposed to go down to the roadblock at noon. I'll just check with Eran to make sure there weren't any changes while I was home."

Meshulam shrugged, as if to say that I could do as I wished with him for the next ten days, as I'd already done the worst thing I could.

In the next four days, Company C had to withdraw from Harbata and prepare for Sukkot, in addition to our routine duties. The name of the seven-day holiday is often translated into English as the Feast of Booths, but a better rendering would be the Feast of Temporary Dwellings. The name refers to the holiday's most visible symbol, the sukkah, a makeshift shack that observant Jews build outside their homes and live in during the holiday as a reenactment of the Children of

Israel's sojourn in the desert after the Exodus from Egypt. According to the sages, rabbis, and commentators, the temporary dwellings are supposed to remind the Jews that they hold all their possessions—including the Land of Israel itself—only at God's pleasure. He can take them away in an instant if we do not remember that we were slaves in Egypt and that God took us out of the house of bondage on condition that we never do to others what the Egyptians did to us.

Jewish law never has dining or napping far out of mind; living in a sukkah is thus defined as eating and sleeping in a dwelling that meets certain technical specifications of temporariness. For example, unlike our army tents, the roof of a sukkah has to be open to the elements and composed of reeds, leaves, sticks, or branches. Company C would need one next to our mess tent. Falk asked our battalion chaplain to provide poles, tarpaulin, and thatching.

The battalion chaplain was a personable scribe and scholar who did his best, but he didn't know the art of cajoling and desk banging necessary to the army requisitioning process. He showed up at the Route 443 base with a kit containing all that was needed to build a hut measuring two by two meters.

Falk's respect for the learned did battle with his contempt for the unresourceful. "That's all you could come up with?"

"It's the standard army sukkah," the chaplain said. "It'll be big enough for your religious soldiers to eat in if they take turns."

"In Company C," Falk admonished him, "our religious and nonreligious soldiers don't eat separately. We need a sukkah that's big enough for everyone."

The chaplain shrugged. "That's all I can get you."

"Then we'll build our own sukkah," Falk declared. He grabbed Barak, got into the red Falk et Falk van, and drove to Jerusalem. They returned a few hours later with boards, canvas, and palm branches. They soon had a dozen guys banging nails and stringing electric wires. On Sunday we moved the tables from the mess tent into the sukkah, and that night Company C celebrated together, religious and nonreligious, left and right, in its spacious temporary dwelling.

In the meantime, I was organizing reinforcements for Platoon One in Harbata, which we were to evacuate on Friday. It had seemed counterintuitive when Elnatan ordered us to send more soldiers into Harbata in order to remove the ones we already had there, but I'd never organized a withdrawal. Under Eran's direction, I put together a force led by Yoni, and on Friday morning it took up positions alongside Efi's men. Eran went to the village in his commander's jeep while I remained in charge at the largely emptied Route 443 base.

The operation went smoothly, but like nearly everything done by the army, it took much longer than planned. The Israeli civil administration workers slowly loaded their files and computers and furniture onto trucks that were late in coming. The Palestinian Authority officials and policemen who were to take over were delayed. By the time the handshake that gave the Harbata office to the Palestinians happened, Company C's soldiers were too tired and hungry to really give a damn that they were participating in history. They couldn't see the handshake in any case, since they were stationed at various points around the village to ensure that the Harbatans did not use the opportunity to wish us a violent farewell. As far as our men could see, however, the good citizens of Harbata couldn't give a damn, either. It was olive harvest season, as it had been in Jenin seven years previously, and entire families were out on the terraces surrounding the village, beating the trees and gathering the fruit in blankets. The olive presses, operating day and night, were the center of attention, not the outgoing Israeli soldiers or the incoming Palestinian police.

When our forces returned to the Route 443 base, the guys were grumpy. Dani's usual grin had been replaced by a thin-lipped scowl, which he kept on his face as he got organized on a cot in one of the tents.

"Efi really got on my nerves," he said when I asked him what was the matter. "Took me down in front of the other guys and in front of the locals, too. What's his problem? Tell him to keep his religion out of his army work."

"What happened?"

"I was with a couple other guys covering a position in this grove on a terrace above the village. A family was out harvesting its olives. Simple people, you know, looking forward to a better life now that we're getting out. Everything was quiet, pastoral. A few kids had thrown some pebbles at us earlier but other than that it felt like the occupation was already over. One of the men from the family came over and offered us tea and cake. And there we were drinking the tea and eating the cake and smiling at the Arab family when Efi comes by with his patrol and has a fit."

"Look, you can't be surprised he was tense," I said. "At a time like that your guard goes down, and you become an easy target."

Dani snorted. "'Didn't you hear my orders about not fraternizing with the locals?' he shouts at me. 'Hey, maybe we're conquerors but that doesn't mean we can't be gracious,' I told him. Tell me, where does he get off? He's just upset to see us getting out of there."

On the second day of the holiday, Barak invited Falk and me on a visit to an uncle of his who lived at Kfar Ruth, a five-minute drive from the base.

We found Uncle Na'im wading through a pacific sea of rose and cyclamen in the pungent, humid air of his hilltop hothouse. There was a warm, almost palpable silence, like that between breaking waves on a lonely summer beach. We watched as he bent close to a blossom and examined it, conferring in a low voice with the square-shouldered Thai who stood respectfully beside him. A skinnier Thai man, who like the first looked to be in his midtwenties, cut flowers in the next row of troughs, his fingers swift and nimble. Na'im caught sight of us with a puzzled glance but then made out Barak and smiled. He stood up, brushed off his hands, exchanged a few quiet words with his worker, and walked over to greet us.

"Let's go over to the house and get you some tea," he suggested.

"Couldn't you show us around the greenhouses first?" Falk asked with his usual knack for knowing what the person talking to him really wanted. Uncle Na'im proudly gave us a tour.

"It's the beginning of our busy season," he said. "With winter already starting in Europe they have to import flowers if they want them. It's our opportunity. We're closer than the other exporters so we can get our stuff there faster, in a few hours, but it's hard to compete with their prices."

Baby's breath had been popular last year, he said, and the long-lasting Transvaal daisies—Ilana's favorite—were a growing market. His bottleneck was labor. He had a third greenhouse, but it was closed because he couldn't get enough workers.

He moved up the row with Falk and Barak, but I lagged behind as we passed the first worker. I wondered whether I should speak. After a few moments watching him cut flowers, I finally did.

"Do you have a family back home?" I asked in English.

He looked up and nodded with a polite but apparently authentic smile. "Yes, I have a wife and a little boy."

"Isn't it hard to be away from them?"

He shrugged. "I make money and send it home. Maybe in a few years we can build a house."

"Isn't it boring, this work?"

"No, it's fine work. Mr. Na'im is very nice."

I caught up with Barak and Falk, who were heading out of the greenhouse with Uncle Na'im. My face must have projected my thoughts, because he answered a question I'd thought it rude to ask.

"I read those stories in the newspapers, too," he said as we walked to the house. "I suppose there are farmers who mistreat their foreign laborers. I think they're just hurting themselves. I want my workers to be happy. It's better for me and better for them. They're conscientious and efficient. I just wish they could stay on permanently. Their permits are only for two years, and they can't be renewed."

In the kitchen he made us thick, syrupy Moroccan tea in patterned glasses stuffed with mint leaves.

"I was one of the last farmers here to fire his Arab labor," he told us. "I kept on one of them, Nabil from Na'alin. He worked for me for almost ten years, up until the beginning of this year. It really hurt me to let him go—he's got a family to support. But there have been too many stories of Palestinian workers turning on their employers and murdering them. I couldn't risk it anymore."

"So why not Jewish workers?" Barak asked.

Uncle Na'im waved his hand dismissively. "I tried that. It was a disaster. They cost more, work at a quarter of the pace, and make four times as many mistakes. All they do is complain, show up late, and leave early. My profit margin's too small for that."

He stared at his glass of tea. "Maybe, if this peace really comes to be, I'll be able to take Nabil back on." Then he shook his head. "But I don't believe it."

With the Harabata operation over, tempers cooled and the rest of the stint passed quietly. But I apparently experienced the month differently from most of the other guys. When I later traded recollections with some of them, I discovered that they remembered our time on Route 443 as pleasant, enjoyable, and easy. But it sticks in my mind as the month in which my dreams of peace began to fade.

Our first few days in our sector had proved that the previous year's pressures had not weakened the bonds that kept the guys working together. There was relatively little political debate among the men. The officers and NCOs explained the work, and the reservists did it. There were, however, some dark murmurings that I was too quick to dismiss at the time. The tensions that had been largely kept under the surface in Company C had soon reached a boil in Israeli society. As the withdrawals progressed, the right's rhetoric became strident. The charge that Rabin and his cabinet were traitors was no longer heard only on the extreme right. Politicians and public figures from the mainstream, among them Binyamin Netanyahu, the leader of the Likud, didn't object to the characterization. At demonstrations against the peace process, they accused Rabin, and indeed the entire left, of betrayal.

A couple of weeks after I got out of the army, the Rabin government's supporters organized a Saturday night rally in Tel Aviv to show that the peace process's proponents were as numerous and as passionate as its opponents. I'd originally planned to go and to take my older kids with me, but on Thursday afternoon I got a call for a rush translation job, and I had to spend Saturday night in my basement storeroom-cum-office with the client, making last-minute corrections. At one point he had to call a colleague to clarify an idea. Putting down the phone, he gave me the news. "He says Rabin's been shot."

Ilana had just heard the news as well and kept us abreast over the intercom as we quickly finished. I was upstairs in time to hear the official announcement that the prime minister was dead. The assassin, Yigal Amir, a religious Zionist law student who'd been active in right-wing organizations, had been apprehended.

It wasn't an American-style assassination, perpetrated by a lunatic. A rational, intelligent young man who knew exactly what he was doing had murdered another Jew, the democratically elected prime minister of Israel, because he disagreed with his policies. The fact that the assassin cited the Torah and Jewish law in justification of his act was even more frightening. When extremist rabbis had adduced religious law to justify Baruch Goldstein's massacre of Muslim worshippers in Hebron, I was appalled, and when they used the law to argue that religious soldiers should refuse orders to hand over territory to the Palestinians, I was alarmed. But I always thought that there was one line the extremists would not cross—using Jewish law to justify the murder of another Jew.

The assassination tore Israeli society apart. Leading figures on the left blamed the entire right for the murder, though most opponents of the Oslo accords were no less revolted by the assassination. For a few days, I feared a civil war. But the country mourned, Shimon Peres took over as prime minister, and the debate continued. Elections were scheduled for the end of May.

In February, Company C was called up for three days of maneuvers at Tze'elim. At first, the guys avoided talking politics, as if fearful that the violence we'd experienced as civilians might rear its head in the unit if an argument got out of hand. But late on the afternoon of our second day, as we trudged down a path from Chicago to the bus that would take us back to our tent camp, the emotions boiled over. I don't remember how the exchange began, but Eiger recalls that it was one of the tzfonim who said that the Israeli right wing as a whole was responsible for murdering Rabin. Eiger, no right-winger himself, pointed out that such a blanket accusation wasn't fair. Alon argued that it was, since the right had not disavowed the extremists in its camp. The exchange became heated and ugly. Right-wingers accused the left of recklessly proceeding with a peace plan that was obviously bringing only more terror. Left-wingers accused the right of warmongering. Sheib, who usually stayed out of such arguments, lost control of himself.

"I'm thankful that someone had the guts to stop Rabin. Yigal Amir ought to be paraded through the streets as a hero. He saved the country," Sheib declared.

The rest of us, left and right, fell silent.

Alon, who stood next to me, thought he'd misheard. "Hey, Sheib, I thought you just said that it was right to kill Rabin. "

"You heard me fine," Sheib said in quiet fury.

"How can you say that about another Jew?" I asked him in astonishment.

"That's a Jew?" Sheib hissed. "That's no Jew."

Sheib had never adjusted himself to the interdependent life of a reserve unit. But despite his prickly personality, I had continued to admire
his sharp and unconventional intelligence. Since one of my journalistic
beats was scientific research, I'd occasionally ask him to explain some
concept in his field of theoretical quantum physics. First he'd make a
speech about how he couldn't possibly explain the idea to someone like
me whose mathematical sophistication culminated in high school calculus, but then he'd give me an excellent summary. Although he had little
use for the secular humanities, his knowledge of Jewish religious literature was phenomenal, and he knew how to strip down an issue of Jewish law and analyze it in often unexpected ways.

He was a man of principle but not necessarily in the best sense of
the phrase. When Sheib held an opinion, he held it absolutely. He might
be persuaded that he was wrong, but until he was persuaded, he didn't
budge. The fundamental rules of the subatomic world are statistical, but
there were no statistics in his ethics. He never seemed to make a choice
between two uncertainties. There was always one incontrovertibly correct answer, including on the question of whether any part of the Land
of Israel could be handed over to the Palestinians as part of a peace
agreement. It was absolutely, utterly wrong to do so, and anyone who
furthered such a policy was a criminal.

There were other men in Company C who shared this view, but they
wouldn't justify murder. Alon and I both remember this as a breaking
point, a time when we thought the men of Company C would no longer
be able to work together. No one else had endorsed the assassination,
but wasn't Sheib evidence that the assassination was the unavoidable
product of the theology and politics of the group represented in Company C by the hesder men? Those of us on the left suddenly felt as

though they and we served in the armies of entirely different countries. Had the maneuvers gone on longer, there might well have been a crisis, but within a day we were all home again.

As the May elections approached, tensions between Israel and the Palestinian Authority increased. Hamas staged a series of suicide bombings on Jerusalem buses in which sixty-two Israelis were killed and scores seriously injured. The Islamic extremists wanted to terrify the Israeli public into voting for Netanyahu. For these fanatics, it would be the best possible outcome, for the thing they feared most was peace. They knew that Palestinians living free on their own land would no longer fight to destroy Israel.

Had Arafat and his supporters taken firm action against Hamas and other Palestinian opponents of peace, I believe the greater part of the Israeli public would have been convinced to support the process. But Arafat took only half measures and continued to speak to his own people in terms that made it sound to many Israelis as if he sympathized with the suicide bombers' goals. The Israelis were scared, and when the election came they voted in Binyamin Netanyahu by a narrow margin. Amazingly, despite the suicide bombings and disappointment with Arafat, nearly half the Israeli population had voted to continue the peace process.

Netanyahu had played to the center during his campaign. He positioned himself as a man of the moderate right who would be firmer with the Palestinians than Rabin and Peres had been, and who would be able to produce a better agreement. But it didn't take long for him to revert to his ideological roots. He quickly became the most divisive prime minister the country had ever known, at one point saying that leftists were not really Jews. Netanyahu and Arafat seemed to be in a contest to see who could alienate the other side more quickly and completely. Antagonism increased, and at the end of September 1996, just before Sukkot, Palestinian "policemen"—really soldiers, for all intents and purposes—opened fire on Israeli soldiers, killing a dozen of them. One of the dead was Yoni's eighteen-year-old brother.

I met Barak at the office furnishings store where he worked a few blocks from my apartment, and we drove out to Efrat together. We stopped at Falk's basement apartment and went together to Yoni's. The house was packed with neighbors and friends.

I was afraid that I'd be unwelcome, that Yoni and his family would blame me, a supporter of the peace process, for their loss. But Yoni welcomed me just as he did Falk and Barak. He said that he thought the shootings proved how foolish the peace process was, how foolish it had been to allow the Palestinians to arm themselves. He hoped that Israelis would wake up now. He smiled at me sadly, but he smiled.

A few weeks previous we had received call-up orders for October. Thankfully, we'd be on Mount Hermon. Perhaps a month away from the territories could heal the company's wounds.

"But you'll probably skip this one," I said. "You'll want to stay with your family."

In the end, he never came back. He asked for and received a regiment-level job that didn't involve front-line activity. His parents had been through enough, he told me.

A week later I ran into Meshulam at a grocery store in the neighborhood. His business had collapsed, plunging him deep into debt. While he didn't give me details, I gathered that he'd taken some of his loans on the gray market at exorbitant interest rates. Working three jobs, dawn to dusk, he was slowly paying off his obligations. He and his wife were living in an old caravan home, he told me, one that had once housed new immigrants from the former Soviet Union. They couldn't dream of having children until he got back on his feet financially. It would take a few years, he thought.

"Those ten days in the army really killed me," he said bitterly.

No, I shouldn't take up a collection among the guys. He'd manage on his own. And he was out of the company. He'd be happy never to see any of us ever again.

Chapter Eleven

· ILLUSIONS ·

MOUNT HERMON, OCTOBER 1996

I BROUGHT A CAMERA TO SNOWVIEW IN 1996. THE RESULTING PHOTO-graphs are among the only ones I have of myself as a reservist.

Two of them stand out. The first shows Eiger and me, arms around each other's shoulders, on a rocky Mount Hermon hillock, against the background of the top secret antennas and radio towers of the Yisraeli base. The second shows five members of a mountain patrol as we set out from Snowview: Efi on the right with Bentzi, a young machine gunner, and Dani on the left with fellow tzfoni Dror. I'm in the middle with the radio pack on my back, the long antenna jutting up and out of the picture. Not to be smug, but I *do* look trim and fit. I've got more hair than Efi, who is seven years my junior. In fact, at forty, I don't look out of place with Dani, Dror, and Bentzi, all in their twenties. And except for Bentzi and his machine gun, I'm carrying the heaviest load.

But the exceptional thing about these photographs is not my appearance. It's my rifle, which is clearly visible in both. In every other picture taken of me during my twenty years as a soldier, I deliberately hid my weapon behind my back or outside the camera's field of view. This was a statement of principle—my rifle was a necessary tool, not one to be glorified—and my modest protest against the fact that my years as a soldier had been largely spent in two problematic wars, in Lebanon and in the West Bank.

What was different on Mount Hermon in October 1996? I was taking pictures because this stint marked the end of an era. Efi had decided to take a less demanding post in the battalion. Eran had agreed to become deputy to our new, young, and hyperactive battalion commander before our next round of active duty. And me? I had five years before the army's computer printed out my discharge form, but it was extremely rare for a man of my age to be on the rolls of a fighting company. During my army career, only Jacques had passed the age of forty within Company C, and by that time he no longer went on patrols or other strenuous missions. For me, remaining in the company but abstaining from the hard stuff was not an option. And, in fact, it wasn't hard stuff for me. If anything, my stamina and strength had increased since I'd joined the company. Still, I was five years older than the next oldest man. I was conscious of the age gap between me and Dani's cohort, not to mention the twenty-two-year-olds who had come into the company that month. My mind told me that I was not immortal and that I could not hold out forever, even if my gut said otherwise.

The decision to show my rifle had another cause. The stint at Snowview felt perfect, an exemplar of reserve duty as it ought to be. We oppressed no local population, but guarded a border facing a bellicose enemy. We worked hard, slept intermittently, faced cold and rain and wind. We were alert and prepared for an invasion that, our superiors told us, might take place during our watch. Every patrol and guard shift had the sole purpose of protecting our country and our families back home. This was what a soldier was supposed to do.

Snowview was a concrete citadel on the topmost peak of Mount Hermon. It lay to the north of the much larger Yisraeli fortress. The

Bul'an Valley cut between the two outposts, rising to the saddle on which the road between them ran. The bristling antennas of the Yisraeli made it look like a dragon's head, with Snowview the clubbed tail of the beast. The dragon sprawled on its side, the ridge above the road like spikes on its back and the saddle its vulnerable belly. If the Syrians attacked, their strategy would most likely be to land commandos by helicopter, capture the saddle, and cut Snowview off from supplies and reinforcements.

The citadel was embedded in the limestone mountain. Our living quarters were subterranean and windowless, but the structure had undergone extensive renovation and was much more pleasant than the dismal, endless corridors of the Yisraeli. There we'd been the garrison force for a base devoted to intelligence and command. Here we were kings of the mountain. Snowview was an infantry base, pure and simple. The company served together, with the exception of a small contingent under Vanunu's and Azoulai's command that manned a secondary outpost on the Israeli side of the mountain.

The rooms were well lit and heated. The showers always had hot water. There was a Ping-Pong table in the dining room. A separate common room had a television, VCR, and even a small library. It was as homey as army quarters could get. The officers' room, which also served as my office, had a large table on which I could spread my papers.

An antechamber on one of the Plexiglas-enclosed guard posts overlooking the enemy below us served as the war room. Getting from quarters to the war room required navigating a maze of corridors and stairwells. Soon I knew every turn and shortcut, for the passageways were my exercise route on the days—most of them—when rain or fog prevented me from running outside.

We had come to the mountain at a critical time. The Syrians had mustered forces on the Damascus plain below. Through the binoculars at the war room post we could see the camps and pita fortifications. A high-ranking intelligence officer from Northern Command headquarters arrived to brief us. He reminded us, unnecessarily, that Syria had been able to seize Mount Hermon in the Yom Kippur War partly because Israel had misinterpreted Syria's troop concentrations as preparations for a training exercise. Extremely reliable reports—they came from our best sources on the Syrian side, he said—indicated that this buildup was not merely practice. Hafez al-Assad had concluded that he'd never get back his lost land through negotiations. He was plotting to retake the Golan Heights and Mount Hermon by force. Assad knew that his army was no match for Israel's, especially now that he no longer had a spare parts supplier for his Soviet tanks and weapons. But, the officer said, Assad didn't need to overrun Mount Hermon to get it back. He could isolate Snowview and hold us hostage. The United States and the Europeans, wanting to avoid all-out war at any cost, would pressure Israel to exchange the mountain for our safe return. Helicopters were the key—we were to report any suspicious choppers immediately.

Though we were on alert and there was a whiff of danger, it was not an emergency—as evidenced by the fact that our reserve-day budget was still tight. As always, a handful of malingerers hadn't shown up or didn't return on time from leave. Men had sudden crises at home or at work. And sometimes I had to rearrange leaves for more esoteric reasons. A young, unassuming religious soldier caught me alone one day to discuss a problem that could come up only in this army. His wife's period had gone on a few days longer than expected, and, well . . .

He didn't need to say more. The Orthodox Jewish discipline governing sexual relations within marriage states that husband and wife may not make love during the woman's period or for seven nights thereafter. It's a part of the law not often discussed in public. His three days of leave fell in the week after his wife's period, and the consequence would be a month of celibacy. That was more than I felt I could demand of him, but I couldn't tell Eran, or anyone else, why I suddenly had to change the schedule. A couple of hours of intense work, with Alon helping me count men and days, ensued. In a photograph taken immediately thereafter, I turn toward the camera from my worktable, pen in hand, shirt buttons open, bleary-eyed, with a bemused Alon at my side.

Within a week we were one soldier below our mandatory manpower level at the base. We were in violation of standing orders, and I didn't have enough men to fill the duty roster. The battalion personnel officer told me how to fix the first problem: count our cook as a rifleman. Since the cook was a former Company C soldier whose military abilities were unquestioned, this did not seem unreasonable. But the cook already worked long hours, and I couldn't use him for guard duty or patrols. I finally asked Eran and Aviel to take a guard shift each night. The company commander and his deputy generally needed to be free to command in case of emergency, but Eran and Aviel agreed to help out. I have a photograph of Eran sitting in the command post guard chair, dressed in his hermonit, his rifle on his lap, staring intently out the window into the darkness.

While he admired my resolution of these problems, Eiger was concerned lest I grow complacent. He saw his opportunity when an enlisted medic and a reserve doctor arrived at Snowview to conduct a sick call. This was the first event of the kind we'd experienced. In previous stints, sick men had had to get down to battalion headquarters at the Lower Ski Lift if they wanted to see a doctor. It was so inconvenient that most preferred the semiprofessional ministrations of our company medics. A clutch of guys with sniffles and backaches lined up in the commons room.

I was at my table updating the justice chart when I saw Eiger walk by the open door.

"Hey, whereya going?" I called out, hoping for relief from my drudgery.

"I'm getting my blood pressure checked," Eiger said breezily. I turned back to my papers, then did a slow-motion double take.

"Eiger!" I yelled. "Eiger! Don't do it!" I ran out of my room after him but he disappeared into the commons room. I stood helplessly in the corridor, so haggard that a couple of guys asked if I needed help getting to the doctor.

But the doctor was already striding toward me with a grim air of medical urgency. Eiger walked behind him, grinning sheepishly.

"I have to evacuate this soldier to a hospital immediately," the doctor said. "His blood pressure is 200/140 and he has a history of hypertension. He's on medication. He should never have been allowed to come up to this altitude. He shouldn't be in a combat unit at all. Were you aware of that?"

"He never showed me any medical papers," I said, evading a lie by telling a truth. I glared at Eiger, who shrugged.

"I just thought I'd see what my numbers were."

But Eiger apparently felt I needed a more serious challenge. He grabbed Motti, who was passing by.

Motti was one of Company C's two Ethiopians. Quiet and cooperative, he had the slender frame of a middle-distance runner. His best race was the 2K and he hoped for a place on Israel's national track team. The weight military gear put on his feet led to injuries that kept him from running. Each time he reported for duty, he vowed it was his last. But he always showed up the next time. He was too nice a guy to cause the kind of trouble that would make us cross his name off our list. Sometimes he'd run with Eiger and me, keeping himself to our pace so that we could pretend we were up to his.

"Motti, here's a doctor. Let him check your ankle," Eiger suggested.

"Eiger!" I said.

"Hey, he complained yesterday about some pain," Eiger said. "And he's got a race two weeks after we finish."

"Come with me," the doctor said. He shoved Eiger's papers into my hands.

Diagnosing a torn tendon, the doctor disqualified Motti from service. Motti and Eiger packed up their gear, and the doctor took them to the Lower Ski Lift in his ambulance. Eiger drove Aviel's car from there to the emergency room of Rambam Hospital in Haifa. I was now at minus three soldiers and the Syrians were about to start a war.

I notified the battalion personnel officer that I needed reinforcements. He had none to give. Cancel leaves, he said. Won't do it, I said. We argued. Finally he agreed to send a couple of men from the battalion staff. Eiger returned a day later. The emergency room doctor had written a letter telling the army to discharge him, but Eiger threw it in the garbage, spent the night at home, and drove back to Mount Hermon the next morning. How could I be angry with him?

Then the helicopters appeared. Azoulai was on guard at his base when he spotted them with his night-vision goggles. Intelligence corps observers at other bases seconded his report, and the Mount Hermon outposts were put on high alert. At Snowview we were rousted out of bed to take up positions in the freezing trenches outside the fortress. Now was the time to make use of the information in the training film *Friend or Foe* that we'd been shown endless times in an attempt to teach us to identify the different models of helicopters used by our army and by our enemies. Such identification was not easy, especially through night-vision equipment that made everything green and ghostly. Azoulai reported helicopters to the battalion, which reported them to the Mount Hermon regiment, which reported them to the Northern Command, which reported them to army headquarters in Tel Aviv. Next thing Azoulai knew, the General Staff's chief operations officer was telling him on the phone that this better not be a prank because Prime Minister Netanyahu was on the other line. Azoulai pointed out that he had reported only what he'd seen. The analysis he left to his betters. In the end, before anyone fired a shot, the higher-ups determined that the helicopters were ours.

As a matter of fact, the entire alert was a false alarm, though the story would not hit the newspapers for another year. Yehuda Gil, a senior Israeli intelligence official responsible for espionage against Syria, had been systematically feeding Israel bogus information. Among other things, he reported that the Syrian troop movements of October 1996 were offensive, when they were actually training maneuvers. Gil had served as secretary-general of the extreme right-wing Moledet party, which opposed any compromise on the territories and advocated the transfer of all Palestinians in the West Bank and Gaza Strip to Arab countries, and his motives may have been ideological, aimed at stymieing Rabin's efforts to cut a deal with the Syrians that would involve giving them back the Golan Heights. The information he provided indeed helped convince Yitzhak Rabin to deemphasize negotiations with Syria. On the other hand, the press reported that Gil had received a couple of hundred thousand dollars from his Syrian operators, so ideology was apparently not the whole of it.

But we didn't know that at the time. It was all for the best, really, since the false alert kept us diligent in the fundamentally boring routine of watching the slopes around us.

We had one mission outside this routine that quickly became my favorite, and I assigned myself to it at every opportunity. The foot patrol from Snowview through the Bul'an Valley and up to the Yisraeli asserted our control of this strategic approach to the saddle and also searched the valley for signs of infiltration. A steep descent at the beginning, a climb at the end, and plenty of muddy spots in the middle meant it wasn't a breeze. But neither was it so hard that you couldn't enjoy the view. Eiger, Dani, and I were willing to do the patrol even on top of other duties.

The patrol recorded in my photographs came late in the month; perhaps it was the last we did. As always, we prepared our gear in advance and Efi made sure we packed everything required, including night-vision goggles in case we were delayed past sunset. I assigned myself the radio pack. At our starting point on the lip of the valley, Efi was typically thorough. He surveyed the territory through his binoculars and briefed us on the patrol's purpose and process, both of which we'd heard a dozen times before. After we'd descended he put us through a few drills in which an imaginary enemy attacked from any of several directions. We walked widely spaced in two columns, as standing orders required, so there was little conversation. Here and there I snapped a picture, or passed the camera to a comrade so he could take one of me. The day was overcast and cool, and the rains, which had just begun that month, had not yet brought out what little greenery grows on slopes so high. The mountain was brown and bleak; only vaguely could we discern the Damascus plain below. We walked coatless, and so long as we moved, our bodies were warm. But when we stopped, kneeling watchfully whenever Efi waved his arms earthward, our sweat-soaked shirts chilled us.

I don't know if American soldiers feel what I felt then and every time I patrolled Mount Hermon. With the exception of Pearl Harbor, American men have not had to defend the United States on its own territory for the last 140 years. That all America's wars since its own Civil War have taken place elsewhere is evidence of the country's military strength and of the absence of any comparable power on its borders or, indeed, in its entire hemisphere. When my father fought in Europe at the tail end of World War II, he was defending his country against a real threat, but he battled on land to which he had no attachment. In the early 1970s, when young men only a few years older than I were fighting in Vietnam, they may or may not have agreed with the proposition that America had a vital interest in halting the spread of communism in Southeast Asia. Whatever their views of the war they were in, they could not have felt the same attachment to Vietnam's central highlands that I felt for Mount Hermon. The mountains there were not their mountains.

Mount Hermon wasn't sovereign Israeli territory—it had been captured and recaptured from the Syrians. But it towered over Israel, so its military value was unquestionable. A mountain can be friend or foe depending on who holds it, and the fact that we patrolled its eastern face, and not Syrian soldiers its western face, was integral to the security of our people. I didn't read poetry then—I acquired the habit only after I ceased to be a soldier—but I might have quoted the modern Hebrew poet Natan Alterman, who depicted a mountain—which one, I don't know, but perhaps this one—as a raging bull stopped short in its tracks, and as a pustule in the midst of placid meadows and vineyards, produced by a fever in a foreign land. So the mountain may well have seemed to the Israelis below as long as their enemies held it. When it was ours, however, it was beautiful, pastoral, and quiet.

Company C never guarded another border during my tenure. The frontiers abutting Egypt and Jordan were considered quiet enough to be watched by units less skilled than ours, as was the Syrian border on the Golan Heights. We hadn't had a real border with Lebanon since the invasion of 1982; Israeli forces were deployed to the north of the international border, in Lebanese territory. Lebanese irregulars frequently attacked Israeli bases and patrols there, exacting a steady and heavy toll. The army preferred not to send reservists there at all. Mount Hermon was in between, critical but not deadly; we served there six times in the space of twelve years. Its stark beauty, especially here on the ridge where civilians were usually not allowed, had become a necessary, inseparable part of my life.

"I can't imagine never seeing this again," I said to Efi at the end of the patrol as we surveyed the Bul'an Valley. We sat at the side of the road that led to the Yisraeli, waiting for Falk to come with the truck to pick us up.

Efi wiped his glasses on his undershirt. "The question is how long you'll be willing to pay the price to see it."

I looked at him. He was another fixture in my life, a person I admired and took as a model much more than he perhaps knew. We'd never had deep personal conversations or exchanged confidences, and had no relationship to speak of outside Company C. I realized, with an unpleasant twinge in my chest, that now that he was leaving the company there'd be no reason for us to meet.

"You've had enough," I said.

"I just feel like it's time to move on," he replied. "I'd stay in the company if I could move into a less pressured job. But I'm an officer and I can't. I want a position that won't take me away from my family so many days a year. I've done my part by now."

I settled back on the radio pack, which leaned against a boulder.

"I've been feeling that way myself this time around. Sometimes. Other times I can't conceive of my life without the army. Certainly not without being on top of Mount Hermon every couple years."

"There are other mountains," Efi said. "And you'll have time to find them. And the army doesn't stay the same. Do you really see yourself as clerk under Aviel?"

"Aviel's a great guy," I said, "but chaos isn't my style."

A few days before the patrol, Eran had confirmed my guess that I had had, for a clerk, unusual input into decision making in the company. We agreed I was unlikely to have the same relationship with Aviel. It seemed time to move out of the job. I even knew who my successor should be. Greenberg was dependable and organized, and since he'd gotten married he'd gone from pudgy to heavy. He couldn't lug around his 60mm mortar anymore.

"But, you know, I think I should stay on through next year," I told Efi. "I'll work Greenberg in gradually, help Aviel get on his feet."

"And another year and another year and another year. There's always another year." Efi smiled as the truck pulled up. Barak was driving with Falk in the passenger seat. Eiger jumped out of the back.

"How's your blood pressure?" I asked.

"I'm not dead yet," he said.

"I'll take a picture of the two of you," Efi suggested, and I handed him the camera. I got up, instinctively pulling the rifle strap over my head and laying the weapon on the radio pack. I joined Eiger on the top of a small hillock by the side of the road. Then I held up my hand.

"Wait a second." I retrieved my rifle. Slinging it over my shoulder, I walked back to Eiger, and put my arm around his shoulders.

"Okay, I'm ready," I said.

A few weeks after our Snowview stint, Falk and Barak organized a send-off for Efi. On a Monday night just after Hanukkah, the Company C staff plus some wives—Na'ama was disappointed when Ilana didn't come—gathered in an Oriental restaurant in Tel Aviv. I had a lot of fun, but a couple of painful sores in my mouth prevented me from enjoying the salads, grilled meat, and wine. The sores were remnants of a bout of foot-and-mouth disease, which I'd picked up from my children when I foolishly finished off a container of cottage cheese that one of them had started. The fever that followed seemed worse than the one the kids had had, and the sores that filled my mouth a few days later more numerous. But they had mostly passed, as my doctor said they would, after a week and a half of suffering. The fever was gone, too, but I was still weak. The following Friday, the two lingering sores were still there and I still felt rotten. In the morning I made successive visits to my physician, my dentist, and an ear, nose, and throat specialist. None of them had an explanation or much succor to offer. I halfheartedly attempted my exercise routine at the neighborhood swimming pool's weight room and then headed home to help prepare for the Sabbath.

Ilana was in the kitchen when a lightbulb in the living room burned out. As I climbed a stepladder to change it, a wave of fever swept over me. It was unlike anything I'd ever felt, a debility projecting from the bones. Descending the stepladder seemed to require as much effort as crossing the Bul'an Valley. Ilana called the doctor, who said to phone him at home the next morning if I did not improve. I told Ilana I thought I'd better skip synagogue. An hour later, I felt colder than I ever had in night maneuvers at Tze'elim. I told Ilana to recite the Sabbath blessing on the wine, as she did when I was in the army. I curled up by the living room radiator. The next morning my condition was serious enough for Ilana to make an exception to the prohibition against using the telephone on the Sabbath. The doctor came and spent half an hour checking me out, but he remained puzzled. He wrote a referral letter and said I should go to the emergency room that night if there was no change. There wasn't, and a friend drove me to the hospital. I assured Ilana that I'd be home the next day—no need for her to accompany me.

The emergency room doctors suspected a bad case of flu and might have sent me home had my vital signs not collapsed Sunday morning. The last thing I heard over my own heavy breathing was a doctor explaining that he was giving me a shot to put me to sleep, so that . . . but I didn't catch that part.

It took me a long time to understand that much of what I believed to be true was actually delusion. I never thought about it before, but when you hallucinate, you don't realize that there's anything fantastic or warped about how you see the world. Your mind does its work—it seeks to make sense of the input it receives. As in the instant after waking from a dream full of vivid but incomprehensible scenes, the mind makes connections and arranges disparate images into narrative. Seconds after you wake, your memory of the images has been irrevocably changed by the scaffolding the conscious mind erects to support it, and the discrete images have been overshadowed by a story that was not there when you dreamed.

My earliest memory is flying to the United States to fetch my parents, who are bringing me a critical medical device in the form of a videocassette. The flight attendants are businesslike and accommodating of the passenger with tubes sticking out of every orifice. After I return to my hospital bed, I learn from my doctors that the application of this medical device will be painful. Ilana, who sits at my bedside, suggests that she could undergo the treatment as my surrogate. However, since she has the kids to care for and the apartment to see to, she really thinks it makes more sense for me to do it myself.

I am trying to figure out where I am. To my right, down near my feet, is a glass door and I can see clusters of lights, clearly towns and villages. I learned orienteering in my NCO course, and when we were left on the side of a lonely road in the middle of the night, we often tried first to identify the light clusters around us. By measuring the azimuths to two such points and triangulating, we could get a good read on where we stood. I am lying down, and I wasn't given a map to study beforehand. But there is a large cluster on a hill and several smaller ones here and there. I try to match this arrangements to lights I have seen on those nights in the desert, in the Galilee, in the West Bank, and on Mount Hermon, but none of the ones I recall seem to fit.

Two nurses, a woman with an American accent and a man with an Arab accent, present me with a palette of brown shoe polishes. After I select a shade, they sponge it onto my body and somehow change my bedsheets at the same time. I ask them why I have a tube in my mouth, but they ignore my question, or don't understand it. I am annoyed. Obviously, if they removed the mouthpiece, I'd be able to enunciate.

Daytime. I can see a roof through the window—the top, apparently, of an adjacent wing of the building I'm in. Two soldiers patrol the roof, and I wonder whether they are from Company C. I think they must be. But they are too far away for me to be sure. There is a splay-legged, smooth-skinned, dog-sized creature sunning itself placidly on the rooftop, and I easily identify it as a seymouria, a carnivorous amphibian from the Permian age. I make a mental note to point it out to the staff here, as soon as they take the thing out of my mouth.

The beds hang from a long looped track on the ceiling like that in a dry-cleaning establishment. This way they are not in the way of the staff below. When the doctors or nurses need a patient, they press a button and the beds move along the track until the required patient slides past.

His bed can then be pulled down. At some point, perhaps on this day, perhaps on another, the beds begin to move, creaking and banging like the windows of the guard posts at Snowview. A nurse pulls my bed down and I see that I have visitors. It's Eiger and Eran and a couple of other guys from Company C, though I can't quite identify them. They are talking quietly among themselves. I try to speak and realize with a shock that I cannot communicate. It's not that my words are unclear, but that I cannot form words at all—for my mouth is filled by a thick tube, which I can now see if I cross my eyes and look below my nose. I cannot gesture with my hands because I can lift my right arm only a few centimeters off the bed, and my left arm is so weighted down with something I cannot move it at all. I break into a sweat. Stinging beads of perspiration drip into my eyes. I want to tell Eran and Eiger to wipe my forehead. I try to get their attention by blinking. I recall reading some-where about a paralyzed woman who communicated with her husband this way. I panic because I can't remember how the woman got her hus-band's attention and explained to him how to decipher her signals. My friends continue to speak about, but not to, me.

Eran and Eiger dissolve. It is night again. A nurse wheels a table into my field of vision. On the far side I can now make out two beds. A bearded man lies in the right-hand one, groaning incessantly. The left-hand one is occupied by an elderly man with elastic features who sits erect, gesticulating and reciting lines from Shakespeare. The nurse sits down by the table, takes a clipboard from the foot of my bed, and makes notations. She drinks hot coffee from a cup made of chocolate, and I suddenly realize that I am famished and parched. I haven't had coffee since I got here, and I desperately want her to give me some. I try to catch the nurse's attention, but she finishes off the coffee, eats the cup, and wheels the table away. I cough. She returns and looks into my eyes. She's got the thin, lined face of a strict but kindly grandmother.

"Suction!" she calls. Another nurse, a blond woman who responds with a Russian accent, joins the grandmother. They produce items from behind my head—a rubber contraption like an oversized bicycle horn, and what looks to be a duct tie a meter in length. Then, a pleasant surprise. The grandmother unhooks the tube. The mouthpiece remains in place, but suddenly I can breathe fresh air through it. I assume she's going to bring me one of those chocolate cups of coffee. But then, in a few movements too quick for me to follow, the Russian nurse sticks the duct tie into my mouth and pushes it down my throat. I gag. They attach the bicycle horn and work it; it seems to squirt water into my lungs. In a minute it is over and they reattach the tube. I hate them. I will not stay here another minute. I pull the tube from my mouth, jump out of bed, and head for the glass door, but the grandmother takes me firmly by the shoulder and returns me to bed.

"It helps you breathe more easily," she explains, and my hatred turns to fondness. She has spoken to me.

It is the next day, or perhaps another day. My father sits by my side. He's speaking to me as he did when I was young, looking into my eyes. I realize that he does not know whether I understand him. I try to blink my eyes, move my head, lift my arm, smile behind the tube, to show him that I do. He reassures me that I will recover. The doctors say they will remove the breathing tube soon. Ilana and the kids are doing fine. The members of Kehilat Yedidya have been driving Ilana and my parents to the hospital, cooking meals, helping care for the children. There is nothing to worry about.

The next day, or some other day, the doctors and nurses come by with Dr. David Linton, the head doctor of the intensive care ward on the top floor of Hadassah Hospital. They confer; then Dr. Linton tells the nurses to remove the tube. I will not be able to speak immediately, he tells me, and my throat will burn. He is correct. My bed becomes a pilgrimage site. Groups of doctors come by one after another to smile and congratulate me and ask questions, which I answer by nodding or shaking my head. Apparently my case is a celebrated one.

———

By the time Ilana arrived that afternoon, I could whisper my own questions. She and my parents filled me in. My fever had been caused by Group A *Streptococcus*, a common bacterium that generally causes no more than a sore throat but can cause toxic shock and general organ failure if it overcomes the body's immune system. A massive infection such as mine acts quickly and, lacking any distinguishing symptoms, is often misdiagnosed as the flu. I was lucky to get to the hospital in time.

I began to comprehend the state of my body. The breathing tube was out, but an intravenous shunt and a catheter remained, as well as electrodes on my chest, wired to a monitor above my head. My toes were black with gangrene and my skin scaly and peeling, like that of a molting reptile. My left arm was grossly swollen; I could not move my hand or fingers. When my father brought a mirror, one glance was sufficient. My nose, too, was black and disfigured, my hair wild, my beard scruffy. The face in the mirror, like the body I saw in the bed below me, was starved. I had lost more than seventy pounds, 40 percent of my previous weight. My skin hung on my bones like an old man's.

Our minds suppress bad experiences and magnify good ones, making it possible for us to go on with our lives. When Ilana gave birth to Mizmor, her labor lasted a day and a half—yet an hour afterward she was beaming and had forgotten it all. Only I remained traumatized from having watched her suffer. After my recovery our positions were reversed. Any mention of my illness takes Ilana back to the anguish and fear of those weeks, but my memories of the hospital are mostly pleasant. I remembered talking to friends, cracking jokes with the nurses, and working at my physical and occupational therapy with the same intensity I had once put into my workouts at the gym.

Even in the hospital my natural optimism kept me from acknowledging how sick I was. Despite the evidence of my body and the fact that I was in an intensive care ward where death was not infrequent, I assumed that my condition could not be that bad. One day I remarked to Eiger that I didn't understand why I was in this section of the hospital. The people in the beds across from me seemed to be in much worse shape.

"You almost died," he said. "And you're still not out of danger."

"Oh, come off it," I laughed. "Okay, I was sick. But it was just an infection. How bad could it be?"

"Listen, when you were hospitalized, Ilana called me," he said, pulling his chair closer. " 'I don't know why I'm calling you,' she said, 'but I thought Haim would want me to.' I was here the next morning. I asked the doctor what your condition was. He said, 'There's nothing to do but pray.' So I went out to the corridor and recited some psalms, even though I kept thinking that a rationalist like you would tell me it was pointless. But the doctors didn't expect you to last the day."

Eiger was always the one who told me the truth about myself.

"So why didn't I die?" I challenged him.

"Only God can tell you that," Eiger said. "Although the doctors said you came in with a strong heart and lungs, ones that could take a lot of punishment. All that running on the Hermon was good for something in the end."

"And I thought I was just having fun."

"Not that you shouldn't be thankful to God for getting you through this," Eiger said. "He certainly had a big part in saving you."

I'd thought about this, but having watched the deaths of a series of patients who occupied the two beds opposite me, I found myself unable to say that God had saved me. Even those who hadn't died had been in much more pain than I. Declaring that God had saved me was tantamount to saying that He had wanted them to suffer and die. That was sacrilegious.

"I suppose He did," I said slowly. "But He hasn't said why."

"Any ideas?"

I paused. "Maybe He just thought I could take it better than other people could." It didn't seem an adequate or even accurate answer. But then Judaism, as I understood it, doesn't provide answers for such questions. It expects you to act. I began to say some of the morning prayers again, fulfilling an obligation rather than demanding an explanation.

Over the next two weeks I continued to move between reality and delirium, only gradually learning to distinguish between the two. As waste built up in my blood between dialysis sessions, my mind derailed. I was caught behind a door that an immense beast pressed inexorably to the wall; I was buried alive on a strange, pockmarked planet under a fierce red sun. Or I was in uniform and battle gear, charging a hill against enemy fire.

The army had been a major backdrop to my dreams for the previous fourteen years. But in the hospital the dreams, or hallucinations, were especially vivid and intense. Being in the army was the antithesis to lying in my bed. While I appreciated my other visitors—and my friends at Kehilat Yedidya made sure that I was virtually never alone during those difficult weeks—the visitors from Company C were special to me. They came from all over—Azoulai from Ashdod; Amzaleg from the Golan Heights; Greenberg, Dani, and Alon from Tel Aviv; Efi and Achlama together weekly from Shoham. Eran and the other guys from Jerusalem dropped by frequently.

I had never so appreciated Falk's uncanny ability to read emotions and to know what was needed, even at long distance. He invariably showed up at my most desperate moments to provide encouragement, or brought me a Walkman just when I realized that listening to music could help me sleep.

"Have the doctors said when you'll get out?" he asked during one of his early visits.

"A few more weeks here," I replied. "Then I go to the rehab ward."

"And after that?"

"Home. Back to work and everything," I said vaguely. It was difficult to picture. "They say they have to amputate my toes."

Falk raised his eyebrows and I realized that he may have known this before I did.

"I asked the orthopedist if I'd be able to run afterward. He said no. But the physical therapist thinks I can."

"It probably depends on how much you want to work on it," Falk suggested.

"That's what she said." I looked out the window. "I'd like to go back to the company. At least one more time. I don't want some bacterium to decide for me when I leave the army."

Falk smiled broadly.

So beyond the goals of returning to my family and to my work—challenging enough, given my condition—I took on two others. I pestered the medical staff about running again, and my campaign was a success. When I transferred to the rehab ward after eight weeks in intensive care, running was inscribed in my file as the ultimate goal of my treatment—though I couldn't yet walk very well. Company C was there, too—my physical therapist had served with us for a few years back in the late 1980s.

I told only the people who needed to know about my plan to continue reserve duty and hoped there would be no call-up until I was functioning fully. After three weeks in the rehab ward, I went home. For the next four months I returned to the hospital three days a week for physical and occupational therapy. The other days were devoted to regaining my everyday skills. Sitting at the Friday night dinner table with the kids required more energy than I had ever realized. Typing, once as natural to me as breathing, had to be relearned as the deadened nerves and degenerated muscles in my left hand slowly began to regain dexterity and strength.

My first toeless run, a round-the-block stretch beginning and ending at the swimming pool weight room, lasted five minutes. My feet hurt, but I had proved that it was possible. By September I was running half an hour at a time, and on a Friday in October I ran from my house to Hadassah Hospital in a bit under an hour. Around that time I received my call-up order, for four days of maneuvers in December, at Tze'elim.

Our current battalion doctor happened to be an old friend from Kehilat Yedidya. One Saturday, after services, I took him aside.

"Suppose I show up for maneuvers?" I asked him.

"Where do you stand now?" he asked. "What's the damage?"

I ticked off the items. "The cardiologist says that my heart has healed and that I don't need to limit my activity. My lungs are clear, my kidneys and my liver fully functional. No toes, but I'm running. Limited flexibility in my right ankle, but it doesn't bother me much. My speech was slurred for a while but that seems to have cleared up for the most part. A large perforation in my septum and an ugly scar on my nose, but that has no bearing on my fitness. Another ugly scar on my left arm. I'm partly deaf in my left ear. That seems to me to be the most problematic."

"Look," he said. "The rules say that you're supposed to send in your medical records and ask for a hearing before a military medical committee. They'll review the case and reclassify you. Given your age, you'll probably be excused from further service."

"Suppose I don't ask to appear before the committee?"

"Eventually the records will get sent to the army but, in my experience, that could take years," he said.

"What about you? Do you have a problem with it?"

He shrugged. "I won't stop you. Give it a try."

The night guard woke us for the exercise at 4 a.m. that December morning. In the old days we would have set out at midnight and walked for hours through the desert in full gear before attacking our target. But the new wisdom in the army's central training department was that such a prolonged and intense physical effort could do more harm than good. Most reservists did not exercise regularly in their civilian lives, and long hikes with heavy gear could cause shin splints, back problems, and torn knee ligaments.

I had a hard time convincing myself to get out of my sleeping bag.

The chill night air made my skin feel brittle and numb. I used to unzip the sleeping bag and swing myself out and into my pants in one automatic motion, but I couldn't bring myself to move so quickly now. Back then, the sleeping bag hadn't kept my toes warm, so I was never really comfortable. Now I didn't have that problem.

One of the young guys could carry the radio pack. Looking at it realistically, I was superfluous. I could stay in bed and wake up late. I'd sip hot, sweet Turkish coffee straight off the camp stove with Alon and, as old soldiers throughout history have done, recall times when training was really tough.

The guard was shaking Eiger, who snored loudly. I couldn't remember the guard's name; he was a newcomer who had been initiated into the company by being assigned to guard the last shift, meaning he'd go straight from guard duty into the exercise. Eiger finally shook his head and sat up. If Eiger had sat up, I would, too.

Falk and Barak had a big pot of coffee boiling over a gas dog. We passed around cups and chocolate-spread sandwiches.

"You're crazy," Eiger said.

"I don't mind crazy," I said. "The question is, am I ridiculous?"

He pondered a moment. "No, not ridiculous. Not yet, anyway."

We threw the dirty cups into the now empty pot. Our efods and pakals were already arranged on three sides of a square, a platoon on each side. I stood by Eran on the fourth side and buckled my efod. Alon, yawning in a sweatsuit—he was staying behind to mind the camp—lifted the radio pack so I could slip my arms through the straps.

Eran gave a summary of our route and our objectives.

"This is the last time I'll be commanding this company," he concluded. "So I want it to be good."

Platoon Three led the way. Eran walked behind them, and I followed two paces behind Eran, the radio handset hooked onto my efod's right shoulder strap. In past exercises, I'd had to make sure I didn't fall behind. Now I also had to concentrate on staying to Eran's left side, where my good right ear could catch his commands. My feet were already sore, but I could bear that. The ear problem seemed more serious. A soldier had to be able to hear. I'll just get through this exercise, take one last hill, I thought. Then I'll retire willingly.

The path we were following rose and we reached the top of a low ridge just as the upper rim of the sun broke the horizon to our right. Before us we could see our objective, another hill, one we'd conquered many times. Eran halted, and we went down on our knees. He took the handset from me and tersely enunciated his orders. Platoon One began to circle to the left as Platoon Two took up positions to our right. We had perhaps ten minutes to rest before Eran gave the command to charge. I pushed myself to my feet and ran after him, not even trying to shoot.

Fifteen minutes later, the hill was ours.

"Congratulations," Eiger said to me as we trudged back to camp. "I really respect you for doing this. I mean it."

I smiled, enjoying the feel of the sun on my face. The men spoke in low voices, instinctively respectful of the desert morning. My muscles felt limber and strong.

"I can do it," I said, half to myself and half to Eiger.

He shook his head. "Yes, you can do it. You had to prove yourself, and you did. Isn't that enough?"

"Even without toes I can run faster than most of them," I said stubbornly.

"Even if you had toes, you'd be forty-one. Enough is enough. You've done your share," Eiger said.

"But I enjoy this," I protested.

"Now you sound ridiculous."

I came home from the maneuvers elated but confused. Ilana, like Eiger, had encouraged me to return to Company C, but like him she felt that now was the time to make my exit. I set down my chimidan by the door and sat facing her over the kitchen table, still in my dirty uniform.

"I can do it," I said. "There's no reason to stop."

"It's going to stop sometime," she said. "If not now, four years from now when you reach the maximum age. Why not end it at a high point?"

"My friends are there," I pointed out.

"But you yourself say they're drifting out. And, anyway, you're five years older than the oldest of them."

"It's a good change of pace for me."

"It would be a change of pace for me if you didn't go off to the army. Remember that you spent three months in the hospital. You owe me that time." She warmed her hands on her coffee cup. "Three months."

I fell silent. "I guess I just can't say it's over."

"Why not?"

I had a hard time answering, but I forced the words out. "Because it means I'm getting old. Because it means admitting that the strep beat me."

"You've just proved that it didn't beat you. And you were going to get old anyway."

"I think I should go one more time, for the next round of active duty, to help Greenberg get a handle on things," I suggested.

Ilana was adamant. "If you asked to appear before a medical board, they'd discharge you. That means that from here on out you're for all intents and purposes a volunteer. I was willing to put up with reserve duty when there wasn't a choice. Now there is. You owe me the time."

In the end, I served twice more with Company C. The following spring I went to Snowview for a week, to fill in for Greenberg when he was on leave. I tried to fit into my old job, but I found it no longer interested me much. Greenberg had replaced my justice chart with an Excel spreadsheet; it was much easier to keep track of how many men were on duty and where. But, not having been with the guys from the beginning, I didn't have a feel for what frustrations and personal problems each one was facing. And there were a lot of new men, including three platoon commanders I didn't know at all.

A year later, in 1998, I went back for another week, this time at a West Bank outpost. The work was much like what we'd done at the Route 443 base in the early days of the Oslo agreements, manning roadblocks and patrolling main roads. But these were the years of Binyamin Netanyahu's government, and antagonism between Israel and the Palestinians was growing. Now the work seemed pointless, no more than a holding pattern until Netanyahu or Arafat, or both, decided to trash Oslo and resume open hostilities. I kept away from the duty roster and the Excel justice chart. I was no longer an NCO, either, just a simple soldier going on patrols under the command of much younger men. I didn't know a lot of them, and a number of them didn't make good impressions. On one patrol the commander and driver, both guys who had entered the company over the last two years, parked our jeep in a playground in one of the Jewish settlements and smoked a joint. I protested, but they didn't think much of my opinion on what soldiers should and shouldn't do. Why would they? They didn't know me or my story in Company C. I realized that, in their eyes, I was an uninteresting relic of a past age.

The next time a call-up order came, I phoned Aviel. We had the conversation that we would have each time a call-up order arrived over the next two and a half years.

"If you need me, I'll come," I said.

"If I need you, I'll call you," Aviel replied.

"I mean it. Don't hesitate to call me, even at the last minute. I'll pack up my chimidan and report for duty."

"Don't worry," Aviel said. "If I need you, I'll call."

When people asked, I'd say that I had enough seniority in my unit to write my own ticket now. I went when I wanted to. Of course, if there was an emergency, I'd be there with the rest of the guys.

In my lucid moments, I realized that this was an illusion. But, I thought, maybe I needed the illusion. Maybe, for me, the way to stop being a soldier was to keep thinking I was one.

Chapter Twelve

· REALITIES ·

BETHLEHEM, APRIL 2002

T HE POINT OF INTEREST IN ANY STORY / IS WHERE IT GOES OFF the tracks," writes Sharon Dolin in "Mistake," observing, "That's how we keep track of time / or time keeps track of us."

The news spread quickly among the Passover morning worshippers at the Eigers' synagogue in Zikhron Ya'akov. The town, once a farming village and now a middle-class suburb with pricey houses, lies on Mount Carmel's southern spur, overlooking the Mediterranean coast. Radio and television are prohibited on the first day of the weeklong holiday, but the news had been passed along by nonreligious neighbors. The previous night, March 27, a man had walked into the dining room of the Park Hotel in Netanya, a coastal city twenty minutes south of Zikhron. The room was filled with families waiting for the start of the seder, the ceremony and festive meal that begins Passover. The man, who acted in the name of Hamas, calmly looked around and then pressed the button on his belt of explosives. The final death toll would be twenty-nine; more than two hundred were injured.

Israel had been attacked once before on a holy day. Now, as in

1973, Israelis felt doubly violated—the enemy had attacked not only human beings but also a sacred moment, this time the commemoration of the Jewish people's birth as a nation.

There was a difference, though. The start of the Yom Kippur War had been a blitzkrieg that caught Israel unawares. The Passover bombing of 2002 was but the latest in a series of attacks. On the night of March 9, a suicide bomber had detonated himself in a crowded Jerusalem café around the corner from the prime minister's residence, killing eleven and wounding fifty-four; three days later, Hezbollah gunmen crossed the Lebanese border and ambushed several automobiles on a Galilee road near Kibbutz Matzuva, killing six and wounding seven; on March 20, a suicide bomber blew up on a bus—a favorite target—in Afula in northern Israel, killing seven and wounding thirty. These were the major attacks; many others came between. They were the crest of a wave of terror that had begun a year and a half previous with the second Palestinian uprising, the al-Aqsa Intifada.

Many people we knew had forbidden their children to frequent public places, and when they heard we were traveling by bus and train to be the Eigers' guests for the seder, they called us brave or foolhardy or both. I encouraged my kids to be alert but not to change their habits. To stop riding buses or going to the mall was to hand the terrorists a victory, I told them. Carrying on with our lives would show the bombers they could not scare us.

Still, I was nervous traveling. It seemed all too easy for a young person with death on his or her mind to hop over the fence and onto our train. In fact, the previous July a suicide bomber had exploded at the bus stop opposite the train station where Eiger picked us up in his GMC van.

We had planned to stay with the Eigers for a good part of the week and perhaps do some hiking in the Galilee. It didn't seem likely now. As soon as the first day of Passover ended on Thursday night, we turned on the television. The previous week members of the government had

warned that Israel could not stand by passively in the face of a concerted assault on its civilians. Now Prime Minister Ariel Sharon appeared on-screen to announce that emergency call-up orders would go
out the next morning. The army was going to reoccupy the West Bank.
The operation's codename was "Protective Wall."

The phone call came at noon on Friday. Ilana was helping Na'ama
cook for the Sabbath and I was trying to read the newspaper amid the
noise produced by our combined nine children. It was raining, so we
couldn't have gone hiking even if war were not in the air.

"Hi, Aviel," Eiger said. "I can't say I wasn't expecting to hear from
you."

I put the paper down. Eiger said "okay" three or four times, then, in
response to my gestures, "Here, Watzman wants to talk to you."

I took the phone. "Hi, Aviel."

"Hello, Watzman," Aviel said enthusiastically, as if this were merely
a friendly chat.

"What about me?"

"You're staying home. I'll call you if I need you," he answered.

"But, Aviel, this is an emergency," I said.

"I don't see you on the list of guys getting call-up orders. So relax.
Wait until an order comes."

"Just an oversight. I'll report anyway," I told him.

"If that's what you want, okay. But I hear you're there with your
family. What are you going to do, leave Ilana stranded with the kids?"

I heard Na'ama behind me. "Oh, no, you're not going anywhere.
It's bad enough that Eiger's going. I need you here."

Aviel had hung up—he had other calls to make.

"Don't be ridiculous, Haim," Eiger said. "What are you going to do
there? What are you going to be able to do? Stay here and keep an eye
on my kids for me."

Now it was Ilana's turn. "If you get a call-up order, then I understand
you have to go. But you haven't been called up, so you're not going."

In fact, I no longer had a job to do in the army. And even if I over-looked my nearly deaf left ear, there was my right ankle. A year ago I was two-thirds of the way through the annual Jerusalem half-marathon when I felt a sudden twinge. I pressed on, though the pain evolved from dull and annoying to sharp and debilitating by the time I hobbled over the finish line. I expected to get over the injury as I'd gotten over several other injuries in the previous four years, by sticking to swimming and biking for a month.

But my ankle did not heal. I saw a physical therapist for several months, but nothing worked. In my final session with him the day be-fore my family's trip to Zikhron, he told me he'd tried everything. "I know how important running is for you," he said, "but if you keep run-ning, you might soon be unable to walk."

Until then I'd been stubborn about the injury. I'd followed the doc-tors' advice by changing my exercise habits, but I'd insisted on running once a week. Afterward I'd limp badly for a day or two and pretend that nothing hurt. I knew this was an impossible situation for a foot soldier. I'd never be able to charge a hill or outmaneuver a sniper in an alleyway.

But as Eiger changed into his uniform and threw last-minute items into his chimidan, I felt unbearably guilty. I'd passed the legal reservist retirement age nine months ago, but I hadn't received a discharge no-tice. My own chimidan was packed and ready, down in my basement of-fice. How could I stay home while my friends went to war?

"I can't take it, Eiger," I said. "I've got to come with you."

"Shut up," he said.

Ilana provided the excuse that allowed me to see Eiger off without breaking down entirely.

"You'll call him Saturday night," she told me. "By then he'll know what's going on and what you can do to help. Then we'll decide."

You might think a man who'd consistently opposed Israeli occupa-tion of the West Bank would be glad he didn't have to participate in

conquering it again. Why would a man who'd been led into one unnecessary war by Ariel Sharon follow him into another? But I reluctantly
supported a major strike against the Palestinian Authority. The new
Palestinian uprising was not like the first Intifada. The Palestinians were
armed with rifles and explosives on a scale we had not known in the late
1980s. In the face of nearly daily suicide bombings and regular sniper
fire on one of Jerusalem's outlying neighborhoods, Israel had to take
drastic action.

How did we get to this impasse? How did the promise of the Oslo
peace process collapse into a deadly confrontation between the two peoples? No story of the fall of Oslo can be both coherent and comprehensive. In war and diplomacy the actors are, after all, human, and human
beings are complex creatures. They say one thing and do another; they
maintain contradictory positions simultaneously. Their mind's eye is, as
often as not, more like a fly's than an eagle's—made of dozens of cells,
each perceiving the world from a slightly different perspective. The resulting image can be resolved in the conscious mind only by a process of
simplification. The fallacy of postmodernism is not the recognition that
the picture is indistinct, but the contention that the incoherence the eye
sees is an accurate representation of what lies outside us. A person who
believes this is paralyzed; the world acts on him but he will not change
the world. We must resolve the image—we must tell a story of what
went wrong.

The collapse of the Oslo peace process, culminating in the failure of
the Camp David summit of July 2000 and the outbreak of the second
Intifada two months later, has been analyzed at length. Participants on
both sides of the negotiations, along with outside observers, scholars,
and journalists, have published articles and memoirs and book-length
accounts of the negotiations. What I offer here is how it looked to the
guys in Company C. The men in Company C, myself included, were not
in possession of all the facts in real time. And while the Israeli press is
free and publishes a wide range of viewpoints, most of the guys tended

to accept the version of events given by the Israeli leadership and mainstream analysts. But that outlook explains why these men, no matter what their politics, reported in overwhelming numbers for combat duty in April 2002 after having originally accepted Oslo.

The first Intifada was a success. Not a military success, since Israel retained control of the territories. But when the Palestinians showed themselves willing to fight for their freedom, they earned the grudging respect of the fighters in Company C. They also raised the ante—serving as reservists in Hebron in the spring of 1987 had been a mostly risk-free, boring affair. Serving a year later, a few kilometers distant in Bani Na'im, was dangerous and unpleasant. A large majority of the men in the company, even some of the religious right-wingers, slowly came to see the West Bank Palestinians as a people who, like the Jews, had suffered. They deserved to control their own destiny, and it would be better for Israel to get out of the business of governing this hostile population.

When Rabin signed the Oslo agreement with Arafat, there was a range of opinion in Company C about how much territory the Palestinians ought to receive and how many settlements Israel should relinquish. But most of the guys accepted the agreement's premise.

For me, peace with a Palestinian state meant that the two countries would accept each other's existence and enter into neighborly relations. Most of the guys didn't think that was possible and, after their years in the muck of the Intifada, they wanted little to do with Palestinians. They viewed peace in the terms outlined by Ehud Barak, the Labor prime minister who won a landslide victory over Binyamin Netanyahu in 1999: "We here, them there." I believed that, for the peace to be a lasting one, the two countries would have to develop commercial and social ties that created a vested interest in peace on both sides. But I was not overly disturbed by the "We here, them there" attitude. If hostilities ceased, attitudes would slowly change and the two societies would gradually become closer, I reasoned.

A vocal minority in the company adamantly opposed the Oslo process. Yet even here there was a change. Prior to the first Intifada, opposition to giving the Palestinians territory in exchange for peace had been justified in ideological-religious terms: God gave us the entire land and we were not permitted to give it to anyone else, even to obtain peace. During the Intifada, the arguments took on a practical hue: Arafat could not be trusted, and the Palestinians were dissembling when they said they wanted peace with Israel. I considered this progress, because practical claims, unlike ideological ones, must be substantiated and can change. If we on the left could demonstrate that the Palestinians were sincere and reliable partners in peace, we could neutralize some of the opposition to accommodation.

And this is what happened in the early days after Rabin and Arafat's handshake, as the Palestinian Authority took control first of the Gaza Strip and Jericho, then of other cities in the West Bank. Many guys who'd opposed dealing with Arafat expressed a hesitant willingness to give it a try. Even the right-wingers were largely relieved to get out of the job of policing Palestinian villages.

The men's doubts began when terrorist attacks against Israelis continued, perpetrated by Islamic extremists or by the Marxist opposition to Arafat. Advocates of the Oslo accords argued that attacks committed by the opponents of peace should not deter us. As the Palestinian population began to enjoy the benefits of peace, support for violence would wane and ultimately vanish.

But Arafat's administration continued to speak in aggressive language and did little to suppress the terrorists, who seemed to enjoy broad popular support among the Palestinians. The guys became more fearful of the process. They felt they had been assigned an impossible mission as soldiers—to protect Israel's civilians from terrorists while the terrorists operated freely in the territory of the Palestinian Authority.

These concerns led to Binyamin Netanyahu's narrow victory in the 1996 elections and to three years of stagnation. In early 1999, when I made my last appearance as a soldier in Company C, most of the guys were disillusioned. At our traditional end-of-duty cookout, Marcel Levy stood on a bench and, Hyde Park–style, launched into a lengthy diatribe against the peace process and against me as its personification in our unit. Many of the guys nodded assent and waited for me to reply. I found myself without a strong argument for pressing on with negotiations with Arafat. I could have made a case if my audience had been one of political scientists, journalists, and armchair intellectuals. But the men before me were charged with the day-to-day business of keeping Israel safe.

Yet the first Intifada's fundamental transformation of the guys' perception of the Palestinians had not been overcome. Later in 1999, despite their disillusionment, a majority of the men voted to replace Netanyahu with Barak.

As part of his plan to revive the peace process, Barak promised during his campaign to withdraw all Israeli troops from southern Lebanon within a year of taking office. The troops were there to prevent Hezbollah, the Shiite Muslim militia equipped and trained by Iran, from attacking Israel's northern settlements, but the guerrillas had begun inflicting heavy losses in full-scale assaults on Israeli outposts, raising the question of whether Israel's continued military presence was worthwhile.

Barak also wanted to cut himself clear of the thicket of agreements that had been signed with the Palestinian leadership since the beginning of the Oslo process. The Oslo strategy had been a gradualist one. Difficult issues were put off to a later date with the idea that they would be easier to resolve once the peace process had begun to work. But during the interim period stipulated by the Oslo agreement the two sides had become more distrustful of each other. Barak thought the solution was to sit down with Arafat, under American auspices, and decide all the questions at once.

When Barak went to Camp David to do just that in July 2000,

many in Company C were skeptical about whether Arafat and his associates could be trusted. On the other hand, no major terrorist incidents had occurred for several months, proof that Arafat could control the extremists' violence if he wanted peace. Support for Barak's initiative was cautious but real.

Press reports coming out of Camp David indicated that Barak was offering unprecedented concessions to the Palestinians. The settlements would be evacuated with the exception of a few blocks near the Green Line that would become part of Israel. The Palestinian refugees from Israel's 1948 War of Independence would either be compensated or make their homes in the new Palestinian state. Jerusalem, Israel's capital, would be partitioned. Even I was nervous—the dividing line would run a kilometer from my apartment.

Some subsequent accounts of the Camp David negotiations argued that the plan Barak put on the table was not so generous. But the debate is over small increments. Barak certainly offered much more than any Israeli leader ever had before. From the point of view of the guys in Company C, Barak offered the Palestinians nearly everything—more than these reserve soldiers ever thought they'd agree to give—and the Palestinians said no.

Furthermore, the way the Palestinians conveyed their refusal indicated that, despite their formal recognition of Israel, they viewed the Jews as an illegitimate community without real historical or spiritual connection to the land in which they lived. Arafat and his associates denied any Jewish claim to the Temple Mount, Israel's holiest site, declaring that the Jewish Temple had never stood there. Even the leftists in Company C couldn't agree to the Palestinian demand that Israel accept the right of all Palestinian refugees of 1948, and their descendents, to return to their original homes in Israel proper. Such an influx would turn the Jews into a minority in their own country—the end of Israel in all but name.

When the violence of the second Intifada began at the end of September 2000, the guys of Company C were stunned. The Palestinians said they were fighting to force Israel out of the very occupied territories that Israel had offered to evacuate peacefully. But the guys also felt united, because no matter what one's view of the peace process, all agreed we had to fight back. It seemed to us that the Palestinians had taken Israel's withdrawal from Lebanon to mean that Israelis would no longer defend themselves, that the Jews would run away if enough of them were killed.

The outbreak of violence put an end to any hope that negotiations could resume. In a special election, Barak was beaten solidly by Ariel Sharon. I stuck with Barak, but Sharon got the votes of many disillusioned leftists. Suicide bombings increased, and by Passover 2002, even Company C's most committed advocates of accommodation thought the Palestinian attacks had to be answered.

"It was clear there was no alternative," Dani told me afterward. "The Palestinians weren't going to change their tactics if they weren't forced to."

"We gave it a chance, a serious chance. But it didn't work," Alon said.

Before turning off the radio when the Sabbath began on Friday night we heard reports that reservists were responding to the emergency call-up in record numbers.

Shabbat was dismal. It was rainy and cold, and I was mad at Eiger, at Na'ama, at Ilana, at myself. I was convinced that my staying put was an act of cowardice and disloyalty. Since I'd joined Company C in 1984 we'd been through tough spots, but we'd never had to go into battle in the real sense of the word. Now it was happening. If there was ever a time to be with my comrades, it was now—no matter what I was capable or not capable of doing.

When I called Eiger on Saturday night, he told me virtually everyone in the company had reported for duty, Alon included.

Like me, Alon had not shown up for active duty for some time.

Three years ago he'd been struck with a sudden, disabling fatigue as he drove his two older children to visit their mother and new baby brother in a Tel Aviv hospital. He pulled the car over on the Ayalon Freeway and flagged down a taxi, telling the astonished driver he'd pay whatever it took to get him to leave the cab on the highway shoulder and drive Alon and his kids to the hospital in Alon's car. When they got there, he sent the kids to their mother in the maternity ward and went straight to the emergency room. He was barely functional for several months, but though his doctors never diagnosed the problem, he made a slow recovery. Reserve duty had been out of the question, but he hadn't been able to bring himself to ask the army to reclassify him.

When he responded to the call-up order that Friday, he didn't take a change of clothes or a toothbrush. He planned to submit his medical papers to the battalion doctor and receive a medical discharge. But when he saw all the guys reporting for duty, he called his wife and told her he was staying.

"This is serious business," he said to her. "I can't get out. This is a war to protect our homes. You yourself could get blown up in the bus on the way to work in Tel Aviv." Then he launched into a patriotic speech of a kind she'd never heard him give before.

Hearing a story like this was all I needed to feel even worse about myself. On top of that, Eiger told me about the chaos at our home base near Jerusalem. The emergency gear, supposedly carefully inventoried and maintained by a staff of young soldiers, turned out to be insufficient and in poor condition. The army didn't have enough food for the influx of reservists, and Passover complicated matters, because there wasn't enough *matzah*, the unleavened bread eaten on the holiday, to go around. Emergency rations included cans of leavened crackers, and the religious guys objected when some of the nonreligious ones opened them up. Everyone was wet, cold, and hungry—and of course I felt I ought to be suffering with them, instead of enjoying the warm home and good food Na'ama was providing. When I got off the phone I told

Ilana that the next morning we were all going back to Jerusalem, where I would grab my chimidan and report to the base.

But Sunday morning Na'ama was drained and nervous, and the Eiger kids urged us to stay. Ilana suggested that we do something fun. I suggested that I take the train and bus back to Jerusalem and let Ilana and the kids follow at their leisure, but Ilana wouldn't hear of it. The kids wanted to get out of the house, but the weather was still bad. Given the frequency of the recent terrorist attacks, was any trip to a public place worth the risk? As the adults discussed this, the radio reported another suicide bombing, this in an Arab-owned restaurant in Haifa, death toll fourteen.

"We're going bowling," I announced to the kids. "We're not going to give in."

Na'ama and Ilana agreed, though mostly out of desperation for some quiet. I took the kids in the Eiger van. We bowled, and we returned. Then my family packed up and set out for home. The train was eerily empty for a holiday week, the train station silent, the bus to Jerusalem half full.

Niot, now in fifth grade, announced that he wanted to visit his best friend, Eli, as soon as we got home. Eli lived in Gilo, Jerusalem's southernmost neighborhood. Built on land annexed after the Six-Day War, Gilo stood on a hill overlooking Bethlehem and its sister town, Beit Jala. Eli's house was on the neighborhood's southern edge, with only a green, terraced valley lined with olive trees between it and Beit Jala.

Soon after the second Intifada started, Palestinian snipers began shooting at Gilo from Beit Jala, turning a residential neighborhood into a front line. Eli's house was directly in the line of fire. A lot of parents wouldn't let their kids visit Eli at home anymore, and Eli was put out by this. Like other terrorist actions, the gunfire on Gilo made me angry. I told Niot that if he wasn't scared to go to Eli's house, I thought it was a mitzvah, a good deed, for him to visit his friend. Show the snipers we're not scared of them, I said. Ilana concurred.

One afternoon a few months before Passover, Niot went home with Eli after school. At 6 p.m. I hailed a cab and set out to pick him up. But five minutes into the ride the cab's radio reported sniper fire in Gilo, and the driver said there was no sense continuing—the army and civil defense corps would have already closed off the roads to civilian traffic. As he made a U-turn to take me home, my cell phone rang. It was Niot.

"Dad, I want to sleep over at Eli's."

"It looks like you won't have much choice," I said. "I can't get there to pick you up. The radio says the Palestinians are shooting again. Aren't you scared?"

"Scared? No way!" Niot chortled. "It's great! We're lying on the floor with Eli's mother and we can hear the bullets flying!"

"You're not supposed to enjoy it," I told him.

"Don't pick me up. I want to stay here all night!"

When I talked to Eiger on my cell phone during the train trip home, I mentioned that Niot wanted to go straight to his friend's house in Gilo.

Eiger didn't let me finish. "Not today. Not a good time. Definitely not today."

"Why not?"

"We're moving in."

When we got home I retrieved my chimidan from the office-storeroom and began filling plastic bags with warm clothing, underwear, and books. I wasn't sure where I was to report. I couldn't get any of the guys on their phones—apparently they were mustering close by in preparation for invading Beit Jala, but I didn't know where. If I reported to our home base, I'd get stuck there for a day or two until I found a way to join the unit. Ilana came into the bedroom. I couldn't look her in the eye because I knew if I did I'd unpack the chimidan.

"When are you going?" she asked.

"I don't know. I don't know where they are," I snapped. I threw the half-filled bags into the chimidan and went downstairs to the office. After staring moodily at my computer for a few minutes, I took out my bicycle. The road to Gilo went straight up, a tough climb that had been part of one of my favorite long running routes. I pedaled to the peak, then onto the back road that went by Eli's house. The ugly concrete barriers the army had erected along the road to protect passersby and cars from sniper fire blocked out the view. I leaned my bike against a barrier, walked around it, and looked out over Beit Jala. Just three days before the uprising began, Asor and I had ridden our bikes there. It didn't look like a dangerous place. I saw no sign of Company C. I wanted to cry—because I desperately needed to be with my friends and because I knew that I couldn't, shouldn't, be. And because there was no good reason for the neighborhood in which I stood and the town across the valley not to live in peace. And because I could think of no way to stop the Beit Jala snipers and the suicide bombers except to have my friends invade the town, occupy it, and clean the place out. I picked up my bike to start the trip back before the tears began.

By the time I got home it was raining again. I checked my e-mail. Netivot Shalom, the religious peace movement, had sent a reminder that it was my turn to show up on Friday for the weekly peace vigil the group held outside the prime minister's residence in downtown Jerusalem. My first reaction was disbelief. Only a lunatic would stage a demonstration at such a time. But then I had second thoughts. Perhaps a statement for peace needed to be made most when bullets were flying. I can't deal with it now, I thought. I made a mental note to think about it the next day. In the meantime I tried to piece together the scraps of information I got from my phone calls to the guys.

Sunday afternoon, Company C's regiment had deployed in readiness to move into the Palestinian territories south of Jerusalem. The battalion's mission was to take responsibility for Beit Jala, part of which had been occupied by a paratrooper unit after a spate of sniper fire a few weeks previously. The guys took up positions and patrolled the upper part of the town. There was steady gunfire from upper stories, and the guys shot back to force the snipers away from the windows they were using as positions. Monday night brought orders to prepare for an advance. The guys packed the racks on the outside of the APCs with sandbags to protect the carriers from enemy fire. Tuesday at dawn the forces began to move down Beit Jala's hill and across the Jerusalem-Hebron road into Bethlehem.

Ten or eleven guys were loaded into APCs that were crowded with eight soldiers and their gear. The armored vehicles, steel boxes on treads, moved slowly into the town with all hatches closed for fear of Molotov cocktails, snipers, and antitank rockets. The inability to see outside exacerbated the guys' fear as they waited in the main compartment. The column advanced, then halted for an interminable time before advancing again.

Platoon One was at the head of the column, in two APCs—the first commanded by Eyal, the lieutenant who had replaced Efi, and the second by Dani, who'd replaced Eiger as sergeant. A procession of foreign journalists, foreign peace volunteers, and Palestinians walked up to the APCs and blocked their way.

The periscopes in an APC's command hatch don't allow a full field of vision, and Dani was afraid he'd run someone over. He hadn't been equipped with tear gas for crowd dispersal. Eyal opened his hatch and fired warning shots into the air. Foreign radio and television news programs reported that Israeli soldiers were firing on journalists.

When you are cramped, cold, and frightened, small needs loom large. The guys were desperate to pee, but orders were not to leave the vehicles, and the threat of snipers was enough to keep everyone inside. Azoulai finally radioed his lieutenant.

"We've got eight guys who'll die if they can't piss," he announced. "We've got to storm a house so we can get out of this thing. Get permission from Aviel."

But the lieutenant, a new guy in the unit, wasn't going to bother Aviel, who was busy taking a different part of the town. Azoulai looked behind his APC and noticed a D-9 bulldozer, a monster of a machine with a blade nearly two meters high. Azoulai convinced the D-9's driver to pull up to the APC's back hatch, so that the guys could pop out one by one to relieve themselves, using the bulldozer's blade as a shield.

The battalion's headquarters and support units, along with Company C's administration—the three first sergeants and Greenberg—moved into the leafy campus of Bethlehem University, which sits on a hill overlooking the main road on one side and the Church of the Nativity on the other. Platoons Two and Three deployed nearby.

I managed to catch Greenberg there on his cell phone.

"It's actually a pretty nice place," he told me.

"I know. I used to go there a lot in the 1980s. I'd hang out with students in the cafeteria and the café down the street," I said. "I guess it looks a lot different now."

"No students here," he noted.

"How's it going?"

"I'm fine," he reported. "But I'm in the rear. My main problem is finding a uniform that fits me. My belly's grown a lot since the last time you saw me."

"I figured I'd better come help you with the manpower planning," I suggested.

"There's not much to do," he told me. "Pretty much everyone showed up. There's no duty roster because everyone's in action. You'd be bored." I could imagine him shaking his head, wondering what my problem was.

The guys spent a long day inside the APCs, too scared and too stir-crazy to sleep as rain poured down outside. The battalion's heavy weapons company was facing stiff resistance only a few hundred meters away. Their mission was to take the upper section of the casbah, Bethlehem's broad market street that descends in a series of steps from the top of the university's hill to Manger Square. Either side of the casbah was lined with storefronts that in better days sold souvenirs to Christian pilgrims. Families lived on the second and third stories. I remembered the market glittering with colored lights and tinsel on the snowy Christmas Eve of 1982, when my basic training battalion was sent to patrol Bethlehem for the holiday weekend. There weren't that many tourists—the Lebanon War was on, and times were tense—but enough to create some sense of festivity. Last year, with the Intifada on, there had been hardly any.

Increasingly fearful that the APCs were easy targets for armor-piercing RPG rockets, the guys decided to take shelter in the houses and stores along the street. As they dispersed, they could hear the steady tick of sniper fire coming from all directions, and a bomb exploded in a traffic island Dani had just run past. Eiger and some others broke into a nicely decorated hair salon, where they found a large stock of small-arms ammunition. It was now Tuesday night. The platoon received orders to prepare to move into the casbah. The last day of Passover began at sundown, and before leaving, the guys, soaked and muddy to their shoulders from the rain, unstowed a bottle of sweet wine and Eiger made the customary blessing.

They began their move into the casbah on Wednesday around noon. Individual squads, backs to walls and rifles aimed, took the houses one by one. This was the protocol we'd practiced so often in Chicago, though it called for the use of grenades and none were used here because of the families in these houses.

The guys eventually arrived at Manger Square in front of the Church of the Nativity. The orders were to seize houses and buildings around the plaza and fortify them. Palestinian gunmen and leaders had taken refuge in the church. The army wasn't going to storm a shrine, so the soldiers were to besiege the church compound, keeping anyone from entering or leaving.

I called the cell phone numbers I had. Vanunu and Azoulai had taken what they described as a very nice home. The living room was full of antique furniture and woven rugs, which they moved into a side room. The soldiers slept on the living room floor and used the roof as a guard post, while the family continued to live in the rest of the house. Eiger and Alon and several other soldiers took a French convent. The nuns were furious and wouldn't talk or cooperate. Snipers fired periodically from the houses nearby, and the guys kept up a steady rhythm of return fire.

Because the casbah had been taken but still wasn't secure, Falk, Barak, and Achlama didn't have clearance to use their APC to provision the men at Manger Square, who'd moved out of Beit Jala three days earlier with a minimal stock of canned rations. The campus was stacked with supplies and packages of cookies and candy sent by Israeli schoolchildren who wanted to help, but there was no way to get the food to the soldiers.

I called Eiger, who was on the convent rooftop, in the rain.

"I haven't changed my underwear or socks in three days," he said. "We've barely got anything to eat here, either—our rations are almost gone."

"I have an idea," I said. "Do you want to hear it?"

"There's this huge storeroom of food downstairs but we're not touching it," he said. "We haven't touched any of the furniture either. Though we are using the convent's electricity to recharge our cell phones, Geneva Convention be damned."

"Look," I said, "I accept that I'm not of much use as a soldier. But I think that what's going on now is a key event in the company's history. I thought I'd join you as a writer. As soon as it's safe to get to you, I'll come and start interviewing the guys. Then I'll write Company C's story in the Protective Wall operation. What do you think?"

But Eiger was shouting something at the other guys. I could hear gunfire.

"Ask Aviel what he thinks," I shouted into the phone.

"Aviel, Watzman wants to come and interview us," Eiger shouted.

"Fuck Watzman," Aviel shouted back, cold, tired, hungry, and worried that his men were going to get killed.

Someone was shooting; I heard Eiger calling for guys to come up to the roof, and then he turned off his phone. Admit it, I chided myself. What you are going through is no more than a run-of-the-mill midlife crisis. You're trying to pretend that you are still in your twenties or thirties. It's time for you to stop whining and adjust to your age. The scolding made me feel better. Okay, I breathed in relief. It's over. I know where I'm at. I'll unpack the chimidan. But I didn't.

On Friday at 1 p.m. I biked to the prime minister's residence for the peace vigil. The sun had come out, though heavy clouds created moments of chill and dampness. Only a handful of people came—a couple of professors, a few friends from Kehilat Yedidya. Small left-wing factions can't do anything without an ideological argument, and one was underway when I arrived. A couple of the younger organizers had prepared signs, and one of them read "Stop Operation Peace for the Settlements." The slogan played off the name Sharon had given the Lebanon war when it began, Operation Peace for the Galilee. The implication was that Sharon had concocted the Protective Wall operation solely to protect Israel's settlements in the West Bank.

"That's just not true," an older woman said. "I'm not staying here if the sign isn't removed."

"It *is* true," the young woman who'd made the sign insisted. "If we didn't have the settlements, we wouldn't need the war."

"My unit's besieging Manger Square in Bethlehem now," I said, "and I've been talking to guys there a few times a day. I haven't spoken to one who thinks that they're there to protect the settlements. They think that they're fighting the terrorists who've been sending suicide bombers into Jerusalem and Tel Aviv."

"That's what they think," the young woman said. "But that's not what they are in fact doing."

"We're all against the occupation," I said, "and we're all against the settlements. But the soldiers in the West Bank are acting to protect Israeli civilians from terrorism."

"And you think it's going to work?" she challenged. "A month from now we'll have suicide bombers again."

"If I were prime minister, I'd use the operation to make a major strategic adjustment," I said. "First you prove that we can't be cowed. Then you withdraw the army to defensible lines and evacuate the settlements beyond it. You tell the Palestinians that when they're ready to negotiate reasonably, we're ready, too. In the meantime we do what we have to do to protect ourselves."

"You think that's what Sharon has in mind? He wants to reoccupy the West Bank for good," she assured me.

"You're probably right," I said. "But what should we have done? Not doing anything would have been more dangerous. Withdrawing in the face of suicide attacks would have been even worse. If I were a Palestinian, I'd take that to mean that if they keep up the suicide attacks, we'll withdraw more and more, until we give up the whole country."

The sign was removed. We stood there for half an hour and heard a short lesson about the week's reading from the Torah. Some passersby gave us the finger and called us traitors. We prayed the afternoon service and dispersed. A friend I ran into on the way home told me I'd betrayed the soldiers in the field by demonstrating against the war. I said I was demonstrating for the peace that ought to come out of the war. He said I was naïve. Maybe he was right. But I didn't think I'd betrayed my friends in the company. They could think only about the next hour and the next day. Away from the front, I could think farther ahead than they could, and I'd betray them if I didn't do so.

That day, Company C was rotated out of Bethlehem to take control of a large village southwest of Hebron. The nighttime approach to the village, involving a difficult climb up a mountainside, ended in a dawn invasion that met little resistance. Eiger told me that Aryeh Nasi, our resident Rambo, had inspired everyone with his strength, endurance, and determination. The company set up shop and entered a routine of patrols and guard duty more similar to the West Bank service we'd done in the past. It was serious duty, though—at one point they caught a suicide bomber on his way to Israel.

The day the company was demobilized, Eiger showed up in Jerusalem with Ronny, a young guy who'd joined us at Snowview in 1996. Ronny hadn't made a good impression then—he'd seemed apathetic and sullen. But the current emergency brought out the best in all the guys, Eiger noted. We sat in an Oriental grill down the street from my apartment, and I bought them dinner in exchange for stories.

After three weeks in the field Eiger had lost weight and grown a bushy beard. He and Ronny both looked tired.

I asked how the guys had behaved. The press reported that Israeli soldiers had gratuitously destroyed property, especially in Palestinian Authority offices. The news ran footage of torched filing cabinets and trashed computers. Computer equipment had been stolen and hard disks containing information vital to the Palestinian Authority's educational and health work had disappeared. Sanctimonious leftists, in Israel and outside, were thundering that this was only to be expected from an army whose soldiers were known to be thugs. No less sanctimonious rightists were saying that the charges were all fabrications, as it was inconceivable that an Israeli soldier would engage in wanton destruction. I knew the army well enough to be sure that there were soldiers, too many of them, who had rampaged through Palestinian offices and homes, or done worse. I was also sure that they were a minority. I wanted to know what had happened in Company C.

"I didn't see anything of that kind," Eiger reassured me. "The guys behaved very well."

"You were with Aviel all the time," Ronny corrected him. "When Aviel wasn't around, some of the guys went too far."

"Maybe," Eiger said. "War brings out the worst in people."

"You just said it brings out the best," I noted.

Eiger thought a moment. "It does both. The guys you might expect it from slapped Arabs around and shot more than they should have and acted like assholes. But how many are like that? The great majority didn't do anything you'd be ashamed of."

"Was anyone hurt?" I asked.

"No, thank God, all the guys got through it pretty much un-scratched," Eiger said.

"Great," I said. And after a pause: "I meant on the other side."

"Who knows if we hit anyone when we shot back at the snipers?" Eiger leaned back in his chair and looked at me. "There's one we know of, though. We had a patrol out in Bethlehem, and it spotted two Pales-tinian men. We had intelligence that a suicide bomber was in the area. The guys on the patrol shouted to the men to stop and raise their hands, but they started running. The guys raised their rifles and called again, warning that they'd shoot, but it didn't help. One of our guys—a new kid, you don't know him—fired directly at them. He killed one of the men. It turned out he was armed."

Good thing I wasn't there, I thought. And then I thought, maybe I should have been there.

I looked down at my plate.

"You probably think that's pretty horrible," he said.

"I don't know what I think," I said.

"There wasn't any choice."

I was silent for a long minute.

"What are you thinking?" Eiger asked.

"It just struck me," I said. "I've been in this select combat infantry unit, with all these guns and weapons, for eighteen years. And this is the first time we've killed someone."

EPILOGUE
· *Thoughts* ·

I LATER FOUND OUT SOMETHING I DIDN'T KNOW DURING OPERATION Protective Wall. By the time the operation began, my chimidan was a relic. Had I reported for duty, I would have been sent home. My discharge notice had not yet reached my mailbox—it arrived some weeks after Company C was demobilized—but the army's computer had automatically taken my name off the roster on my forty-fifth birthday.

Maybe it was for the best that I didn't have to risk my life in that campaign. Operation Protective Wall was a short-term success but a long-term failure. It proved to the Palestinians that Israel had both the military ability and the political will to recapture the West Bank cities if the country's vital interests were threatened. The overwhelming public support for the operation, and the near-universal response to the reserve call-up, demonstrated that the Israeli public was nowhere close to collapsing in the face of the Palestinian suicide-attack offensive. Israeli forces captured munitions caches and disrupted the terrorist organizations' chains of command. As a result, we had a few quiet months in which attacks on Israeli civilians nearly ceased.

But Ariel Sharon and his government squandered the victory. Sharon could have used Israel's new position of strength to remake Israeli-Palestinian geopolitics. He could have launched a diplomatic initiative. Or, if he believed that the Palestinian leadership was unable or unwilling to reach a negotiated settlement, he could have unilaterally redrawn Israel's borders. He could have announced that Israel was leaving the Gaza Strip and withdrawing its forces to militarily defensible lines in the West Bank. All Israeli settlers living beyond those lines would be evacuated forthwith. Either policy would have won the support of the Israeli public. Polls showed that a significant majority of Israelis still wanted to get out of the territories, and in the wake of Protective Wall, most Israelis felt strong enough to take the risk of a new peace initiative or a unilateral redeployment. Instead, Sharon chose stagnation. He talked about leaving Gaza and dismantling settlements, but he did not act. It wasn't long before the suicide bombers returned.

Such was the situation when, a few months after the operation, I went to hear three reservists speak in the home of a neighbor and friend from Kehilat Yedidya. The three young men—an immigrant from South Africa and two native Israelis, one religious, one nonreligious—had recently refused to report for reserve duty in the occupied territories. The South African had served time in a military prison, and the others' cases were pending. They believed, they said, that Israel's occupation of the territories was so fundamentally wrong that serving there was immoral.

Any one of them could easily have fit into the Company C I knew. They had not refused to serve because they preferred to pursue private pleasures. They were serious, thoughtful men. Perhaps they were right and I had been wrong. Had my decisions to serve in Hebron, Jenin, Beit Sahour, and Tubas really been correct, or had I allowed my loyalty to my friends to trump the call of my conscience?

The group crowded into the small living room was largely sympathetic to the conscientious objectors. Yet the discussion reinforced my conviction that I had acted properly. In their initial presentation, the three young men stated two axioms. The first was that if Israel withdrew unilaterally from the territories, Palestinian terrorism would cease. The second was that even if terrorism did not cease, it was more moral for Israel to defend itself from behind the Green Line, as it had between 1948 and 1967. If the Palestinians continued to attack, Israel could send its army into the Palestinian territories on specific operations, as needed. The axioms were not new ones. They had been the foundation of my own thinking about the territories before my enlistment in the army.

The first axiom was easy enough to refute. While many Palestinians accepted the premise of a Palestinian state in the West Bank and Gaza Strip that would live in peace alongside Israel, many others believed that the ultimate goal of the Palestinian national struggle was the elimination of the Jewish state. Hamas's and Islamic Jihad's leaders stated explicitly that they would continue to fight if Israel withdrew from the territories. Had they not done so in the mid-1990s when the Oslo process was in high gear? If Israel withdrew to the Green Line, either as part of a peace agreement or unilaterally, it would still have to defend itself against terrorist attacks.

The second axiom made some sense. As long as our army was deployed within the borders of the state of Israel, it was self-evidently in a defensive position. But with the army deployed beyond our borders in the West Bank and Gaza Strip, we were occupiers. In the latter case, we could not say that our military actions were only defensive. Inevitably, the purpose of some proportion of our activity was to maintain the occupation rather than to defend Israel proper. Defending ourselves was morally acceptable, while maintaining our rule over an alien population was not morally acceptable. Therefore, we should defend ourselves at the Green Line and not beyond.

But this thinking, I now knew, was based on a fallacy. It assumed that, in a hostile environment, an army could adequately defend its country from behind the country's borders. It also assumed that there was a clear and obvious distinction between defensive and offensive actions.

Our moral choices would be much simpler if the world worked that way. But armies that fortify themselves behind their defenses in the face of a belligerent enemy lose more often than they win. And in a small country with borders abutting major population centers, an army would betray the people's trust if it simply waited for the enemy to attack. Offensive operations are thus part of a defensive strategy.

All things being equal, a country's position is certainly more moral if the army carries out offensive operations from bases within the country's borders. But caution is in order. Such incursions into enemy territory are not necessarily more considerate of the lives of the civilians on the other side. When Ariel Sharon conducted a cross-border raid into the West Bank at Qibya in 1953, he left behind sixty-nine dead Arabs, half of them women and children. Such missions are much riskier than raids conducted in territory that your army controls. You have less intelligence and must use more firepower to ensure your own soldiers' safety. In comparison, occupation may save lives and thus be the morally superior option—assuming that the occupation is temporary, pending the conclusion of a peace treaty. That being the case, being a soldier in an occupied territory is not prima facie immoral. Therefore, an Israeli soldier should not refuse to serve in the West Bank simply because it is occupied territory.

But the three conscientious objectors made another point that I had a harder time refuting.

"The last time I was called up for duty in the West Bank, my unit was stationed in a Jewish settlement. None of the roadblocks and arrests and guard duty we did had anything to do with protecting Israel against terrorism. Everything we did was aimed at protecting the settlement, not Israel proper," the South African man said.

"That's not typical," I responded. "I served in the West Bank many times during the first Intifada, and we had almost nothing to do with the settlements."

"You don't understand. It's different now," said one of the other men. "There are a lot more settlements now than there were then."

He was right. Settlement had continued apace during much of the previous ten years, under governments of both parties. According to a report by B'Tselem, an Israeli human rights organization, in 1993—the year the Oslo accord was signed and the year of Company C's last stint of first Intifada duty, in Kabatiyeh—100,500 Israelis lived in the Palestinian territories. By 2000, the year of the abortive Camp David summit, there were 191,600. (These figures do not include the Jewish neighborhoods in East Jerusalem, which the Palestinians consider settlements but which Israeli law and the vast majority of Israelis consider part of sovereign Israel.) The construction of new settlements—and, in existing settlements, of new, often distant, neighborhoods—required the army to keep secure a growing network of access roads. Policing these roads had the effect of isolating Palestinian villages from the cities that served as commercial and service hubs and of making travel between Palestinian cities a harrowing and time-consuming journey that involved waiting at multiple roadblocks.

In other words, the Jewish population in the territories was nearly double what it had been when I was an active reservist, and spread out over a larger area. Simple military logic meant that more soldiers were needed to protect the settlements and that a much larger proportion of reservists' time and efforts in the territories was being devoted to activities that would not be necessary were the settlements nonexistent. It was thus considerably harder for a reservist who believed that the settlements were wrong and detrimental to Israel's interests to explain his West Bank service by saying he was primarily protecting his family, friends, and country. The three young conscientious objectors were certainly not unjustified in feeling that the pain and suffering that they as soldiers had caused Palestinians was not the regrettable but necessary minimum intrusion needed to keep terrorists out of Israel.

Yet there was still the argument that, like it or not, the Jewish settlers had made their homes in the territories with the acquiescence and encouragement of democratically elected Israeli governments. Furthermore, those who supported Jewish settlement in the territories did so on the basis of an undeniable and profound historical, emotional, and religious connection to these lands. Jewish settlement was not simply avaricious colonization imposed on defenseless natives, as many leftists would have it. But if Jews and Palestinians were to live together in peace, Jews must surrender their aspiration to include these lands in the state of Israel, just as the Palestinians must surrender their aspiration for a Palestinian state that includes the territory that is now Israel. We who opposed the settlements were free to campaign against them as civilians and to attempt to influence our government to dismantle them. As soldiers, though, we were not individuals but part of an army charged with carrying out the will of the country's elected civilian representatives.

The three conscientious objectors did not reject that premise in principle. But, as one of them said, his years of political activity had been a failure on this score. The settlements continued to burgeon. His refusal to serve in the territories was, he said, in many ways an act of desperation. There seemed no other way to catch the public's attention and make them open their eyes to the indefensibility of Israel's settlement policy.

I could sympathize with that desperation, but I thought it was wrong to act on it. Israeli democracy is flawed (as is every democracy on earth), but Israel is nevertheless a country in which individuals can express their views freely. Opponents of the settlements and of the occupation could demonstrate, write letters, form political organizations, and vote for candidates of their choice. So long as that was the case, I could not justify a blanket refusal to serve in the West Bank and Gaza Strip.

The three young men also voiced an argument I'd heard during the first Intifada: Say we accept your premise that a soldier's point of refusal has to be the specific immoral or unlawful order he receives. What if such an order is given in a tense, dangerous situation, as your unit prepares for a difficult operation? To refuse an order at a sensitive juncture might well put your comrades at risk. And in those moments when there is no time for moral discussion—while a battle is in process, for example—any hesitation may give your enemy an opening to hurt or kill you and your friends. In such a situation it would be nearly impossible to exercise your own independent moral judgment, the conscientious objectors said. So a soldier should not allow himself to get into such a situation in the first place.

A military unit cannot operate without loyalty. No individual can fight a battle on his own, so each soldier's security rests on his trust that his buddies are doing their jobs in the best possible way. And he knows that their trust in him requires him to do his assignment properly. If he doesn't, he is endangering the lives that others are risking for him.

Life is sacred—perhaps more so in the Jewish tradition than in any other. The Torah says that God's commandments were handed down for us to live by, not to die by, so the law requires a Jew, no matter how pious, to violate the Torah's commandments if observing them will result in his death. But this law, like all others, has its exceptions. If the violation in question is a fundamental moral wrong—if to save his life, the Jew must commit an act of idolatry or of sexual immorality, or he must commit a gratuitous act of murder against a another human being who is not threatening his own life or those of his family, friends, or nation—then he must choose to die. In democratic societies, we also accept that the fundamental freedoms on which democracy is based cannot be guaranteed unless citizens are willing, when called on, to die in order to preserve them. A citizen might be required to do that while serving as a soldier in his democratic country's army. But he might just as easily be required to risk his life as a civilian to preserve fundamental democratic values, such as the right to speak his mind, to publish an opposition newspaper, or to participate in a free election.

There are times when such choices ought to be clear. In cases where a soldier receives a manifestly immoral order—for example, to shoot defenseless civilians for no other reason than that they defied a curfew or don't have a necessary permit, or to murder subdued prisoners—he must set aside his loyalty to his comrades just as he sets aside his obedience to his commanders, and disobey. It's precisely this standard that allows me to condemn Palestinian suicide bombers as immoral. Their attacks on buses and restaurants are aimed at civilians who are no direct threat to them or their people. The sole purpose of their actions is to wreak havoc and fear. A Palestinian ordered to carry out such a mission ought to refuse, as should an Israeli soldier ordered to go into a Palestinian village and spray live fire indiscriminately at homes and passersby. In such a situation, the soldier may, in the short run, put his comrades at risk and earn their opprobrium. He may even risk death or injury at their hands. But the morality in whose name he acts is no less a pillar of military strength than is loyalty to his comrades. In the long run, he is doing them a favor.

But most choices soldiers face lack this kind of clarity. I was never given a manifestly immoral order and, thanks primarily to the leadership of officers such as Elnatan, Efi, and Eran, Company C's men never, during my tenure in the unit, found themselves in circumstances that even came close to requiring this kind of momentous decision.

Instead, we faced many small decisions, day by day, when we served in the West Bank. When you tell a Palestinian shopkeeper to paint over the slogan splashed on the wall outside his store, do you slap him around? When you run into a pack of Palestinian youths who want to make trouble, do you ignore or confront them? When you see another soldier treating a Palestinian with contempt, do you say something or keep quiet? Sometimes we decided correctly and sometimes we didn't. It wasn't always easy to know the right choice. I disagreed in general with the policy of collective punishment on which the standing orders were based during the first part of the first Intifada. I thought the standing orders were wrong and counterproductive. But as bad as I thought they were, they were certainly not so depraved that I felt an imperative to disobey them.

Facing such dilemmas is not morally execrable. What is wrong is to refuse to face up to the choices your life in your country requires. It's wrong to decide to keep yourself pure while letting others get sullied in the muck of moral uncertainty. A man who refuses to enter a morally ambiguous situation out of fear that he might make the wrong decision is not pure. He is cowardly.

Did I really believe, when I became a soldier, that peace between Israel and the Palestinians was certain to come? Did I believe that my own children would never have to serve in an army? Or that if they did, they would be, as the Hebrew expression has it, chocolate soldiers—who'd put on uniforms, shoot a few bullets at a target for the sake of protocol and tradition, and then go home?

I wasn't quite that naïve, but I did think that peace was there for the taking if only our leaders and the Palestinians' leaders would be courageous enough to sit down and talk out their differences. And I thought that it couldn't be all that difficult to get them to do so. When I decided to make my home in Israel, which I knew meant that I would be a soldier, I really did think that Israel's state of siege was an anomaly, a temporary situation rather than a permanent one.

I am no longer so certain. I can still draw borders and list arrangements that I think constitute a reasonable compromise between the two peoples. But I'm no longer all that optimistic that I, and people like me, can get a majority of Israelis and Palestinians to agree with us. And I admit that, in recent years, I have acquired some of the suspicion of the other side, and some of the cynicism, that so puzzled me when I first came to Israel and encountered it among older and more experienced Israelis.

By the time this book is published, my oldest daughter, Mizmor, will be a soldier. She's turning my choice into a family tradition by enlisting in Nachal. My oldest son, Asor, will be at the end of his last year of high school, facing conscription. He wants to serve in an elite commando unit. They will not be chocolate soldiers. While Ariel Sharon is currently talking about evacuating all of the Gaza Strip and part of the West Bank, the Israeli army will still be occupying a good part of these territories as Mizmor and Asor perform their service. In fact, the way things look now, they will serve in a particularly tough and dangerous time, a time when the way to peace looks more convoluted than ever.

As a father must be, I will be frightened. I'll fear for their physical safety, and I'll fear for their moral compass, because I know that when you're a soldier it's all too easy for that compass to go awry. I'll also be proud of them, because I know that they will face challenges and problems and dilemmas and overcome them, and be better people for having done so.

Mizmor almost certainly won't be a reservist, as few women serve in the reserves. While Asor presumably will be, the nature of the reserve force is changing. The work of soldiering has become more complex and costly, and many recent studies suggest that a smaller, professional reserve force would do a better job than the current setup. Israel can't afford a second-rate army, so such a shift might be necessary. But something will certainly be lost. The citizen-soldier may not be the best soldier for the modern battlefield, but he is certainly a better citizen. The citizen-soldier can't sit back and ignore what the army is doing in his name, for he is part of that army.

For that reason, I will probably recommend to Asor that he join the reserves, even if he doesn't have to and even if it means he'll be in more danger. My advice to all my children when they go to the army will be as follows. Be loyal to your friends, determined but cognizant of your actions. Do your duty toward God, if for no other reason than it gives you the right to argue with Him and with those who claim to know exactly what He wants. Consider the moral implications of everything you do, for God expects that of us. But don't let your moral concerns paralyze you, for a person who makes no choice cannot make the right choice.

ACKNOWLEDGMENTS

Through my work as a journalist, translator, and editor, I know that every book is a collaboration, even if only a single author's name appears on the cover. It's thus only proper to recognize the important contributions that others have made to this memoir.

My agent, Simon Lipskar, and Ethan Nosowsky, who accepted this project for Farrar, Straus and Giroux, were instrumental in convincing me to write about Company C. Ethan's guidance in the early stages of the project set me in the right direction. Rebecca Saletan, my editor, and her assistant, Stacia Decker, offered sound advice and applied a sharp but always friendly red pen to my pages. Cynthia Merman copyedited thoroughly and professionally. Eric Chinski and Kathryn Lewis guided the manuscript through the process of publication.

I received valuable comments on my early drafts from my good friend Neal Feigenson and from my sister, Nancy Watzman. My father, Sanford Watzman, who has always been my toughest and best editor, carefully marked up my initial draft and forced me to reconsider every sentence.

Special thanks also go to Neal Feigenson and to my mother, June Watzman, for having the foresight to save the letters I wrote over the years. Their prescience has allowed me to check my memories against my own contemporary accounts of stints in the army.

My friends from Company C were also extremely helpful in confirming facts and correcting errors. I interviewed many of them at length and consulted many others on specific points. Some of those who gave generously of their time do not appear as characters in this book—not because their friendships and contributions to Company C were inconsequential, but simply because narrative economy required me to leave out many stories. Several members of Company C read drafts of all or part of these chapters. They all gave me enthusiastic encouragement, but two in particular took the trouble to make detailed comments—Company Commander Eran and my good friend Eiger, whose phenomenal memory for detail has been an invaluable resource.

I have made every effort to be accurate in my accounts of events. However, even with the help of my letters and interviews with my comrades, much is based on memory. I report events from my own point of view, and others would no doubt have told these stories differently. Any errors are my sole responsibility. I have done my best to portray my fellow reservists accurately and hope that none will be offended, for I feel that I have learned much from each and every one of them, including those whose opinions on politics, religion, and military service are far different from my own.

My sister, Nancy, and her husband, Mark Nitczynski, my brother, Saul Watzman, and his wife, Kyle, and my friends Nancy and Jeff Heller provided encouragement and more when it was needed. Col. (P) Albert Bryant Jr. of the U.S. army helped me find the right English translations for military terms I knew only in Hebrew.

The reader of this account may get the misimpression that my military service has been at the center of my life. In fact, that place is occupied by my family and by my community, Kehilat Yedidya. My life's task is Kehilat Yedidya's effort to create—in practice, not just in theory—a Judaism that is faithful to our heritage but open to the world at large, committed to both tradition and innovation, to God, the Jewish people, and to all of humankind.

Throughout my work on this book, my four children, Mizmor, Asor, Niot, and Misgav, have been constant reminders that they, and not anything I might be writing at the moment, are the most important things in the world. My wife, Ilana, to whom I owe more than I can ever put into words, has been an anchor and an inspiration as I wrote this book, as she has been ever since this dazed and drifting demobilized soldier met her one fine May evening so many years ago.

Jerusalem, May 2004